FORTY YEARS IN CANADA

FORTY YEARS IN CANADA

REMINISCENCES OF THE GREAT NORTH-WEST
WITH SOME ACCOUNT OF HIS SERVICE
IN SOUTH AFRICA

SAMUEL B. STEELE

THE RYERSON ARCHIVE SERIES

McGRAW-HILL RYERSON LIMITED

TORONTO
MONTREAL NEW YORK LONDON SYDNEY
MEXICO PANAMA JOHANNESBURG DUSSELDORF
RIO DE JANEIRO KUALA LUMPUR NEW DELHI SINGAPORE

REISSUED BY McGRAW-HILL RYERSON LIMITED, 1972.

This book contains the complete text and illustrations of the original edition. The illustrations have been grouped in a sixteen-page section. The title page of the first Canadian edition is shown overleaf. The note which follows was inserted in all copies of the original edition.

THIS BOOK WAS PRINTED AND BOUND READY FOR PUBLICATION IN AUGUST, 1914; BUT WAS POSTPONED OWING TO THE WAR. SINCE THEN THE AUTHOR HAS BEEN PROMOTED TO THE RANK OF MAJOR-GENERAL FOR DISTINGUISHED SERVICES TO CANADA.

FORTY YEARS IN CANADA

REMINISCENCES OF THE GREAT NORTH-WEST WITH SOME ACCOUNT OF HIS SERVICE IN SOUTH AFRICA BY COLONEL S. B. STEELE, C.B., M.V.O., LATE OF THE N.W.M. POLICE AND THE S. AFRICAN CONSTABULARY EDITED BY MOLLIE GLEN NIBLETT WITH AN INTRODUCTION BY J. G. COLMER, C.M.G., & 17 PLATES

TORONTO
MᶜCLELLAND, GOODCHILD & STEWART LIMITED
LONDON
ℐ ℐ HERBERT JENKINS LIMITED MCMXV ℐ ℐ

INTRODUCTION
BY J. G. COLMER, C.M.G.
WRITTEN AT THE SPECIAL REQUEST OF THE LATE
LORD STRATHCONA, G.C.M.G.

THE late Lord Strathcona promised to write a foreword for Colonel Steele's projected book, but his lamented death intervened. Although not able to carry out his intention, he did not forget the promise ; and among his last words was a request to me to undertake the duty for him and in his name. Lord Strathcona had a sincere regard for Colonel Steele, and never forgot the services rendered by him as commanding officer of " Strathcona's Horse " during the South African war. When his name was mentioned for that position, Lord Strathcona at once accepted the nomination, as he recognised that Colonel Steele was one of the most suitable men for the command, in view of his long experience in that famous force the Royal North West Mounted Police. I write with some knowledge of the subject, as it was my privilege to assist Lord Strathcona in the organisation of his distinguished regiment ; and, besides, I can look back on twenty years or more of personal acquaintance with the author of this volume. In this connection, I may say in passing that it was a gracious act on the part of the Canadian Government to perpetuate the name of " Strathcona's Horse " by the formation of the permanent western regiment which now bears that honoured name. Lord Strathcona was much gratified by this mark of consideration, and it was especially pleasing to him that Colonel Steele was selected for its command. The reader of Colonel Steele's book will be impressed with the simplicity and vigour of the man. His life during the last forty years, except for the time he was in South Africa, is synonymous with the progress and development of the western territories of the Dominion of Canada, now one of the leading agricultural countries of the world. He was there in the early days before there were railroads or settlements or wheat fields—when the country was largely in possession of the Indian and the trapper, and covered by herds of hundreds of thousands of the buffalo. What a change these forty years, or thirty years, or even a lesser period has brought about! In the decade from 1870 to 1880, and even up to 1890, it was possible to travel over many parts of this vast area without seeing a house from morning till evening ; while at the present time passengers on the thousands of miles of railway that now intersect the western provinces in every direction are hardly ever out of sight of cities, towns and villages, huge grain elevators, and thriving homesteads.

It is impossible to give too much credit to successive governments, to the Hudson's Bay Company, and to the Royal North West Mounted Police for what they have done to assist in the peaceful and wonderful development of what was once the red-man's country, and described, later on, by Lord Beaconsfield as " an illimitable wilderness." It is true that there were some troubles in 1869–70, when the country was transferred from the Hudson's Bay Company to the Dominion Government, and again in 1885 ; but these arose rather from the misdirected ambition of a few prominent men among the half-breeds and Indians than from any really deep-rooted grievances. The Hudson's Bay Company had always instilled into the native mind that fair treatment would be extended to them, that the word of the Great White Company and its officers could always be relied upon and kept. The Government continued this policy, and it soon became known that justice was being administered equally to the red man and to the white. Herein lies the explanation of the excellent relations it has always succeeded in maintaining with the red population —which enabled the country to be opened up for settlement and cultivation with so little friction and difficulty. The North West Mounted Police was the channel through which this wise policy was carried out, and the tact and discretion it has always shown in keeping law and order within so

immense a territory, and the confidence felt in the force
both by the Indians and the settlers, afford ample evidence
of the manner in which such duties have been carried out.
Few are aware of the part played by the Mounted Police
in connection with the construction of railways in, and the
immigration movement to, Manitoba and the other western
provinces since the early seventies. The men employed
on the construction work, especially in the earlier days, were
not exactly angels, and a good deal of tact, good temper and
determination had to be shown in handling them. And further,
immigrants of all races have been pouring into the country
in their thousands and tens of thousands, and many of these
settlers must be grateful to the Mounted Police for timely
help and counsel. The force has also been of much use to
the Indian Department in its successful efforts to transform
the red man into a useful citizen and a worker. My experience
—and I have travelled over a good deal of the country—is that
the officers and troopers of the North West Mounted Police
are welcomed wherever they go. Their work has not been
confined to the settled districts, or districts in course of settlement ; they have done splendid pioneer work in the Yukon,
and are still similarly engaged round the shores of Hudson's
Bay, and in the far northern boundaries of the country.
Colonel Steele has taken no small part in the course of events
to which reference has been made, and has a record of which
most men would be proud. His life has been full of incident,
but he is a modest man, never accustomed to blow his own
trumpet, preferring the more sterling satisfaction of doing well
whatever duty was entrusted to him. He is a splendid example
of the man who puts deeds before words, and this is shown not
only in his record in Canada, but while in command of Strathcona's Horse, and in his subsequent work in the South African
Constabulary. For all these reasons I have no doubt that this
volume of reminiscences will have a wide circle of readers in
the many parts of the Empire in which the name and sterling
qualities of Colonel Sam Steele are well known and appreciated.

                                                J. G. COLMER.
Dominion Day,
   1st July, 1914.

CONTENTS

CONTENTS

CHAPTER VIII

CHAPTER IX

CHAPTER X

CHAPTER XI

CHAPTER XII

CHAPTER XIII

CHAPTER XVII

CHAPTER XVIII

CHAPTER XIX

ILLUSTRATIONS

FORTY YEARS IN CANADA

CHAPTER I

My birth and ancestry—A fighting family—My father's career in the
navy—The *Leopard* and the *Chesapeake*—His first marriage—He
emigrates—His life of public service—A tedious journey—His
second marriage—Our early education—The training of a back-
woodsman—My half-brother, John Steele—A crack shot—Fenian
raids—My military training—The Clarksburg Company—The Red
River rebellion.

I WAS born on January 5, 1849, at Purbrook, township of
Medonte, county of Simcoe, province of Ontario. I was
the fourth son of Captain Elmes Steele of the Royal
Navy, by his second wife, Anne, the youngest daughter
of Neil MacIan Macdonald, of the Ardnamurchan branch of
the Macdonalds, who was a native of Islay, Argyllshire, Scotland, and was a grandson of Captain Godfrey MacNeil of Barra,
and nephew of Colonel Donald MacNeil of the British Army.

My grandfather was Dr. Elmes Steele of Coleford, whose
brother, Colonel Samuel Steele, served at the capture of Quebec.
My father was one of seven sons, three of whom served in
the navy and three in the army during the great war, and one,
William, adopted his father's profession and practised in
Abergavenny, where his descendants are still residing.

My father served in the navy during the days of Nelson and
later, and was present at many engagements on board some of
the most famous ships. He entered the service in the last
decade of the eighteenth century as a midshipman on board the
Triton, thirty-two guns, in March, 1798. In 1800 he was transferred to the *Cambridge*, seventy-four guns, the flagship of
Sir Thomas Pasley, and then to the *Atlas*, ninety-eight guns.
In November, 1802, he was nominated master's mate of the
Caroline, thirty-six guns. During the passage of the *Caroline*
to the East Indies a prize was taken, and my father was placed

B 1

on board with, very naturally, the worst of the crew, to take her home, his only assistant being a young middy of sixteen years, named Curran, a nephew of the great Irish lawyer, John Philpot Curran. On their way to Cork the British crew broke into the spirit-room one night and got drunk. In the midst of their disorder the ship was retaken by the enemy, but she did not remain in their hands for many days. They had lost their reckoning, and my father was called upon deck to assist them in working it out, and as a reward was permitted to walk the deck. Curran was also allowed to come up to keep him company. Finally, when in sight of the Scilly Isles, the ship was retaken by a ruse and her course changed to Cork. For this service my father was made a freeman of the city of Gloucester.

Early in 1805 he was nominated lieutenant of *L'Aimable*, and between August following and December, 1812, he was employed on the coast of North America and in European waters. He was on the *Leopard* at the time of the famous " incident " with the *Chesapeake*, when they enforced the right to search foreign ships for British deserters, and commanded a broadside in the encounter. This extraordinary action was brought about by the direct orders of the British government through the admiral commanding the North American squadron, but the powers that controlled the navy at that time went back on their officers, and meted out some punishment to all, including my father, although he was only acting under the orders of Captain Humphries, whom if he had not obeyed, he would no doubt have been tried by court-martial and shot.

His hottest time was in the Basque Roads under Cochrane, and he commanded a forced landing and destruction of guns and signal-stations at Baignio, on the coast of France. He continued on the active list for some years after Waterloo, but Europe was tired of war, the navy was reduced, and, as there was little to do, he took to the land and interested himself in civil affairs. After his marriage with Miss Coucher of Bath, and for several years he lived in Paris and Coutances and Normandy. There were six children of the marriage, who were given every advantage in France until the Revolution of 1830, when he and his family returned to England.

In 1832 my father and many other British officers of the

army and navy were induced by Lieutenant-General Sir John Colborne, at that time governor of Upper Canada, to emigrate with a large number of soldiers and sailors to that province and and settle on the vacant Crown Lands. He proceeded there with his second son, John, and took up 1000 acres of land in the picturesque county of Simcoe, cleared off the forest, built at his own expense the first Anglican Church in the township, and eventually became the first member of parliament for the county, his election being one of the most hotly contested in the records of the county. During the remainder of his long life, he devoted himself enthusiastically to everything that would benefit his adopted country, and became a magistrate and colonel of the militia. The old soldiers and sailors who had emigrated had commuted their pensions to realize sufficient money to make a start in the new land, and at one time they, like many others, were in sore straits to make ends meet. While my father was in parliament he took the lead in inducing the home government to restore their pensions.

The year after he had settled at Purbrook, Mrs. Steele and all but one of the family, his eldest son, Elmes, afterwards a doctor in Abergavenny, joined my father, the sailing ship which brought them to New York taking two and a half months to cross the Atlantic. They then came by the Erie Canal to Rochester, whence the only railroad in America, the short line from that place to Oswega, took them to the only steamboat on the Great Lakes. My father met them at Little York, now the fine city of Toronto, and they crossed Lake Simcoe on the sloop which carried passengers to the little Indian village of Orillia. They went cheerfully through the inconveniences of pioneer life in the backwoods, and no doubt enjoyed a great deal of it.

Mrs. Steele, a much beloved lady, died in the forties, when her family were well settled in life, the girls in Toronto, and in 1848 my father married again. At the early age of twenty-nine my mother died, leaving six children, the eldest myself, only eleven years old. Our years were very happy before that, but there came afterwards much sorrow and a great deal of unhappiness, brightened, of course, at times by the kindly sympathy of our relations. Previous to our sad

bereavement we had moved into Orillia, which was no longer
the red man's home, and there the older ones of the family were
sent to school.   My brother Dick and I went to one kept by
a talented old English gentleman, Mr. Edwin Slee, whose wife
taught French, but before I went there I had the benefit of my
father's excellent teaching and a large stock of books, and was
in consequence able to slip into the top class with the older boys.

In those days every man and boy, and many girls and women,
could shoot, swim, and find their way through the forests,
which were then a trackless wilderness, and all men and boys
could ride well.   I had the benefit of all this, and in winter
could skate, play any game, wrestle and box ; our bouts at
school were without gloves, as all boys could not afford to
purchase any, and we had to do without.

My riding and shooting I learned under the auspices of my
cousins in the township of Oro, Captain Hugh Clarke, then only
a lad, being my preceptor, assisted by my cousins of the MacIan
clan, who were kind comrades and teachers.   With my cousin,
J. B. Clarke, now K.C. of Toronto, I roamed the woods during
the holidays, built boats and rafts, assisted Hugh to make
gunpowder and ball, using the heavy rifle or fowling-piece as
soon as we could carry them.   There was nothing in the life of
the backwoods pioneer that we did not know and desire to
learn.

I was thirteen years old when my father moved into the
country again, and in 1865 he died full of years, and I lived for
a short time with my half-brother, John, who had a leading
place in the country, and was thirty years or more my senior.
An association with him was a great advantage to any lad, for he
was kind and cultured, a true gentleman, admired by all who
knew him.   He was one of the best shots that I have known,
and a good sportsman, who could shoot, run or ride, and he
joined the young men and boys in their games.   He used the
heavy octagon barrelled rifles, with their weighty iron ramrod,
and I have often-known him shoot the heads off two partridges
at once.   On such an occasion his Highland Scotch companion
used to suggest sagely to his neighbours that the Evil One must
have loaded John Steele's rifle !   In those days the farmers
would assemble at some " corners " and shoot for geese,

turkeys, and even horses and cows, at so much per shot, and if the Council were sitting in the neighbourhood he would sometimes have to adjourn to shoot for some old gentlemen who had been bred under different conditions.

As a boy I shared in that sort of life, and when the Fenians began to threaten Canada, and made raids on our honest, loyal people, I joined the militia at about sixteen years of age. As I had been given a commission in Number 6 company of the 35th Regiment, I had to qualify for the highest rank, and did so with the 2nd battalion Leicestershire Regiment, taking the best certificate going, and making one hundred per cent. of marks on drills and dicipline. I did not remain long with that company, however, as circumstances compelled me to do better for myself, and I got employment as a clerk in the business of a Mr. Turnbull of Clarksburg, co. Grey. While there I raised and trained the Clarksburg company of the 31st Regiment, and was asked by the leading people to take command, but I felt that I was too young and not prominent enough to take a company when there were fine men there to undertake it. I left there after putting the company in good order and well organized, parting from them with much regret. I was still interested in the force, however, and made a close study of all military matters, at the same time looking well after the interests of my employers, until the disturbances of the Red River Metis under Louis Riel changed the course of my life.

CHAPTER II

The Red River settlement—The transfer to the Dominion—Dissatisfaction of the Metis—Louis Riel—Capture of Fort Garry—Attempts at conciliation—Mr. Donald Smith—Riel's violence—Murder of Scott—Public indignation—Organization of an expedition—Colonel Wolseley—I join—Preparations—A narrow escape—Prince Arthur's landing—Jack of all trades—The voyageurs—The advance—The difficulties of the expedition—Donald McKellar—Captain Redvers Buller.

D URING the autumn of 1869 and for many months of 1870 the Red River Settlement of the North West or Hudson's Bay Territory was in the throes of rebellion. This then remote colony was situated in what is now the fertile province of Manitoba, and extended for a considerable distance along the banks of the Red and Assiniboine rivers. Its inhabitants were the descendants of Scotch settlers, who had been placed there by the famous Earl of Selkirk, and French Metis, descendants of half-breeds, the renowned " coureurs de bois " of Canada, who had been in the employ of the North West Fur Company of Montreal. The settlement had at different times been reinforced by retired Hudson's Bay Company's officers and other employees. At Portage la Prairie, about 60 miles up the Assiniboine from the Red River, there had settled in the early sixties a considerable number of British Canadians from Ontario. Fort Garry, near the confluence of the Red and Assiniboine rivers, was the principal post of the " Great Company," and the residence of its governor.

Shortly after the confederation of the provinces in 1867, an arrangement was made for the transfer of the North West Territory to the Dominion of Canada. The Hudson's Bay Company, which had held sway over it for nearly 200 years, agreed to annul their charter for a consideration, and the transfer was fixed for December 1, 1869. The Hon. William

McDougall was appointed Lieutenant Governor of the vast country, and on September 1 he left Ottawa for the settlement to assist in the transfer.

Survey parties had been sent by the Canadian government to Fort Garry, and were already laying out the lands in sections and townships. This greatly offended the French Metis, and on October 10 a party of them, under the leadership of Louis Riel, stopped the work of the surveyors. The chief of the survey party appealed to Governor McTavish of the Hudson's Bay Company, but without effect. Riel flatly refused to allow the work to proceed, and the surveyors were withdrawn.

The French Metis then formed a provisional government, with a man named John Bruce as president and Louis Riel as secretary. The latter, being the stronger head and the better educated of the two, soon assumed the leadership, and was elected president. Soon after this government was formed an armed force was sent to Scratching River, about 15 miles south of Fort Garry, where a barricade was erected to oppose the entrance of Mr. McDougall by the Pembina trail. The following letter was sent forbidding him to enter.

Le Comité National des Métis de la Rivière Rouge intime à M. Wm. McDougall l'ordre de ne pas entrer sur le territoire de Nord Ouest sans une permission speciale de ce comité.

Disregarding the letter, Mr. McDougall kept on his way to the Hudson's Bay post at Fort Pembina, inside the North West Territory. Three days later an armed party of mounted men arrived from Fort Garry, and sent into the post two of their number to inform Mr. McDougall that by order of the Metis' provisional government he must leave the North West Territory by nine o'clock the next morning. This was enforced, and the Lieutenant Governor took up his residence in the village of Pembina, on the American side of the border. On November 24 Riel took forcible possession of Fort Garry with its stores, food supplies, arms, ammunition and money. He made the post the base of operations, and fed and paid himself and his men at the expense of the Hudson's Bay Company.

On December 1 Mr. McDougall took formal possession of

the North West Territory in the name of the Canadian government, and issued proclamations to the people. The first was to the effect that he had been appointed Lieutenant Governor, and the second confirmed all public officers in their appointments, except Governor McTavish. He gave Colonel Dennis, chief surveyor, authority to raise a force to put down the rebellion. This Colonel Dennis proceeded to do, taking possession of the Stone Fort, 20 miles north of Fort Garry, and placing some men there ; but at the solicitation of some of the leading persons of the settlement, he caused his men to lay down their arms so that unnecessary bloodshed might be avoided. Soon after this, Riel increased his force to about 500 men, and had the promise of many more if required. To maintain them he continued to draw on the provisions and funds of the Company.

With affairs at this pass, Mr. McDougall deemed it useless to remain in the north west, and returned to Canada. In the meantime two delegates were sent from Ottawa to conciliate the rebels. A few days later, Mr. Donald A. Smith, better known as Lord Strathcona, chief officer of the Hudson's Bay Company in eastern Canada, followed as special commissioner to inquire into and report upon the causes of the disturbances, and to assist Governor McTavish. He arrived in the settlement on December 27, and, gaining admission to Fort Garry, met Riel and his councillors, and was soon, to all intents and purposes, a prisoner. He found the British flag hauled down, and the *fleur de lys* and shamrocks floating over Fort Garry. He learned that the desire of several of the rebel leaders was to bring about the annexation of the country by the United States. However, he took the people of the settlement into his confidence and succeeded in convening a mass meeting of the settlers, where he explained to them the views of the government. About 1000 men were present, and the convention lasted for two days, January 19 and 20. It was held in the open air, with the temperature about 25 below zero, and resulted in 40 delegates being chosen. On February 10 it was decided to send three of their number to the government at Ottawa with a bill of rights. These persons were Father Richot, Judge Black and Alfred Scott, men whose names are intimately connected with the history of the Red River Settlement.

Riel burst into violence while the delegates were in session, and placed a guard over Governor McTavish, who was confined to his bed by a serious illness, threatening to have him shot before midnight. He also arrested Dr. Cowan, chief officer of the Hudson's Bay Company in the district, and placed him in the fort with 60 prisoners whom he had confined some days previously. He threatened to shoot Dr. Cowan if he did not take the oath of allegiance to the provisional government. A few days later he calmed down, and on February 10, the last day that the 40 delegates were in session, he set the Governor and Dr. Cowan at liberty, and on February 11 and 12 released a few more of the prisoners, promising to set free the remainder in a few days.

Before Riel had an opportunity to do so, however, the people of the British Canadian settlement at Portage la Prairie assembled and were joined by some hundreds of the old settlers under Major Boulton, an ex-officer of the 100th Royal Canadian Regiment of the British Army. These men were determined to take Fort Garry by assault. Major Boulton endeavoured to dissuade them from the enterprise, as they were very inferior in numbers to the rebels, and were not well supplied with arms or ammunition. Seeing, however, that the people were determined to make the attempt to release the prisoners, he decided to try to surprise Riel in the night, the only plan which could have the slightest hope of success. The enterprise was frustrated, however, by a blizzard which sprang up on the night on which the attempt was to be made, and they were unable, owing to the storm and deep snow, to reach Fort Garry before daylight. Finding that they could not surprise the place, and being short of food, they departed for their homes on February 17, but on their way to Portage la Prairie, Major Boulton, Thomas Scott and 45 others passed too near the fort, and were captured by Riel and placed in confinement in the post.

Major Boulton was tried by court-martial on the 18th and was sentenced to be shot at noon on the same day, but, on the petition of some friends, the execution was postponed until the 19th.   Poor Boulton was kept in suspense.   He was given the last rites of the church, and was fully prepared to die when at the last moment Riel yielded to the earnest solicitations of Mr. Donald Smith and pardoned him.

The elections in the Scotch and English parishes were held on February 26, and on the 28th Riel promised to release the prisoners who were captured with Major Boulton ; but on March 4 he ordered the trial of Thomas Scott.   The court-martial was presided over by Ambrose Lepine, and Scott was condemned to be shot on the same day.   He was accused of being unruly and insolent to the guards who were placed over him, and Riel stated that an example must be made of him. Mr. Donald Smith did all that a human being could do to turn the rebel leader from his purpose, but without success.   In his report he wrote :   " It was now within a few minutes of one o'clock and on entering the Governor's house the Rev. Mr. Young joined me and said, ' It is now considerably past the hour, I trust that you have succeeded.'   ' No,' I said.   ' For God's sake go back to the poor man, for I fear the worst.' " He left immediately and a few minutes after he had entered the room in which the prisoner was confined, some guards marched in and told Scott that his hour had come.

His dreadful position now for the first time flashed upon him.   Poor Scott turned to his fellow-prisoners and said good-bye to them, and was led out accompanied by his faithful and kind pastor, Mr. Young.   His eyes were bandaged, and when he was outside the gate on the east side of the fort near the north west bastion, he asked Mr. Young where he should place himself, and then knelt down on the snow, facing north, the firing party of six facing south.   At the signal they fired, and three bullets passed through poor Scott's body.   He fell, but as he still showed signs of life, the commander of the firing party drew his revolver and fired a shot into his head, the bullet entering the eye and passing round the skull.   Mr. Young then asked for the remains, so that they could be interred in the Presbyterian burying-ground, but he was refused.   The Anglican Bishop also asked, with the same result.   The body was taken into the fort, confined in a rough pine-box, and left for the night in one of the bastions.   Before daylight, it is said, the murdered man was heard to groan, and a guard was sent in to finish the bloody work. It was supposed then that the remains of poor Scott were buried within the walls of the fort, but it has since been clearly proved that this is not so.

On the way to his execution Scott prayed fervently and continued to do so until he was unconscious, and he said, as he was led down the steps, " This is a cold-blooded murder." The news of this atrocious crime produced a great sensation in eastern Canada, particularly in the province of Ontario. Public meetings were held all over the province, and the government was urged to send an expedition to restore the authority of the Queen and punish Riel and his companions in crime. As soon as the three delegates from Fort Garry arrived in Ottawa, two of them were arrested as accessories before the fact to the murder of Thomas Scott, but as nothing could be proved against them they were released.

At this crisis, Mr. Donald Smith recommended that a military expedition should be sent as soon as possible in the spring. His suggestion was approved, and it was decided to dispatch a force of regulars and Canadian militia under the command of Colonel (afterwards Field-Marshal Viscount) Wolseley, who had served many years in Canada. His appointment was very popular with the Canadian people, and as he had commanded large camps at Thorold on the Niagara frontier and at La Prairie near Montreal, he was well known to the Canadian militia and thoroughly understood conditions in the country.

The route chosen for the expedition was that formerly used by the Great North West Fur Company before its amalgamation with the Hudson's Bay Company ; but nothing larger than a birch-bark canoe had been employed for the first 200 miles westward from Lake Superior. The route had been considered impracticable for boats. Troops had previously been sent to Fort Garry by Hudson's Bay, the Nelson River and Lake Winnipeg.

On May 1 I received a message from Lt.-Col. Alexander Mackenzie of the 35th Regiment to the effect that Captain D. H. McMillan would be at Barrie, co. Simcoe, at four o'clock, and that if I cared to go to Red River he would give me a place. I had previously held a commission in the 35th, had organized and drilled a company of the 31st Grey Regiment, and had obtained from the Military School field officers' certificates of qualification for cavalry and infantry, but I had resigned my commission.

Accordingly I joined, and was pleased to find myself a member of No. 4 Company 1st Ontario Rifles,[1] under the command of Captain McMillan, with Lieutenant N. Kennedy and Ensign Stewart Mulvey as th. subalterns. We were already well drilled, but as yet the N.C.O.'s were only " acting," and as it was necessary that all should have officers' certificates, the order came out one afternoon for all men with Military School certificates to fall out to the right, but I did not do so, as I had made up my mind to serve as a private. The men were very kind and cheerful companions, always ready to do a good turn for a comrade, so that as far as experience went I was better off without chevrons and learned how to appreciate the trials of other men to an extent that I should never have been able to do had I been promoted.

On May 16 my company arrived at Sault St. Marie, and marched over to the camp ground near the old Hudson's Bay Company's quarters. This place was directly opposite Fort Brady on the United States side of the river, and as at first all the troops and supplies had to be brought over the Sault portage, we were stationed there to prevent any interruption by the Fenians who were then active in the United States.

At this time, through a foolish misunderstanding, none of our vessels were allowed to pass through the canal on the American side of the river, but later on this was settled amicably on the protest of the Governor General through the British ambassador at Washington. The ships were then permitted

---

[1] The Ontario Rifles consisted of 7 companies for service and one at the depot, Kingston, Ontario, and was commanded by Lt.-Col. S. P. Jarvis, a Canadian of the British Army. The battalion earned the admiration of Colonel Wolseley by its steadiness on parade and aptitude under instruction. The appearance of the corps on parade was very striking, the rank and file being remarkable for their physique ; the flank men of the companies were almost gigantic, the right-hand man of No. 2 being 6 feet 8 inches in height, and perfectly proportioned.

to go through with ordinary supplies, the troops and contraband of war going across the Canadian portage. Since then a splendid canal, far superior to those opposite, has been constructed over the portage road, and a well-built, bustling town of many thousands of inhabitants, with fine factories and other works, has taken the place of the village which at that date compared very unfavourably with the pretty and clean American town opposite. We did not realize then that we were the pioneers of the Western Canada of to-day.

On May 23 Colonel Wolseley arrived at the Sault. The troops and military stores were landed at the wharf and the *Chicora* passed up, the first to get through the canal after consent had been given, although she had brought the horses, boats and ordinary stores with her. The screw steamer *Shickaluna* also arrived, accompanied by the schooners *Pandora* and *Orion*. Colonel Wolseley and the troops embarked on the *Chicora* and with the fleet left for Thunder Bay, but, much to our disappointment, we were left behind.[1]

The American troops at Fort Brady consisted of two companies of infantry, and I am pleased to say that the greatest harmony existed between us, the American soldiers often coming to see us after our work was lightened by the ships being allowed to pass the canal.

[1] The force consisted of detachments of the Royal Artillery, Royal Engineers, Army Hospital Corps and Army Service Corps and seven companies of the 1st Battalion 60th Rifles. There were also two battalions of militia. The daily rations issued to N.C.O.'s and men were : 1 lb. biscuit or $1\frac{1}{2}$ lbs. soft bread ; 1 lb. salt pork or $1\frac{1}{2}$ lbs. fresh meat ; 2 ozs. sugar; 1 oz. tea ; $\frac{1}{2}$ oz. salt, when fresh meat was used; $\frac{1}{3}$ pint beans or $\frac{1}{3}$ lb. preserved potatoes ; $\frac{1}{6}$ oz. pepper. Tobacco and soap were provided by the Control Department for purchase by the troops. In consideration of the special nature of the service, the Secretary of State for War sanctioned the issue free of cost to all N.C.O.'s and men of 1 serge frock, 1 pair serge trousers, 1 pair outside boots, 2 pairs worsted socks, 2 flannel shirts, 1 housewife, 1 woollen nightcap, 1 cap cover with peak, 1 piece mosquito netting, 1 clasp knife, 1 tin cup, 1 tin plate. There was an extraordinary field allowance for six months for all officers, who, however, were not allowed under any circumstances to take private civil servants with them. They were permitted a limited amount of mess stores and cooking utensils as far as Fort William. Beyond that place each officer was to be allowed 90 lbs. weight only, to include bedding, cooking and mess utensils. All company officers were to be armed with rifles, and to carry 60 rounds of ammunition like the men.

We were at the Sault longer than any company in the expedition, and were glad to join the others. We arrived at Thunder Bay on June 13. The place where the troops disembarked had been named " Prince Arthur's Landing " by Colonel Wolseley when he arrived, in honour of Prince Arthur[1] who was then serving in the Rifle Brigade at Montreal. On our way up Lake Superior we had a very narrow escape from shipwreck. We were saved by the presence of mind of Harry Stavely, one of our privates, who had served in the navy for a number of years. He was sentry on the fore-part of the upper deck in front of the wheel house, when, in the midst of the dense fog through which the *Chicora* was ploughing at an early hour of the morning, he saw a large rocky island looming up before the vessel and only a short distance ahead, whereupon he gave the word " Hard a port ! " The helmsman obeyed, and the *Chicora* passed the rock, missing it by only a few feet. If a landsman had been on sentry we should most likely have been wrecked and all hands lost.

The day after our arrival we were set to work on a stockade fort which had been under construction for some weeks. It consisted of a strong palisade with a ditch, and a magazine was built inside with small bastions at the corners. Employment on this was the only task which seemed to be distasteful to the men. Canadians dislike the pick and shovel, and if they can get anyone else to use them, they are never to be found digging ; any other occupation, no matter how severe, seems to be preferable.

Sometimes in the evening, when the day's work was done, Colonel Wolseley provided a few boats, and encouraged races, and generally acted as starter on these occasions. In addition to the rowing there were competitions in hornpipes and fancy dancing on a platform erected in the vicinity of the canteen of the 6oth. Foot-races and other sports were also indulged in after a hard day's work, but, as a rule, the majority were quite content to be spectators of the various events.

The appearance of the country in the vicinity of Prince Arthur's Landing, now Port Arthur, was most forbidding. For some time before the troops landed and probably several

[1] The present Duke of Connaught.

years previously, the forest for many miles had been swept by fire. Enormous quantities of fine timber had been destroyed, and thousands of acres were covered by the blackened trunks of trees. Several stretches were still burning when the rain began in June. These fires had destroyed many of the culverts and bridges over the small creeks on the Dawson Road, as the road to Shebandowan Lake had been named.

More than 700 voyageurs, whites and Indians, had been hired in different parts of Ontario and Quebec, selected on account of their great skill in handling boats, canoes and rafts of timber in the great rapids of the St. Lawrence, Ottawa, St. Maurice, Saguenay and other rivers. These men were accustomed to bush work ; their winter employment being cutting, sawing and hewing timber for the English and home markets. There was no work in the woods to which they could not turn their hands, and as they landed they were sent up the road, and were soon hard at work. A few of them, but very few, gave trouble because of their objection to work on Sundays, but when matters were explained to them they accepted the situation and laboured with a will, and a better lot of men it would be impossible to find. They were a motley crowd ; and more than half were Indians, or had Indian blood in their veins ; the whites were Scotch or French Canadians. The Iroquois took first place for skill in navigating boats and canoes in surf waters. It was thought at first that the voyageurs and soldiers would not understand one another, and consequently not work well together, that the officers, especially those of the regulars, would not know how to handle men unaccustomed to unquestioning obedience, but as a matter of fact the officers got on admirably with them, and the men anticipated every wish and combined with the soldiers to make a success of the expedition.

On the day the headquarters of the Ontario Rifles disembarked at Prince Arthur's Landing, Colonel Wolseley, dissatisfied with the progress being made by the land transport in hauling the boats by road, made up his mind to try the water route to Shebandowan, and detailed Captain Young, of the 60th Rifles, with his company and the proper complement of voyageurs and Indians to make the attempt. Six boats were taken with two voyageurs to each, to steer and guide, and a crew of soldiers to track or tow them along the rivers.

From the mouth of the Kaministiquia to the Matawin bridge are 12 miles of quiet water and 33 miles of rapids, with now and then short navigable sections. Boulders of all shapes and sizes and sharp rocks set on edge were encountered along that part of the stream, which could be traversed with little or no risk to men, but which was very dangerous for boats. Great care had to be taken to prevent damage to keels and bottoms, and the labour of getting the boats safely over the portages and tracking them up the stream was exceedingly trying. None but men of strong physique were of use here.

From the Matawin bridge to the Oskondagee Creek by land was 12 miles. To a point known as Young's Landing it was navigable, but from here on there was a succession of rapids, the most difficult on the route, and a deep canyon with perpendicular walls, through which the current dashed at a great speed. The boats had to be taken up this part of the river for 8 miles. These rapids end at Calderon's Landing, and this place was connected with the main road by a bush trail two miles long, called Browne's Lane, after an officer of the corps. By this trail supplies were hauled from the Matawin bridge to the Landing and transported by boats to Ward's Landing.

From Calderon's Landing to the Oskondagee the river was navigable for lightly laden boats, but the current was swift and the work severe, the men having to track along the high rocks, sometimes poling or wading in the swift and shallow water up to the armpits. From the Oskondagee to Ward's Landing, over 4 miles, the boats and supplies had to be taken by waggon. The total distance by water from Fort William to the Oskondagee is about 70 miles, and prior to this expedition no boats had ever passed up. The bark canoe was the only craft considered suitable by the Great Fur Company's voyageurs, and with good reason. Mr. Dawson reported unfavourably of the route on account of the danger of damaging the clinker-built boats, but Mr. MacIntyre, of the Hudson's Bay Company, was of the opinion that we could make use of the route, though with difficulty. The torrents of rain which fell during the time the expedition was bringing up the boats certainly made it much easier, for, although the river was swifter on that account, the boats avoided many rocks which in ordinary seasons were uncovered, and would have damaged them. Even so the difficulties of that trip up the Matawin were stupendous. It was hard enough on the soldiers, but it was still worse for the voyageurs, who were kept continually coming and going until the last boat had passed up.

When Captain Young started up the Kaministiquia on June 3, rain was falling daily and the rivers were rapidly becoming torrents. The Kaministiquia, fed by smaller streams, rose 6 feet in one night. There were 7 portages to pass as far as the Matawin, one of them, at the Kakabeka Falls, being nearly a mile long and the fall 110 feet. The heavy boats had to be dragged up the hill at an angle of 45 degrees, and the load carried upon the men's backs over the portage. The rain fell continuously, while the black flies worried the men during the day and the sand flies and mosquitoes at night.

The method of bringing the boats across the portages was by skids (short poles), cut and laid across the track at intervals of a few feet. When the boats were ready the long towline was secured to the forefoot or stem and passed over double to a ring bolt on the kelson, back again to the forefoot and there secured. Then a man would take the end of the towline over his shoulder to lead in the right direction ; two of the most powerful of the crew, generally voyageurs, placed themselves at the bow with their backs against the side of the boat, seizing the towline where it passed above the stem, and braced themselves, while two more of the strongest men were at the stern. The rest strung themselves along the towline or supported the sides of the boat by holding the gunwales. Those on the towline placed themselves in pairs or half sections, dividing the distance to the end of the line, fastening their tumplines (portage straps) to the rope, passing the flat part over the outward shoulder, and hauled on the rope, bearing outwards a little. As the boat went along the men at the bows lifted the stem over obstacles, such as stumps, stones or high skids, and in this manner they crossed the portage.

This was hard work, but drawing the boats across was mere child's play compared to the labour of carrying the stores and

c

tracking or poling up the torrent. Even on the few navigable stretches the current was often much too swift to admit of rowing or even poling; consequently tracking had to be resorted to in many places. When at this work the voyageurs were in the bow and stern of the boat, each with a pole to keep it out from the rocky shore or to steer clear of boulders. The remainder of the men took hold of the line, one of them leading it the best way over land or along the shore, while the rest passed the line over their shoulders. Often when the water was too deep near the shore they ascended the bank, the leader passing the rope in front of the trees while the others hauled on the line as was most convenient, running along and passing one another when necessary. As a rule wading was preferred to taking to the high banks. Frequently, owing to the swiftness and depth of the water, one would miss his footing and would have to hang on to the towline whilst the other men steadied themselves until he had regained his feet.

Captain Young and his party reached the Matawin bridge in 7 days from Fort William. The voyageurs reported that they had agreed to go as far as, but no farther than, the Matawin, and were sent back by road and tug boat to Fort William. They stated before leaving that it was impossible to take the boats higher up the river, but a few days later Captain Young made the attempt without voyageurs. He took only one boat, and after great difficulty reached the gorge on the canyon already described. He returned, convinced that it was useless to try to bring the boats up further by water. It has been stated by Captain Huyshe that no boats were taken up that part of the river, but this is an error difficult to account for, as all were brought up the bad stretch and on to the Oskondagee Creek. Mr. Dawson, who was in charge of the transport, etc., was much annoyed when he was informed that they could not be taken up, but took immediate steps to prove that with voyageurs it could be done.

There is no doubt, however, that the difficulty was such that not one man in a hundred could have succeeded. It was left to Mr. Donald McKellar, a Highland Scotch Canadian, and now a leading citizen of Fort William, Ontario, to prove that it could be done. There were several brothers

McKellar living at Thunder Bay, all experienced in the rivers and forests, with a thorough knowledge of the capabilities of the Indian voyageurs. Mr. Dawson knew them well and sent a messenger for Mr. John McKellar, and when he got a reply that John was not at home, he sent back the messenger to get *any* McKellar to come to him without delay, as he had very important business under consideration. Mr. Donald McKellar, at the time the only one at home, went in to see him and was told how things were at the Matawin. Mr. Dawson said: " I want you to go up to the Matawin station and get the boats up the Matawin and Shebandowan rivers to the Oskondagee. Take with you a crew of local Indians from the mission at Fort William. Here is a letter to the foremen along the line, authorizing them to give you any men, boats or supplies you may want ; see that you get the best, so that you will be sure to open up this route." Mr. McKellar suggested taking Iroquois and Sault St. Marie Indians along with the local Indians, and selected ten Fort William Indians, ten Iroquois and ten Sault St. Marie Indians. When they arrived at the Matawin he chose three boats. While he was fitting them up for the trip, Captain Young, who was encamped on the opposite bank of the river, came across to where they were working and said to him : " You can save yourself all this trouble, for there are not men enough in the expedition to take the boats up this river."

At four o'clock next morning Mr. McKellar started with ten men to each boat, he taking the lead with the Fort William Indians. Mr. T. A. P. Towers followed with the Sault St. Marie Indians and Captain Pritchard with the Iroquois brought up the rear. At nine o'clock in the evening they arrived at Ward's Landing on the Oskondagee, which was their destination. Captain Ward, of the 60th Rifles, was encamped there and rushed down to meet McKellar and his party. He was delighted and surprised, thinking it impossible to get the boats up the river so far. The feasibility of the route from the Matawin bridge was now assured, and it proved a great success. The news soon spread, and there was great rejoicing along the line, for the success of the trip removed a load from the minds of all concerned.

When, on June 20, Colonel Wolseley inspected our regiment he expressed himself very much pleased with the way we turned out.   It looked odd on these parades to see our officers armed with rifles, but they are certainly a more useful weapon than the sword.   A few hours after the parade the *Arctic* came in with the last of the detachment which had been at the Sault St. Marie.   These were the last troops to land, and they came at a time when the thunder had for many weeks rolled round the vast solitudes where the white man was practically unknown.   The rain was almost incessant, and the road was in constant need of repair.   Bridges were swept away and transport trains cut off, so that they could neither advance nor retire.   The ingenuity of everyone was taxed to meet the situation.   The boats were going up the Kaministiquia, and large parties of men were posted at intervals to repair damages to the road.   When they had finished one tedious job, knapsacks were strapped on, rifles grasped, and the company moved on to the next place needing repair.   This road work was the hardest task in my experience in this land of severe trials and strenuous pioneering, but it was carried out under the direction of one of the most capable of commanders, whose example and tactful treatment of his troops inspired them to face cheerfully and remove every difficulty in their way.

One of the brigades of boats sent up the Kaministiquia left on June 14, under the command of Captain (afterwards Sir) Redvers Buller, who was soldiering for the love of it, and setting his men an example of self-denial not often seen.   He was a great favourite in Canada and the Old Country to the day of his death.   On arriving he reported :

The boats, nine in number, are arranged according to merit and capacity, durability, and speed; 2 white clinker-built boats marked R. Abbott, 2 large carvel-built, 2 small grey ditto ; 2 marked T.S., painted grey inside, and one clinker-built from a maker in Barrie.   The carvel-built are undoubtedly the strongest, but their weight renders them liable to rough treatment in portaging.   They have no well holes, and therefore carry a large quantity of water, which it is impossible to bale out.   A large quantity of the cargo consisted of flour in barrels, the hoops of which not being nailed on, came off during the rough usages which they received in portaging.

The axes supplied as camp equipage were so blunt that they were worse than useless.

The felling axes to which Captain Buller alluded were the old army ordnance pattern, and were served out to us although quite useless. As it was impossible to do any work with them, they were condemned and the excellent Canadian felling axe was supplied instead.

The *Algoma* arrived at Prince Arthur's Landing on the night of June 29 with Lt.-Gen. Sir James Lindsay [1] on board. He landed at once, and went over to Fort William,[2] the solitary Hudson's Bay post under the direction of Mr. MacIntyre. A tremendous storm arose which forced the general and his staff to return to the Landing. It was the worst we had yet experienced ; the thunder and lightning were incessant ; the road and every hollow were rivers of muddy water rushing down to the lake, and all work at the Landing had to cease for the day. Everything seemed to have conspired against us to cause our discomfiture ; but nothing disturbed the troops, officers and men were united to push on to the great west. '' On to Fort Garry ! '' was the word. We left Prince Arthur's Landing on June 30.

[1] Commander-in-Chief of the forces in British North America.

[2] This post took its name not from one of the Royal Family as most people suppose, but from Mr. William McGillveray, a leading officer of the Great North-West Fur Company, by whom it was built before the amalgamation with the '' Great Company.''

CHAPTER III

FROM the day of his arrival, Colonel Wolseley had been incessantly on the move. Had the men required it they could not have had a better example. When the first brigade of boats started for McNeill's Landing on Shebandowan Lake, Colonel Wolseley was there to see that all went well. The 18th found us still at Calderon's Landing with little to do. The next day we prepared to make a final start and loaded our boats that we might be off early in the morning.

The boats moved in regular order, Captain McMillan in front, then Lieutenant Kennedy, Ensign Mulvey, Sergeant Doidge and Major Macleod, *The Flying Dutchman* bringing up the rear. This was the worst boat in the lot, two feet shorter than any, and at least a foot wider in the beam. I was one of her crew, and had something to do with suggesting her name, which was received with derision, as it required nearly twice as much effort to move her through the water as any other boat in our brigade, except, perhaps, *La Belle Manitoba*, an immense boat navigated by Major Macleod, which gave him much trouble on all the portages, and in rapids was very clumsy and difficult to steer. .

Our voyageurs were white men. The bowman did not last long, but the steersman, Big Neil McArthur from near Owen Sound, was a success ; he was a splendid man, tall, strong, good-tempered and all that we could desire. None of us were novices at handling boats under any circumstances, which was fortunate. By the time we reached Kasheboiwe portage we had developed splendid appetites for our dinners, and eagerly disposed of our rations of pork, beans, hard tack and strong black tea, of which Colonel Wolseley saw that there was an unlimited quantity, a very good substitute for beer or spirits, of which there were none. There were many of Mr. Dawson's voyageurs, boatmen and axemen busy on the portage, and four carts had been provided to assist in transporting the loads, but they proved to be of little service to us after all.

The work of portaging was done with a rush, the officers and men running back after depositing their loads, all working alike. Major Macleod, a tall, graceful men, was the first of all of us to shoulder a barrel of pork, a heavy load, each barrel weighing 200 lbs. The flour and biscuit barrels weighed 100 lbs., the arm-chests 200 lbs., and the beans 100 lbs., the lightest loads being the boxes of ammunition, 500 rounds in each, which weighed 64 lbs. The arm-chests were the most awkward burdens.[1]

On July 29 we reached Baril portage. We found it very rough, with a high hill in the centre like a hog's back or barrel, but it did not get its name from that. It is derived from an incident which occurred in the early days of the fur trade. Two brigades owned by rival traders or corporations were on

[1] The loads in every boat weighed nearly 4,000 lbs., made up of—

					lbs.	lbs.
Biscuits, barrels	8 each	..	..		100	800
Flour,	,, 6 ,,	..	..		100	600
Pork,	,, 8 ,,	..	..		200	1600
Sugar,	,, 1 ,,	..	..		80	80
Tea, chests	1 ,,	..	..		50	50
Beans, sacks	2 ,,	..	..		100	200
Potatoes, cases	2 ,,	..	..		50	100
Ammunition boxes, 2 each	..	..			64	128
Arm chests, 1 each	..	..			200	200
Ball pouches, 10 rds.						
,, ,, large, 50 rds.						
Tents, 1	..	..	..	..	75	75
Soap, cases, 1	..	..	..		50	50
Candles, boxes, 1	..	..	..		25	25
Boat nails, 1 keg	..	..	..		10	10
Mosquito oil, 1 bottle	..	..				

3,918

their way west in bark canoes laden with goods. One brigade was a few days ahead of the other and had on board of one of the canoes a barrel of rum, which the leader feared might be taken from them by the rear brigade if it caught up, as it was stronger in numbers. He therefore caused a grave to be dug and the barrel of rum carefully and decently interred, and a hewn headboard placed, on which was inscribed, *A la mémoire de Monsieur Baril.* The rear brigade saw the grave and thought that some good voyageur had been buried there, and as they were pious fellows after all, some of them offered prayers for the repose of the soul of Monsieur Baril. On the return trip of their rivals his remains were exhumed and his health drunk with many a laugh at the success of the trick.

The Deux Rivières portage was one of the worst on the route. It was 750 yards in length, and there was a large hollow in the centre which had been bridged by Ignace, Colonel Wolseley's favourite voyageur, and some of his men. Two tall pines had been thrown across the hollow and skids laid on notches to enable the boats to be dragged up the slope over the ravine. This was nicknamed " Jacob's Ladder."

The advance of the expedition arrived at Fort Frances on August 4, and the last of the brigades of the 60th passed on the 7th. Lieutenant (afterwards Sir William) Butler, who had gone incognito to Fort Garry via the United States to find out how matters stood in that settlement, met the commander of the expedition at the outlet of Rainy Lake, three miles above the fort. He had seen Riel and had the latest news from Fort Garry. It was far from reassuring to those who desired peace ; both parties were at daggers drawn and afraid of the Indians, who at that time were very powerful, but always loyal and peaceful if justly treated.

After we arrived at Fort Frances, the crew of *The Flying Dutchman* exchanged her for a slightly damaged but much lighter boat, which was soon repaired, and this addition to our fleet we named *The Girl of the Period.* On Saturday, the 13th, we loaded our boats with frenzied eagerness, lest on the arrival of our colonel next day we might be ordered to remain behind. We received no orders, but there seemed to be something in the wind, and as soon as each boat was loaded it departed with all speed and was quickly beyond recall.

When we reached Rat portage we found orders for us regarding the navigation of the Winnipeg River, which we were now to descend, and here we had news of the leading brigades and heard that Colonel Wolseley in crossing the lake without a guide had missed his way in the maze of many thousands of lovely islands. It was a difficult task to undertake, and it was indeed fortunate that he happened to meet some Indians, who guided him to Rat portage. He had sailed round the lake for two days, had waited for us the same length of time, and, hurrying on to overtake the leading brigades, had been gone only two hours when we arrived.

The navigation of the Winnipeg River by boat or canoe is one of the most difficult in the world. In its course to Lake Winnipeg it falls many hundreds of feet by a succession of cataracts, most of which are of a very difficult and dangerous character. The portages on the route enabled the force to pass a number of those places, but many rapids had to be run and many risks taken before we arrived at Lake Winnipeg.

On approaching a rapid which has to be run, the bowman always stands up in his place and steers, long paddle in hand, braced against the stem, his keen and practised eye on the rushing water. The voyageur in the stern, who has shipped a long oar in the stern-rowlock, a ring securely fastened so that it cannot jump out, keeps the boat from swinging in the current. Down the torrent the craft rushes, propelled by the desperate efforts of the six oarsmen. They row as for their lives so that there may be steerage way for the bowman who, by skilful use of his paddle, brings the vessel safely through the rocks and whirlpools of the passage. The boat seems to spring beneath its crew, the speed being so great that the oars seem like feathers in their hands, no pressure of the water being felt on the blades as the boat careers down the incline. At a very early hour the next morning we were at work and had our boats and their cargoes across before breakfast. The ground was rough and stony but level, and on this portage we saw the heaviest load carried. One of the Company's guides, a tall, dark, and powerful-looking voyageur, with a full black beard and moustache, hearing of the exploits of the Iroquois and others in our brigades, was anxious to show what he could do, so he carried two barrels of pork and 1000 rounds of ammunition across. The load had to be carefully secured and placed so that he could stand well under it. The weight was 528 lbs., but the burden was an awkward one and nothing to be gained by it except to show the man's great strength, which was patent to everyone as he moved quickly under the load without any apparent distress. Many heavy burdens were carried by the officers and men ; nearly every boat had several who carried their barrel of pork or arm-chest of 200 lbs. without any difficulty. Many conveyed a barrel of pork and a sack of beans on their backs as one load. I always carried my share of pork with either my knapsack or another pack, of equal weight added. One of the officers of the 60th Ensign St. Maur (now the Duke of Somerset), a tall, handsome young man, nicknamed " Anak," because of his great strength, frequently packed two barrels of pork on his back, 400 lbs., and Captain Redvers Buller always took at least 200 lbs. and sometimes 300 lbs. at a trip. Everyone of us, on account of the training given by the heavy work, became much stronger than when he started, although he was then in good condition.

At the rapid called Le Grand Descharge we met with what at one time promised to be a serious mishap. Big Mike, the powerful and skilful Iroquois, although of Major Macleod's boat, took the bow of ours also, and Captain McMillan, who had remained at the summit to see his boats safely through, came in our craft, which was the last, and sat in the stern sheets near Big Neil McArthur. I had the stroke oar (we took turns at it), and, as we approached the crest, set the pace, but just as we passed over it, rowing our best, Neil's oar snapped like a pipe stem and the boat swung into the tremendous waves on our right, rolling and pitching over them, and hurling several of the crew from their oars into the bottom of the boat. Captain McMillan tried to hold my oar down in the rowlock to enable me to row, but it was impossible ; we were quite helpless, and death stared us in the face as we surged past the rocks and whirlpools at a great speed, while Big Mike stood towering in the bow wielding a heavy oar as if it were a light paddle.

His long hair streamed in the wind, his coal black eyes glared at the angry waters, and he handled his oar with such effect that the boat came safely through, landing us far below, and his compatriots on both sides of the Descharge, who, with our comrades of the brigade, were watching the outcome with great anxiety, joined him in wild whoops and shrieks of triumphant laughter.

At Fort Alexander, which we reached at sundown on the 25th, we found Mr. Donald Smith with news of the Red River Settlement. Colonel Wolseley and staff had arrived on the 20th and were met by Mr. Donald Smith, who had come there for the purpose. Lt.-Col. Feilden and the whole of the regular troops had reached there on the 18th, and on Sunday, the 21st, they had left for Fort Garry in 50 boats via Lake Winnipeg.

We were off early on the morning of the 27th, and the next day as we ploughed our way up the Red River numbers of the Scotch settlers and Indians came to the bank to welcome us to the " Great Lone Land " and the church bells rang merrily as we passed on.

The brigades arrived at Lower Fort Garry, " The Stone Fort," early in the afternoon. Colonel Wolseley, Mr. Donald Smith and Lieutenant Heneage, R.E., had been there that day to inspect the fort and arrange for the accommodation of the 2nd Quebec Rifles for the coming winter. Major Wainwright and his two brigades of the Ontario Rifles had passed up at noon on the 26th. We left Lower Fort Garry early next morning and tracked up the St. Andrew's rapids. Numbers of people came, as on the previous day, to welcome us as we rowed along. We arrived at Fort Garry at sunset on August 29, just 38 days from Shebandowan, and encamped on the level, grassy stretch of plain between the mouth of the Assiniboine and the fort.

When we arrived Colonel Wolseley and staff were busy making arrangements for the return of the regular troops and the retention of the Canadians as a garrison until the following spring. The Ontario Rifles were to be quartered at Fort Garry and the Quebec Rifles in the Stone Fort. The colonel and his officers were the guests of Mr. Donald Smith in his commodious quarters at Fort Garry.

The advanced troops had landed on the 23rd on the left bank of the Red River, six miles by land and nine by the river from Fort Garry, with the intention of moving upon the fort the next morning. But a violent gale sprang up, accompanied by torrents of rain, which continued all night, making the roads nearly impassable, and the commander was obliged to change his plans and take to the boats. The scouts sent into Winnipeg during the night brought the information that the rebel flag still floated over Fort Garry that evening and that Riel evidently meant to fight.

Early the next morning the force landed about two miles north of Winnipeg and advanced on Fort Garry, going round the west side of the village, but although guns were seen protruding from the embrasures in the bastions and the gate on the north side was shut, there were no signs of life, and the rebel flag had been hauled down. Scouts were sent round the fort at a gallop and found the south gate open ; Riel, Lepine and O'Donoghue were seen escaping over the bridge of boats in front of the fort. We then took possession of the place, hoisted the Union Jack, fired a salute and gave three cheers for the Queen.

Fort Garry, which has taken such a prominent place in the history of the west, was originally given the proud name of Fort Gibraltar. It was erected in 1806, and destroyed in 1816. In 1822, when the Hudson's Bay and North West Companies were amalgamated it was rebuilt and named Fort Garry. In 1835 it was rebuilt in stone, running 280 feet east and west and 240 feet north and south. There were circular bastions at each corner with embrasures for guns and loopholes for muskets. The walls were about 12 feet in height and had a wooden banquette round the inside to enable the defenders to fire over them.

In 1850 a second part was extended 300 feet north with double walls of oak bolted together about two feet apart, filled in with broken stone, mixed with earth. The foundation of the new addition was of stone, the banquette was continued, and a north gateway of stone was built with a platform and embrasures for guns. This was no doubt the gateway on the north side of the stone portion of the fort, and was shifted when the addition was constructed. I have no authority for this, but it seems to me that there must have been such a gateway for the stone fort, and that it is only natural that the same material should be used. The south gateway of the fort was but a short distance from the Assiniboine and had no gun platforms ; the gates were of heavy oak timber, clamped with spikes. The buildings inside the fort consisted of a store, or sales-shop, on the east close to the south-east bastion. A large house, two stories in height with a stoep, or platform, along the front of it, and used as officers' quarters, stood in the centre of the older part of the fort.

The residence of the Governor of the Hudson's Bay Company faced the north gate, a short distance from it. At the west side of the fort, not far from the wall, there stood four long buildings, each two stories in height and large enough to accommodate 100 soldiers. Three of these were handed over to the Ontario Rifles as soon as they were put in order, and behind the doors of each room the roll-boards of the last troops who had come in by Hudson's Bay were still hanging. On one of them was entered the name of Bugler Coyne, our sergeant-major !

The south-east bastion was now in use as a guard-room and the others were filled with military stores left by the former occupants of the fort ; these were Brown Bess muskets, bayonets, kegs of bullets, powder and shot. Other buildings were on the north-east side of the fort, and during our stay were used as commissary stores. There were a few small buildings in secluded nooks. As soon as the public works department officers arrived a large building was erected between the front gate and the south-east bastion, and contained the orderly-room, sergeants' mess, library, etc.

Outside the fort communication with the south was by means of a bridge of scows and a ferry over the Assiniboine ; both were in constant use until winter set in. Large numbers of creaking Red River carts, without a particle of iron in their construction or grease for their axles, came in every day from St. Cloud, Minnesota, the nearest rail point in the United States, laden with merchandise for the Hudson's Bay Company and the merchants of Winnipeg. The United States points were reached by the steamer *International*, a flat-bottomed river boat propelled by a stern wheel, which went to the highest point navigable on the Red River. Running in opposition to her were flat boats, which brought in flour, butter and eggs ; when their loads were discharged they were broken up and sold, the lumber bringing good prices.

The Winnipeg of that day was situated about half a mile north of Fort Garry and consisted of about forty houses of every shape and size lining the Stone Fort trail for about half a mile. That old road is now the beautiful main street of the city of Winnipeg. The first house from the fort was that of the Rev. Dr. Young, the truly Christian pastor of the little Methodist church. There was one fairly good hotel kept by a Mr. Davis, who was, later on, premier of the new province of Manitoba. Nine stores, three chemist shops, one saddlery, one hardware store, and, of course, several saloons, with such names as " Hell's Gates," " The Red Saloon," etc., were situated in the village.

The village of St. Boniface lay on the right bank of the Red River, and was the residence of Bishop Taché, a prelate of the Oblate order ; his residence and the cathedral were for that time very fine buildings, and there were several comfortable houses and a convent. The cathedral was well attended by the Metis, large numbers of whom could be seen going to and from it every Sunday. Each would be respectably dressed in the costume of the country, the men in long blue coats with bright brass buttons, gay sashes, and fur caps, which would now be worth 1000 dollars, corduroy or moleskin trousers, leggings and moccasins beautifully ornamented with beads or worked in silk. The women wore, as a rule, dark-coloured skirts of silk, beaded or silk worked moccasins, and they had dark-coloured shawls over their heads instead of hats or bonnets.

North of Winnipeg, St. John's Anglican cathedral was the principal church of that denomination, and there was a Presbyterian church in the Scotch settlement of Kildonan, some miles further. The clergy of the settlement were broad-minded and on excellent terms with everyone, and the people, when we got to know them, were kind and true friends.

For several days after the leading troops reached Fort Garry, the main street, which was a trail from the fort to the lower settlements through the little village of Winnipeg, was a sea of black mud, caused by the recent rains. In it voyageurs, whites, half-breeds and Indians fought, wallowed and slept in all stages of drunkenness, induced by the poison dispensed over the bars of the vile saloons of the place. They made the day and night hideous with their yells, shrieks and curses, and it became necessary to detail strong pickets to patrol the village, and Mr. Donald Smith posted at various spots special constables to maintain the law. Happily these precautions had the desired effect, order was restored and the victims of the debauch returned to work.

On August 31 the last of the corps arrived under Lt.-Col. Jarvis, and Captain Buller left with his company for the north-west angle of the Lake of the Woods. On September 1 the last of the 60th Rifles departed for the east, followed two days later by the detachments of Royal Artillery and Royal Engineers. Mr. Dawson, the indefatigable, brought our first letters from the east. Mr. Archibald, the newly-appointed Lieutenant Governor of Manitoba and the North West Territories, arrived at the Indian settlement at the mouth of the Red River in his huge bark canoe manned by Indians. From there he sent on in advance a letter to the commander of the expedition, congratulating him on its " magnificent success," and saying that it was " impossible not to feel that the men who have so triumphed over such difficulties must not only themselves have worked wonders, but also must have been well led."

Mr. Archibald was a Nova Scotian, a clever lawyer, handsome and benevolent in appearance. He was installed in his office of Lieutenant Governor on September 6. Mr. Donald Smith, who had carried on the civil government of the North West until Mr. Archibald's arrival, Colonel Wolseley and staff, and a large number of the leading people of the settlement were present. Lieutenant Butler and Dr. Schultz arrived together, both remarkable for their magnificent physique and almost gigantic stature as well as for the contrast they afforded, Butler being dark-haired and bearded, Schultz golden-haired like a Viking of old. When the governor appeared a large band of Saulteaux and Cree Indians appeared to do honour to the occasion. They were on foot, decorated, feathered and painted, and the chief was mounted on a pony and painted white from head to foot.

Among the amusing incidents that occurred before Colonel Wolseley and his staff left Fort Garry was one which took place when I was on sentry early in the morning at the rear gate of the Government House. I had only just been posted when a colonel on the staff, noted for his kindness of heart, capability as a soldier, hot temper and lurid language, appeared unshaven and in his shirt sleeves, carrying in his hand a letter. He addressed me with, " Sentry, have you seen my orderly ? " I replied, " No, sir, not yet ! " upon which he broke into his favourite style of conversation when disturbed, saying, " Blank the blank to h—l and d—n ! " I acquiesced as a good soldier should, and he returned to his quarters, but soon reappeared just as Stavely, his orderly, who was an ex-naval man, came swaggering along the walk, spick and span, as if he owned the country and there was nobody like him. When the colonel sighted him he said pleasantly, " Ah, Stavely ! Take this letter to ——, and here's 50 cents to drink my health ! "

During his stay at Fort Garry, Colonel Wolseley promulgated a farewell order to each contingent of troops. The regulars he thanked for enabling him to carry out the Lieutenant General's orders so successfully. After referring to the " excessive fatigue in the performance of a service that for its arduous nature can bear comparison with any previous military expedition," to the 600 miles traversed, to the road-making, to the 47 portages, " entailing the unparalleled exertion of carrying the boats, guns, ammunition, stores and provisions," he went on :

The whole journey has been made through a wilderness, where, as there were no supplies of any sort whatever to be had, everything had to be taken with you in the boats. I have throughout viewed with pleasure the manner in which officers have vied with their men in carrying heavy loads. It has rained 45 days out of the 94 that have passed by since we landed at Thunder Bay, and upon many occasions every man has been wet through for days together. There has not been the slightest murmur of discontent heard from anyone. It may confidently be asserted that no force has had to endure more continuous labour, and it may be truthfully said that no men on service have been better behaved or more cheerful under the trials arising from exposure to inclement weather, excessive fatigue and the annoyance by flies.

To the militia he addressed a separate farewell in which he paid them a compliment that must awaken a thrill of pride in every Canadian's heart.

I can say without flattery that, although I have served with many armies in the field, I have never been associated with a better set of men. . . . You have only to attend as carefully to the orders of the officer to whose command I now hand you over, as you have done to mine, to become shortly a force second to no corps in Her Majesty's service. . . . I bid you all good-bye with no feigned regret. I shall ever look back with pleasure and pride to having commanded you, and although separated from you by thousands of miles, I shall never cease to take an earnest interest in your welfare.

In his *Story of a Soldier's Life*, Field-Marshal Viscount Wolseley says :

I can draw no distinction between the relative merits of the military value of the regular soldier and the Canadian militia man who went with me to Red River ; each had arrived at Prince Arthur's Landing with special attributes peculiarly their own, but by the time Fort Garry had been occupied each had acquired the military virtues of the other. What it is that a large army of such men under some great leader could not achieve, I, for one, know not.

Colonel Wolseley left Fort Garry on September 10, but before his departure a banquet was given in his honour at Government House.

Arrangements were made for the two battalions of militia to garrison the Red River Settlement for the winter of 1870-1. The 1st Ontario Rifles were stationed in Fort Garry, with No. 1 Company under Captain Cook at Fort Pembina on the border, the 2nd Quebec Rifles in the Stone Fort, and in the

D

short space of 17 days from the date of the arrival of the troops everything had been put right, the Lieutenant Governor had been duly installed, the garrison settled down and the regulars despatched to eastern Canada.

Soon after Colonel Jarvis took over the command an incident occurred which disturbed the community and caused bad blood in the settlement for some time, in fact the feeling did not die out for more than a year. The Ontario Rifles were out on fatigue, taking the boats out of the Assiniboine where they had been moored, and placing them on skids near the camp. Suddenly two travel-stained horsemen, one on a black horse the other on a grey, rode up to us and asked if we had seen a man named Elzear Goulet who, one of them stated, had commanded the firing party which shot Thomas Scott. As we could give no information they wheeled quickly and rode off at full speed towards Winnipeg. The same night it was reported in camp that they had found Goulet seated on a bench at the Davis House, a hotel in the village, and when they had accosted him he had taken flight towards the Red River, pursued by his accusers. When he arrived at the bank he turned and threatened to shoot, but they called to him " Fire away ! " Seeing that they would not be denied, he jumped into the river, and when he attempted to swim across, shots were fired and he sank. The horsemen had been followed by a crowd of people, amongst whom were two of our buglers, mere lads. No other soldiers were present, and neither of these took part in the chase, nor is it likely that any of our men would have taken part in the pursuit of the unfortunate man, even had they known that he was one of the murderers of Scott. We had amongst us about a dozen very wild spirits, but they were kept in control by the strict discipline maintained in the regiment, and, what is sometimes better, the fear of the displeasure of their comrades, who in ways which soldiers have, could make their lives intolerable. At the time of this occurrence a strong party of military police was in the town night and day, and as they were remarkable for their attention to duty, it is a certainty that they would be aware of any part taken by soldiers and would have arrested the delinquents on the spot.

The next day our commanding officer, misled by reports made to him by interested parties who wished to put the blame on the military to save others, paraded us in camp and fiercely attacked us, accusing us of being a lot of hot-headed fanatics who had aided and abetted the death of Goulet. No doubt he believed the report, for it came to him from persons in high places, but they were persons who would not hesitate to make political capital out of the circumstance, and, able staff officer though he was, he took no steps to inquire into the charge which, had he done so, could easily have been disproved. He believed the words of enemies in disguise, and the evilly-disposed persons, to whom Colonel Wolseley had referred in his farewell order to us, were thus fortunate enough to have the blame shifted from their shoulders to ours. Thus, for party reasons, we were branded throughout the eastern provinces as a band of murderers, and when the papers from Ontario and Quebec arrived and were read in barracks, there was a strong feeling of indignation which it required a steady hand and tactful mind to keep within bounds. As a matter of fact it never died out so long as the regiment lasted, and was carried into civil life.

It was supposed up to this time that the body of poor Scott was buried within the walls of Fort Garry, but this was disproved one morning before we had gone into barracks. I was present when an officer of the public works department with a fatigue party opened the grave which was situated between the officers' quarters and the south gate. An oblong, pine box was found, but there was no body in it; the box was empty, and had no doubt been buried in the fort to deceive people as to the true disposal of the remains of the murdered man. After this discovery there was a strong impression that his body had been taken away during the night after the murder, weighted with chains and forced through a hole in the ice of the Red River, but the mystery has never been cleared up.

For several months before the advent of the troops to Fort Garry smallpox had been raging on the plains of the far west from the Missouri to the North Saskatchewan. This scourge, so fatal to the red man, was brought into the country on a Missouri steamboat plying from St. Louis to Benton, Montana. A white man, who had the disease, left a blanket behind him on the steamboat. This was stolen by an Indian of the Gros Ventre tribe and started the contagion. He caught it and gave it to his people, amongst whom it spread until many camps were depopulated, and a war party of the Bloods, a tribe of the Blackfeet nation, who had gone south to steal horses, found in one camp nothing alive but the ponies grazing round the tents. The dead lay as they had fallen.

The Blood warriors, knowing nothing about the disease, appropriated as many of the ponies and buffalo robes as they could take, and returned with their spoil to the north, no doubt well pleased with the results of their foray. It proved, however, to be a fatal one to them, and to the majority of the dusky inhabitants of the great plains. By the time they got back to their people, the infected robes had given them the disease and it spread through their tribe, depopulating their camps and sending destruction through the Peigans, Blackfeet, Crees and Stonies; in fact through all our Indian tribes. From them it spread to the plain hunters, Company's employees and the families of the missionaries. Many of the latter did their best to induce the Indians and half-breeds to scatter so as to escape the dread germs, and all who obeyed them succeeded, but unhappily there were many who paid no attention to the advice, and suffered the consequences. Some of the missionaries, well-meaning but unpractical men, encouraged their flocks to keep together in large numbers, and they were soon surrounded by sick and dying people. To make matters worse there were neither doctors nor medicines, and this state of affairs continued until enormous numbers of Indians had died. Every important chief of the Blackfeet nation had gone, leaving few fit to lead the people. One tribe which, a few years previously, had 2,000 lodges in their principal camp, each lodge averaging at least eight persons, was reduced to one-tenth of its number. It was particularly virulent amongst the Crees, who were said to have contracted it from the Blackfeet in the same way that the latter had caught it from the Gros Ventres.

A Company's officer at Edmonton reported the circumstance to his chief, with the result that Lieutenant Butler was despatched west with a stock of medicines and directions for their use, these to be given to the officers of the Company, missionaries and other persons of intelligence. He had also orders from Lieutenant Governor Archibald to report upon the extent of the scourge and its origin, as well as upon all matters about which it was necessary for the government to be informed.

The whisky trader had already penetrated the southern and western portions of the North West Territory, and his pernicious influence was already felt amongst the tribes in those regions ; he had to be dealt with, and Lieutenant Butler was expected to devise means to teach him that British law was supreme. He performed his task with great skill and sound judgment, returning to Fort Garry on February 18, 1871, having travelled on horseback and by dog train 2,700 miles and endured many severe hardships, sleeping under the sky with the thermometer indicating many degrees below zero. His book, *The Great Lone Land*, gives a clear account of his journey and work.

Soon after Goulet's death Colonel Jarvis went on leave, and until his return to Fort Garry in the winter, Lt.-Col. Casault took over the command of the 2nd Quebec Rifles, whilst that of the Ontarios fell to Major Wainwright. The quarters were being put in order for our occupation when Captain McMillan sent for Private Grady and myself, and gave us a page of a novel to write from dictation. When we had finished, he looked over our work with the remark, " That is very nice," and dismissed us. A few days later, when the regiment had moved into barracks, both of us were in orders for promotion to corporal.

I reported for duty to Sergeant R——, a kindly man and an able civil engineer and land surveyor, but too good for some of those with whom he had to deal. The majority of the company were very fine men, but there were several as bad as I have met, and strange to say they were located in one room in charge of Corporal A——, who seemed to have been selected for the job

of keeping them in order as much on account of his physical
as his mental powers. The men were afraid of him. The *élite*
of the company, with few exceptions, had been able to induce
their kindly Sergeant R—— to permit them to be together in
the other room, and to that I was posted. I was young in
comparison to the majority of the men in the lower room where
the wild spirits were quartered, and I went to Number 7 with
some misgivings. As I expected, I was not well received by
the rough element. The men of the upper room were comrades
from the first, and the officers treated me kindly, but the
" toughs " regarded me as an interloper who should not have
been promoted from another company. One of them, who had
been drinking when I reported to the senior sergeant, made no
bones about telling me so and a great deal more. He was one
of the greatest ruffians that I have ever seen out of gaol, but
our mild senior N.C.O. let him rave away in his drunkenness,
instead of letting him see the inside of the guardroom.

I was not pleased with my reception, but bided my time.
For the first month the bad lot in the company left nothing
undone to compel me to commit myself and be paraded " on
the carpet." Their attempts were useless, however, and I took
my own way, making them toe the mark. Some of them, when
warned for duty, would object that it was not their turn, but
they were made to find that such conduct was useless. I was
firm, laughing off much of their nonsense, with the result that
in less than a month they ceased their stupid manœuvres and
showed signs that I had at least gained their respect. But it
did not cure them of acts of insubordination for which they were
noted, and one morning a strong, stalwart fellow of the group
had a narrow escape from being charged with murder.

I had just come off guard and was resting on my cot, and
Jack Kerr, a favourite in the company, was busy polishing the
huge Carron stove when this fellow came upstairs, dressed in
review order without his rifle, conversing with some of the men.
There was a long table beside him on which lay several sheath
knives which had just been cleaned. The cook, nicknamed
" Rattledy W——," came in and began skylarking with Kerr,
who made a black streak across his nose with the brush he was
using on the stove. W—— laughed at this and the other man

smiled, but with a sinister look said to Kerr, " You could not do that to me." " Oh, yes, I could ! " replied Kerr, and sprang at him with the brush, making a motion about a foot from his face, but without touching him, nor did he mean to do so, as .the fellow was in review kit. But this was no safeguard ; the other seized one of the long sheath knives and, rushing at Kerr, drove it into his thigh. Before I could get round the stove to interfere, he made another rush at Kerr, knife in hand, but the latter was too quick for him ; he seized the huge tongs, used for the big stove, and brought them down with full force on his assailant's head, felling him insensible to the ground with such force that the building shook.

His comrades in the room below, hearing the noise, dashed up the outside stairway, the only entrance to the room, and seeing Kerr seated on a cot holding his bleeding thigh, and their comrade lying senseless on the floor, they made for Kerr like madmen. On hearing them coming up the stairs I had armed myself with a rifle, and when they charged, met them with it clubbed, and drove them out of the room and downstairs by sheer force. I then sent for the surgeon's assistant, in the meantime doing my best for both. When Dr. Codd arrived he sent them to hospital, where both spent some time. This scrimmage seemed to clear the air, and we had no more trouble in barracks.

Soon after the regiment had settled down, and the Indian summer with its delightful sunshine was at its height, our commanding officer began our annual training. Being young and strong with good appetites, we found our rations insufficient, and when we could afford it we turned to Devlin's prolific bakery, not far from the barracks. We paraded for drill two or three times a day, once in the early morning under the adjutant, again in review order until noon, and in marching order at half-past two with our 70 lb. packs and ammunition. This would have been a severe enough test, but, owing to our work on the portages, we had a contempt for any load less than the weight of a barrel of pork. In the afternoon, as in the morning, the drills were those of a rifle regiment of that time, every movement had to be done very smartly, double time was the rule, and from extended order we occasionally made rushes of 1000 yards or more to assemble on the reserve. After about 2½ hours of this amusement the proceedings wound up with a march-past at all the paces, to the music of the regimental band and the intense satisfaction of a bevy of fair damsels and their mothers who sat on the balcony on the north side of the parade ground. Fortunately we were in good trim for the work, and none showed any signs of fatigue, but it was not encouraging to our ravenous appetites to return to a cheerless barrack-room and make our evening meal off a bucket of cold tea and the attenuated remains of the morning loaf of bread.

These manœuvres did us a great deal of good, brushed us up until we were wellnigh perfect, and taught us how little food a healthy Anglo-Saxon really requires. The afternoon drills in marching order were in fun styled " Ladies' Parades," on account of the interest that the fair sex took in our movements, particularly the pretty wheels on and off the passing line. One of the young ladies remarked to an officer, " It is charming to see the regiment out in the afternoons; the men look so nice with the little boxes on their backs ! "

CHAPTER IV

Winnipeg forty years ago—Dances—Weddings—Funerals—Sundays—
Schools—Buffaloes—The new province of Manitoba—Election
riots—Our relaxations—We leave Fort Garry—Home again—
The Canadian artillery—A good record—An active veteran—
The inception of the North West Mounted Police—" The wild
and woolly west "—Whisky traders—" Whoop up "—" The
Spitsee cavalry "—A treacherous attack—The Peigans, Crees, and
Assiniboines—The state of things in the west.

THE Red River Settlement[1] in 1870—consisted of parishes
which were subdivided into narrow farms about four
miles in length, the rear half of which was held as a
hay privilege. The houses being close together gave the
settlers the advantages of a water front and easy communication for social intercourse. The rivers during the summer
were the highways for their boats, and those of the Great
Company, and during the winter became a sheltered road for
their sleighs and dog trains. The houses were chiefly of squared
logs let into a frame, and were roofed heavily with thatch ;
the farms were fenced with rails and posts as far back as
required for agriculture. Near each house were the outbuildings
and sheds, whilst huge piles of poplar poles stood on and in the
vicinity of the clay-oven, almost invariably to be seen near the
house.

The chief social events in the life of the settlers were dances,
weddings and funerals, whilst church-going was a duty never
neglected, the people being in the habit of walking five or six
miles to service, or riding or driving twice that distance.
Weddings were as important then as now, and were one of the

[1] My kind friend, the Hon. Colin Inkster, High Sheriff of Manitoba,
whose father was one of the first to welcome the troops on their arrival
in the vicinity of his residence, Seven Oaks, Point Douglas, has given
me much valuable information, which added to my own experiences
has enabled me to write a short sketch which may be of interest to those
who have not had the great pleasure of meeting those delightful people,
the first settlers of the Great Lone Land.

occasions on which wines and liquors were drunk. They took place during the winter months, as the long nights were conducive to the proper execution of the Red River Jig, the Scotch Reel and other dances requiring vigour.

To be a good jig dancer required much speed and endurance. When the first surveyors arrived a dispute arose as to the distance to Sturgeon Creek, about six miles west of Winnipeg. In order to settle it they agreed to send one of their dog drivers to the creek and back with a pedometer in his pocket. This was at night, and before he had come back the surveyors had gone to bed. Next morning their dog driver produced the pedometer and to their astonishment the instrument indicated 60 miles ! He was at once questioned as to where he had been, and his reply was that he did not go farther than Sturgeon Creek, but finally he admitted that when he arrived there a dance was going on, to which he was invited, and he had danced all night, walking home in the morning.

Weddings generally took place on a Thursday ; the father of the bride or some person representing him went from house to house, inviting friends and neighbours on a day prior to the wedding, not later than the Monday. It was short notice, but such was the custom. On these occasions it was not unusual for the guests coming from a distance to arrive the night before, and have a sort of preliminary canter for the following day. The bridal party drove in carioles, another reason for not celebrating weddings in the summer months, as it would not be becoming to see twenty or thirty well-dressed couples going to church in squeaking Red River carts. The horses were decorated with coloured ribbons, and when the party arrived at the bride's house they were received with a salute of firearms. The men then put away the horses, and the ladies doffed their French merinos and substituted muslin gowns. Dancing then commenced and was kept up all night. The music was supplied by relays of fiddlers, and the only interruptions were for meals. These consisted of roast beef, roast mutton, buffalo tongues, plum puddings, mince pies, etc., and as one house was too small for the entertainment of such a large party, two were generally brought into use, one for dancing and the other for feasting. The following week the groom would take his bride to his father's house, and a repetition of the festivities ensued, called the " home wedding."

Funerals were conducted with great solemnity and decorum, friends were invited as at the weddings and refreshments partaken of. The coffin, home-made and covered with a black cloth, was carried by four men at a time, whilst four others walked by their side, ready to take their places when the patriarch who led the procession should halt and call out · " Relief ! " The carriers would then fall out, and others be ready to relieve those who had taken their places. Funerals proceeded in this way for many miles, a halt being occasionally called for refreshments.

Sunday was kept with Puritan exactness and, however great their need, no windmill would grind on that day. As for cards, they were prohibited as an institution of the Evil One.

Of churches and schools the settlers had sufficient, and, thanks to the missionary societies, the salaries of the Protestant ministers were paid, and those of the teachers in part, especially in the poorer settlements. In St. John's, where the people were well off, the parents paid 15s. per child per annum and supplied sufficient firewood to warm the schoolhouse. In that school, besides the three R's, geography, history, grammar, Latin and French were taught, and Bible history was one of the most important branches. At one time school material was so scarce that old slates had to be broken up for slate pencils and tea-chest lead beaten into shape to take the place of lead pencils, but these were, of course, extreme cases. Quill pens were often used, the teachers cutting them into shape every morning, and each pupil's name was scratched on the back of the quill.

In 1870-1 the buffalo were about 300 miles west of Fort Garry, and nearly half the people lived by hunting them. There were two classes of hunters, one that lived by the chase, called " winterers," the other that had small farms and lived on them during the winter ; the former class usually arrived from their winter quarters and encamped west of the fort, the product of their hunt being mostly buffalo robes and wolf and fox skins.

After the sale of their robes money circulated freely ; they had no idea of economy and never thought of putting anything aside for a rainy day. They would pay £40 or £50 for a good horse, as the possession of a good buffalo runner would raise the owner from poverty to affluence in one season. After they had sold or traded their robes and furs, they outfitted again and went off to their summer hunt early in June. The class with the small farms did likewise and returned with what they called " dry provisions " in August. The product of the summer hunt would be pemmican, dried meat, tallow, dressed skins, sinews and hides. The " winterers " then outfitted and left for the west and did not return until spring. Those with the little farms, after they had harvested their crops, went out for the fall hunt and came back in November to spend the winter in the settlement.

The first cattle were driven into the settlement from the south by Americans ; cows sold at £30 and oxen at £18.

Such was the Red River Settlement, and up to the date of the rebellion of the Metis I believe there were no more truly happy people in the world than the inhabitants of this region. In the words of Longfellow,

> Neither locks had they to their doors, nor bars to their windows,
> Their dwellings were open as day, and the hearts of their owners,
> There the richest was poor and the poorest lived in abundance.

During the winter of 1870-1 party feeling ran high in the new province of Manitoba. Old sores were re-opened and real or imaginary grievances made the most of. The elections came off on November 20 and produced much rioting, which kept the excellent little civil force, our military police, and inlying pickets very busy. Fortunately, it was not considered necessary to call out the troops. The pickets were strong, the police resolute and tactful, and the very numerous disturbances which took place during the winter were quelled with a firm hand.

The civil police force was a fine body of men under the command of Captain Villiers, of the Quebec Rifles, who had served in the 13th Hussars. The constables were selected from the two rifle regiments, and there were a few young fellows from the settlement. They were drilled and uniformed as cavalry. In all their dealings with the rival parties they displayed sound judgment, thus gaining the confidence of the public. As for the men of the regiment, there were few who gave trouble while the elections were in progress. The colonel did not confine the corps to barracks, as was customary in those days ; he put us on our honour and had very little cause to regret it, although considering the bitter party feeling one might think that the indulgence was risky.

When the rioting began I was on picket. The call for help was sounded, and the picket hurried to the town before I could fall in, as my quarters were outside the fort. I ran all the way to join it, however, and was met by three hostiles who tried to stop me ; but I clubbed my rifle and easily brushed them aside ; they were not prepared to try conclusions in that way. When I fell into the ranks the riot was at its height and many arrests were made. Our officer ordered us to load with ball, and it seemed at one time that we might have to fire ; but, fortunately, the disturbance was quelled without it, though there were many broken heads.

In spite of our regular round of garrison duties, we contrived during our spare evenings to have a pleasant time. There were dances in the settlement, the reading-room was full of men every night, reading the papers and writing letters home, which had to be carried 500 miles by dog-trains and sleighs before they would reach the nearest railway. There were readings from his favourite authors by Ensign Stewart Mulvey, who convulsed his audience as he rendered humorous passages from " Handy Andy," " Rory O'More," and " Charles O'Malley." Amateur theatricals, nigger minstrels and concerts, in which the officers and men took part, were held in town and well attended by the citizens and soldiers. The vocal talent was above the average and much appreciated.

Even on guard the time did not hang heavily, although on the cold nights the sentries had to be relieved every hour, which necessitated a good deal of walking, but when one returned to the guard-room there were many yarns to amuse us. There were a couple of dozen old soldiers in the regiment, one of whom had been through the Central Indian campaign under Sir Hugh Rose. On one of these occasions, he said,

" I was in the 86th Royal County Down in the Mutiny, and whin we tuk the fort of Jhansi there was a big pile of goold and dimonds in the middle of the big square, but I would not go near it, do yez think I wud ? Not a bit av it ! But there were dozens who did, and were busy filling their pockets whin there was an explosion, which blew them all to the divil ! It was jist as I expicted, there was a mine undernayth the goold and dimonds, put there to blow us up whin we wud be hilpin' ourselves to the stuff ! "

The first Legislative Assembly of the new province of Manitoba consisted of 24 members, and the inaugural session was opened on March 15. It was convened in due form by Mr. Archibald in person, the usual salute was fired, and the Ontario Rifles furnished a guard of honour.

A short time before the snow had disappeared orders had been received for the officer commanding the district to select from each of the two regiments a company of 50 men, who would volunteer to remain in the service to garrison Fort Garry for another year, or longer. All the soldiers who desired to enter civil life in the west were to be discharged, and those who did not wish to settle in Manitoba were to be sent back to Toronto or elsewhere in the east. The discharges entitled the recipients to a free grant of 160 acres of prairie land. If they decided to farm they could have a homestead of 160 acres and a pre-emption of the same area, the latter at a trifling cost per acre, and three years in which to pay for it.

No difficulty was experienced in getting 100 men to volunteer for the service companies, and Major Irvine, of the 2nd Quebec Rifles, was placed in command. The discharges of those who wished to settle were soon in their hands, and the necessary arrangements made for those who were returning to the east. We left Fort Garry on June 11, and on the morning of July 14 we arrived at Toronto.

The Quebec Rifles manned the walls of the old fort and gave us three hearty cheers as the train rushed by. This was the only welcome we received, but a veteran officer of the British Army, who was on a visit to Canada, was at the station when we detrained, and he remarked, " Well, those are something like soldiers ! " We were discharged in a few days, and departed for our homes, whence the majority soon returned to the west.

Captain Scott was sent to Manitoba the same autumn to reinforce Major Irvine's companies. A Fenian raid had been attempted on the province of Manitoba a couple of months after the return of the expedition. Major Irvine had taken very prompt steps, but the American troops had been set in motion and nipped the affair in the bud, before he had a chance to give them a drubbing. This could easily have been done, as the whole of the officers and men of the Red River expedition who had settled in the west, backed up by a large number of settlers and Hudson's Bay employees under Mr. Donald Smith and other leading citizens, rallied to his assistance and marched under him to the frontier. Captain Scott's command, which had started late, and went by the north-west angle of the Lake of the Woods, underwent a good deal of hardship at an inclement season of the year, but on their arrival were soon settled down comfortably in old Fort Garry, and were stationed there for a considerable time, rendering the settlement perfectly safe from attack.

In October, 1871, the new battery of artillery and school of gunnery, the first of the Canadian Permanent Force, was being organized, and my younger brother Richard and I went to Kingston, Ontario, the headquarters of the corps, for the purpose of taking a twelve months' course.

The battery had few men when we joined, my brother and I being the twenty-second and twenty-third members of it. When fully up to strength it would consist of long-course N.C.O.'s and gunners from the field and garrison batteries of the militia, and be able to receive and instruct short-course officers and men. Lt.-Col. (now Maj.-Gen. Sir George) French of the Royal Artillery, commanded the battery and school of instruction, and the next senior officer was Captain Cotton.

The commandant began the formation of the battery by selecting the best N.C.O.'s and privates from the disbanded depot of the Ontario and Quebec Rifles, which had been stationed at Kingston while those corps had been in the west. These were given a good course in gunnery, and were obliged to pass their examinations and prove their fitness in every way. The chief instructor and sergeant-major was John Mortimer, late sergeant-major of the school of gunnery at Shoeburyness, England. He was the first man to instruct on the Armstrong gun when it was invented, and was considered one of the ablest of his rank in the R.A. I always congratulate myself on having served with him and profited by his precept and example. Mortimer had been twenty-two years in the army, which he had entered at the age of sixteen in the R.H.A., and when the short service system was introduced he was obliged to leave while he was still in his prime. It was related of him that when he had his papers he marched to the parade ground, and facing to his proper front, addressed himself thus:— " Sergeant-Major John Mortimer, you have served your Queen and country faithfully for two and twenty years ; your services are no longer required. Right turn ! Dismiss ! " On these commands from himself he turned to the right, took a side pace to the left, and marched briskly through the barrack gate, to be seen no more in England. He proceeded to Canada by the first ship, enlisted in the Red River force, and when he was discharged was appointed to the rank of brigade sergeant-major in the battery, where he certainly left his mark, as he did afterwards at the Royal Military College.

In the spring we were reinforced by some first-class instructors and other staff N.C.O.'s from England. They came fresh from courses in instruction in their branches of the service. They were soon busy and left their impress on the battery and the militia artillery. Among them was Staff-Sergeant (now Lt.-Col.) Clarke, who, in addition to his work as a laboratory foreman, had charge of the drivers of the battery, and soon had that part of the work on a sound basis. He had served in the Crimea, and had the medals and clasps. His yarns about the Russian war were interesting and his experiences varied, for he had taken a turn at everything done by his famous battery, the Grey, of the 4th Brigade.

By June there was a large camp of instruction assembled at Kingston under the command of my former O.C., Colonel Jarvis, and it was visited by the Earl of Dufferin, the Governor General, accompanied by Colonel P. Robertson Ross, the adjutant-general of militia, who gave the battery its first inspection.

The corps supplied the guards of honour for Lord Dufferin. They presented a very fine appearance, nearly all of the fifty men in the front rank were decorated with medals, and the guard averaged at least five feet ten inches. We handled our arms with smartness and precision ; an Irish soldier near me muttering between his teeth, " Holy Moses, what a prisint ! I tell ye, I tell ye ! " I was sandwiched between two ex-colour-sergeants of the British Army, one had the Crimean, Turkish, Indian Mutiny medals and Legion of Honour decorating his broad breast, and the other showed the same medals and the French decoration for Valour and Discipline.

After the militia camp broke up a brigade of garrison artillery was stationed in Fort Henry for training, and five instructors, myself included, were sent there to train them. Our quarters were in the casemates, and damp from long disuse, but we were strong, and if our boots became blue-moulded during the night from the effects of it, they were easier for the batmen to polish ! I was very fortunate in having a very good battery to instruct, though none of the men understood English. At the final inspection, however, their record was the best in the brigade for gunnery and discipline. Their officers belonged to the old seignorial families of the province of Quebec.

I was next sent to Toronto with a strong party to be stationed in the New Fort, as the Stanley barracks were then called, to put the artillery stores, guns and ammunition in order, and I was given the selection of my men, a very great compliment. I found everything in the worst state of confusion, disorder, and neglect, in fact as bad as could be. The stores were piled in heaps on the floors, but before we had been there a month order was restored, thanks largely to our hard-working district gunner, Billy Mitton, a man of more than twenty years' service in the army, but who would never accept promotion. After the stores were put right, we made the obsolete cartridges into modern ones to suit our guns, but before this was done the Toronto garrison battery came into barracks for their annual training, and I took charge

E

of their instruction, assisted by several of my detachment. The corps was excellent, and its training a great pleasure to us. The officers were good disciplinarians, but kind to their men, who were bright and well-behaved.

When the last evening in barracks arrived the battery gave a smoking concert, which Lt.-Col. Goodwin, the military store-keeper, a position now held by the senior Ordnance officer, attended, and contributed much to our pleasure by dancing Irish jigs and hornpipes, and singing " a Waterloo song by a Waterloo man," as he called it, and he also gave the fugle exercise which had been abolished in 1826, a graceful handling of the old Brown Bess musket. It was marvellous to see this officer of 82 years performing this feat as if he were still in his prime. He had served in Bull's troop of the R.H.A. at Quatre Bras and Waterloo, and at the former received a lance wound through the left arm while fighting hand to hand with Kellerman's cavalry when they made their fierce onslaught upon the British squares and guns.

After Waterloo he served in Paris in the army of occupation under the Duke of Wellington, and while there made the acquaintance of several of Napoleon's most noted *maîtres d'armes*, with the result that he became not only a good French scholar, but one of the best swordsmen in Europe, fencing well in both the Italian and French styles. Duelling was in vogue, of course, and in his travels three men who insulted him by saying that no Englishman could fence, were carried off the field. The old gentleman was now devoting his declining years to making a competence for the widow and young child of his son Henry, who had died while attempting a severe gymnastic feat.

In those days the Old Fort possessed a canteen for the sale of ale, porter and groceries, and we got our supplies from the Irish couple who had the privilege of keeping it. The husband was an ex-sergeant of a famous regiment, and he and his wife had been with the corps in all quarters of the globe. We liked them, and had no reason to think that there were occasional lapses from the path of sobriety, but one dull morning Gunner Phillips had cause to visit them for the day's groceries, and found the interior of the canteen in a most ruinous state.

The old man, still active and in his prime, had " broken out " and taking an axe, an excellent weapon for the purpose, had demolished the unoffending beer pumps, the clock, and in fact everything within reach, but when Phillips arrived he had sobered, and was going about amongst the wreckage wringing his hands, bemoaning his foolish escapade, while his faithful spouse, who had also returned to the prosaic present, sat on the floor in the midst of the ruins, dissolved in tears, and when the visitor appeared broke out into lamentations, ejaculating, " Pheelips, I'm a luniac ! "

We found Toronto very pleasant, but were kept busy during the spare hours. After work I attended the Commercial College for a course in business, telegraphy, etc., and when that was concluded I returned to Kingston, the colonel having found himself short of instructors.

In the battery there were many things to amuse ; every kind of sport was indulged in during our spare hours, there were also amusing tales to tell of scenes in the orderly-room when prisoners appeared before the commandant. A gunner, whose time was to be very short, had given the N.C.O. of his room much trouble, and the sergeant in testifying against him delivered himself thus : " I do not know what to make of this man, sir ! He goes out when he likes, comes in when he likes, gets drunk when he likes, in fact he might be an officer, sir ! "

It was not all fun, however, even when we tried to have it, as we found to our regret when the battery had its annual picnic, which came off in the summer. This was held on an island east of Kingston, and we proceeded there in our numerous boats, one of which, a very cranky little craft, with two masts, was steered by an ex-naval man. After luncheon he started off east with three others in the boat, and when they had gone a few miles before a very fresh breeze, they attempted to luff. I was watching them from a high point, and saw the sails disappear and then come up again. This was repeated several times, and I told an officer and several others that the boat had upset, and the men were trying to get on the bottom and turning her over. They would not be convinced, however, so, calling for volunteers, I jumped into a boat, and we rowed

hard for the overturned craft, which I saw in the distance.
When we reached it we found the sailor seated in the stern
with his boots, a pair of Wellingtons, held between his teeth,
while he kept the boat before the wind ! There was no sign of
one of the men, but the other two were on the bottom of the
boat making agonized efforts to retain a hold of the keel over
which the waves washed with great force, and it was evident
that had help not come, their end would have been soon.
The sailor by his own efforts had turned the boat, and repeatedly placed his comrades on it when they were washed off.
With some difficulty we got the three men on board. Soon
after we landed I asked our sailor gunner why he took the
trouble to hang on to his boots under such circumstances.
" They cost me two dollars," was his practical reply, " and if
the lads had drowned in spite of my efforts to save them,
I could swim ashore and have the boots to carry me over the
gravel. I had no fears for myself, but it was almost certain
that the men would drown if help did not come soon."

Apart from this unfortunate circumstance, the spring and
summer of 1873 passed off pleasantly enough. I had many
friends, and at the week-ends had trips to Gananoque to visit
the family of Mr. J. B. Mitchell, or would take a run down to
Alexandria Bay, a pleasant summer resort among the Thousand
Islands, where Generals U. S. Grant and Phil Sheridan were
to be seen, seated under the trees in quiet converse or strolling
about enjoying their cigars and the music of the bands, as if
the roar of battle had never troubled them.

In August at Ottawa I learnt that the North West Mounted
Police Force was to be raised and sent to the north west
very soon. I obtained an introduction to Major Walsh,
who, it turned out, was well known to my relatives on the
St. Lawrence. He was to commence recruiting for " A "
division of the force, and I arranged to go with him as his
sergeant-major if I could get my discharge. So we went
to Colonel French, who was in the city, and with a twinkle
in his eye, as if he knew all about it, he gave four others and
myself permission to leave the battery and join the police.
We returned to Kingston as soon as possible to get our discharges and examinations, and left for Brockville by steamer,

but before we departed our messes gave us a jolly send-off I was sorry to leave, for I had been very well treated by all ranks, and I liked the work, but there were no prospects, and I had the Great Lone Land before me, where it is a man's own fault if he fails while he has health and strength.

We were met on the arrival of the boat by Major Walsh, and in the afternoon we passed the medical examination, and were sworn in as members of the North West Mounted Police Force. Major Walsh left for Ottawa the same evening and directed me to take any desirable recruits who might present themselves, and, on October 1, I took over my duties as sergeant-major of the division.

Before going further with this narrative I must give some idea of what we were, what we were going to do, and why the North West Mounted Police Force was organized. Many persons of high attainments who have only seen the results are under the erroneous impression that there never has been in Canada, as in the United States, what is commonly called "The Wild and Woolly West." Such is not the case, for the state of affairs in the west at the time of the organization of the N.W.M.P. was infinitely worse than in the days when none but the officers of the Hudson's Bay Company and the numerous tribes of Red Indians inhabited the territory.

One cause of the lawlessness was the settlement of the territories of the United States to the south of us. Here large numbers of reckless men found their way, and simply did what they pleased, ruined the Indians, and brought on quarrels with them for the sake of gain. No steps had been taken to restrain them, and the consequence was that there were many who traded to the Indians improved arms and "fire water" in exchange for buffalo robes and furs. These men moved over into Canada, and established palisaded posts as a protection against the Indians whom they were destroying, and systematically continued their nefarious traffic.

The Indians, although much reduced by the ravages of smallpox, were still powerful and of a warlike character. The territory formerly under the rule of the Hudson's Bay

Company had been transferred to the government. The Red River expedition had only enabled the government to be properly carried on in the then small province of Manitoba, which at that time extended not more than 100 miles west of Winnipeg. The south of the territory had not even a justice of the peace, nor dared one set foot in that region.

Travelling across the prairies was fraught with danger. Near Edmonton and on the east slope of the Rocky Mountains the Indians were friendly. A Methodist mission had without difficulty been established well up in the foothills of the Rocky Mountains by the Rev. George McDougall, one of the most noted and enterprising missionaries of his church, but south and west from these foothills, where the city of Calgary is now situated, through the country where the thriving cities of Medicine Hat, Lethbridge and Macleod are located, and along the south branch of the Saskatchewan it was necessary to travel with an escort of armed men.

One of the principal posts of the traders in that region was Fort Hamilton, commonly known as "Whoop Up," situated at the forks of the Belly and St. Mary's rivers. There were two walls, about a dozen feet apart, built of heavy squared logs, braced across by heavy log partitions about the same distance from one another, dividing it into rooms, which were used as dwellings, blacksmiths' shops, stores, etc., the doors and windows opening into the square. There were bastions at the corners, and the walls were loop-holed for musketry. Iron bars were placed across the chimneys to prevent the Indians from getting in that way. There were heavy log roofs across the partitions, and a strong gate of oak, with a small opening to trade through. All other posts merely had palisades, but they were strong enough for the purpose. The trader stood at the wicket, a tubful of whisky beside him, and when an Indian pushed in a buffalo robe to him through the hole in the wall he handed out a tin cupful of the poisonous decoction. A quart of the stuff bought a fine pony. When spring came, wagonloads of the proceeds of the traffic were escorted to Fort Benton, Montana, some 200 odd miles south of the border line.

There were a few legitimate American traders in the country, who traded to the Indians Winchester repeating rifles and ammunition, which enabled them to hunt the buffalo with success, and thus increase the quantity of robes to be traded. The whisky-traders objected, and to put a stop to it organized a body of men styled "The Spitsee Cavalry," after the river of that name, now the well-known High River, Alberta. Spitsee means tall timber, and, consequently, High Wood was the name by which we knew it at first. These people ran some of the legitimate traders out of the country in spite of their protests.

In 1872 a party of men, most of whom had taken part in the great Civil War in the South, came from Fort Benton, Montana, to the Cypress Hills, about 40 miles north of the border, near where Fort Walsh was afterwards built. These men traded large quantities of whisky to a band of Assiniboine Indians who were encamped along the creek on a flat piece of prairie, now known as "The Massacre Ground." When night came these fiends in human shape decided to " clean out " the Indian camp, and accordingly proceeded to a cut bank on the south side of the creek. Here they could stand on the gravel, breast high, rest their Winchesters on the top and fire from good cover. The Indians were in the midst of their orgy, every lodge lighted up so that a good view of each could be had. Fire was then opened, with the result that over 30 of the Indians were killed, many wounded, and the rest, not knowing where their assailants were, took to the hills for refuge. This occurrence was seen by Abe Farwell, a respectable American trader who had a post close by, and who was married to a Crow squaw known as Big Mary. After the Indians had fled the ruffians had made prisoner a young squaw who had crossed the creek to take refuge with the Farwells, and were in the act of carrying her off when Big Mary appeared upon the scene, covered them with a revolver, and, backed up by Abe, dragged her from them and took her to their post.

From time immemorial the Indians of the west were at war with one another, and many fierce and bloody conflicts took place. One of these came about in this way. There was a trading post named Fort Kipp, after Joe Kipp, a well-known scout and interpreter of those days. It was situated at the forks of the Belly and Old Man's rivers, half-way between the present towns of Lethbridge and Macleod, and was in charge of a well-known and respectable trader named Howell Harris. Up the Belly, close by, there was a camp of North and South Peigans, a branch of the Blackfeet, composed of about 500 warriors. At the time the Assiniboine Chief Piapot, with a large number of Cree and Assiniboine Indians, had gone into the Blackfeet country to hunt buffalo, and had camped on the left bank of the Belly, opposite to where Lethbridge now flourishes. Piapot sent his scouts up the Belly to where a small party of old Peigan men, women and children were encamped, and these unfortunates were all put to death, except a boy of thirteen, who took to the bush, and eventually found his way to Kipp, where he warned the trader and the Peigan warriors.

The Peigans came to the Hudson's Bay Company's post and persuaded Jerry Potts, a remarkable scout and interpreter employed there, to take command as their war-chief. The next morning at dawn Potts took Piapot's camp by surprise, and after a desperate fight drove the Assiniboines and Crees out of the country. Mr. Harris and another, who followed Potts out of curiosity, were in full view of the battle. The Crees and Assiniboines, driven out of their camp ground, took to the ford near the coal banks and, being crowded, suffered heavily from the rifles of Potts' warriors, who pumped bullets into them and followed them across the Belly, keeping up the fight as long as an enemy was in sight. Four hundred dead were counted on the field, apart from those who were killed in the ford and on the other side. At the close of the fight Potts was knocked senseless by a stone in the hands of a Cree squaw. For many years Potts acted as police interpreter, scout and guide, and was one of the most remarkable men I have known, having a most extraordinary eye for country.

Before the arrival of the N.W.M.P. no Hudson's Bay Company's trading post could be maintained with safety south of the Red Deer. Even the whisky-traders could not have established themselves in the Blackfeet country had they not been led by men who knew war and palisaded their posts. There was incessant warfare between the tribes, and this condition, enhanced by the abundance of whisky brought in by unscrupulous traders, provided a decidedly wild and woolly atmosphere south of the Red Deer and South Saskatchewan rivers. The Indians burnt Old Bow Fort near a Hudson's Bay Company's post on the Bow, which is really the head of the South Saskatchewan, and Chesterfield House, built below the confluence of the South Saskatchewan and Red Deer at a cost of £40,000. In consequence, the Hudson's Bay Company built Rocky Mountain House, about 100 miles above Edmonton, on the North Saskatchewan. This was done to pacify the Blackfeet, as they were determined that intruders, both white and red, should be kept off their hunting grounds. When they met at Edmonton for trade, the Crees and Blackfeet invariably fought, causing the occupants of the fort to close the gates and man the banquette until the fight was over. In 1870 seven Blackfeet who went to Edmonton to trade were slaughtered by the Crees, in spite of the efforts of the officer in charge of the post, assisted by hired half-breeds from St. Albert Mission.

The Drunken Lakes, a few miles from Edmonton on the north side, were the scene of orgies, brutalities and crimes beyond description, all caused by " fire water." Murder was common and the perpetrators stalked abroad in open day without the slightest fear of arrest. In 1870 a whole party of Blackfeet, who were on the south side of the Saskatchewan, were slaughtered by the Crees, and a war party of Blackfeet shortly afterwards came up to avenge them. Seeing there the carts of the Hudson's Bay Company and Mr. David MacDougall, they looted the goods and furs, burnt the carts, and after firing a volley at the closed gates of the fort, left for the south. There were many massacres and outrages of the most dreadful description in the vicinity and under the walls of Forts Carlton, Pitt, Edmonton, and Mountain Fort, as the Rocky Mountain House was named. The murderers went scot free unless the families of the murdered men contrived the death of the murderer. Scalping and horse stealing were considered virtues. The Indian who could boast of his coups of stolen horses and scalps taken was the envy and admiration of his tribe.

Only the traveller who courted death went west of where

Regina now prospers, in the midst of smiling farms, without an escort.   When exploring the west in the late fifties, Captain Palliser had to go out hunting a whole winter with Old Sun, the Blackfoot Chief, that he might become acquainted with the tribe and be permitted to take his observations without molestation. The half-breed hunters and others of the Red River settlement never ventured west of the Moose Jaw, except in well-organized, armed bands, with written rules and regulations, guards, scouts and pickets.   An experienced hunter styled " The Captain of the Hunt " was responsible for the scouting.   Whenever they halted in the Indian country their carts were formed in circular corrals, or laagers, the shafts turned inwards and the hubs touching.   Tents were pitched inside and the horses corralled in the same enclosure.   These people often fought with the Indians, particularly the Sioux and Blackfeet, and they considered themselves " far out," when at Swift Current Creek, where there is now a prosperous town.   If they ventured to the Cypress Hills they did not stay long, for the game being plentiful and in great variety, the Indians made that a favourite hunting ground and would swarm to the destruction of the intruders as soon as they were aware of their presence.

CHAPTER V

THIS was the state of affairs when Canada took possession of the Great West, and steps should have
been taken at once to remedy it. The horrors referred
to were brought to the notice of the government in 1871
by the officers of the Hudson's Bay Company; remedies were
suggested by the Revs. George and John MacDougall, Father
Lacombe, Captain Butler, Colonel P. Robertson Ross and Sir
Sandford Fleming, all of whom had taken trips through the north
country.

Many exaggerated reports of the state of affairs in the north
west reached the ears of the government at Ottawa, and no
doubt caused them to put off doing what should have been
done as soon as Lieutenant Butler's report had been submitted.
However, on May 3, 1873, Sir John Macdonald introduced a
Bill for the establishment of a police force in the North West
Territories. This body was not to exceed 300 men, " who
should be mounted as the government should from time to
time direct," the commissioner and superintendents to be *ex-
officio* justices of the peace. The salaries were small when
considered in relation to the hardships of the service and the
banishment from the advantages of civilization ; but the
government probably relied on the spirit of adventure regard-

less of compensation which is innate in every Anglo-Saxon in his early manhood.

One of the clauses in the North West Mounted Police Act[1] was that " No person shall be appointed to the Police Force unless he be of sound constitution, active and able-bodied, able to ride, of good character, able to read and write either the English or French language, and between the ages of 18 and 40 years." Recruiting was commenced in September under Inspector Walsh. It was decided to despatch to Fort Garry in October three divisions of 50 men each, so that they might arrive before winter set in. Lt.-Col. W. Osborne Smith was to have temporary command of the force until the arrival of the commissioner.

From Prince Arthur's Landing there travelled with us on their way west the last party of settlers of that year, consisting of a man, his wife and family and a couple of spans of horses. They were very nice people and lucky in having us for their fellow-travellers to assist them along. Thus within a month of its organization the N.W.M.P. began the work of assisting the immigrant to his destination.

At the Stone Fort we were soon settled fairly comfortably in the store buildings which had to answer for barracks. The officers were quartered in the Hudson's Bay Company's officers' mess, which still stands in the centre of the square, and as soon as all were located Lt.-Col. Osborne Smith came down from Winnipeg and swore us in, each man being given a warrant with his name and rank, the first and last issued to the force. When my turn came Inspector Walsh said to the colonel, " I wish to recommend Sergeant-Major Steele to be confirmed in his rank," and Colonel Smith replied, " I am very glad, for my friend, Colonel French, who is commissioner, has requested me to appoint him."

Supt. Jarvis was left in command after Colonel Smith returned to Winnipeg. Inspector Walsh took over the duties of adjutant, veterinary surgeon and riding-master. Griesbach took charge of the discipline and instructed the divisions at foot drill in the square of the fort. I took over the breaking of the horses and instructed the N.C.O.'s and men in riding. Our work was

[1] Passed May 20, 1873.

unceasing from 6 a.m. until after dark. I drilled five rides per day the whole of the winter in an open *ménage*, and the orders were that if the temperature were not lower than 36 below zero the riding and breaking should go on.

With very few exceptions the horses were bronchos which had never been handled, and none but the most powerful and skilful dared attempt to deal with them. Even when we had them "gentled" so as to let recruits mount, the men were repeatedly thrown with great violence to the frozen ground; but no one lost his nerve, they always "had it with them." With plenty of such exercise, when spring opened they were very fine riders, laying the foundation of Canadian horsemanship in the wild and woolly west.

Lt.-Col. French arrived in November and assumed his position as commissioner of the force. The difficulty of organizing the force under the Act was very great, it being quite evident that our lawgivers must have been under the impression that we were plaster saints, not Canadians of blood and brain, with a number of the peculiarities and weaknesses of poor human nature. The only punishment that could be awarded was by fine, and strange to relate the pay of all N.C.O.'s from senior to junior was the same. This, of course, Colonel French had rectified during the next session of parliament, but he could not get everything put right, and it was not until two years later that the officers were given proper disciplinary powers over the force, which in every respect had more the characteristics of a first-class cavalry regiment than those of an ordinary rural police.

The junior officers were not successful recruiting agents; "tough nuts" had been enlisted without regard either to character or physique, but this was remedied by a rigid medical examination and the undesirables were weeded out, so that those who were left were as fine men as any one could desire.

It had been the original intention of the government to send out only 150 mounted police, a quite inadequate number, for there should have been at least 1000 well-mounted men; but to ask for even 500 would have been considered an absurdity. The needs and possibilities of the west were not understood except by those on the spot, and they unfortunately had little weight at that time. Colonel French's representations, however, resulted in the force being increased to 300.

The work of training the force was kept up in the Stone Fort until May. The left wing, when raised and horsed, was stationed in the barracks at Toronto. Several new officers were appointed: Walsh got command of " D " division; " E " division was later assigned to Supt. Carvell, an able officer who had served with the southerners during the great Civil War in the United States. Horses were purchased in Ontario and Quebec to make our strength up to our requirements. We had purchased very good mounts from the Hon. James Mackay, of Deer Lodge, and from Colonel Shaddock, of Iowa, U.S.A., and arrangements were made for a few more when the commissioner should return.

Although we had much work at Stone Fort there were some amusements, such as balls, parties, and rifle matches; but with the thermometer in the thirties below zero there was little pleasure in shooting. There was a Quadrille Club for the N.C.O.'s and men, but I never attended, as I much preferred an evening either with the old settlers, who could tell me something about the country, or in attending their dances and weddings. I took notes of all the information I received, and was pretty well acquainted with the customs of the Indians, hunters and traders before I left Fort Garry.

During the winter a grand ball was given by the sergeants of Lt.-Col. Irvine's corps at Winnipeg, to which I was invited. The day was cold when two of us, mounted on Colonel Shaddock's horses, rode to Winnipeg. In spite of the fact that we had a head wind and the mercury stood 20 below zero the ride on the trained American trotter was one of the warmest that I have yet experienced. The seat was the military one, which all soldiers practised, every stride raising us several inches off the saddle and bringing us down with a bump which would have been fatal to any one with a weak heart. The ball was held in the new barracks and was a great success.

When the Queen's birthday came round athletic sports were held in a pleasant little park not far from the Stone Fort. The principal feature was a cricket match between a local eleven captained by Thomas Sinclair, an old settler, and one of the force captained by Constable Tetu. He and Killaly, of the Mounted Police, were a great acquisition, both having played against W. G. Grace's eleven during his tour in 1872.

On June 7, 1874, the detachment of the Mounted Police left Stone Fort with considerable regret, but with high hopes. We were now under the command of Major Macleod, who had been promoted to assistant commissioner on June 1. I was placed in charge of all arrangements for the march, encampments, etc., and directed to carry out these to the best of my ability until we should arrive at Dufferin, near Pembina, North Dakota, where we awaited the arrival of the commissioner and the three divisions from Toronto, which he had obtained permission to move through the United States on account of the difficulties of the Dawson route. On the 19th they encamped beside us. They corralled their horses inside a ring of loaded wagons, where they were secured to the picket lines. Our horses, mostly bronchos, were kept at their old lines, a fortunate circumstance, as was afterwards proved.

The left wing was composed of a fine, carefully selected and well-educated body of men with exceptionally good horses. These were all over fifteen and a half hands, with almost perfect forms, and were admitted in Toronto to be the best ever shipped from that city. But they were soon to have a hard time, and their perfect forms were reduced to living skeletons.

About ten on the following night a terrific thunderstorm burst upon us, the worst that I had seen in the west since 1870. I was riding near the large corral at the time, the incessant flashes of lightning making every object visible for a long distance. A thunderbolt fell in the midst of the horses. Terrified, they broke their fastenings and made for the side of the corral. The six men on guard were trampled underfoot as they tried to stop them. The maddened beasts overturned the huge wagons, dashed through a row of tents, scattered everything, and made for the gate of the large field in which we were encamped. In their mad efforts to pass they climbed over one another to the height of many feet. At the time Constable Colman had just cleared the gate with his team, which ran away at its utmost speed ; but the powerful driver hung on to the reins and brought them to a halt in about half a mile. The stampede continued south over the Pembina bridge. Crazed with fright, the horses crossed the river and continued their flight on the opposite bank, and the majority were between 30 and 50 miles in Dakota before they were compelled by sheer exhaustion to halt.

I shall never forget that night. I had full view of the stampede, being not more than 50 yards from the horses as they rushed at the gate and attempted to pass it, scrambling and rolling over one another in one huge mass. This and the unceasing flashes of lightning, the rolling of the thunder, the loud shouts of the troopers as they vainly attempted to stop the horses and the mad gallop of Colman's team, gave to it a weird and romantic complexion, typically suggestive of the wild west.

Our bronchos and Shaddock's horses came in now that the other steeds had taken flight. We started after the runaway horses the next morning, covering over 100 miles during the following twenty-four hours. The fugitives were brought in with only one missing. When they reached camp several of them lay down and rested for some days.

This stampede had such an effect on the horses that for the remainder of the summer they were ready to repeat the performance on hearing the slightest unusual sound, and every thunderstorm brought us out of our tents at night, and in the daytime we had to be amongst them to calm their fears.

As soon as we were equipped there were parades to test us. The Sioux Indians in Dakota gave us an opportunity one day. They raided an American village near the border, and took some scalps. The alarm coming to the commissioner, we were turned out ; the horses were grazing more than a mile off, and at the sound of " boot and saddle " they were driven in and we were off in twenty-five minutes to the south west, in case the force could be of any assistance to the poor people, but when we had gone some distance news came that the redskins had decamped. These Indians had been on the warpath for some time, and when our horses stampeded into Dakota there were fears that if we did not hurry to get them back into Canada we should have them run off with by the Sioux.

We left Dufferin on July 8. The first camp was merely a "pull out," commonly called for many years a "Hudson's Bay Start," very necessary so that before finally launching into the unknown one could see that nothing had been forgotten, or that if one had taken too much, being so near to the base, the mistake could be easily corrected. The column made only 10 miles the next day. It was about 2½ miles in length when closed up, and advance and rear guard, scouts and some flankers were thrown out. It must have presented a curious appearance with its motley string of ox-carts, ox-waggons, cattle for slaughter, cows, calves, mowing machines, etc.[1]

At the Turtle Mountains, a range of low, partially-wooded hills, a heavy shower of rain came on, which was followed by a hailstorm, but this did not last very long, and the sun came out brightly, but the pattering noise on the tents continued. This proved to be caused by the visitation of locusts, which afflicted the province of Manitoba so sorely that year. The air for the height of hundreds of yards was full of them, their wings shining in the sun, and the trees, grass, flowers, and in fact everything in sight, were covered by them. Even the paint and woodwork of the waggons, and our carbines were not free from their attacks, and our tents had to be hurriedly packed away to save them from destruction. This swarm destroyed the crops of the majority of the settlers in the province, and seed grain had to be distributed for the next season's crop. From the Turtle Mountains as far west as the extremity of the path of the locusts the grass was very scanty ; the pests came with the south west wind from their breeding grounds on the great plains. Fortunately their path did not cover the country beyond the Moose Mountains.

On July 23 the force was halted at Rivière des Lacs, near the Hill of the Murdered Scout, a forbidding spot not far from the

[1] Colonel French's report of this occasion stated that : " To a stranger it would have appeared an astonishing cavalcade, armed men and guns looked as if fighting was to be done. What could ploughs, harrows, mowing machines, cows, calves, etc., be for ? But that little force had a double duty to perform, to fight if necessary, but in any case to establish posts in the far west."

F

border. The hill is named on account of a story, the truth of which can be vouched for. A Cree scout in his search for his enemies perceived a Mandan ascend the hill on the same errand and, having taken a survey of the horizon, lie down and sleep. The Cree then approached the spot with the usual stealth of the redman and killed him. He cut in the hard clay with his hunting knife the shape of the Mandan's footsteps, of his own where he crept up the hill, and that of the murdered scout's body where he lay asleep. Although the occurrence had taken place many years previously every mark was as clear when we visited the spot as when made, and no doubt can be traced to this day, the clay being almost as hard as brick, and not likely to be much affected by the rainfall.

Rivière des Lacs was the scene of a good joke on one of our most active divisional commanders. During the march the commissioner had caused the divisions to take turns in leading the column, that each might take their share of the dust. Later he directed that the first ready to march would move at the head. This inspired our hero to turn out his men before reveille that morning that he might be ready to move off before any of us were up. The noise made, though purposely suppressed as much as possible, woke me and I hurriedly dressed, horrified lest I had overslept myself. I was much relieved, however, to hear the trumpet call a few minutes later, but the others were in their saddles and the drivers in their seats ready to trek. It was no doubt a great disappointment to their commander to be ordered to have his men dismount and stand easy until all were ready to pull out. We were the first, but he was permitted to move off before us. He had trusted to watering his horses at a lake on one side of the trail. When he arrived opposite it, he outspanned his teams and moved towards it in hopes that he would have finished watering before the remainder would have time to pass him, but he was still on his way to the lake and not half-way there when we passed his waggons. He had forgotten how deceptive distances are on these high plains.

At St. Peter's springs we found only a group of dirty mud holes, so had to set to work to make several wells. Sawing barrels in half, we bored holes in the bottoms of them, and set them in the spring, and soon had them running over with fine clear water.

At Short Creek, on the banks of the Souris, by La Roche Percée, "A" division under Inspector Jarvis left the rest of the train, to proceed to Fort Edmonton via Forts Ellice and Carlton, a distance of 875 miles by trail. The commissioner was compelled to transfer the majority of the men and all of our horses except the officers' chargers to other divisions, and Jarvis received in their stead the quartermaster and several of the youngest and weakest men, 55 sick and almost played-out horses recovering from a severe attack of epizootic, 24 waggons, 55 ox-carts with 12 drivers, 62 oxen, 50 cows and 50 calves to help us on to Fort Ellice.

The commissioner with the main force left La Roche Percée on July 29. We were a disconsolate lot when we saw the force depart on their long trek, but we had a much harder time before us than any experienced that year. There were no oats for the horses, although they had never before done work on grass alone. Erroneous reports of travellers in the northern part of the prairie region had been made to the effect that horses could do 40 miles a day on grass. The people forgot to say that they had ridden and driven on horseback and in buck-boards with a herd of acclimatized native ponies driven behind them, and none of them were obliged to be under saddle or in harness for more than a couple of hours in the day at most.

We remained in camp getting everything put in shipshape order until August 3, when we started for Fort Ellice. Every man, including the sick, was employed. The latter drove teams, and as we went on improved in health. We had a bad time of it for several days after we left La Roche Percée, the horses being so weak that they had to be changed twice both forenoon and afternoon to enable our little force to make 8 miles a day, and the cows and the calves became so footsore that they would lie down every few yards unless a goad were constantly applied. The guide was able to keep ahead of the transport at a slow walk, leading his little pony and cart. The cart train and the yoke oxen followed, while we drove the herd of cows and calves before us. The country over which we passed, now covered with fine farms and comfortable homes, was gently undulating and luxuriant with grass, which caused our horses and cattle to show signs of returning vigour.

We reached Fort Ellice on August 14. It was a large fenced enclosure, with the usual style of dwellings and stores, and stood on the bank of the Assiniboine about 300 feet above the river, surrounded by bluffs of aspen and poplar. The valley, which is more than a mile wide, was very pretty, partly timbered, and there were occasional grassy bottoms on which large herds of ponies, many of them pintos (piebald), and numbers of cattle were grazing. Our horses and cattle were turned out on the flats, and as there were quicksands in different places we had a good deal of practice hauling them out of those death traps, which the Indian ponies knew enough to avoid.

On August 18 we pulled out from Fort Ellice towards the west, leaving behind us the quartermaster, the sick men, half of the cows and calves, a large quantity of provisions and stores and several horses, which were not in good enough condition to be brought with us.

Our stock had now recovered their strength, and, as we had not enough men to furnish night herders, they wandered considerable distances. As we did not know the ground, the round up took us a considerable time. One morning I jumped a fine creek with grassy banks, and found my horse up to the neck in a shaking bog with a tough sod on top and quicksand beneath. Fortunately the horse must have been in such a place before, as he did not exhaust himself with vain struggles. He took things easily and waited till I called him to come, which I lost no time in doing. I had, as one should always do in a quicksand, thrown myself face downwards, and struggling as if swimming, took the lead, and the horse when called made a plunge forward, and resting for a second, gathered himself for another effort until we were extricated from our predicament. I noticed afterwards that this horse and another which was always with him and had the same colour and marks avoided all soft places when they were turned out to graze.

There was one man, the shortest man in the force, who was noted amongst us for his hearty appetite, which, on account of the quantities of game which fell to our guns, he was able to indulge to the fullest extent. Stewed prairie chickens and ducks usually formed part of the evening meal, and after eating, in addition to his rations, at least a brace, he would say, " I wish I were in Toronto, at Gus Thomas's English Chop House, where I could get a porterhouse steak and a bottle of Guinness ! " He was worth all he ate, for there was no more useful man in the division in his own line, that of a horse trainer.

There were signs of prairie fires having run over the country the previous autumn. These had done a good deal of damage to the islands of poplar. At that time there were no laws against this destruction. The Hudson's Bay Company had no jurisdiction now, with the lamentable result that people had become careless. Travellers left their fires burning, tenderfeet threw matches into the grass after lighting their pipes, Indians and the half-breed buffalo hunters wilfully set the prairies on fire so that the bison would come to their part of the country to get the rich, green grass which would follow in the spring. Large tracts of country had been burned every year, consequently no trees were to be found except where the lakes and creeks were numerous enough to prevent the fires from running.

A change was soon to come over this, however ; ordinances were passed and rigidly enforced, with beneficial results ; but there is much to be done to prevent the dreadful waste of timber in forested parts of the country, where millions of dollars' worth have been destroyed. In the Rocky Mountains the mischief has been chiefly caused by railroad engines, careless travellers, prospectors and green hunters. Steps are now being taken to conserve the timber, and when there are a sufficient number of foresters who know their work the Dominion will save many millions per annum.

On the Salt Plain we met several brigades of carts driven by hunters, freighters and traders with packs of buffalo robes, dried meat and pemmican. Inspector Jarvis bought a supply of pemmican, which is the best food in the world for the traveller, soldier and sailor, either on the plains of America or in the Arctic regions. It was cooked in two ways in the west ; one a stew of pemmican, water, flour and, if they could be secured, wild onions or preserved potatoes. This was called " rubaboo " ; the other was called by the plain hunters a " rechaud." It was cooked in a frying-pan with onions and potatoes or alone. Some persons ate pemmican raw, but I must say that I never had a taste for it that way.

After eight long weeks of weary days we reached Fort Carlton. Here perfect discipline existed. The offices and stores were neat, and over each door was painted in French and English the name of the store and office, together with the class of goods in the buildings. After a week's rest we pulled out of Carlton. As we left we were informed that the Blackfeet and Crees were again on the warpath. The country through which we went was a good stock country, but we found the cart trail very rough with roots and stones, and the horses were now beginning to show signs of the long march without grain. Game was very plentiful, and the cranes, white wild geese or wavies were in profusion, with considerable numbers of the grey Canadian goose. Our guns and rifles were kept busy during each halt, Corporal Carr on one occasion shooting eleven wild geese with one barrel.

Carr was a young man of 26 years, who had been at Trinity College, and was for a considerable time assistant agent on an Irish estate, but conditions were so distasteful that, although he was well treated and had the shooting, he decided to emigrate, and like a good man and true worked at anything he could get until he had the opportunity to go west.

The evenings were fine, and the half-breed drivers had great fun after supper. One of them had a violin, and to its music the remainder in turn danced a Red River Jig on a door which they carried in their carts for the purpose. Tired of ducks, geese, prairie chickens and pemmican, these strange fellows caught skunks, boiled them in three waters and then roasted them, thinking them preferable to any other food !

Our O.C. was a great favourite with all. When in the evening they sat round the camp-fires, he would tell amusing yarns of his experiences in South Africa during the Kaffir wars in the fifties. I took mental notes of all that he told us about the customs of the country, and found it useful when I served there many years after.

One morning as we were struggling up a hill, we found that one of the teams was in difficulties. The driver was a most original chap hailing from Belfast, where he had been educated by two careful maiden aunts and had lived for many years. In his recitals of experiences he always dated events from outbreaks that had occurred in Belfast. For instance, " It was just before the '65 riots," or " that was just one month after the '69 riots." He always took notes in his diary if anyone used strong language, happily a rare occurrence, but he omitted nothing. On this particular occasion the fiery temper of our good O.C. showed itself in a tirade of lurid expressions, many of which were said to have been learned while he was on the staff of a celebrated general, whose name shall go down to posterity as long as Britain lasts, and of whom it is said that when an exalted personage asked if he had taken over command at Aldershot yet, he received the reply, " Oh, yes, he swore himself in yesterday ! " This our comrade could not stand. Here was a chance which must not be overlooked, so he jumped off the seat of the waggon, went down on one knee and entered the words in full ! The O.C. had passed on by this time, and did not hear the roar of laughter that greeted the incident.

Horse Hill, close to Turtle River, was, a few years previous to our visit, the scene of a desperate fight between the Crees and Blackfeet. The Crees were encamped near the foot of the hill when a party of Blackfeet, who had recently made a successful raid, discovered them and charged. The Crees were waiting for them, and sent a large body of warriors round the hill at full speed, and they drove the Blackfeet into the ravine, where they were surrounded. Many escaped, but the plunder was retaken and, remarkable to relate, 40 horses were killed. The Blackfeet Indians were always noted for reckless daring. Long acquaintance with them has taught me that they are the most straightforward and least crafty of the plain Indians. There are many tales to prove that this is their character. Sometimes they will exercise strategy, but often no more than the average white, who to the Indian is simplicity itself.

From now on the trouble with our tired horses and oxen

increased. Heavy rains had fallen, reducing the trails to a deplorable state, and the poor horses in the waggons staggered along with marvellous pluck. They suffered much more than the oxen and, as the nights became colder, when they lay down to rest the unfortunate brutes became so stiff that they could not rise without help, and I had to call the men up many times during the night to lift them by main force and rub their stiffened limbs to restore the circulation. This occurred so often that the men themselves became exhausted from fatigue and want of sleep.

To add to our troubles, some of the teams would be hours behind the leaders, and we who were in the rear with the cattle and worn-out horses, had to stay and help them along. Axes and spades were in constant demand to repair the numerous bad spots on the trail, long stretches of which were under water, often for hundreds of yards. There is a saying that Canadians are born with an axe in their hands, and the way everyone used his on this trek proved to me its truth. In the rear our party were obliged to walk all the time ; our horses could carry us no longer. The loose ones we were driving would sometimes fall, and be unable to rise. Carr and I, with a pole under the brisket, had to lift the wretched brutes to their feet while the shoeingsmith assisted to steady them.

At last, however, we reached Victoria, a Company's post with a palisaded enclosure, situated on a narrow ridge along the Saskatchewan. There was a mission founded by the Rev. George McDougall, one of the pioneers of the Methodist church, and round the fort and on the river bank clustered the thatched log houses of the Scotch and English half-breeds who had followed him to the place. These people made a living by hunting buffalo, fishing and freighting. They sowed their crops in the spring, and never saw them again until harvest. If the crops failed it did not matter, for the distance to the herds of buffalo was not far, and the numerous lakes of white fish were near at hand, Whitefish Lake Mission being located about 60 miles north of Victoria.

We enjoyed the halt here among the good people of the settlement. The Cree Indians who had recently come in to trade at the fort came to see and wonder at us. One of them was known by the breathless title of " Sky-Blue-Horn-Sitting-Down-Turning-Round-On-A-Chair ! " Before we left Victoria the O.C. made arrangements to leave the cows, calves and weak oxen there for the winter months, under a contract with one of the settlers at 15 dollars a head for oxen and cows and 10 dollars each for calves.

Our progress from here to Edmonton was slow and the going very difficult. Our loose horses very often fell, one fine animal being lifted bodily by Carr, the shoeingsmith, and myself at least a dozen times by means of a pole. The other horses had to be helped along in the same manner until we arrived at the outspan. We had not been halted very long when a messenger arrived from Inspector Jarvis directing Gagnon to bring the division into Fort Edmonton the same afternoon. Some of the horses could not go on, and a marquee was pitched to shelter them at night, and two men were left in charge. I inspanned the remainder, leaving no transport behind. Gagnon went ahead with the yoke oxen and was soon out of sight, and I pushed on with the horse teams and had the hardest trek that I have yet undertaken. The trail was worse than any we had encountered. It was knee-deep in black mud, sloughs crossed it every few hundred yards, and the waggons had to be unloaded and dragged through them by hand. Many small ponds covered with a thin coating of ice lined the sides of the trail, and gave us much trouble while we were engaged in unloading the waggons. The poor animals, crazed with thirst and feverish because of their privations, would rush to the ponds to drink, often falling and having to be dragged out with ropes from where they fell. One of the men would hold up their heads while I placed the hitch. It mattered not how often they were watered, the same performance had to be gone through time after time.

Determined to carry out my orders to get to Fort Edmonton, which was only 12 miles on, I kept my willing men going in spite of the darkness, which frequently caused us to miss the trail. On one occasion the ambulance driver, who was ahead, took his team out into an extensive marsh covered by thin ice for several hundred yards until the increased depth of water warned him of his mistake.

This struggle to obey orders continued until five o'clock the following morning, when we arrived at Rat Creek, a small stream about 4 miles from Edmonton. Gagnon was there with the two ox teams which, of course, walked through the sloughs without much difficulty. I informed him that it was useless to continue, the men and horses having been constantly on the move for at least 21 hours, exclusive of the noonday halt, and they all needed rest. They appeared to have reached the limit of their endurance. Gagnon agreed to this, and went on to Fort Edmonton, while I had the tents pitched, caused two rows of fires to be built of the quantities of dry wood in the vicinity, and had the horses washed, dried and rubbed down and turned out to graze with two herders to watch them, while Sam Taber prepared our meal.

We had just got ready to turn in when the herders called out that a horse was in difficulties. I seized my rope and rushed to the spot, followed by the men, and found the animal partly through the ice in a large, round hole with high banks. I gave the men one end of the rope and had secured the horse by the lasso with my usual hitch round the neck and hindquarters, when the ice broke and horse and men sank in about ten feet of water. The men hung on to the rope, however, and so did I, and after a few hearty pulls we were once more on dry land. This accident was the last. The men were sent to rest, and I changed my clothes. As it was after six o'clock, and I was not tired, I cut poles to make a bridge across the creek, which was only a couple of yards wide, but awkward for the horses. I was engaged in laying them when the O.C. arrived. He was cheerful, expressed himself well pleased with our work, and told me that he had secured winter quarters for us at Fort Edmonton.

We inspanned immediately and, passing over the first dry piece of trail, reached the fort in fairly good time. When they sighted the welcome roofs the poor horses pricked up their ears and made a feeble attempt to trot as we moved down the hills. Mr. Hardisty, one of the kindest and best of men, met us at the gate of the fort and assigned us our quarters and stabling at once. He gave the officers' mess to Inspector Jarvis and Gagnon. The men were given a comfortable row of houses with bunks along the walls and fire-places in each. I had good quarters in another building, which I shared with Carr, and our horses and cattle were provided with stables and large corrals. Inspector Jarvis showed me his report, very kindly stating that he was pleased with my work, and hoped that it would be recognized. The paragraph relating to the division stated: " Had it not been for the perfect conduct of the men and real hard work, much of the property would have been destroyed. I wish particularly to bring to your notice the names of Troop-Sergeant-Major Steele and Constable Labelle. S.-M. Steele has been untiring in his efforts to assist me, and he has also performed the manual labour of at least two men. The attention paid to the horses by Constable Labelle has saved many of them."

The distance covered by the division since it left Fort Garry amounted to 1,255 miles.

We had parted from Colonel French at La Roche Percée on July 29. His march need not be related at length. They went via Wood End depot, across Long River and Dirt Hill to Old Wives' Lakes, and on to Old Wives' Creek, where they rested several days. At Cypress Hills they halted from August 25 to 31, waiting for supplies which Lt.-Col. Macleod had secured. At first he had experienced some difficulty with the guides. Doubting their reliability, he had been forced to keep a check upon them by observations taken night and day, route sketching, and checking the distance by odometer.

On September 4 a party of Sioux Indians visited the camp and, as usual, showed themselves very friendly. The commissioner made them presents of tea, buffalo-meat and biscuits, which pleased them exceedingly. The guides soon began to show reluctance to investigate the country, knowing that hair from the top-knots of Crees and half-breds was in much demand among the Blackfeet, who roamed in every direction.

Buffalo were now seen in vast numbers on all sides, moving south west, 60,000 or 70,000 being estimated from one hill, but as the country as far as the horizon was black with them, no doubt this count was much under the mark. The same extent of country has since had about 100,000 cattle grazing on it, but they were very thinly scattered over it in comparison to the enormous numbers of bison that there were seen on that trek to the Sweet Grass Hills.

At Fort Benton, an important trading centre at the head of navigation on the Missouri, and a station of the American army, which had many posts in Montana at that time, Colonel French received telegrams approving of his recommendation to leave a considerable number of men in the south west of the territory, and informing him of the decision to make Swan River the headquarters of the force. He also engaged Jerry Potts, a half-Scotch, half-Peigan scout and interpreter, and made arrangements for horses, ponies and supplies for the wing of the force established in the south west. He then returned to the boundary trail and started on his march eastward to the Swan River, while Lt.-Col. Macleod at the same time set out westward for the post on Old Man's River.

Jerry Potts accompanied the latter party. He was a short, bow-legged man, with piercing black eyes and a long straight nose. He was silent and laconic, and people said he was a fighter, and he looked it. He won the confidence of all ranks the first day out, and when morning came he rode out boldly in front of the advance guard. It was noon when the party reached Milk River, and found him there sitting near a fat buffalo cow which he had killed and dressed for the use of the force. To those new to such life he appeared to know everything, and their good opinion of him was confirmed when on the second day he turned sharp to the left towards the Milk River ridge, selected a camp ground, and then led the force a short distance to some fine springs containing the best water that they had tasted for many a long day.

During that night mysterious rumblings were heard, which were explained in the morning by the sight of vast numbers of bison. As far as the eye could see to the north west there was a black mass moving eastward ; hundreds of them were to be seen crowding down into the coulee to the springs. On Jerry's advice orders were given that not a shot was to be fired at the buffaloes in case the report of the guns might stampede the great herd. The men had to crowd them back from the springs as quietly as possible so that a sufficient supply of water for man and beast could be obtained.

Upon the order to march being given the advance and rear guards were not sent to their stations. The waggon train and guns were closed up to one yard distance, the men marching quietly alongside the train, and thus all day long they thrust their way through the immense herd. Throughout the day the buffalo kept very close, and sometimes a fierce young bull would gallop along not many yards away, tossing his head and snorting in defiance of these strange creatures in such extraordinary garb, that he had never seen before.

The Rocky Mountains had been in full view for many days, and they seemed like a great wall to the west. Chief Mountain, like a huge square block many thousands of feet in height, reared its remarkable head through the clouds. Potts had been telling them something of the people and conditions of this part of the country, and all were anxious to see Whoop Up, Slide Out, Stand Off, and other traders' posts, and to meet those who were at the time causing so much trouble in the north west by selling liquor to the Indians.

A specimen of the work that was going on was seen on one side of the trail, where an Indian lay dead, his body riddled with bullets, and Jerry Potts, when asked the cause, in his laconic but effective way replied, " Drunk ! "

The scenes which had been enacted round Whoop Up and other trading posts were just what might be expected when the wild redman obtained the " fire-water." The Indians who came to those posts to trade were soon maddened by drink, and settled old scores and family feuds by shooting or butchering one another in their camps or other places where they obtained the intoxicants. When the police arrived the victims of these orgies were to be seen lying dead in the vicinity.

The first raid on the persons engaged in this traffic was made during the same month in which the force established itself on the Old Man's River. Three Bulls, a prominent Indian of the Blackfeet tribe, and later a chief, informed the assistant commissioner that a coloured man named Bond, who had a trading post at Pine Coulee, nearly 50 miles north of the police camp, had given him a couple of gallons of whisky ₃ in exchange for two of his horses. Potts obtained the necessary information, and arranged that Three Bulls should meet him next evening about dark on the trail to Pine Coulee. Inspector Crozier and a small party of well-mounted men, guided by Potts, left camp a little before dark with instructions to seize all robes and furs of any description which he suspected had been traded for whisky, and in addition a sufficient amount of goods and chattels to satisfy the fines which might be imposed.

Crozier executed his task, and two days later appeared in camp with Bond and four others in custody, all of whom had been captured about 45 miles distant. They had waggons laden with alcohol, 16 horses, 116 buffalo robes, and a Winchester Henry magazine rifle and a Colt revolver each. The assistant commissioner confiscated the robes, destroyed the alcohol, fined the two principals and Bond, who was their guide and interpreter, 200 dollars each, and the other two, who were hired men, 50 dollars apiece. Next day a well-to-do trader of Fort Benton came to Lt.-Col. Macleod and paid the fines of all but Bond.

There were many raids to capture whisky outfits. These were very exciting and almost always successful, the traders being fined or imprisoned. Their furs and buffalo robes obtained through the trade in whisky were confiscated and, as the force was in need of bedding, a sufficient number was issued for the purpose. The hides of the younger animals were made into coats and caps, one being issued to each member of the police.

Meanwhile the barracks were being constructed, officers and men alike busy early and late until they were completed. As the weather became very cold it was decided to build the hospital and stables first, the men's quarters next, and the officers' last. The quarters for the force were built of rough, round cottonwood logs, placed upright in the ground, and the roof covered with about a foot of mud ; the cracks had to be filled with the same material. As gloves could not be worn at that work, the men's hands hardened with the exposure, but if the thermometer indicated 10 below zero they were allowed to cease " mudding " and go to another job.

While all this was going on several chiefs of the Bloods and Peigans paid the assistant commissioner a visit, upon his sending them a message that he wished to speak to them. None of the Blackfeet came until the last week of November, when a fine looking young Indian brought a message from a number of their chiefs. They had heard that the North West Mounted Police were their friends, but desired to be assured of this before they came to see him. Lt.-Col. Macleod told the young man that he had been expecting to see the chiefs for some time past, gave him to understand what were the principal objects of our mission to the north west, and made him a present of tobacco for each of the chiefs as a token of friendship.

On December 1 Chapo Muxico, or Crowfoot, Chief of the Blackfeet, came in to visit him, and a few days later all the chiefs of the Bloods, Peigans and Blackfeet, headed by Crowfoot, came for a pow-wow with " Stamixotokan," as they called him on account of the bull's head over his door. Some say they gave him this name because of the crest of the Macleods which he had in his Glengarry cap. Upon being introduced by the interpreter, Jerry Potts, they all shook hands and expressed their pleasure at meeting him. They then sat down and Jerry Potts lighted a pipe and handed it to the principal chief, who took a few puffs and then passed it to the others. All remained silent and waited to hear what the white chief had to say.

He explained to them why the government had sent the force into the country, and gave them a general idea of the laws that would be enforced, telling them that not only the white men but Indians also were to be punished for breaking them. He impressed upon them that they need not fear being punished for what they did not know to be wrong, and assured them that the force did not come to take away their land, an intimation which they received with great satisfaction. He told them that when the government wished to speak to them, their great men would be sent to meet the chiefs of the tribes, and that they would know the intentions of the government before anything was done.

When the assistant commissioner had ended, Crowfoot,

the personification of grace, rose and shook hands with the white chief and all the white men present. Then he bared his right arm and, with eloquent gestures and eyes flashing fire, made a long speech, thanking the One Above who is our Chief and the Great Mother for sending the Mounted Police to save them from the effects of the cursed fire-water, which was destroying their young men, and for the peace that was to come. At the conclusion of the speech Potts interpreted it, and Crowfoot departed, followed by the other chiefs.

When rendering the Blackfeet into English Potts was very laconic ; but his interpretation of what Lt.-Col. Macleod said was eloquent, and his eyes gleamed as if his soul were in it, and as if showing that he felt that every word of it was good for the Indians. Several of the chiefs besides Crowfoot stated that they were delighted at the arrival of the force, and they told how they were being robbed and ruined by the whisky trade ; how their wives, horses and robes were taken from them ; how their young men were continually engaged in drunken riots, and numbers of them shot dead ; how their horses were gradually decreasing in numbers, so that before long they would not have enough to chase the buffalo and would have no means of procuring food. Now all that was to be changed. One chief said, " Before you came the Indian crept along, now he is not afraid to walk erect." This pow-wow had a good effect. The war between the Blackfeet and the Crees ceased from the time the force arrived.

The Blackfeet were a fine race, of splendid physique ; the men tall and well formed, pleasant in their bearing and very straightforward. The legend of Hiawatha was not known to them, but they had one which told of a battle between a hero who came from the east and the Great Spirit of the West Wind who had his seat in Chief Mountain. The large stones, which form at equal intervals a straight line from north to south about 40 miles from the Rocky Mountains, were said to be the missiles which the latter hurled at his enemy. The Blackfeet were polygamous, and their wives seemed to live happily together, and in those days chastity had a high place amongst them. At their great spring meeting the wives went down on one side of a long line of men, the young women and children on the other, to where sat the medicine man of the occasion Each married woman received a piece of the sacred tongue, specially prepared, and then returning to where the sun could shine upon her, she held it up before the people, calling all of them to witness that she was true to her husband and children, asking the Great Spirit to bless them and keep her virtuous until the next great meeting.

There were many strange characters in the country at that time who soon became acquainted with the Mounted Police. One old trader had a store not far from Fort Macleod. His trade had been largely in whisky, and when he was arrested a great number of buffalo robes obtained in that way were confiscated and he was fined and imprisoned. When he came before Colonel Macleod and was convicted, he said, " Colonel, I'll make them wires hum to Washington when I get loose ! " The magistrate calmly replied, " Let them hum ! " He did his six months ; but instead of making the wires tingle with his messages to the President of the United States, he became quite fond of the force, who had always treated him kindly, as far as lay in their power. He was given leave to go once a week to his store to see that his books were being kept correctly and the business going on as it should, returning with a treat of California tinned fruit for " the boys."

Another strange character was a stalwart German who had served under Colonel Mosby in the American Civil War. He and his partner in the robe trade, a Spaniard, had quarrelled. One night, returning from an inspection of the stables, he looked through the window and detected his amiable Spanish friend going to bed with a large knife under his pillow. " Dutch," as the German was nicknamed, entered the cabin, picked up a heavy gun barrel which had been in use as a poker and broke his partner's head with it. He then departed hastily for Fort Macleod and confessed to the assistant commissioner that he had killed his partner in self-defence, which he no doubt had, for had he not made such good use of the poker the Spaniard's knife would have put an end to him. He was allowed to go, with orders to come before the court when called upon.

Peace now reigned in the Old Man's River country. The war amongst the Indians had ceased with the arrival of the

G

force. The whisky trade was dead in every part of the north west, and a more peaceable community could not be found in any part of Canada. Large numbers of Indians encamped near the fort for weeks at a time, exchanging their robes for the goods in the stores. Thousands of horses, the produce of the whisky trade, had gone out of the territory, and the Indians were now busy buying all that they could get and would sell none. Before the arrival of the force, gates and doors were fastened at night. The Indians' passion for whisky was so great that they could not be kept out of the traders' stores, and even when friendly to the traders of the fire-water, they would climb the roofs and find their way down the chimneys to steal it.

When Colonel French reached the site for the Swan River barracks he found to his amazement that the barracks were being erected on a high hill covered with huge granite boulders which were firmly embedded in the ground. To add to his chagrin, the prairie fires had burned half the hay, and the Hudson's Bay Company had lost 300 loads which the Mounted Police might have purchased, and there was no more to be had. Good work had been done on the barracks considering the late start, but machinery had to be hauled from Winnipeg, more than 300 miles, over a very bad trail, consequently the buildings were not nearly ready for occupation. He left one division there, and with the rest went on to Winnipeg. There the men had to sleep in the lofts of stables until authority was received for them to winter at Dufferin barracks, which the Royal Engineers had vacated the same autumn, after completing the survey of the international boundary. In his annual report, made in January, Colonel French wrote :

For the credit of the Dominion and humanity, it was absolutely necessary that a stop be put to the disgraceful scenes which were daily enacted on the Bow and Belly rivers and in the Cypress Hills. The immense distance to those places and the shortness of the season for operations necessitated a mounted force being dispatched. The Mounted Police were being organized for the preservation of law and order in the North West Territories, but consisted of about 120 men and

50 horses at the time this expedition was contemplated. Nevertheless it was decided with very good reasons that the work of establishing law and order where all was lawlessness and violence should be entrusted to the Mounted Police.

Tied down by no stringent rules or articles of war, but only by the silken cord of a civil contract, these men by their conduct gave little cause for complaint, though naturally there were several officers and constables unaccustomed to command and having little experience of tact, yet such an event as striking a superior was unknown and disobedience of orders very rare.

Day after day on the march, night after night on picket or guard, and working at high pressure during four months from daylight until dark with little rest, even on the day sacred to rest, the force ever pushed onward, delighted when occasionally a pure spring was met with. There was still no complaint when salt water or the refuse of a mud hole was the only liquid available, and I have seen this whole force obliged to drink liquid which when passed through a filter was still the colour of ink. The fact of horses and oxen dying for want of food never disheartened or stopped them, but pushing on on foot with dogged determination they carried through the service required of them under difficulties which can only be appreciated by those who witnessed them.

Where time was so valuable there could be no halting on account of weather, the greatest heat of the July sun or the cold of November in this northern latitude made no difference ; ever onward had to be the watchword, and an almost uninterrupted march had to be maintained from the time the force left Dufferin with the thermometer 95 to 100 degrees in the shade, until the remainder of the force returned there in November, the thermometer marking 20 to 30 degrees below zero, having marched 1,959 miles.

Thus ended the Mounted Police march of 1874-5, the longest on record of a force carrying its supplies. So well was the work of that year performed in every part of that vast country where the presence of the force was required that in a very few months the situation was under our control.

CHAPTER VI

SHORTLY after we had got settled at Fort Edmonton, Mr. Donald Macleod arrived by the same trail by which we had come from Fort Ellice. He was a fine fellow, one of the characters of the early days of the north west. His house was always open to his friends and neighbours, and every one liked him. One of the men who during the winter would always be seen in his chimney corner, smoking or frying buffalo steaks for the numerous guests, was an old placer miner, known as English Charley. He had made good-sized fortunes, and lost them, in every mining camp from California in '49 to Caribou in the early sixties. He came to a halt at the age of sixty-five with his old comrade Scotch Charley, and together they worked on the gold bars of the Saskatchewan, near Edmonton, where they washed out fine gold in a machine called a " grizzly," or prospected up the river as far as the mountains until the storms of winter compelled them to desist. When winter closed in he would take refuge with the kind-hearted Donald and other hospitable pioneers. Scotch Charley died before we came west ; his loss nearly broke the warm heart of his old comrade, but he never lost faith and believed that there was a great fortune in store for him in the mysterious recesses of the great range, but the poor fellow did not live to see his dream of wealth come true.

On the approach of Christmas Inspector Jarvis gave me permission to get up a ball in the fort, as it was thought to be a good thing to introduce ourselves to the people in the settlement and to return some of the hospitality which we had received. A meeting was held and all voted a month's pay towards the dance. Chief Factor Hardisty gave us the use of a large store-house, in which there was an enormous fire-place, and loaned all the crockery and other table necessaries required for the feast. Large quantities of fresh buffalo tongues, humps (or " boss ribs," as they were called), buffalo hind quarters, venison, prairie chickens and wild geese were purchased, and the *chef*, Sam Taber, with his assistants, was set to work to make plum-puddings and mince-pies, for which there was an ample supply of material in the Company's store.

Invitations were sent to every settlement and every hunters' or traders' camp for 100 miles round, and on the appointed day, Christmas Eve, the guests began to arrive and were put up in the fort and in the neighbouring houses. First, they were entertained to supper and a dance, which lasted until nearly morning. The next day after breakfast the company went to church ; then came the dinner, presided over by Inspector Jarvis and Sub-Inspector Gagnon. The Queen's health was drunk in good tea, the beverage of the north west in those days, and after the repast dancing was resumed with vigour to the lively music of several violins.

The Red River Jig, Lord Macdonald's Reel, the Eight Hand Reel and other dances were all performed to very fast music. The men sat on one side of the room and the women and girls on the other, and, when the fiddlers had finished the preliminary tuning up and scraping, one of the men advanced to the centre of the room, gazed at the partner of his choice, closed his right hand and pointed at her with his thumb, whereupon, no matter what her wishes in the matter might be, she placed herself beside him and he took her hand. The jig struck up forthwith, and the couple took a few steps forward and back, dropped hands and, facing one another, stepped to the music, usually with great skill, now and then relieved or cut out by others. If the man were conceited or a foolish person the men let him dance until his limbs almost refused to move and the perspiration rolled off his face in streams, while if he were a favourite he was allowed sufficient to satisfy him. When the dance was over breakfast was served, and all went home, after expressing their delight at the entertainment which had been offered them.

During the first week in January Inspector Jarvis learned that an illicit whisky outfit was en route from Belly River to the large buffalo hunters' camp at Buffalo Lake to trade with the half-breed hunters and Indians. He made up a party composed of my brother Dick, Carr, myself and ten men. We hired a dog-train and ponies and set off, the weather being very cold. As we proceeded the cold increased, our thermometer indicating from 42 to 56 below zero for 15 days, the severest weather known for at least thirty years, according to the Company's records.

We took no tents, as we were better without them, and we had no stoves, such luxuries being then unknown in the west. Our halts for the night were made about an hour before dark, so that the ponies could be made snug and a large quantity of firewood cut. The snow was then shovelled away, a large fire built, buffalo robes laid down, and after a supper of buffalo steak, bread and tea, we lay in front of the fire like herrings in a barrel and slept well.

We arrived at Buffalo Lake after dark, and were searching amongst the four hundred cabins to find John Ashon's store when we heard the sound of dance music and directed our steps to a large log cabin in which a lively wedding dance was going on. Two rows of young men and women were on the floor footing Lord Macdonald's Reel to the most rapid time possible, as was the custom among the hunters. Inspector Jarvis and I entered the room and were directed to Ashon's place, where we received a hearty welcome.

We remained four days in the camp and enjoyed the novelty of the situation. Mrs. Ashon, a young woman about twenty years of age, took good care that we should not suffer from starvation, for she kept the fire going and the pot boiling the whole time. The intervals between meals are very short, for every now and then we would be asked to " draw in " and despatch buffalo tongues, bannocks, strong tea and tinned fruits.

Inspector Jarvis did much to obtain intelligence from all

parts of the country, which he caused to be visited for at least
100 miles to the south, east and west, and as the hunters and
traders liked to talk we kept their tongues wagging. We
secured a great deal of information of all sorts which was
afterwards of good use to us.

To the south between Buffalo Lake and the Hand Hills,
vast numbers of buffalo covered the country, and, although the
snow was deep, made a good living off the grass, until the new
crops came in the spring. Many buffalo were killed and the
robes bartered for by the Company and the free traders.[1]
White hunters were few in number, but when they went to
hunt for the purpose of obtaining a supply of fresh meat, they
committed the most wanton destruction, killing enough for a
whole settlement or a regiment of soldiers. They were, as a
rule, poor horsemen, and did their hunting on foot. Concealed in a bluff of timber, or behind a snow drift, they would
shoot down hundreds without the poor animals having a chance
to see the direction from which the shots came.

The Metis and Indians gave the buffalo a chance for its life ;
they were splendid horsemen, the equal of any in the world,
and killed the game from the saddle, a dangerous operation in
the winter, owing to the numerous badger holes concealed by
the snow. The most successful of the half-breed hunters
during that winter was Abraham Salois, who killed 600 ; in
one run 37 fell to his rifle, no doubt the best on record.

Shortly after our return to the fort, the Company's packet
came in with the first mail for us since July 8. It contained
news of the rest of the force and general orders, which assigned
rewards to a number of N.C.O.'s and men. I was fortunate
enough to be one of the number mentioned for " upright and
conscientious discharge of duty." The commissioner, under
the Act, was supposed to have the power to distribute such
marks of appreciation, but after 1875, in spite of the remarkable
services of the force, the custom was more honoured in the
breach than in the observance, nearly all the fund being distributed evenly throughout the division, for the purchase of

---

[1] Men who had completed a term of service with the Company and
then went trading on their own account were known as " free "
traders.

newspapers, games, etc. Perhaps this was the best way, as no member of the force worked any the less conscientiously on account of there being no prospect of individual reward.

The remainder of the winter of 1874-5 passed off quietly enough at Fort Edmonton. We had only one party of visitors from the west, Mr. E. W. Jarvis and his assistant civil engineer, who came from Fort George, British Columbia, across the Rocky Mountains, looking for a pass for the Canadian Pacific Railway. The surveys for this had been going on in the north and west through the Yellowhead Pass for some years without any route having been decided upon. The trip was a hard one on snow shoes, the party subsisting part of the time on rabbits, the only game seen in the mountains. A few days' rest at Edmonton was a great relief, particularly to Mr. E. W. Jarvis, who in our O.C. met a cousin whom he had not seen for years.

Another mail came in during the winter with orders from the commissioner for our commanding officer to prepare to build barracks for us on a site to be selected on the right or south bank of the Saskatchewan, anywhere between the present fort and Sturgeon Creek, some 25 miles east. These instructions were soon known and a deputation of the people of the settlement came to Inspector Jarvis with blood in their eyes to interview him and to demand that the barracks should be built at Edmonton. They did not use much tact, and they were trying to coerce the wrong man. Our O.C. was of a fiery temperament, and would carry out his orders as he pleased, and was the last man to let himself be browbeaten. I have no doubt that if the settlers had let him alone he would have built the new post on the opposite side of the river. As it was, he chose a position 20 miles east, where he thought there would be a good railway crossing.

The site selected was a good one, but very inconvenient at that time, being quite out of the line of travel by trail. The ground opposite Edmonton was equally good and in other respects better, but at that time, one must remember, the preliminary survey of the C.P.R. passed 40 miles south, at a point known as the Hay Lakes, and crossed the Saskatchewan many miles west of Fort Edmonton, thus giving the impression that the main line would not touch Edmonton. Inspector Jarvis had quite a different opinion, however. He knew that Edmonton had a name already, and had large quantities of coal beneath the fort, in veins which extended and improved all the way up the river for many miles, but he knew that the crossing at the new site was easier and believed that a good town would spring up there in the future, as well as at Edmonton, which should have had a through line 25 years ago.

In April, 1875, we set to work to build our new quarters. The men's building was 90 feet by 22 feet, whilst the officers' quarters were of a size suitable for two or three. To these were added a guard-room and stables.

We made our own shingles, raised the walls, put on the roof, a new experience to many ; but a few of us had been bred in the rural districts in the east, where every boy in those days was supposed to have an axe in his hands within a few weeks of his birth, and where, in the early days of our boyhood, retired army and navy officers might have been seen on the roofs of their log barns, shingling them or handspiking at the log heaps to make homes for their sons. So there were we teaching ex-graduates and Irish land agents' sons to place shingles.

Our food at this time consisted of pemmican and mountain trout. The smallest trout weighed 5½ lbs., and many were over 12 lbs. These fish have a flavour quite equal to salmon, but one does not so soon tire of them. As an addition to our larder large quantities of wild duck eggs were obtained from the shores of the lakes in the Beaver Hills, to the south of our post, and an old Indian moose-hunter, who lived in the hills, brought us quantities of game in exchange for flour and tea. The favourite was beaver, which when roasted is delicious food.

In July the Company's steamer *Northcote* arrived on her maiden trip, the first steamer to navigate the Saskatchewan. She brought great quantities of mails for our division, the first mail of any consequence since we left our camp at Dufferin more than a year before. Amongst the official correspondence received were the general orders of the force, one of which was to the effect that I was to proceed to Swan River to take the position of Chief Constable, to which I had been promoted, to replace Chief Constable Griesbach, who had been appointed sub-inspector. I had to start for Swan River at once. I was sorry to leave the division and my kind O.C., but the orders were imperative and all arrangements had been made for my successor to come from Fort Macleod.

I had pleasant companions on the *Northcote*, and the time passed quickly. Joe Favel, the pilot, had been for years on the Mississippi and Missouri, which he had found difficult at times. The Missouri, he asserted, was not so good a stream as the North Saskatchewan. He had toiled on the river for years before, and the change from " tracking " from the mouth to Edmonton was very agreeable to him ; he knew every stone, bar and shallow in the river.

The steward was a character worth studying, a French Metis with the aristocratic name of Xavier de Mont-Ferron. This cognomen was a puzzle to the chief engineer, who substituted " Mor-fe-daw," which did not matter to Xavier, who came with alacrity when called.

At the Grand Rapids we were to be met by a new steamer from Lower Fort Garry, but there was no sign of it, and ere long our bill of fare consisted of fat sturgeon and tea alone, other supplies having run out. Eventually, two large boats, manned by Indians, arrived from Norway House at the head of the lake, and as they were bound for Lower Fort Garry, I took passage by one and left the next afternoon.

On Lake Winnipeg we ran into a headwind so strong that we had to turn into a little creek and wait for a change. It kept up for several days, and as we had only a few pounds of flour we were soon out of rations and had to shoot seagulls. These and tea were all we had to keep us from starving. At last the wind changed, and we lost no time in setting sail across the lake.

At the mouth of Berens River there was a Company's post, and here we procured a small supply of pemmican, tea and flour, sufficient, with economy, to last us until we reached the Stone Fort, now better known as Lower Fort Garry.

We sailed wing and wing down the lake, from point to point, and, when meal time came, landed to cook our stew of pemmican and flour and boil our tea, and when the kettles were on the fire we all knelt down to pray, led by the chief pilot, if both boats could get berthed in the same cove ; if not, each pilot led his own crew in fervently delivered prayer. When the meal was cooked all hands embarked and ate it in the boats to save loss of time.

I was naturally much impressed with the piety of the Indians, and it had often struck me what a curious scene was that assembly for prayer. The red-coated white in the kneeling circle of Indians, the wild surroundings of rock, forest and lake, the deep and impressive tones of the praying pilot lending solemnity to it all. I shall never forget it.

Talking of red-coats, one day when I was seated beside the chief pilot, a man of sixty or thereabouts, he looked at me with a roguish expression, and laughingly said, " Ah ! Soldiers is wild mans ! " " How is that, Baptiste ? " I enquired. " Aha," said he, " I was one of the pilots of the soldiers who came to Fort Garry by Hudson's Bay in 1846 (meaning the 6th Warwicks under Colonel Crofton), and when we ascended one of the rapids one of the soldiers was drowned, but that made no difference, in a few minutes all were singing as if nothing had happened. Ah, soldiers is wild mans ! "

On our way through the narrows of the lake we saw a light passing, which proved to be that of the new steamboat on her way to meet the *Northcote* at the Grand Rapids. She was very much behind time, and I was fortunate in more ways than one in taking passage with the Indians.

We arrived at Lower Fort Garry in three or four days from Berens River, and there I parted from my Indian friends with much regret. I should have liked to sail, fish or hunt with them all the summer long.

Next morning I decided to walk to Winnipeg, as the distance was but 22 miles. I took my room, on arrival, at the Grand Central Hotel, and next morning reported to the Mounted Police supply officer, a somewhat peppery old gentleman who did not receive me with urbanity. He read my credentials from Inspector Jarvis, which stated that I was en route to Swan River barracks on promotion. The latter word did not seem to please him, for he gazed disapprovingly at me, saying, " Take care you do not get the Irishman's hoist ! " Being disciplined I made no remark, but spoke cheerfully about

the trip in such a way that he seemed sorry for his out-
burst of temper, and promised me transport in a few days.
In the meantime I called at the sergeants' mess of the
battalion on duty at Fort Osborne, where I found several
old friends.

The next afternoon I left for Swan River with the teams
of the Public Works Department carrying artisans and supplies
for the men employed there.   The weather was fine, with the
exception of a hailstorm near Fort Ellis, which lasted but a
few minutes, and I found the men very kindly, cheerful fellows,
most of them from my own county in Ontario.

I noticed on this trip that a great change was taking place
beyond Portage la Prairie, 60 miles west of Winnipeg.   Homesteads had begun to dot the prairie at intervals as far as the
" Beautiful Plains," 100 miles west, most of the new settlers
being from Huron and Bruce, Ontario.

On my arrival at Swan River the adjutant and Colonel
French gave me a hearty welcome and promised me plenty of
work.

I then learned that the commissioner and a party of 50
officers and men had been at Carlton the previous month, with
Major-General Sir E. Selby-Smyth, G.O.C. of the militia,
who was on an inspection tour of the north west and British
Columbia, with instructions to report on the North West
Mounted Police and other matters of importance.   On his
arrival at Swan River barracks he was overtaken by Lieutenant
Cotton, of the Artillery, who brought a despatch, which caused
him, after consultation with Colonel French, to proceed to
Carlton without delay.   The reason for this hurry was a report
that Gabriel Dumont, a great leader of the plain-hunters,
had set up a sort of provisional government on the banks of
the South Saskatchewan, 18 miles east of Carlton, and that
he claimed independence of the Dominion.

The general met Gabriel at Batoches crossing on the south
branch, and had a conference with him, which resulted in
clearing the air.   He then passed on to Carlton, crossed the
North Saskatchewan, and continued his march west.

The true reason for all the fuss was that Gabriel Dumont had
enforced the law of the plains on one of the band of hunters

to which he belonged, and of which he was virtually the chief. Information was laid against him for assault, etc. A warrant was issued by a local J.P., recently appointed, and an attempt was made to arrest him, but without success. No violence was used, however, nor were any of the police employed. The law of the plains was necessary that there might be a proper system when the large number of plain-hunters were out. No member of the band was permitted to leave camp until all were ready to run the buffalo, lest the herds in the vicinity should be stampeded and the hunters have to break camp, and make a long march before they could overtake them. It will thus be observed that the law was not only necessary, but should have been provided for when the country was taken over by the Dominion government.

Gabriel Dumont was a remarkable Metis, who, with careful and just treatment, might have been educated to become one of the most loyal citizens of Canada. He was very much of the red man, far from faultless, extravagant, never looking out for the morrow ; but, as with his copper-coloured relatives, his good qualities far outweighed his bad, and he was a man whom many leading white men were glad to call friend. An old comrade of mine who had starved, hunted, feasted, and worked with him, and knew him in his hours of play, joy and sorrow, considered him one of the kindest and bravest of men. His equal as a hunter and horseman it was difficult to find. He was a great scout, and knew the plains as well as a housewife knows her kitchen.

One might travel the plains from one end to the other and talk to the Metis hunters and never hear an unkind word said of Dumont. He would kill bison by the score and give them to those who were either unable to kill or had no buffalo. Not until every poor member of the hunting-parties had his cart filled with meat would he begin to fill his own. When in trouble the cry of all was for Gabriel. His father and uncle, the former known as Kanpiew, the latter as Kanhow, were great hunters, though very old men, and were very much respected, but all turned to Gabriel when there was any grave crisis, the oldest paying attention to his word. He had, however, one fault, a grave one, but common amongst the hunters and Indians, that of gambling. Sometimes he would play for three days on end, stopping only to eat.

The life of the plain-hunter of those days is almost forgotten, and I shall give some account of it. I have seen a great deal, and my experiences have been and are corroborated by others who lived with them before the bison were exterminated.

The spring hunt began as soon as the snow had melted, and usually continued for a month or six weeks. Then came the summer hunt, until the middle of September, and lastly the fall or winter hunt, which did not cease from the time the ground was frozen until the hunters had sufficient fresh meat laid up to last them all the winter. This they kept frozen either in their outbuildings constructed for the purpose in the vicinity of their log-houses, or on stages or scaffolding erected to keep it out of reach of the numerous dogs.

The spring hunt engaged most of the hunters, though a few stayed at home to plant small patches of garden stuff. The remainder who did not go hunting took to the trail with their carts laden with prime buffalo robes, furs and pemmican secured during the previous summer and winter hunts. They would bring back to their homes from the Company's posts supplies of tea, sugar, tobacco, clothing, guns, rifles and ammunition.

The summer hunt found everybody out on the plains, young and old. The men of the band were divided into heads, councillors, and soldiers. The councillors met each day, discussed matters pertaining to the hunt, the camp, etc., and appointed a leader for the next day. His duties resembled those of the officer of the day and commanding officer combined. He took charge of the line of march, selected the halting-place for noon and night ; if the band was not on the move, he took the lead when the buffalo hunt began. For the day his word was law. At night he called his soldiers, of whom there were several detailed to each captain and under his orders, who formed a corral or ring with the carts in a circle, shafts inwards, hub to hub, into which all the horses were driven at dusk, to be let out to graze at daybreak. Outside this defence fires were lighted at intervals, and inside the lodges or teepees were pitched in a circle close to the carts. The soldiers remained on guard all night, passing from one fire to the other, keeping them alight and watching over the camp generally. There was seldom any wood, and buffalo chips took its place.

Every evening after the halt, when the corral had been formed, an old man, the crier of the camp, made a round of the enclosure calling out, " Oh, ho, oh, ho, le conseil ! " and after the council had assembled and made their selection of a leader, he would go the rounds again calling out, " Oh, ho, les soldats ! " and they would assemble under their respective captains. These camps were often very large, sometimes 300 or 400 lodges together, including Indians and plain-hunters. The diameter of the corral was often as much as 1000 feet.

When a buffalo run took place, the hunters would form up in line at intervals and canter slowly to an advantageous point, generally to leeward and behind some rising ground, the captain always in command. Very often they would dismount under cover of the rise and, before making a dash, one of the older men would repeat a prayer, all the rest responding. After that they would mount, but no other move was made until the captain gave the word to " let go," when it was every man for himself after a herd often of 50,000 or 60,000 buffaloes.

The winter hunt was for robes and meat ; the spring and summer hunt for pemmican and dried meat. The hides were tanned for leather to make harness, saddles, tents and moccasins. To make pemmican, the meat was dried, then finely pounded. For first-class pemmican, the marrow of many buffalo bones was taken, the whole put in a sack of the skin of the animal, the hair outwards, and well mixed together. When the sack was full the mouth was sewn up with threads of sinew. The second-class pemmican was composed of meat of the same quality, but mixed with the best of fat melted, while the third-class was of meat not quite so good nor so finely pounded ; but it was mixed with melted fat in the same way. This preparation of dried meats and pemmican would keep in perfect condition for decades. I do not know what the record is, but I have seen sacks of pemmican which had been worn smooth by transportation, not a hair being left, and yet

it was as good as the best made within the year.   It is first-class
food for travellers, hunters or soldiers, and, now that the buffalo
no longer roam the plains, it can be made from the meat of
the domestic animal, and is much superior to the " biltong "
of South Africa.   Both dried meat and pemmican were the
favourite food of the traveller on the plains and far north,
and the Mounted Police used it for years.

The Swan River barracks—Livingstone was the name on the
official record of the government, but never used by the force—
were built on a most extraordinary spot.   How on earth any
person in his senses could have selected such a situation it
is difficult to imagine.   When the builder arrived he found a
board marked " site for barracks," and was obliged to commence.   It lay on a high point between Snake Creek and the
Swan River, which lay in a wide and deep valley.   The surface
of the ground was covered with very large, firmly embedded
boulders, a considerable portion of them showing above
ground, only a few feet apart, and before enough space could
be cleared to enable the men to form properly on parade
we had to build large fires over the rocks and adopt the
primitive method of causing them to split when heated by
pouring water on them.

At the end of the barrack reserve an extraordinary spectacle
might be seen in the autumn or the early spring.   There
were several beds of stone about 25 feet square, on which lay
a huge mass of garter snakes basking in the sun.   The reptiles
took refuge there when the nights became cool, and for the
most part paid no attention to intruders.   When summer
came these snakes left their beds, and were found in every
direction for miles round, and some of them were even found
in the barrack-rooms.   Fortunately they were quite harmless,
if unpleasant, and the children gathered boxes full of them,
or amused themselves chasing their playmates with a snake
in each hand.   These beds gave the creek its name and had
been the resort of snakes from time immemorial.

The members of the force were a mixed lot.   Many were
smart young fellows from the old country and eastern Canada,
well-educated, but unaccustomed to manual labour, lured

to the wild west by the halo of romance which surrounded the lives of the pioneers. These men proved themselves equal to the very best, and helped to build up the reputation which the force now possesses.

There were also sons of Ontario farmers and the like, who, by their resourcefulness under all circumstances, were an excellent leaven to the whole lump. They seldom remained in the force for more than one term of service. They had come from the east to make homes for themselves and, as soon as their time expired, took their discharges and settled down to farming or business pursuits, generally in the vicinity of one of the police posts.

Such were the rank and file of the Mounted Police in 1875. Each had his own virtues and was different from the others, but in a short time all had absorbed the best characteristics of the others, the few faults soon disappeared, and the corps, although ridiculously weak in numbers for the work it had to do, became a powerful engine for the government of the west.

The mails were brought once a week from Winnipeg to Shoal Lake by our men with sleighs, and thence on to Swan River barracks, 140 miles, by a French Metis named Antoine Geneille, with the police dog trains On several occasions he made the distance in 36 hours' continuous travel, running behind the trains, and when he arrived at the orderly-room Colonel French would often say to him in fun, " Why, Antoine, you are ten minutes behind time ! What was wrong ? " and Antoine, taking him to be in earnest, would make all sorts of excuses and apologies for not having made more than 100 miles per day ! The dog drivers of the north west were marvels of endurance ; they are no longer to be seen on the plains, dogs have been superseded by horses and railways, but it will be many a long day before they will cease to be of use in the north.

The telegraph line constructed through by Swan River the previous summer was a great convenience. The operator gave us every day the latest news from the east, in a bulletin which he posted up in a convenient place, an advantage which no other post except Battleford enjoyed for many years. The

H

western terminus of the telegraph was at the Hay Lakes, 40 miles south of Forts Edmonton and Saskatchewan, on the projected line of the C.P.R., which was not intended to touch those places. The former, however, owing to later and better plans, is now one of the most important cities in Canada, and has three great railways passing through it.

Major-General Sir E. Selby-Smyth's report on the N.W.M.P. was published in general orders during the winter, and was read with interest. It was complimentary on the whole, but contained several erroneous statements. The drill of the force was commented upon most favourably ; the endurance of the men, their resourcefulness under all circumstances he considered greater than that of any force with which he had travelled during his many years of service on every continent. He had a good opportunity afforded him to test the mettle of the men. The trails, where there were any, were bad ; rafts had to be made daily to enable him and his staff to cross the numerous rivers.

During his trip the general was impressed by the kindly and firm methods of the Hudson's Bay Company in its dealings with the Indian tribes. The lawless invasion of the southern country had been followed by the organization of the N.W.M.P., whose work was now in evidence over the whole of the Great Plains. The west had never seen so many and useful changes. Strong posts had been established at Swan River, Saskatchewan, Calgary, Macleod, Shoal Lake, and the Cypress Hills. Law and order prevailed ; the quarters in all stations but one had been built by our own hands, officers and men vying with one another to get the work done ; surveyors were busy, a telegraph line, 900 miles in length, had been almost completed, geologists were boring for coal, the explorers of the government went about their business safe in the knowledge that we were near when wanted, and people had settled near all of our posts except in the Cypress Hills ; the Hudson's Bay Company had navigated the North Saskatchewan by steam ; and all this in the short space of fourteen months.

The lessons of Stuart and Sheridan fell on good soil, and we were far in advance of the times as mounted riflemen. Ten years later, when the mounted infantry instruction came out, it was too antiquated for us, and had to be improved upon to bring it up to the old standard, as in its original form it was never intended for first-class horsemen. In everything military or civil our commissioner led the way. Our equipment was comfortable ; full dress, grey cork helmets, scarlet Norfolk jacket, with loops for the belt so that it would not fall when unbuckled, Bedford cord flesh-coloured pantaloons, blue overalls, black boots for parade, brown for the trek, German silver hunting spurs, brown belts, gauntlets ; undress, scarlet serge, the same pantaloons, blue overalls, with double white stripes, black and brown boots, heel and hunting spurs, forage cap with gold laced band for officers and sergeants ; fatigue, brown jackets of duck ; winter, fur caps, mitts, moccasins, buffalo coats, and long stockings.

Lt.-Col. Irvine, who succeeded Lt.-Col. Macleod as assistant commissioner, had been in the far west all the summer. On his journey to Fort Macleod from Winnipeg his travelling companions were, with others, Abe Farwell, a fine type of American frontiersman, and one of the old hunter *coureur de bois* class, named Alexis de Bombard. The party had the usual buffalo skin tent or lodge for shelter at night, and the custom, common and necessary, was to stretch a string across the tent at a good height above the fire and hang thereon any moccasins or other articles which had become wet through travel in the deep snow. When the party turned in a stew of buffalo tongues, prairie chickens and rabbits was put in a camp kettle over the fire to simmer all night so as to be ready for breakfast in the morning. Alexis had for a head covering a tuque, or thick woollen cap, commonly used in the woods in winter. It looked as if it had been an heirloom from his grandfather, and as it had got wet that day he hung it up to dry with the rest of the articles. In the morning it was missing, but at breakfast Abe Farewell fished it out of the stew ! One of the party objected to stewed nightcap and contented himself with a survey of the horizon, but de Bombard donned his tuque as if it were not the first time it had been cooked, and Abe went on eating his breakfast as if nothing had happened, saying that he could not hit the trail on an empty stomach.

In July, Colonel French, our good and capable commissioner, resigned and returned to duty with the Royal Artillery in England. The sergeants at headquarters presented him with an address and a gold watch and chain, which he is still proud to wear, and the corporals and constables presented Mrs. French with an address and a service of plate.[1]

[1] Colonel French and his family left Swan River in August. On his arrival in England he was decorated with the C.M.G., and soon afterwards appointed Inspector of War Stores for Devonport and the Channel Islands. Later he organized the defence force of Queensland. On his return to England he was appointed Commandant of the School of Gunnery at Shoeburyness, then of the Artillery in Bombay. He was subsequently in command of the troops in New South Wales during the Boer War, and organized the whole of the troops sent out to it from that State. He left his mark on the North West Mounted Police by laying the foundation of its splendid efficiency.

CHAPTER VII

IN July we heard that Lt.-Col. Macleod had been offered
and accepted the commissionership of the force, and
had been gazetted on the 20th. He started for the
west at once, accompanied by the adjutant, Captain
Dalrymple-Clark.

They arrived at the Swan River barracks at 6 a.m. on
August 6, and gave orders for the headquarters and all but a
handful of " D " division to start by 9.30 a.m. for Fort Carlton,
where the Indian treaties were to be concluded in August.
It was a march of 1,150 miles, and we were to have all that
we required to enable us to halt anywhere and spend the
winter ! We had to see to the shoeing of the horses, transfers
of men who were to be left behind, as well as the hundred
and one other matters. The whole of these arrangements
fell upon the shoulders of the orderly-room clerk, the orderly
sergeant and myself, but at 8.45 I was able to report that
the division was ready to march, and we pulled out at 9 a.m.,
with half an hour to spare. Sub-Inspector Dickens, a son of
the great novelist, accompanied the division. Before we
trekked we learned that the Swan River barracks had been
found to be unsuitable for headquarters, and the place was
in future to be a mere outpost of the force.

On August 18 at sunset we arrived at Fort Carlton. We
found there a very large number of Indians of different bands

in one huge camp with the tents in a great circle. Near at hand many traders had assembled to get the benefit of the large sums of money that were to be paid to the Indians at the conclusion of the treaty.

The first day's proceedings were over when we arrived. The commissioners for the treaty were the Hon. Alexander Morris, Lieutenant Governor of Manitoba and the North West Territories, the Hon. W. J. Christie, and the Hon. James Mackay ; the two latter were well known in the country, had been born in it and spoke the Indian languages with ease and fluency. Mr. Christie had served in the Hudson's Bay Company for the greater part of his life ; Mr. James Mackay, a man of enormous size, weighing nearly 400 pounds, was perfectly familiar with every phase of life in the great west, and knew the Indian character intimately ; no better men could have been chosen to carry out the work than these able councillors of the north west. The secretary of the commission was Dr. Jackes, of Winnipeg ; the interpreter, a dignified plainsman named Peter Erasmus.

The council tent was pitched on an eminence about a quarter of a mile from the Indian camp, which contained upwards of 2,000 redskins. These assembled soon after the arrival of the commissioners, firing rifles, beating their tomtoms, dancing and yelling, the whole band chanting to the accompaniment of their drums.

When quite ready they advanced in a semi-circle, preceded by a large number of mounted warriors giving an exhibition of their magnificent horsemanship. These braves had been painted by their squaws in the most approved Indian style, some like zebras, others like leopards, each according to the skill and fancy of the artists. It was a fine show, well worth coming many hundreds of miles to see. Nothing so fine or barbaric can be seen nowadays ; the exhibitions one sees at fairs and shows being a mere sham and a disgrace to the red man.

The Indians gradually approached in the same semi-circle to within 50 or 60 yards of the Council Tent, where they halted and began the " Dance of the Stem." This was commenced by the chiefs, medicine men, councillors and musicians coming to the front and seating themselves on robes and blankets spread there for the purpose. The bearer of " The Stem," which was a gorgeously adorned pipe with a long stem, walked slowly along the same semi-circle of Indians and advanced to the front. He then raised the stem to the heavens, turned slowly to the four cardinal points and, returning to the group on the robes in front of the Council Tent, handed it to one of the young warriors, who commenced a slow chant, at the same time performing the stately dance, accompanied by the musicians and the singing of the men and women in the semi-circle. This was repeated by the other men, the main body steadily advancing. The commissioners then left the Council Tent to meet them, the horsemen still performing their wonderful feats. The bearer of the pipe of peace presented it first to the Lieutenant Governor, who gently stroked it several times and passed it to the other commissioners, who repeated the ceremony. This when repeated meant that the friendship of the Indians had been accepted.

The interpreter then introduced the chiefs and headmen. After that the Indians seated themselves before the Council Tent, and the commissioners placed themselves at a large table within it and faced them, while the sides of the tent were drawn back to enable the parties to the treaty to have a clear view. The Lieutenant Governor then addressed the Indians, announcing the mission of the commissioners through Peter Erasmus, who stood at the end of the table facing them, his position graceful and dignified, his voice deep, clear and mellow, every word distinctly enunciated. On hearing what the Lieutenant Governor had to say the red men requested leave to adjourn to talk it over in their council lodge, and the commissioners returned to the fort.

On the 19th the council was resumed. There were present the principal chiefs, Mis-Tah-Wah-Sis and Ah-Tuk-Ah-Coop. When all were placed the Lieutenant Governor again addressed the Indians, asking them to present their chiefs so that they could address him and the other commissioners. These were then brought forward by their braves. They represented 456 lodges.

Chief Beardy, of Duck Lake, 16 miles from Fort Carlton,

was not present with his band, having refused to meet the commissioners. His demeanour had been so unfriendly that Inspector Walker had to send an escort to bring the Lieutenant Governor and his colleagues from the south branch of the Saskatchewan to the fort. The refractory chief also sent a messenger to the commissioners to find out the terms of the treaty, but the Indian was told firmly that if he wished to know anything he must sit and listen to what they had to say. The terms of the treaty were then given out to the assembled Indians, and when the Lieutenant Governor had concluded his address Mis-Tah-Wah-Sis came forward, shook hands with him and asked for time to go and think over his words. It was arranged that they should meet again on Monday morning, the 21st.

The Indian camp was on a level plain and presented a very picturesque appearance. The lodges or tents were of tanned buffalo hides, many of them large enough to allow 20 or 30 to sit comfortably inside. The fire was built in the centre, the smoke finding its way through an aperture in the top, the proper draught to prevent the occupants from being smoked out being secured by a triangular wing of the tent being held in the right direction by a pole. The skin of the tent was stretched on long spruce poles trimmed quite smooth ; these, when the Indians were on the move, became part of the means of transport by being passed through the loops of the saddle or back band and trailed along the ground behind the pony ; two pieces were lashed across behind to form a sort of hammock-like stretcher, in which were carried the babies, the sick, the wounded, puppies, food, or any camp utensils, etc. On the outside of the lodge the Indians had painted the figures of birds, beasts, or reptiles representing their totems. Like the rest of their race on the plains, the Indians had many thousands of horses, the hills and prairie being covered with them, each family having its own herd and band of ponies. These were driven regularly to water at the Saskatchewan, and on the way back the herders invariably had a quarter-mile race on the level ground from the river to the bench land. The ponies were in first-class condition, and numbers of pinto or piebald ones were to be seen amongst them.

The Indians again asked for more time for deliberation, but on the 23rd, after a few preliminaries, the treaty was signed by the Lieutenant Governor, the Hon. James Mackay, the Hon. W. J. Christie, and by Mis-Tah-Wah-Sis, and Ah-Tuk-Ah-Coop. On the 24th, at the same place, the Lieutenant Governor invested the chiefs with their uniforms, medals and flags, and the headmen received theirs in the evening. The uniform of the chiefs was a scarlet frock coat braided with gold lace and a top hat of felt with a gold band. The headmen were given blue frock coats with gold lace, with hats similar to those of the chiefs. The medals were very large, with the Queen's head and a suitable inscription thereon.

On August 26 the whole of the Indians assembled in the fort, led by their chiefs, headmen and councillors, in uniform and with their medals. Each of them came forward in turn, shook hands with the Lieutenant Governor and the other commissioners, at the same time expressing gratitude for what had been given to them and the courteous treatment they had met. After this the Lieutenant Governor had some small pow-wows with lesser bands of Indians, some 5 miles from the fort, who assembled to meet him and sign the treaty.

We then went on to Fort Pitt, which we reached on September 5. A large number of Indians were assembled but, as there were many more still to come, the treaty was postponed until the 7th.

The same method of procedure was employed as at Fort Carlton. The Indians performed the " Dance of the Stem " in a very elaborate manner. Several " Stems " were used on this occasion, the bearers advancing gracefully to the beat of their tom-toms ; ermine skins festooned the " Stems," which were stroked in turn by the commissioners and Lt.-Col. Macleod. The pipes were smoked when that was concluded, the Lieutenant Governor, chiefs and commissioners passing the stem from one to the other, the chiefs pointing it to the north, south, east and west before smoking.

The horsemanship of the warriors as they advanced was even more daring than at Carlton. Each Indian was beautifully painted and mounted on his war horse or buffalo runner. They formed in line about 500 yards from the tent, broke away from the flanks in a double serpentine, the horses at their utmost speed, and finally halted in line about 50 yards from the tent. Two of them on this performance met with an accident through one of the horses putting its foot in a badger hole, this causing a collision which put the hip of one of the warriors out of joint and seriously injured both horses. Fortunately our surgeon was present,·and gave immediate relief to the injured man. The ceremony did not cease for a moment owing to this accident, nor was the least surprise manifested.

The Lieutenant Governor addressed the chiefs and headmen as at Fort Carlton. He told them that the red-coated servants of the Queen had come to protect them when it was learned that a large number of Assiniboines had been murdered at the Cypress Hills by the American traders, and that they would protect them from fire-water and from murder, would preserve peace, and prevent whites from injuring the Indians ; they must know, therefore, that when they met the red-coats they met friends. Sweet Grass, a fine Indian, was the principal chief, and, on the conclusion of the Lieutenant Governor's speech, shook hands with him and asked for the full terms of the treaty. These were carefully explained, and received with the " how-how " of approval from the assembled Indians, who next day considered the treaty in council.

On September 9 the treaty was signed, uniforms, flags and medals were presented, and the band played " God Save the Queen." The Indians were paid the same afternoon and presents distributed, the numerous traders realizing a large harvest of dollars. Amongst the chiefs who had come to Fort Pitt was Big Bear, whose band afterwards massacred the people at Frog Lake, only 28 miles from Pitt. He did not sign the treaty, nor had he any intention of doing so, but he signified to the Lieutenant Governor that he agreed to its provisions.

On September 13 Sweet Grass and others came to say good-bye to the commissioners. Big Bear did his utmost to extract a promise that there would be no hanging. He seemed in great fear of the rope, but was given to understand that anyone who took life must die for his crime.

Swan River having proved unsatisfactory, it was decided to make Fort Macleod the headquarters of the force, at any rate for a time. Accordingly, soon after the treaties had been made, we set out thither, and arrived on October 22. We had travelled on the prairie, from the time we left Swan River, at least 1,149 miles, and were sorry the trek was over.

There was also another reason for the change to Fort Macleod. The Sioux Indians and the American troops were fighting not very far from the boundary line between Canada and the United States. On the previous May 25 Major-General Custer, of the U.S. Army, with the 7th Cavalry, attacked Sitting Bull, the head soldier of the Sioux Indians, but the gallant general was slain and his regiment, fighting against enormous odds, was almost annihilated. The survivors, under Major Reno, were forced to take refuge on a hill in the vicinity and entrench as best they could until the arrival of General Terry, with whom Custer was to co-operate in the attack. I heard the account of this battle from Spotted Eagle, who was with Sitting Bull, and will give it in his own words :

" The Sioux were encamped in the valley of the Big Horn River, their lodges extending for some miles, when a cloud of dust was seen in the distance, and their scouts sent word that the ' Long Hair ' (General Custer) was coming. Sitting Bull ordered the Indians present to prepare for battle, and galloped down the valley to rouse the rest of the camp. The Indians assembled in large numbers and General Custer, sending part of his force round the hills to cut them off, advanced to fight on foot. The action with this part of the force did not last long. The soldiers were jammed in a crowd and, although they fought with great courage, were dispatched by the Indians with their " coup " sticks.[1] Some of the soldiers tried to escape on their horses, but in vain, the Indians crowding about and clubbing them to death. The last stand was made by Custer and a small party of his men, who stood together to the end. He was the last to fall, and died like a true soldier."

Spotted Eagle expressed a sincere admiration for the " Long Hair," who, he believed, would have been able to lead his

[1] " Coup " sticks are weapons having an egg-shaped stone secured to a stick by raw hide tied round a groove in the stone, and with a loose end at the other extremity which was coiled round the wrists like a sword knot. A blow from this was fatal, if received on the head, a fracture of the skull being certain.

regiment through them had they been armed with swords. The fight with this part of the force was over and the soldiers all dead before Sitting Bull returned.

Fort Macleod was situated on the island formed by the Old Man's River and a channel called " The Slough." The force had been located there for two years, and trails had been made to Fort Benton, 245 miles, and to Fort Shaw, Montana, 210 miles, both places garrisoned by United States troops. A fortnightly mail kept us in touch with Ottawa, via Fort Shaw, Helena, Ogden, Utah, and the Union Pacific Railway, the letters being one month in transit. There were mails to and from Forts Calgary and Edmonton, the former once a week, the latter at longer intervals. All these were run under our own contracts ; there were no post offices, and all letters had to have United States stamps, the nearest post offices being at Forts Benton and Shaw. Letters came to the orderly-room both ways, were sorted by our men and distributed, civilians getting theirs free of charge.

All freight for the Mounted Police and the traders' stores in the little collection of houses designated a town were brought from Fort Benton in ox-waggons, commonly called prairie schooners. These were very large and hauled by spans of 10 yoke or pairs of oxen of huge size. The vehicles were in trail, that is, coupled as freight cars, and carried from 10,000 to 15,000 lbs. of goods. The first waggon had about 6,000 lbs. the second 5,000, and the third carried 3,000 lbs. They were always neatly painted and had a nice cooking outfit to each span or team, the canvas cover fitting so well that everything was brought to its destination in perfect condition. The bull-trains, as they were styled when there were several, came in brigades of 10 or more teams, and in some parts of Montana I have seen them to the number of 50 or more moving in their slow and regular way across the prairie. One firm in that state had over 1000 oxen and 300 waggons on the trails. This system was very good in a country without bridges or roads, as the west was in 1876 and for many years later. When the teams came to bad places the waggons could, if necessary, be uncoupled and taken over one at a time. One crossing in the west, that on Milk River, south of Fort Walsh, was so bad through quicksands that on several occasions during the spring rains 40 or more oxen were required to drag one waggon across the stream.

The town lay in close proximity to the fort. It had gradually increased in size during the past two years, and contained, in addition to two excellent stores, many small log buildings roofed with mud, which were occupied by small traders, gamblers and others who made a living by smuggling whisky for the use of the whites and half-breeds. This stuff was retailed on the sly at the price of 50 cents per glass. It was a vile decoction which soon showed its effects upon those unwary enough to use it. Many of the gamblers in the place married Indian girls according to the custom of the aborigines, which was to give the father a present of a gun, a pony or ponies, according to the value he placed upon his daughter when he gave her to the white man in marriage. These marriages the Indians considered binding, but the white men took quite another view of the transaction and in most cases tired of their Indian wives and threw them aside when they left the place. This offence should have been severely punished, as it had a bad effect on both Indians and whites, causing them to become lax in their morals, and it was the origin of much mischief.

Crimes of a serious character had decreased, but there was no law against gambling until 1877, and the majority of the gamblers were professionals who, when they lost all, would depart for new fields in the south. They were replaced by others or were " set up " again by their friends for a fresh start, for with all their faults they were a generous class.

As at Fort Walsh, I. G. Baker & Co. were our contractors and bankers, and supplied us with forage and rations. Our men deposited most of their pay with them and received a large percentage per annum. This was done to save the firm the trouble and risk of bringing large sums into the country, and was no doubt profitable to both parties. Everything in the stores was expensive ; money, owing to the long distance from the base of supplies, was only turned over once a year, and a profit of about 100 per cent. was expected upon goods sold to the whites. The Indian trade was more profitable, however; enormous numbers of buffalo robes were taken, the Indians receiving not more than two dollars in trade, while the robes realized five times that amount in Chicago. Thus there was always a large profit both ways, 100 per cent. on the goods and at least four or five times that amount on the robes.

The timber suitable for fuel had disappeared from the river bottoms, but the pioneer coal-miner of the west, Nick Sheran, located a vein near where the city of Lethbridge now stands, and supplied us from that by ox waggons. This was a great thing for the post and town, and was the origin of the immense colliery at Lethbridge.

There was a good trade going on at Fort Calgary, the buffalo being plentiful to the eastward of the post. The Hudson's Bay Company and I. G. Baker & Company had stores, and Mr. David Macdougall had a good trading outfit, by which he dealt with the Mountain Assiniboines or Stonies, a very good tribe, whose conduct had been much influenced by the Rev. George Macdougall. He was one of the ablest of the missionaries of his church, but unfortunately was frozen to death near Fort Calgary the previous winter, when out hunting. His son, the Rev. John Macdougall, succeeded to his labours at the mission near the old Bow Fort, and became chairman for the whole of the north west. Near Fort Calgary Father Constantine Scollen established a mission as soon as the Mounted Police were firmly located, and a Methodist mission house was built on the flat near the barracks.

This short description of the country adjacent to the foot-hills of the Rocky Mountains will give an idea of the change which had come over the region in less than two years, the results being, no one will deny, due to the work of the Mounted Police. It was indeed pleasant to see everyone going about his work as peacefully and free from molestation as if he were on an Ontario farm. Whites and Indians rode the plains on peaceable terms, all tribes of Indians camped near one another, the redman and his family were rich again, well fed and clad. They thought nothing of the morrow, when, owing to the fact that everyone was at peace with his neighbour and could go where he pleased, the buffalo would soon disappear.

We found on arrival at Fort Macleod that the assistant commissioner had prepared for headquarters to be located there for a time at least. Log buildings were under construction to shelter us, and these were soon completed and made comfortable. The officers and men, at their own expense, however, lined the walls with factory cotton to keep the dust out and make the rooms look neat, and for the first time in two years floors of plank took the place of mud.

We all had a very busy time. As for myself I had not a moment to spare. In addition to the endless routine, a party under my supervision was employed broncho busting. The remainder of the force was kept busy at the barrack routine of a cavalry regiment, guarding prisoners, heading off whisky traders and horse-thieves, visiting Indian camps and traders' posts.

The court-room was crowded nearly every day ; the assistant commissioner and Inspector Winder were frequently on the bench and, in addition to my numerous outdoor duties, I attended court regularly, producing witnesses and preparing all details. Scarcely a night passed without an excursion after some criminal cases, and our men were continuously on the trail of law-breakers.

Some of the Indian witnesses had extraordinary names, such as " Double-barrelled Scissors," " Waggon Box Julia," and the nicknames of the white men who were before the court were quite as odd. Almost every white man went by a nickname which either connected him with some occupation or " outfit," by whom he was employed, or some personal peculiarity gave him the cognomen, such as " Yeast Powder Bill," " Self-rising William," " Red Waggon Jim," " Mormon Mike," " Diamond R. Brown," or " Liver-eating J." This last had killed an extra brave Indian warrior and devoured that portion of his anatomy, in hopes that he would absorb some of the red man's courage, not that he himself was lacking, but he wanted more !

In carrying out our duties that winter we were fortunate in having very mild weather. There was a slight fall of snow, and the weather grew cold near Christmas, but the chinook came in January, leaving the prairie bare for the remainder of the winter. This extraordinary wind has a great influence on the climate of the prairie region, and is even felt as far east as Winnipeg. Many were of the opinion that it came from the south west through the Rocky Mountain passes, and it was years before the true origin was known. It is from the Pacific Ocean, whence it rises in a damp wind, discharging its moisture on the mountains of British Columbia, Idaho and Montana, in snow and rain. It then descends dry to the plains, taking up all the moisture in its course until it exhausts itself far east. Its influence causes the isothermal line to run north west and take in the Peace River country. Even in the far, cold Yukon one day in 1899 it had the effect of melting the snow off the roofs of the houses. Its velocity is sometimes quite 100 miles per hour, and it is then somewhat unpleasant. Three feet of snow with a crust has been melted in one night, and its coming is heralded by a heavy bank of dark clouds on the Rocky Mountains, and its cessation is signalized by their disappearance. The weather then, if in winter, gets gradually colder until the heavy clouds again gather and the chinook comes roaring on to the plains.

My first Christmas at Fort Macleod was very pleasant The sergeants were a right good sort, united in everything which goes to make life pleasant. There were among them three university graduates, a Blue Coat boy, three N.C.O.'s, Royal Irish Constabulary, a West Point cadet, who had been rusticated for objecting to a coloured student from Virginia, and an ex-sheriff of New Brunswick.

Our Christmas dinners in the Mounted Police were always in the evenings, no daylight dinners for us. All, from the commissioner to the latest recruit, realized that Christmas comes but once a year, and that we must have a good time. Our civilian friends, to the number of 20, sat down with us, and our bill of fare consisted of turkeys, wild geese, antelope, other venison, buffalo tongues, boss rib, plum pudding, California fruit, raisins, nuts and milk punch, for which a permit had been obtained to enable us to pass the Christmas satisfactorily. The proceedings were enlivened by songs, speeches and toasts, the Queen, the Governor General, the army and navy and other loyal toasts being duly honoured. The

President of the United States was toasted in honour of our guests, who with few exceptions were citizens of the great Republic, and was responded to by every American at the table. Several of these are now British subjects and well satisfied with their new country.

One fine fellow, who has departed for the Great Unknown, was Hiram Upham. " Hi," as he was affectionately called, was a tall, good-looking man from Vermont, and of great western experience. He once took a trip in the Indian country when the red man was looking for scalps, taking with him old Vielle, the interpreter of his firm. They were only out a few days when a party of their red brothers on the warpath approached. As it would have been madness to run for it, Hi and Vielle took to a large buffalo wallow and prepared to fight. But the latter, who was not noted for his pluck, and was married to a squaw of the same tribe as the Indians, thought that his skin would be safer if he left Upham to take care of himself and returned to a coulee in the vicinity. As he could not get away without some valid excuse he suggested, " You stand 'em off, Hi, and I'll ' rustle ' a bit on the side." It was no good, however, for Hiram replied, " You rustle here, you angel, or I'll relieve you of your top hair ! " This decided Vielle to remain with him, and Vielle's red relatives, seeing that the white men presented a bold front with their rifles ready for use, concluded that their scalps would be too expensive and drew off to look for easier prey.

During the winter large numbers of Blackfeet, Bloods, Peigans, Stonies and Bobtail's band of Crees came to trade at the stores. These people were armed with magazine rifles and many had revolvers. The Blackfeet were with few exceptions dressed in buffalo robes, with the hair inside, the outside coloured with red ochre, and the whole secured by a large black belt studded with brass nails. The Bloods and Peigans wore gay American blankets, the latter had theirs neatly arranged with a hood at the back to pull over their heads in stormy weather. All wore leggings and were painted with ochre according to their fancy. Bright brass rings were fastened round their well-braided locks. The Crees and Stonies wore the durable white blankets of the Hudson's Bay Company

I

wrapped round them, but they took very little trouble to adorn themselves.

Great numbers of buffalo robes were brought in by the Indians, those furnished by the Blackfeet and their kindred tribes were very fine ; the skin of the heads and tails and the horns and hoofs well polished were left on them and made them much more valuable. The Crees and Stonies did not take the same trouble until they found that they must follow the example of the Blackfeet or be unable to sell the skins.

Quay-we-den, the gigantic medicine man of Bobtail's band of Crees, was at Fort Macleod during the greater part of the winter, and Chief Crowfoot at Blackfoot Crossing, " The Ridge Under the Water," became unwell, and sent word to this Cree medicine man that he must be using his " long medicine " on him, in other words, bewitching him, and that there was no excuse for doing this, as their tribes were at peace with one another. This tickled Quay-we-den, who, being a cute Indian, played upon the superstitious fears of the Blackfeet chief until the latter bought him off with presents and was restored to health.

During the winter we had proofs of the ease with which buffaloes and antelopes can be tamed. We captured two yearling buffalo calves, which within a few weeks would go out to graze on the prairie every morning and in the evening before dark return to the corral, where they would play with the men. Several times I met them a mile from the fort without exciting in them the slightest alarm. Some antelopes were secured and ere long could be turned loose, and would frolic with the Indian children and the only white child in the post, circling round them like kittens. They would encourage the dogs to chase them, keeping them within a few feet, and then by a sudden burst of speed distance them like a flash.

I was in T. C. Powers' store one day when one of our antelopes, not more than a month in captivity, came into the building. As it was not wanted Mr. Williamson, the accountant, got a biscuit from a box behind the counter and coaxed the little beast outside. Next day it returned, went round the counter to the biscuit box and helped itself.

It is a great pity that no attempt was made in those days

to domesticate the buffalo on a large scale so that such a useful animal should not be lost to us. They could have been easily captured at a small cost per head, and no doubt the plain-hunters and Indians would have been glad to do the work. In the hunts the calves were left far behind and when the hunters returned the calves ran round the horses' legs, taking them for their mothers, and would follow them into camp, where they were killed for their meat and hides.

We had by this time become very well acquainted with the Indians and had a very great influence over them. They were learning to shun the low white man and look to us for protection. The Blackfeet Nation, viz., the Blackfeet, Bloods and Peigans, were an open, frank, bold people, with very little of the craft supposed to be in the Indian character. The Crees were quite different, very distant and less inclined to make friends except for selfish reasons. The physique of the Black-feet Nation, especially the Blood tribe, was very fine, the men were tall and graceful in bearing, and were pleasant and cheerful. Their horsemanship was of a high class and their ponies, buffalo-runners and war horses of a good type. From two years of age the children rode without assistance, and the women also rode well and took charge of the trains of ponies when on trek from one camp to another, pitched the tents, dressed the buffalo robes and cooked the food. The more wives an Indian had the richer he was !

The Indians had a name for every white man they knew and were very clever in noting any physical peculiarity. A handsome young man, for instance, might get the name of " Pretty Young Buck." Colonel Macleod was a great favourite with them, and the fort was called " The place where the ' Bull's Head ' stays." He was regarded by the Blackfeet Nation as the personification of justice. I doubt if any one ever had such influence with them, and, as a matter of fact, it could not be otherwise. He kept his place, never accepted a present, never gave one, and was respected by them all the more for it, his word being law from the time he appeared amongst them.

One of the most important aids to us in our management of the Indians and the carrying out of our duties, both military and civil, in the great west was our remarkable scout and interpreter, Jerry Potts. He had been in many Indian fights, in which he had led large bands of warriors. He was indispensable as a teacher of the mysteries of the plains and the ways of the red man. He was only fifteen years of age when he lost his father, a Scotchman of education, who had charge of one of the American Fur Company's posts on the Missouri, and was murdered by an Indian who mistook him in the dark for one of the employees of the Company with whom he had quarrelled. From that time on Potts was employed as an interpreter, scout and guide, and at all our posts was trusted implicitly in all dealings with the Indians. The officers and men treated him with the greatest consideration and received in return the most loyal assistance and support.

" The 17th of Ireland," as our friends call the day of their patron saint, was kept by the Irishmen at Macleod in the most patriotic manner. Green ribands were to be seen everywhere, and many a whisky *cache* or hiding-place was raised to enable Pat and his many admirers to do honour to the occasion. About midnight on the 17th I was reading in the mess, wondering if I could soon retire to rest, but afraid that I should have something to do in town, when a man rushed excitedly into the room with the information that a small trader had a row going on in his cabin and was dispensing firewater, whereupon I got the farrier-major to come with his men.

When we arrived at the door of the cabin we found a party of civilian toughs there to warn the proprietor. Tuke, the farrier-major, seized the largest and shook him as a terrier would shake a rat, while I, on being refused admission, kicked the door in. We had to be prompt in those days ! We found the trader and several others in a hilarious state. No sooner did he see my informant than he made a rush at him with fury in his eyes, and no wonder, for the young rascal had been enjoying his hospitality, had quarrelled with his host and then out of spite had informed upon him. The trader was arrested, however, and a *cache* discovered amongst a huge pile of buffalo robes.

Just as we were leaving Tuke saw a stockinged foot protruding from a pile of robes in a dark corner and dragged the owner forth. He proved to be a poor fellow, commonly called Paddy, a graduate of a famous university, who in the weakest moment of his life had fallen to the seductive wiles of the trader. There was no help for it, he should not have played the ostrich and been caught by Tuke's eagle eye. He was before the assistant commissioner next morning, and met the fate of all in the force who sacrificed duty at the altar of Bacchus.

In 1877 the Dominion Government decided that a treaty should be concluded that year with the Blackfeet and other Indian tribes who roamed the Great Plains from the North Saskatchewan to the international boundary in what is now the province of Alberta. The Indians' title to their hunting-grounds was to be extinguished and the red man to receive reserves and other compensation.

The treaty was to be styled Number 7, and the commissioners appointed to represent the government of Canada were the Honourable David Laird, Lieutenant Governor of the North West Territory, and Lt.-Col. Macleod. The place decided upon was the Blackfeet Crossing, or " The Ridge under the Water," of the Bow River, about 80 miles over the prairie from Fort Macleod.

On September 19 the majority of the chiefs and minor chiefs of the Blackfeet, Blood, Peigan, Stoney and Sarcee tribes seated themselves in front of the Council Tent, and about a third of a mile beyond them some 4,000 men, women and children were on the grass watching the proceedings with interest.

Mr. Laird then addressed the Indians in the following words :

The Great Spirit has made all things, the sun, the moon, the stars, the earth, the forests and the swift running rivers. It is by the Great Spirit that the Queen rules over this great country and other great countries. The Great Spirit has made the white man and the red man brothers, and we should take each other by the hand. The Great Mother loves all her children, white men and red men alike ; she wishes to do them all good. The bad white man and the bad red man she alone does not love, and them she punishes for their wickedness. The good Indian has nothing to fear from the Queen or her officers ; you Indians know this to be true.

When bad white men brought you whisky, robbed you and made you poor, and through whisky made you quarrel amongst yourselves, she sent the Mounted Police to put an end to it. You know how they stopped this, and punished the offenders, and how much good this has done. I have to tell you how much pleased the Queen is that you have taken the Mounted Police by the hand and helped them and obeyed her laws since their arrival. She hopes you will continue to do so, and you will always find the police on your side if you keep the Queen's laws. The Great Mother heard that the buffalo were being killed very fast, and to prevent them from being destroyed her councillors have made a law to protect them. This law is for your good ; it says that calves are not to be killed either in winter or spring, except by the Indians when they are in need of them for food. This will save the buffalo and provide you with food for many years, and it shows you that the Queen and her councillors wish you well.

Many years ago the Great Mother made a treaty with the Indians, far away by the great waters of the east. A few years ago she made a treaty with those beyond the Touchwood Hills and the Wood Mountains. Last year a treaty was made with the Crees along the Saskatchewan, and now the Queen has sent Colonel Macleod and myself to ask you to make a treaty. But in a very few years the buffalo will be destroyed, and for this reason the Queen wishes to help you to live in the future in some other way. She wishes you to allow her white children to come and live on your land, and raise cattle and grain, and thus give you the means of living when the buffalo are no more. She will also pay you and your children money every year, which you can spend as you please. By being paid in money you cannot be cheated, as with it you can buy what you think proper.

The Queen wishes to offer you the same as was accepted by the Crees. I do not mean exactly the same terms, but equivalent terms that will cost the Queen the same amount of money. Some of the other Indians wanted farming implements, but these you do not require, as your lands are more adapted to raising cattle, and cattle perhaps will be better for you. The commissioners will give you your choice, whether cattle or farming implements. I have already said we will give you money. I will now tell you how much. If you sign the treaty, every man, woman and child will get twelve dollars each. This year's chiefs and councillors will be paid more than this. Chiefs will get a suit of clothes, a silver medal, a flag, and every third year you get another suit. A reserve of land will be set apart for yourselves and your cattle, upon which none other will be permitted to encroach. For every five persons one square mile will be allowed on this reserve, on which they can cut brush and trees for firewood and other purposes. The Queen's officers will permit no white man or half-breed to build or to cut timber on your reserves ; if required, roads will be cut through them. Cattle will be given to you and potatoes, the same as are grown at Fort Macleod.

The commissioners strongly advise you to take cattle, as you understand cattle better than you will farming, for some time at least, and as long as you continue to move about in lodges. Ammunition will be issued to you each year, and as soon as you sign the treaty, 1,500 dollars' worth will be distributed among the tribes; and, as soon as you settle, teachers will be sent to you to instruct your children to read books like this one (a Bible), which is impossible so long as you continue to move from place to place.

I have now spoken. I have made you acquainted with the principal terms contained in the treaty which you are asked to sign.

You may wish to talk it over in your council lodges, you may not know what to do before you speak your thoughts in council. Go, therefore, to your councils, and I hope you may be able to give me your answer to-morrow. Before you leave I will hear your questions and explain any matter which may not be clear to you.

After a few questions the proceedings closed for the day.

Next morning the commissioners proceeded once more to the Council Tent and found the chiefs awaiting them. The proceedings continued all day, with short intervals, in which the band played. All the chiefs spoke and asked questions, to which the commissioners replied, explaining any point that the Indians did not quite understand. On the following day the terms of the treaty were agreed to and several of the chiefs made speeches. Crowfoot, being the paramount chief, spoke first and said :

While I speak be kind and patient. I have to speak for my people, who are numerous, and who rely upon me to follow that course which in future will tend to their good. The plains are large and wide ; we are the children of the plains ; it has been our home, and the buffalo have been our food always. I hope you look upon the Blackfeet, Bloods, Peigans and Sarcees as your children now, and that you will be indulgent and charitable to them. They all expect me to speak for them, and I trust the Great Spirit will put into their breasts to be good people, into the minds of the men, women and children, and their future generations.

The advice given to me and my people has proved to be very good. If the police had not come to this country, where should we all be now ? Bad men and whisky were indeed killing us so fast that very few of us indeed would have been left to-day. The Mounted Police have protected us as the feathers of the bird protect it from the frosts of winter. I wish them all good, and trust that all our hearts will increase in goodness from this time forward. I am satisfied. I will sign the treaty.

Crowfoot then seated himself, and Button Chief, an Indian who made stupid remarks during the conference, asking that the Indians be paid for the wood used by the Mounted Police for fuel, etc., rose and said : " I must say what all the people say, and I agree with what they say. I cannot make new laws. I will sign." Thereupon Red Crow spoke and said : " Three years ago when the Mounted Police came to the country, I met and shook hands with Stamix-oto-kan (Colonel Macleod), at Belly River. Since that time he made me many promises, he kept them all ; not one of them was broken. Everything that the Mounted Police have done has been good. I entirely trust Stamix-oto-kan, and will leave everything to him. I will sign with Crowfoot." Father of Many Children, the oldest Indian present, said : " I have come a long way and far behind any of the bands I have travelled with these traveaux that you see outside with my women and children. I cannot speak much now, but I agree with Crowfoot and will sign." Ancient Sun addressed the commissioners also, saying : " Crowfoot speaks well. We were summoned to meet the Great Mother's chiefs here, and we would not disappoint them. We have come and will sign the treaty. During the past Crowfoot has been called by us Our Great Father. Great Mother's Chief (Mr. Laird),

everything that you say appears to me to be very good, and
we hope that you will give us all that we ask, cattle, money,
tobacco, guns and axes, and that you will not let the white men
use poison on the prairies ; it kills horses and buffalo, as well
as wolves, and it may kill men. We can ourselves kill the
wolves and set traps for them. We all agree with Crowfoot."

Red Crow was one of the very best of the Indian chiefs. He
was head chief of the Bloods, the most powerful of the three
Blackfeet tribes, and was loyal to the last. The putting out
of poison for wolves was much objected to by the Indians, but
at the time of the Blackfeet treaty there was not so much of it
done as in former years, when a considerable number of white
men, styled " wolfers," made a living by that means, and their
cabins were to be seen along the rivers. Laws had been already
passed to prevent the careless use of poison, and the Mounted
Police kept a sharp look out to prevent " wolfing " in a reckless
way, viz., throwing poison about wholesale. It had been a
common thing a few years before the law was passed to see
dozens of wolves lying dead near the poisoned carcase of a
bison.

A great many chiefs followed Red Crow, all in favour of the
treaty, and on September 21 the whole of them and their
councillors signed it beneath the signatures of the commissioners, and the usual salute of thirteen guns announced the
conclusion of the last treaty with the Plain Indians of Canada.

The next three days were spent in paying the Indians their
treaty money. Some very odd requests were made during
these payments, such as premiums for the babies that were to
come, and for blind brothers and sisters who could not attend.
On the last day of the payments the chiefs presented an address
to the commissioners, expressing their satisfaction at the way
its terms were carried out, and their best wishes to the Great
Mother, the Lieutenant Governor, Colonel Macleod, and the
North West Mounted Police. They spoke in the highest terms
of the officers and of the force in general, and assured the
commissioners of their firm determination to adhere to the
treaty and abide by the Queen's laws. Jerry Potts stated
that he had never heard Indians speak their minds so freely
before.

Mr. Laird, in reply, said that he was much pleased to receive such an address from the Blackfeet Nation; it was to the Great Mother, for whom he was acting, as he was only carrying out her wishes.

Colonel Macleod said:

The chiefs know what I said to them three years ago, when the police first came to the country—that nothing would be taken away from them without their consent; you all see to-day that what I told you was true. I also told you that the Mounted Police were your friends and would not wrong you, or see you wronged in any way; this also you see is true. The police will continue to be your friends and be always glad to see you.

On your part you must keep the Queen's laws and give information to them in order that they may see the laws obeyed and offenders punished. You may still look to me as your friend, and at any time when I can do anything for your welfare I shall be only too happy to do so.

You say that I have always kept my promises: as surely as my past promises have been kept so surely shall those made by the commissioners be carried out in the future. If they were broken I should be ashamed to meet you or look you in the face. But every promise will be solemnly fulfilled, as certainly as the sun now shines down upon us from the heavens. I shall always remember the kind manner in which you have to-day spoken of me.

CHAPTER VIII

The Sioux in Canada—Major Walsh and Sitting Bull—Grievances against the United States—The commission—General Terry—The conference with the chiefs—Sitting Bull's reply—Failure of the commission—Work at Fort Macleod—Buckskin Charlie—The Assiniboine sun dance—The initiation of the braves—Indian signs —An awful journey—Big Bear's band—Leveillée—Jerry Potts—An adventurous youth—A triumph of strategy—Indian honesty—An intelligent goose.

COLONEL Macleod had now another important duty to perform. The governments of Great Britain, Canada and the United States had arranged that commissioners from the latter country should visit the North West Territory in October, 1877, and endeavour to induce the surrender to the United States of Sitting Bull and the Sioux Indians, who had taken refuge in Canada after the fight in which they had almost totally destroyed the 7th Cavalry under the gallant General Custer. It was necessary that the commissioner of the N.W.M.P. should represent Canada and arrange for the Sioux chief and his colleagues to meet the American commissioners and discuss proposals.

The Sioux had crossed the boundary line in December, 1876, and in March, 1877, Medicine Bear and 900 lodges of Yankton Sioux followed. The latter were not concerned in the Custer massacre, nor were they regarded as hostiles, although they belonged to the Sioux Nation. Major Walsh had met the Sioux, who asked for ammunition; but he would give them only some food for themselves and their families. They had no ammunition left with which to kill buffalo, and later on he allowed ten rounds per man on a permit signed by an officer of the Mounted Police. No trader could sell more than the number of rounds authorized. This was a wise arrangement, it being known that there were petty traders in the buffalo country who would, if they dared, sell all that the Indians

123

desired, and, provided that their own scalps were safe, were quite regardless of the safety of those of the " Mela Hoska " (Long Knives, *i.e.*, United States soldiers) or the " Shagalasha " (Mounted Police).

About the 29th of the same month Lt.-Col. Irvine was met by some Sioux Indians at Fort Walsh, who reported that three Americans were in Sitting Bull's camp near Pinto Horse Butte, and on the last day of the month he proceeded to the camp, accompanied by Major Walsh, the adjutant of the post and another officer. When he arrived he saw three white men, the Abbé Martin, an interpreter, and an alleged scout of General Miles, of the U.S. army. These persons had seriously offended the Indians, who looked upon them as spies who had no right to be present, and had it not been for the orders of Major Walsh they would have put them to death. The Abbé was desirous of having them return to their reservations in the United States. The other two men stated that they had accompanied the Abbé for protection, but that they intended to find out from the Mounted Police if the Sioux purposed crossing the international boundary. This was a very absurd excuse, for if it was their wish to meet the officers of the force they could have done so without going to the Sioux camp, which was a very strange proceeding if reliable information was to be obtained. In fact, to say the least of it, their actions had the colour of stupidity or deceit. Had they gone to Fort Walsh to interview the commandant they would have been treated with courtesy, and he would have known the best course to take in the matter. The officers and men of the force, from the date of the arrival of the Sioux until the time of the surrender of Sitting Bull and the last of the hostile Sioux, in 1881, maintained perfect touch with every move of those Indians, and succeeded by their constant vigilance in preventing them from raiding or annoying any settlements of the U.S.A.

The assistant commissioner's council with Sitting Bull and his chiefs was conducted with the usual ceremony, the pipe of peace was smoked and the ashes buried. At this conference the chiefs present were Sitting Bull, Pretty Bear, Bear's Cap, Eagle Sitting Down, Sweet Bird and Minnieonzon.

Major Walsh, having already met Sitting Bull, informed him

that the assistant commissioner was the highest authority in that part of the country, and that he had come to hear what he had to say. Lt.-Col. Irvine then addressed the chiefs, explaining to them that now that they were in British territory they would have to obey the laws, and that they must not cross the border to fight the Americans and then return to Canada. He told them that they would be allowed enough ammunition to hunt buffalo for food, but that not one round of ammunition was to be used against either white man or Indian. He said that they had done well to send information of the Americans who had come to their camp, and that he would go and see them, and take them away with him ; they had nothing to fear from the Americans, as they could not cross the line after them.

Sitting Bull came to Lt.-Col. Irvine's tent about 11 o'clock at night and sat there until an early hour in the morning, relating his grievances against the " Long Knives." His band was small at first, but soon grew, being recruited by many hostiles who had not yet taken refuge in Canada. The numbers from first to last have been under estimated. With Medicine Bear's Yanktons, there were well known to be double the number reported. It was this state of affairs which brought about the visit of the American commissioners and Colonel Macleod's trek from the Blackfeet Crossing to meet them.

We found everything bustle and hurry at Fort Walsh. General Terry, of the U.S. army, was expected to arrive shortly with his staff. There was another cause for excitement. Chief Joseph and his Nez Percée Indians had dug up the war axe and were fighting the American troops a few miles south of the international boundary at the west end of the Bear Paw mountains. The red men had already fought a battle with Major-General Gibbon, and were attempting to reach Canada for refuge. They had up to date behaved in a remarkably civilized manner, no farmers or other civilians had been molested, and, with the exception of a few stores at the Coal Banks of the Missouri at Cow Island, where they had a fight with some volunteers who had turned out under the command of an officer of the regular army, they had done no plundering.

Several columns were soon in pursuit of the Nez Percées, to

prevent them from getting across the Canadian border, and General Miles in command of the forces had brought them to bay. They had entrenched to make their last stand and faced the troops with great determination. This outbreak had given much alarm to the settlers in Montana, and the despatch riders from Fort Benton to Fort Walsh in connection with the rising and the movements of the commissioners to meet Sitting Bull demanded and received as much as 500 dollars for the trip of 160 miles. On our side, however, no such sum would have been paid. The despatches were carried by our men without extra pay, and all were anxious to be employed.

When we arrived we found that Major Walsh had gone to Pinto Horse Butte, about 150 miles east of Fort Walsh, to meet Sitting Bull and the other Sioux chiefs and escort them in. The following day our party went out to meet him and lend more importance to the occasion. When Major Walsh appeared he was accompanied by the Sioux chiefs, 20 in all, and one squaw, a tall, powerful looking woman in the prime of life.

He reported that he had seen a party of Nez Percée Indians, who had succeeded in escaping through the American lines to Canada. Many were wounded and in a destitute condition. They stated that the rest of their party had been either killed or captured.

Early next morning we were on our way back to Fort Walsh, the Indians jogging along at a fox trot beside us. The chiefs were very frank and friendly in their demeanour, and we soon learned that no matter how much the Canadians and Americans desired it, the Sioux had not the slightest intention of giving themselves up to the United States government. In fact, nothing but force or starvation would induce them to cross the border. These chiefs were the most noted of the Teton Sioux, handsome in appearance, all having the dark and intensely piercing eyes peculiar to the Sioux.

After supper one of the Sioux started to run buffalo, and a fat cow was killed and dressed by the squaw, who cut the meat into thin strips and broiled them on the coals for the Indians, who washed them down with copious draughts of strong tea. The Indians sat up all night round the buffalo chip fire, singing, eating and drinking, until the whole carcase had been devoured, every one of them stowing away at least twenty pounds of the well-cooked meat. This gastronomic feat may seem incredible to those who do not know the capacity of the North American Indian to eat large quantities of food when favourable opportunity presents itself. He has to be ready for the morrow, and it should be borne in mind that the flesh of the buffalo is much easier to digest than beef.

The day after our return to Fort Walsh Colonel Macleod met General Terry at the border. Permission was given for the American general's escort of infantry to come with him to the fort. This company travelled in mule waggons, and was very interesting ; several of them had been through the battle with the Nez Percées at the Bear Paw mountains. Many were old and seasoned soldiers, one having been through the Mexican War, more than 20 years before. They were supplied with comfortable tents with good stoves ; the latter were luxuries unknown to us at that time. The camp fire and our blankets were the best we could have. Stoves were introduced many years later and proved to be a great comfort.

There were several professional scouts in General Terry's party, one of them, an Englishman of an old family, Howard by name, a very bright, well-informed man, but, like many, averse to hiding his light under a bushel   He took no pains to conceal his dislike of the red men

The day after his arrival, General Terry and General Lawrence, who accompanied him, were met at the officers' mess-room by Colonel Macleod and his officers, and received Sitting Bull and his chiefs in council   A number of American and Canadian newspapers were represented, and the squaw who came with the Sioux was permitted to be present, although it is against Indian etiquette for a woman to take part in a council. In fact, it was an affront to the commission, but whether intentional or not I cannot say.

The proceedings began by Colonel Macleod stating that General Terry and his staff were present by invitation, and that the Sioux chiefs had been summoned to meet them. General Terry then addressed the chiefs, through an interpreter who, it is to be regretted, did not know even his own language and was in no manner to be compared with those who did duty at the great Blackfeet and Cree treaties   Few men of good education had opportunities of learning Sioux, consequently the fine display of oratory of some of the chiefs was cut down to laconic remarks even coarser than one sometimes heard in the magistrate's court at Fort Macleod.

The general told the chiefs that their band was the only one that had not surrendered to the United States, and that it was the desire of his government that they should return to their reservations, give up their arms and horses, and receive cattle in exchange for the money realized by the sale.   In reply Sitting Bull said :

For 64 years you have kept me and my people and treated us badly.   What have we done that you should want us to stop ?   We have done nothing.   It is the people on your side who have started us to do these depredations.   We could not go anywhere else, so we took refuge in this country.   It was on this side of the country that we learnt to shoot, and that was the reason I came back to it again.   I should like to know why you came here.   In the first place I did not give you the country, but you followed me from one place to another, so that I had to leave and come over to this country. I was born and raised in this country with the Red River half-breeds, and I intend to stop with them.   I was raised hand-in-hand with the Red River half-breeds, and we are going over to that part of the country, and that is the reason that I have come over here.   (Here Sitting Bull shook hands with Colonel Macleod and Major Walsh.)   That is the way I was raised, in the hands of the people here, and that is the way I intend to be with them.   You have got ears and you have got eyes to see with, and to see how I live with these people.   You see me, here I am.   If you think I am a fool, you are a bigger fool than I am.   This house is a medicine house.   You come here to tell us lies, but we do not want to hear them.   I do not wish any such language used to me, that is, to tell me such lies in my Great Mother's house.   Do not say two more words.   Go back to where you came from. This country is mine, and I intend to stay here, and to raise this country full of grown people.   See these people here, we were raised with them.   (Again he shook hands with the Mounted Police officers.)   That is enough, so no more.   You see me shaking hands with these people.   The part of the country you gave me you ran me out of. I have now come to stay with these people, and I intend to stay here. I wish to go back and take it easy going back. (At this point he took a Santee Sioux Indian by the hand.) The Santees, I was born and raised with them. He is going to tell you something about them.

"The One who runs the Roe," a Santee Indian, then said : "Look at me ! I was born and raised in this country. The people away north I was raised with. I have lived in peace with them. For the last 64 years we were over in your country and you treated us badly. We have come here now, and you want to try and get us back again. You did not treat us well, and I do not like you at all."

The Sioux squaw then got up and remarked : "I was over in your country. I wanted to raise children over there, but you did not give me any time. I came over to this country to raise my children and to have a little peace. That is all I have to say to you. I want you to go back to where you came from. These are the people I am going to stay with and raise my children with."

Flying Bird then spoke, saying : "These people here, God Almighty raised us together. We have a little sense and we ought to love one another. Sitting Bull here says that whenever you found us out, wherever his country was, you wanted to have it. It is Sitting Bull's country, this is. The people sitting all round me, what they committed I had nothing to do with. I was not in it. The soldiers find out where we live and they never think of anything good. It is always something bad." He too shook hands with the Mounted Police officers.

The Indians then arose and were about to depart when the interpreter was directed by General Terry to ask : "Shall I say to the President of the United States that you have refused the offer he has made to you ? Are we to understand from what you have said that you refuse those offers ?" to which Sitting Bull replied : "I could tell you more, but that is all I have to tell you. If we told you more, why, you would not pay attention to it ; that is all I have to say. This part of the country does not belong to your people. You belong to the other side. This side belongs to us."

K

Sitting Bull than left the room, followed by the Indian chiefs, and encamped outside the fort for a day or two. During their stay they visited the barrack-rooms and were fed by the men on the best they had. In one room they were regaled with plum-pudding and one of them, Bear's Cap, had a severe attack of indigestion, necessitating the loan of a tent, in which he was treated in a very drastic manner for the complaint.

While the American soldiers remained with us I made the acquaintance of the officer commanding their company and the smart German sergeant. I was shown their system, interior economy, books, pay sheets, etc., all of which they carried with them in neat pigeon-holed chests which, when the company was halted, could be opened and used as desks.

General Terry and his officers were smart soldiers, very punctilious in their bearing towards us. The general was the hero of Fort Fisher, which he captured during the great war between the Northern and Southern States, and when the war was over was rewarded by high rank in the regular army. He was very erect and at least six feet six inches in height, well proportioned and with a very kindly expression of countenance. It was a great pity that his mission was so unsuccessful, but nothing else could be expected. The buffalo were still plentiful, the country attractive, and as long as the Indians behaved themselves there was no trouble.

The day after the council broke up General Terry and his staff departed for the south, escorted by Major Walsh as far as the border. They expressed themselves delighted with their visit and the pleasant time they had with Colonel Macleod and the force under his command.

The winter of 1877–8 we spent at Fort Macleod. The weather continued delightful during the whole of that season. I have never seen finer anywhere. New Year's Day was like midsummer and cricket was played outside the fort. But it was not all play ; the force was worked to the limit of its powers to keep down crime. I never went to bed before midnight and, like the rest of the men, was often up all night. Parties had to be sent off on patrol at all hours of the day and night to look for horse-thieves, to make sudden raids on Indian camps, to capture lawbreakers, to lie in ambush at far coulees or at lonely fords to head off criminals making south with their plunder or trying to escape the service of a warrant, or to intercept whisky outfits on their way north to carry on their illicit trade. I paraded all parties and went with some of them. Life was so busy and the hours so uncertain that no one knew when he could get a night's rest. Our guard-rooms were gaols and penitentiaries, and even long term prisoners sentenced in the winter had to be kept until spring, when they could be sent by trail to Winnipeg.

These expeditions were excellent practice, and our force could now produce a large number of first-class scouts. Every man of two years' service had so much of it that he could find his way to any point required for hundreds of miles round.

In May, 1878, headquarters had to be moved to the Cypress Hills on account of the large numbers of Indians hunting buffalo near Fort Walsh.

In June a strong party of recruits arrived. Mr. James Christie came from Idaho with a large band of bronchos and, as few of them ever had a man's hand on them, some of our men and a fifteen year old broncho buster, known as " Buckskin Charlie," were put to work to " gentle " them. " Buckskin " was a handsome lad. I believe he had a history. He had suddenly appeared at a horse ranch in Montana, clad in buckskin from head to foot, and asked for work. He was promised that, if he could ride, he would be given plenty to do and good wages, and there were a large number of untamed bronchos to break. There was a narrow door to the corral with high side posts and a cross bar on top, upon which Charlie mounted and requested the rancher to drive his wildest horse through it. This was done, and he proved his horsemanship by dropping on the animal's back as it passed beneath him and riding it without saddle or bridle, in spite of its wild bucking, until it was tame. Charlie had taken part in a buffalo run the previous year and, riding alongside a large bull, sprang from the saddle to its back and, hanging on to its long hair, rode it until he was tired, finally shooting the buffalo to enable him to dismount.

Some of Christie's wild horses were very good jumpers, although raised on the plains. One of them, when I was drilling a ride in a log corral which answered for a manege, suddenly broke away from the circle and, galloping down the enclosure some 80 yards in length, jumped the fence at the farthest end. The recruit, afterwards one of our best riders, threw himself off after he had safely landed on the other side. I asked him why he had done so, and he replied : " For fear of going over the fence ! " He meant this, for he did not know that he had cleared the obstacle. I measured the fence at the place where the horse jumped it and found it to be six feet eight inches. The same horse some years later cleared seven feet two inches.

The first white women came to Cypress Hills during the spring. They were the mother and sisters of ex-Constable Graham, from Mulmer, co. Simcoe, Ontario. Graham and his two brothers came with them and settled down to work. One of the young fellows joined the force.

The Indians encamped in and hunting round the Cypress Hills when we arrived from Fort Macleod, were Sioux, Assiniboines, Saulteaux, Blackfeet, Sarcees and Crees. These Indians had fought fiercely amongst themselves from time immemorial, but were now at peace. The Crees style the Sioux " Po-en " or " Po-el," *i.e.*, Enemies, and the Assiniboines, on account of their relationship to the Sioux and their custom of using hot stones to generate steam for a sort of Turkish bath, they call Stone Enemies—" Assinee Po-en," or " Assinee Po-el." The Assiniboines were handsome and more frank and open than the Crees, who were of a crafty, cunning character. All the Indians liked to visit the fort and the stores in the valley, where they amused themselves with pony races. In these there was no jockeying for a start ; they rode hard from start to finish, and the best horse won.

A short time after the force had settled down in the fort the Assiniboines held their annual Sun or Medicine Dance on the north side of the Cypress Hills, and I rode over there with several others to witness the ceremony, which is for the initiation of warriors, and gives one a good idea of the endurance of the red man.

I have seen many Sun Dances by different tribes, but none of them equalled the dance in the Cypress Hills. In the centre of the Medicine Lodge was a large post which supported the fabric, and a railing of rough saplings ran three-quarters of the way round the inside of the lodge, from the left-hand side of the door or entrance. Behind this was a single rank of braves close together, each with a whistle in his mouth secured by a string tied round the back of his neck. These neither ate nor drank until the ceremony was concluded. The whistles were kept going to the beat of the tom-toms.

The Medicine Man of the tribe, naked to the waist, stood near the centre, ready to administer the torture, and when the proper time came the candidates, partly stripped and painted, came forward, accompanied by their female relations. They were taken hold of by the medicine man, who, with the aid of the women, drove sharp skewers of hard wood through the thick muscles of the breast, secured them to the double tails of a lariat (raw hide lasso) attached to the upper part of the post, and when this was completed the young brave, to the low, deep chant of the warriors, the shrill whistling and drumming of the musicians, and the unearthly shrieks of the women in the lodge, threw his weight back upon the lariat until the skewers were torn from the flesh. This ordeal made him a warrior, and the next candidate came forward to go through the torture, which was occasionally varied by attaching to the skewers passed through the muscles beneath the shoulder blades a couple of heavy buffalo skulls, which were dragged round till the flesh parted and the skewers came out. Sometimes skulls of buffalo were fastened to skewers passed through the muscles of the back and chest, the candidate being compelled to dance until the weight of the skulls tore the skewers out of the quivering flesh. These severe tests of endurance were borne by the young braves with the greatest fortitude ; no cry or moan escaped their lips, their teeth were set and drops of agony stood in beads on their foreheads, but there was nothing more to indicate that they were in pain.

During this weird performance large numbers of braves belonging to the tribe, all in feathers and war paint, stood round the Medicine Lodge viewing the proceedings with great interest, to all appearance anxious that the young braves should pass successfully through their severe trial ; for if they failed they could not be warriors, and when the braves went on the warpath would be obliged to remain in camp with the women and children.

Each tribe of Indians has a sign of its own which they will make when they are asked what they are. The Crow sign is both hands held extended beside the head, palms to the front, flapped up and down as the wings of the crow. The Pawnees, or Wolves, hold the hands above the ears with the knuckles of the forefinger of each hand held to represent the sharp ears of the wolf ; the Peigans, or " Painted Faces," rub the knuckles of the right hand on the right cheek as if applying paint ; the Bloods draw the forefinger of the right hand along and through the closed lips from left to right ; the Blackfeet make a motion with the extended hand towards the feet, and so on throughout the whole of the red men of the plains. The Crees, Ojibbeways or Saulteaux, having been for centuries, one may say, in closer contact with the white man, and the latter having learned the language, are not quite so good sign talkers as the other great tribes.

The winter of 1878–9 in the north west was exceptionally severe. Blizzards were common. After Christmas orders were received to take a census of the half-breeds in the north west. I was detailed to take that in the vicinity of Fort Macleod and Calgary. I left Fort Walsh in the afternoon of January 3, taking with me two constables and a fine old half-breed plain-hunter named Foley as an interpreter. Foley and I were riding and the two men, Mills and Holtorf, drove jumpers (small sleighs with shafts), each drawn by a pony. Mills was a small, active Irishman, Holtorf a tall, strong German Canadian. We took with us eight days' rations and forage in the belief that it would be sufficient.

The weather was extremely cold and our provisions and forage ran short. To make matters worse, the ponies in the jumpers showed signs of " playing out," and on Belly River we got into a maze of coulees very difficult to pass and very deep, so I decided to leave the sleighs and baggage there and mount Holtorf and Mills on the ponies. As Foley said he did not know the way to the Old Man's River I took the lead and we struggled along through the deep snow for some hours.

Darkness and a blizzard came upon us, and presently my horse halted and refused to go, whereupon I dismounted and found that the wise brute was within a yard of the high precipitous bank of the Belly River, some distance below old, abandoned Fort Kipp, and another step would have launched us on to the ice at least 100 feet below.

Next morning the blizzard still raged; the snow was too deep for them to walk, and as Foley's horse and mine were very strong and in good condition, the men were mounted behind us. In the teeth of the blinding snowstorm we rode up the valley until we reached Fort Kipp, where we had hoped to light a fire; the effort was in vain, however, there was no fuel, and the dry cottonwood logs of the old buildings were so smooth and hard that had we tried to set the place on fire it would have been impossible. There was, therefore, no help for it but to push on to Fort Macleod, 17 miles distant.

The blizzard became worse as we mounted the hill to the westward, and there was no sign of a trail, but with a good idea of the right direction I led the way until Foley cried out, "The man behind you is freezing to death." Holtorf was behind me, and when I dismounted I found that he was going into the death sleep, and I pounded, shook and slapped him, saying, "A nice fellow you are, to try and steal off in this way! You must wait a while, you are too young to die yet, wait a while!" These exhortations had the desired effect, and we pushed along for some time at a slow walk until I had to call out to Foley, who was now riding on my left, "The man behind *you* is freezing to death!" whereupon Mills was dragged off the horse, shaken, cuffed and reproached for his apparent willingness to leave this world of care and cold. This sort of thing had to be repeated several times, and I began to have misgivings as to our chances of bringing the poor fellows through.

I had Holtorf dismounted for what seemed to be the last chance for him, when I saw Mr. Joseph Macfarland's Pioneer ranch, four miles east of Fort Macleod. Letting the horse follow me, I supported the man to the door, where we were met by Mrs. Macfarland with a kindly Irish welcome. We had been nearly four days without food, but neither Foley nor I felt any ill-effects from the storm and lack of food.

A short time after my return, one of the Mackays of Fort Walsh, who had been out hunting buffalo near the forks of the Red Deer, 100 miles north of the fort, brought in some Cree Indians, who complained to Lt.-Col. Irvine that Wandering Spirit, the head soldier of Big Bear's band, had enforced the old law of the plains upon them when they were hunting, by confiscating their ponies, cutting up their harness and committing assaults upon them and their women.

On hearing this a strong party was sent out under my charge. We had with us two interpreters, Potts and Leveillée, Blackfoot and Cree ; they were both tough enough, but the latter seemed to care nothing for the cold, his only covering at night being a thin, single blanket, which he wrapped round him when he turned in for his night's rest. He was tall and well knit, about 66 years of age, with all the vivacity and politeness of his French ancestors. Being good natured, he was much chaffed by the men, with whom he was a great favourite. One of them, an Irishman, invariably called him " father-in-law," and proposed in jest for the hand of one of his numerous daughters, a suggestion which was taken in earnest, but refused for the reason that his daughters had to marry men who would settle down to a quiet life, not wanderers like the men of the force.

Leveillée would never fail to bow to the officers or touch his hat gracefully and politely to any who addressed him, no matter who they might be. When first with the force in 1874 he was employed to hunt buffalo near Fort Macleod. When he came into the post at night he would report direct to Colonel Macleod saying, " Three fine buffalo, my dear Curnell, all for you, my dear Curnell ! " He had, like his compatriots, hunted on the plains from childhood, and had been in many fights with the Sioux, whose country was nearest to the half-breeds. The marks of these encounters he bore on his body ; several bullets had passed through his chest, and it was marvellous to our surgeons how he had survived them. He had once been unhorsed by a buffalo bull and had lain on the ground as if dead, while the huge beast turned him over with his nose, trying to gore him. He had sufficient presence of mind to lie perfectly still. A short time before, one of his relatives had been caught in the same way, but, being of a nervous disposition, he could not remain quiet, and, half-rising to escape, was gored to death.

Potts was of an entirely different temperament from Leveillée, seldom smiling when a joke passed ; no one attempted light conversation with him, although he was very good tempered. It was difficult to get from him an account of his very eventful life, but occasionally, when few were near, he might be drawn out. I have had many chats with men who had been in all sorts of adventures on the western plains from the Gulf of Mexico to their northern limit, but none were more interesting than our favourite Jerry Potts.

He had been thrown on his own resources from the age of sixteen, when his father, a fine old Scotchman, had been murdered by an Indian. Old Mr. Potts was of a very respectable family, had relatives in Edinburgh who were of the learned professions, and it had been his intention at one time to send his son there to be educated. He was in charge of the American Fur Company's post at Benton at the time of his death, and had with him, amongst the employees of the Company, a man who one day quarrelled with an Indian. The man's duty was to close the shutters of the store at night, and the Indian, still angry and determined on revenge, went out and lay in the brush outside the fort, whence he could see the upper windows of the stores and shoot his enemy when he came to close the shutters. On this occasion, however, Mr. Potts had something else for him to do, and himself went to the window. As he stretched out his arm to unhook the shutter, the Indian, taking him for his man, fired with fatal effect, then fled to his camp several hundreds of miles away. Young Jerry was soon in hot pursuit of the murderer, whom he followed to the midst of his people, and shot him dead before the whole band. The Indians, in admiration of the lad's pluck, and also liking his father, spared his life and ever after looked upon him as Big Medicine.

One of the most remarkable adventures in which Potts took part was during the days of prospecting for precious metals in Montana. He had been hired as a guide by Major George

Steell, known to the Indians as " Sleeping Thunder " on account of the fiery spirit that lay beneath a calm exterior. They went prospecting, taking a young tenderfoot with them. After a long time the little party found nothing and were returning home, but still far from it, when a band of about 200 Sioux warriors on the warpath rode out from a coulee and gave chase at full speed. The three white men rode for their lives for a short distance, whilst they consulted as to what course they would pursue, and finally decided that as the Indians would make the running and thus eventually get them, it would be best to turn suddenly, charge through the red men, firing right and left, and make their way as fast as possible to a deserted log cabin about two miles further back. No sooner decided than acted upon. They dashed through the Indians at a great rate, taking them quite by surprise, and reached the cabin in time to off-saddle and let the horses go, which they had to do as the door was too low to admit them, and hurry inside.

The door was off its hinges, so they placed it on its side across the entrance, braced it with some logs left beside the fireplace by the former occupant, and stood rifle in hand and revolver ready for the assault which was sure to come. At a considerable distance from the cabin the Indians dismounted and rushed at them, receiving the fire of the defenders of the hut. Several were killed, but a number of attacks were made. Potts killed five Sioux with his revolver through the chinks between the logs. The first assaults failing, the Indians drew off some distance and waited for darkness to come, so that they could burn them out, but Potts knew a trick better than to wait. He took one of the saddle blankets, wrapped it round him in Indian fashion, crept out of the cabin when it grew dark, went round behind it on hands and knees and walked a quarter of a mile back, keeping the cabin between him and the Sioux. He then strolled round to a point behind them, went amongst them as if he were one of themselves and, finding some of the horses loose, took three of them back the way he had come, brought them close behind the cabin, where he and his comrades mounted and made off. As they galloped over the hill, Potts could not resist a war whoop of defiance. It was too late for the Indians to pursue now, their prey had too long a start !

We reached the forks of the Red Deer and South Saskatchewan, three days from Fort Walsh, and on arrival encamped amongst the trees.

Next morning we secured a few of Big Bear's men, who were concealed in lodges up the valley of the Red Deer, and in the evening sixteen of us pushed on to where there were some Indian lodges amongst the trees. We surrounded the lodges and secured the last of the gang.

On our return we picked up our *caches* of provisions as we went along, and in one of them we noticed that a handful of biscuits had been taken from the box. There were moccasin tracks about, but knowing that they must have been extracted by some one who needed food, nothing was thought of it. When we returned to the fort an Indian came to offer payment for the biscuit which he had taken " because he was hungry and knew that we had enough." Such was the Indian before he came in contact with the low white. It was perfectly safe in those days to leave anything out of doors, neither Indian nor white man would touch it. The former, and sometimes the latter, would steal the horses of their enemies, but the Indian looked upon that as war and an honourable act.

Our prisoners were tried by Colonel Irvine the day after our return, and were given several months' imprisonment, which might appear to be sufficient punishment, but after events proved that the longest term that could be given to the wretches who composed Big Bear's soldier lodge would be none too much for them.

There was a strange bird in the fort which gave the lie to any assertion that a goose is not highly intelligent. It had been caught by one of the men and soon became a great pet. During the winter it was fed in the barracks, in summer-time it grazed on the parade ground outside the post, and when first post sounded came in and placed itself on a flat stone near the guard-room door. It was to be seen there both winter and summer until the reveille sounded. The beat of the sentry extended to the gate and he had orders to leave it occasionally to visit the stables, and, if anyone had any doubts as to the regular performance of that duty, the goose removed them by setting up a series of yells in goose language from the moment the sentry left his beat until he returned. On very cold nights the bird would tap on the guard-room window with its beak until admitted to have a warm at the stove, and when sufficiently comfortable it left the room on the first opportunity given to it by some one entering or leaving, and resumed watch on the flat stone. In the daytime, when inside the fort, the goose kept its eye on strange dogs, and when one appeared there was an immediate attack and fierce flapping of wings until the intruder departed through the gate !

CHAPTER IX

THE postal communication of the southern half of the North West Territories in 1879-80 had not changed from what it had been some years previously. There were no post offices between the Rocky Mountains and the western boundary of Manitoba, a distance of at least 750 miles. Everyone posted his letters in the orderly-room of the Mounted Police at Calgary, Fort Macleod, Fort Walsh and Wood Mountain. United States postage stamps were used, the nearest post offices being in the United States. The orderly-room clerks made up and sorted the mails, which were carried to their destination by contract with the Mounted Police. Fort Walsh, Fort Macleod and Calgary had weekly mails to the south. From Wood Mountain to Fort Walsh and thence to Fort Macleod they were once a fortnight, and from Battleford, 300 miles, once every three weeks, and with few exceptions, had only official mails for the force. In the north mails were sent out by contract with the Post Office Department and picked up at the Hudson's Bay and Mounted Police posts en route.

In June, 1879, I was ordered to the Coal Banks of the

Missouri to meet a large party of recruits who were coming up that river from Bismark, Dakota.

Four companies of United States infantry were encamped close to the bank of the river on the cactus-covered alkaline flat. I called on Captain Durham, the commanding officer of the detachment, and reported to him my business at the Coal Banks and the number of men with me, and I had not been long in his tent when a number of officers called to have a game of whist. Mr. W——, a well-known citizen of Fort Benton, came at the same time, and we sat down to the game. He took a hand in with the rest of us and made himself very agreeable. He had a contract for the supply of wood to the camp for the coming season.

The game was going on very pleasantly when the quarter-master reported to Captain Durham that there was something very peculiar in the construction of the piles of wood supplied by the suave contractor, and Captain Durham asked me to accompany him to the spot, where an examination of them showed that they were hollow, except those outside. These and the ends were so closely piled that without the careful inspection which we then made this could not be easily detected. Captain Durham expressed himself very much surprised that any respectable man would be guilty of such deception, but old W—— protested that his men had done it without his knowledge and were a bad lot. No one believed him, however, and he had to set his men to work and rebuild the whole of it. Some people seem to think it is no disgrace to rob the government.

The officers of the 18th called next day in a group and asked me to dinner. I found them very pleasant and kindly men of large experience. All had fought through the great battles in Virginia during the Civil War. The senior lieutenant had commanded the 62nd New York Infantry from the time he left West Point Academy in 1862 until the end, and another had been in the whole of the operations for the capture of Richmond and had been wounded several times.

On our return we were held up at Fort Benton by incessant rain. It was garrisoned by the 3rd Infantry, and during our halt I met some remarkable characters. One of the most interesting was a veteran of the Civil War who had been on General Grant's staff at the siege of Vicksburg and was an intense admirer of that distinguished soldier. The gallant major, for such was his rank, was a great talker and stayer, very interesting to me, but there were others who had heard his yarns before and had not time for a repetition of them. One of these men pinned a paper skeleton in the inside of his coat with the inscription above, " This man was talked to death ! " and, when the major was deep in one of his yarns, exposed it to view, by putting his thumbs in the arm-holes of his waistcoat and drawing back his elbows. After that for some time they passed without speaking, until the major, in his good nature, had forgotten the incident.

The brothers Conrad were very hospitable and did a great deal to make us comfortable during our stay in the frontier village. They belonged to an old Virginian family and had served in Stuart's cavalry during the Civil War. The town of Fort Benton had been the scene of many strange doings from the time when it was first a trading post of the American Fur Company. Even in our day short shrift had been given to many a horse-thief. There was a magistrate, a sheriff, and deputies, and unless the accused was a horse-thief he would get a fair trial. Five years later, however, there were 40 genuine or alleged horse-thieves hanged by the vigilantes improvised for the occasion. The magistrate was a man who, having led a Fenian Raid on Manitoba in 1871, had no liking for Britishers and made a practice of measuring their fines by the amount of money they had in their pockets when arrested.

When we got back to Fort Walsh we found that many changes had been arranged for the force. Inspectors were to be known in future as superintendents ; sub-inspectors as inspectors ; and military ranks, which had always been customary with the N.C.O.'s instead of the cumbrous official terms, were confirmed by law. The pay for those who wished to re-engage when their time was up had been lowered to 50 cents a day. The recruits who had just arrived were being paid 75 cents ; they were to be the last, however ; the next lot were to receive only 40 cents. The consequence of this remarkable regulation was that none of the old hands would re-engage to get less pay than the recruits. No high-spirited man would submit to such treatment, and the result was that the force was given a blow from which it took some years to recover.

I have never been able to fathom the reason for this change, but before that I heard senior officers state that our men were too well educated, that a rough lot would have been better, and there were frequent arguments on the subject. A trial of the class advocated proved how foolish it was to take such men, and the pay had to be raised again by a sliding scale to 75 cents per day.

In July there were many Indians in the Cypress Hills— Assiniboines, Sioux and Saulteaux—who had been hunting to the south-east. " Little Child," the Saulteaux chief, was a very fine Indian, with the dark copper colour and keen eyes of the tribe. The Indian custom of buying wives was very much in evidence at this time ; some of the younger squaws were held by their fathers at high prices, and one Saulteaux girl was valued at thirty horses, although the usual price or present was a rifle or one horse !

Many stolen horses were brought into the hills that summer. The American owners generally came after them and reported at the fort ; then there was some careful scouting for the stolen property, which was invariably found and restored to the rightful owner. Much time was taken up by these claimants, but they always went away well pleased with the promptness of the force. For these services no charges were made against the owners, their sole expenses being their trip into Canada. The foreigner received the same treatment as our own people, but in our case we could get no criminals of the horse-stealing class extradited from south of the border line. The neighbouring States made their own laws, but had forgotten to provide one which would permit them to return our neighbourly act, and the extradition treaty between Canada and the United States was the worst that the British Empire had with any country. It is better now, I am pleased to note.

The Indian treaty payments came in September, and the usual escorts, under the command of an officer, had to be sent to protect the agent and other officials and assist, if need be, in the work. This left the barracks with but few officers and, as there was danger of the horses being run off with by a raid of thieves, it was necessary to have an officer in charge of the horse camp. I was detailed with only one old hand in the party, the rest, having joined in the spring, were not yet capable prairie men, consequently we had to exercise a great deal of care.

The herd stampeded one night, and the old hand and I had to go out in every direction to round them up. I was " loping " along in the Six Mile Coulee, east of Fort Walsh, when my horse turned a somersault through putting his foot in a concealed badger hole, and struck me between the shoulders with the oak cantle of the saddle, breaking it and twisting the ironwork. The poor animal rolled over my head and remained there several seconds before I could extricate myself, and when he staggered to his feet the blood poured from his nostrils, as his head had struck the gravel and stones, giving him a severe shock. When I got back to camp he had to be put off duty for a few days.

My next misfortune was a severe attack of fever, typho-malarial they called it. I had been in bed only a few days when I felt well enough to go and pay a visit to my friend, Frank Clark, who had been stricken down with the same disease. The state in which I found him will give an idea of the hardships of the pioneer, and when I saw him I pictured to myself the contrast between his surroundings and those of his childhood in his happy southern home. The sight would have driven any doctor or nurse distracted, but there was no help for it, for our hospital was full already, and there was no other. There was no ventilation, there was no nurse, and the poor fellow lay in the corner of his log shack, a group of Indians sitting in one corner of the room and along the wall, whilst myriads of flies buzzed round him in the stifling atmosphere. I tried to cheer him up, but I could see that it was useless, as he had, no doubt, made up his mind to die. I turned the Indians out, however, and persuaded an Indian boy to fan the flies off ; but I suppose he gave up the task as soon as my back was turned.

When I returned to my quarters I had a relapse and was

L

soon at death's door. Our doctor did his best for me, but was soon in the hospital himself with the same disease, and Surgeon Kennedy had to be sent for from Fort Macleod. When Kennedy arrived he had his hands full, with 60 patients to attend to, and no nurses except our own men, who did their best. My nurse was my man Holtorf, the young German Canadian who was in the blizzard with me the previous winter, and a good, kind one he was, going to all sorts of trouble to make me comfortable. I liked cool spring water, and he would ride several miles up the mountain every day to get me a pailful of it. I became very weak, however, in spite of all the kindness and attention of Kennedy and his staff, and at last, as I appeared to be near my end, he asked me if I had any message to send to my relatives, but I had not, for although I had every bad symptom I would not give in. I felt a confidence that was not warranted by my appearance, for I was a perfect skeleton, and the others had no hope of my recovery. I learned this one night when Holtorf opened the door stealthily and crept in on his hands and knees, dragging a blanket with him to the foot of the bed, where he lay awaiting my departure. This actually amused me, and I laughed at the idea, but the effect of this was good, and I was out of danger in the morning. It was, however, many a long day before I was able to walk about without the aid of a stick, and when I returned to duty and had to parade the guard I had temporarily lost my memory.

After the treaty payments, large numbers of the Indians came to the hills to hunt buffalo, but there were none. They were south of the border on their way north, and if left alone would have returned to Canada. Lt.-Col. Irvine did his best to induce the Indians and the Metis hunters to remain near Fort Walsh, and rations were issued to them, but all was in vain. The Sioux from Wood Mountain, Pinto Horse Butte, and other points east of us along the border line began to hunt on the north side of the great herd, turning it back into the United States, whence it was never to return.

About the end of November one of the men of the force, a mere lad, named Greyburn, was murdered by a Blood Indian. He had been on duty at the herd camp, three miles up the creek from the fort, and had been sent to get a picket rope and an axe which had been forgotten at the last camp a mile further up the creek. As the lad did not return when expected, a search was made and, no trace of him being found, a report was sent into the fort. From there a party reinforced the men at the herd camp, and patrols circled for trails in the vicinity until darkness compelled them to desist. Next morning we were at it again, and Jerry Potts finally came upon the trail, which had been covered up with snow. His horse walking through it exposed blood, and a further search revealed the lad's hat hanging on a bush, and in a ravine below it the body was found where it had been thrown by the murderers. The lad's horse had been led into the woods near by, tied to a tree and shot dead.

We tried to track the murderer out on to the open prairie, but a chinook had sprung up and melted the snow, and, the ground being frozen, not a trace was left. Patrols and scouts of the force searched every hollow where snow might still lie, but in vain. Sufficient had been learned, however, to prove that the murdered man, after leaving the herd camp, had been joined by two Indians and had ridden along with them, no doubt conversing, when one of them halted suddenly and fired a shot into his back. He had fallen head foremost, but there would have been no trace of it there had not Potts' horse kicked up the snow. The motive of this outrage was revenge, but for a long time it was a mystery. No one would believe that the poor young lad had given the murderer the slightest cause for it. He spoke the Blackfeet language well, although he was a recruit of the previous spring, and was a favourite with his comrades and appeared to be so with the Indians.

The winter of 1879–80 set in with as great severity as the previous one, and the numerous Indians who had come to the Cypress Hills in the autumn would have starved to death had it not been for our efforts. Rations were issued to at least 500, whose horses were unable to proceed after their trek from the north, but inducements were held out to the remainder to follow the buffalo into the United States before travelling became too difficult on account of the depth of the snow. The majority took this advice, but a considerable number, knowing that we would not permit them to starve, remained in the hills round the post. Their lodges were to be seen in every hollow or sheltered spot in the vicinity. Starvation stared them in the face, and the force were put to a severe test to prevent it. Two hundred of the Indians were sent to the Island Lake to the north of the hills to be near some cattle herded there by the Indian Department. Provisions were hauled to the camp through the deep snow by our teams, often a distance of 70 miles, the condition of the Indian ponies being such that they could not transport their own supplies. Fish nets were purchased, and some of the men were out all winter to teach the Indians how to manage them, an art of which the plain Indians knew nothing.

Towards spring fish were plentiful in the small creeks, and many of the Indians were issued rations and ammunition to enable them to hunt the smaller game, such as antelope and deer. In this way starvation was prevented until they would be able to travel to their reserves, where they would find food provided for them. In the spring large numbers of them, who had gone south, came back to Fort Walsh, their search for buffalo having been unsuccessful. The herds had been almost totally destroyed by the large number of Indians and ruthless white hunters who had been sent by the merchants of the United States, who were in the robe trade, to slaughter the noble animals for their hides alone. This resulted in the wretched Indians, once the wealthiest and happiest of primitive races, being forced to loiter about frontier posts and villages, to live on garbage or the contents of swill barrels not fit for hogs to eat.

Messengers had been sent by Major Crozier to ask the Indians to return to Canada as soon as the prairie was passable, and when they began to move north our teams were sent to meet them with provisions. During the winter and spring our men were constantly on the trail to assist them, and when the last of the Indians had assembled round us, they numbered at least 5,000. These consisted of every tribe of plain Indians, Crees, Assiniboines, Blackfeet, Bloods, Peigans, Sarcees and Sioux. Some of the trips taken by the members of the force in connection with Indian affairs and other duties were of the most trying character.

This is not to say that the men of the force were the only persons to endure hardships. The whole of the inhabitants of the south, and many of the north, were obliged to travel on the plains, and often underwent much suffering. In the winter of which I write an instance came under our notice which is worth mentioning. A young man, who had come to Fort Walsh from Montana early in the winter, obtained employment as a trader for I. G. Baker & Co., who had placed him in charge of their east end post, many miles from Fort Walsh. On one occasion he was obliged to visit the post for more supplies. On his way back to his camp he halted for the night at the coulee, six miles from Fort Walsh, picketed his horse and lay down. Unfortunately he took off his moccasins, a mad thing to do, and which no one of experience would attempt. He woke during the night to find that the pony had broken loose from the picket line and was some distance off. He ran after it, picketed it again and lay down, to be again aroused by the animal breaking the picket line and getting beyond his reach. He tried to rise, but in vain ; his feet were frozen. There was nothing for it but to crawl to Fort Walsh *on all fours*, and he had reached a point within one mile of the post and was sitting exhausted in a snowdrift, when found by one of the constables, who lifted him on his horse and brought him to our hospital, where, had his heart been strong, he would have recovered. This was an exceptional case, and could not have been the experience of anyone accustomed to prairie travel in winter, and for us the rules were so strict and the men so suitably clad for any season that as long as they had food they were safe. We were never allowed to travel alone, no matter how much we were accustomed to the plains, and wherever Major Crozier was in command all hands had to show kit before they left the post, so that nothing they required would be left behind. He was always anxious about his men when they were out in stormy weather.

It must not be supposed from what I have written that it was all work and no play at Fort Walsh. An ex-member of the force, who had served as a French conscript through the Franco-Prussian War, had erected a large hall, which we used to his great profit as a theatre, dance hall and church.

The first Masonic banquet in the north-west was held at Fort Walsh in 1880 ; Major Crozier was chairman and I was vice-chairman.   There were no Masonic lodges in the territory at that time, and it was felt that something should be done to show that there were masons, if there were no lodges.   The banquet was quite a large affair and proved to be a great success, all taking part enthusiastically without regard to creed, nationality or language.

It was late in the winter when we had a clue to the murder of Constable Grayburn, but at last, by occasional talks with the interpreters, who in turn sounded the Indians, two Blood braves, who had been charged with horse-stealing, were arrested and confined to the guard-room cells.   Crozier remanded them for some days, and while they were awaiting trial we learned that they had been encamped near our herd at the time of the murder and knew all about it.   There was at this date a large camp of Bloods on the rising ground before the fort, and in it the wives of the two Bloods were living, during the time they were in prison, and were permitted to see them at intervals of a few days.

The prisoners soon came to the conclusion that they had more than horse-stealing against them, and made up their minds to escape as soon as possible.   This they attempted one very fine spring afternoon, when, with another of the same tribe, they were taken out for exercise, escorted by two of the guard.   No sooner had they cleared the gate than they made a bold dash for liberty, leaving the other Indian, who knew nothing of the attempt, standing aghast at the sudden break. They were followed by the escort in their long boots, poor footwear for a race after moccasined red-skins.   As the escaping Bloods rushed swiftly through the camp on the hill, their wives, who were on the look-out, handed them their Winchesters and belts of ammunition.   The other Indian, thinking that he should follow their example, fled in the opposite direction.

Crozier, Cotton and Kennedy were playing tennis in front of the post and, when they saw the escape, followed the fugitives.   I sent the first men who turned out after them, mounted. They caught up to the Indians in about half a mile.   Ignoring their levelled rifles, they rode at them and soon had them back in their old quarters in the guard-room. Their attempt to escape having failed, the two asked to see Crozier at midnight in his quarters, and, after the windows had been covered with blankets so that no light could be seen from the outside, they gave him the name, description and full particulars of the Indian who had murdered Grayburn.

A despatch was then sent to Colonel Macleod, who was in Benton, to the effect that the murderer was lurking in the fastnesses of the Bear Paw Mountains, and he asked the American authorities in legal form for his arrest, but, unless he could pay at once 5,000 dollars in cash, the sheriff would not make the attempt, and we were, in consequence, obliged to wait until the accused would venture back to Canada, for an opportunity to capture him. This did not present itself until 1881, when Sergeant Patterson at Macleod learned that he was in the Blood camp, and proceeded there, accompanied by Jerry Potts and two constables. They arrived at dawn and went to the lodge in which the murderer, Star Child by name, was concealed, their intention being to take him without alarming the camp, which, it was believed, was hostile. The Indian came out at dawn, fully armed ; covering Patterson with his rifle he told him that he would shoot if he moved hand or foot, but the sergeant, as a ruse, spoke as if addressing someone behind Star Child, causing him to turn his head, whereupon Patterson threw himself upon him. In the struggle the rifle went off, rousing the whole camp, and the Indians turned out in hundreds. In the meantime Patterson had the murderer beneath him half choked, and finally handcuffed him while Jerry Potts, Chief Red Crow, Strangling Wolf, One Spot and Constable Wilson, by threats and exhortations, kept the remainder at bay. The sergeant then took Star Child towards Macleod at the full speed of his horse, supported by Potts and the constables, followed by the majority of the band as far as the fort, where they were forced to halt and turn back.

Star Child confessed to the murder, and there was corroborative evidence, but in spite of it all the jury disagreed and he was set free, to be arrested for horse-stealing a few years later and sent to the penitentiary for five years. There is no doubt that the jurymen who were for acquittal were afraid that the conviction would bring on an Indian war, or cause the Bloods to kill their stock out of revenge. This idea was sheer nonsense, of course, but it was certainly in the minds of some of the jury.

The day following the recapture of the two Bloods, the young horse-thief, who had escaped at the same time, was found in a dying condition in the backyard of one of the married men, living a few hundred yards from the fort. The weather, which had been delightful for some weeks past, became stormy, accompanied by sleet and snow, and the poor Indian lad, not being clad for such an emergency, perished within easy reach of aid. The occupant of the cabin heard him groaning for a long time, but was afraid to go outside at first to see what was the matter ; at last, however, he plucked up his courage and reported the circumstances to me, and I sent a stretcher and bearing party to bring the Indian in, but by the time he was brought to the hospital he was beyond human help. This caused some excitement amongst the Blackfeet who were in the vicinity, and they asked to see the remains, having got the idea into their heads that we had hanged him. Kennedy went into the case, and with some difficulty persuaded them that their relative had died a natural death.

The large number of Indians now in the hills round the fort gave us a great deal of anxiety. Horse-stealing became prevalent amongst them, many of them coming over from the United States to run off the herds. Our own Indians were not free from the offence, and the Sarcees began the trouble by stealing from the Assiniboines. They came to the fort to lay a complaint, and one night, with a strong party and the interpreter, I went after them. The whole of the Sarcees were in the camp, and to take them by surprise we stole cautiously up a coulee. The scouts crept up the hill at the head of the coulee and reported all quiet.

The Indians seemed to be in deep slumber, and keeping a small reserve on the outside I threw a circle of men round the camp, which we then entered. The whole of the Indians by this time were out in the centre of the large ring of tents, the men with their rifles in their hands, but the chief and headmen, recognising me, called out, "How, Manistokos!" They shook hands and said that they were ready to obey my orders. I knew that the tribe were worth watching, and would do anything to permit the horse-thieves to escape, visits to the penitentiary near Winnipeg not being at all popular. I ordered all the tribe to assemble in the middle of the circle whilst some of our men searched the lodges and others watched every movement of the Indians from one lodge to another. We caught the thieves at last in the act of creeping back to lodges which had been searched from those that had not been inspected. Placing each thief between two men we galloped to the fort by another trail, arriving there about noon.

Some days later Major Crozier persuaded the Sarcees to leave for their reserves near Fort Calgary. An ample supply of provisions was served out to them before they left and we soon learned that they had taken with them a number of horses which they had stolen from the Assiniboines. I sent Staff-Sergeant Fraser and a party of six constables in pursuit. He overtook them near the Seven Persons Coulee, about 40 miles west, and, galloping to the front of the Sarcees where the horses were being driven ahead, cut out the "bunch" on the hill on the left. He was pursued by the majority of the Indians, who fired several rounds upon the party, but without effect, except to wound one of the stolen horses, and they were back in the fort within twenty-four hours, having covered 80 miles. We were very glad to be rid of the Sarcees, the most unprepossessing of the plain Indians. They were originally from the north, where they had quarrelled with some of their relatives about a dog, and departed for the prairies. There they were surrounded by so many strange tribes and were so weak in numbers themselves that they learned the Cree and Blackfeet languages, and, having to hold their own against odds, became very self-reliant.

We heard that winter that many of the Sioux Indians were in a starving condition and obliged to eat their horses, which had died of the mange caught from the buffalo robes which had been placed on their backs as substitutes for saddles or pads. It had spread through the whole of the north west, Montana and Dakota, destroying thousands of horses and ponies, and, despite our veterinary staff and great care, it got amongst ours and was stamped out with difficulty.

In the spring we took steps to induce the Indians who had not yet left to make an effort to go to their reserves, where they could find food and be instructed in agriculture, raising cattle and building houses for themselves, but none of them departed before June, and then were with difficulty persuaded to leave. They would take their supplies, make a show of moving, eat them and, making ridiculous excuses for their delay, return for more, until at last our men were placed in charge of the rations and issued them as they were required when the Indians were on the march.

On June 17 I left Fort Walsh for Fort Qu'appelle with eight four-horse waggons very heavily laden. The remainder of the men were mounted, and we had with us everything necessary to enable us to camp and make ourselves comfortable anywhere.

The seventh day we were at Moose Jaw Creek or, as they called it then, the Moose Jaw Bone, the Cree translation being " The place where the white man mended the cart with the Moose Jaw Bone," the reason being that the Earl of Mulgrave, then an officer in the Guards, who was on a buffalo hunting trip, spliced the broken felloe of one of the carts of his party with a moose jaw bone which he picked up in the vicinity and used as a splint.

We reached Fort Qu'appelle in nine days, having covered 300 miles. Fort Qu'appelle was an important centre, where several trails met. One led north to the Swan River barracks through the Pheasant Plain ; one followed the valley for 30 odd miles, and then ascended the bench land and so on to Fort Ellice ; another led to Winnipeg via Portage la Prairie, and a trail to Fort Carlton via the Touchwood Hills left the valley through a narrow coulee on the north side. There was also connection with Winnipeg by other routes.

The north west was not divided into Mounted Police districts at this time, but all knew well that when a crime was committed the first one hearing of it had to proceed and bring the accused to the nearest and most convenient post. Our division, roughly speaking, had to keep an eye on an extent of country about 400 miles square. Within this extensive tract of country the Indians were being placed upon their reserves, escorted by us, most of them having arrived from the south, west and east during the previous two months. Some of the reserves were more than 150 miles distant. There was no white settlement for about 140 miles east. In that section a number of Ontario farmers, chiefly from the counties of Huron and Bruce, were settling on the homesteads and taking up their pre-emptions of the same area. They were a good type of pioneer, hospitable, industrious and law abiding.

At this date Lt.-Col. Macdonald, the Indian agent, was absent on a tour of inspection and paying Indians, and his sub-agent not being at home I had to take charge of the agency for a few days. One of the Cree chiefs, Pasqua, " The Plain " or " Prairie," came to me for rations to take him and a party of young bucks to the United States. He had already been refused them, when I was present, but had forgotten that I had been with Colonel Macdonald when he applied. I, of course, refused, and he went off very much annoyed. The colonel's reason for refusing was that he was certain to get into mischief over there and cause serious trouble, and this proved to be correct, for, in spite of the rations being denied him, he took a small war party over. Near the Missouri he came upon a Mandan camp when the braves were away hunting, and killed and scalped some of the old men, women and children, and fled north. Before he had gone far the Mandan warriors returned and to the number of 60 gave chase, following the trail, which forked, one branch going north west, the other in the direction of Moose Mountain. They took the latter and, after a long ride, caught up to a strong hunting party of Assiniboines who were halted in their corral on the trail. On riding up and seeing that they were not Crees, they were passing by when an Assiniboine called out in Cree, " Where are you going ? " The Cree tongue caused them to be suspected, and they were attacked at once and a sharp fight was kept up for some time until the Mandans were defeated with loss. This was the last fight between Indians on Canadian soil. Old Pasqua, fortunately for him and his gang, had taken the left-hand trail, and escaped to his lair on the Qu'appelle lakes, and it was some time before we got news of his misconduct, no one having come north to us to complain of the outrage.

On August 6 the division had as guests, with quarters in the guard-room, two English gentlemen, settlers from the vicinity of Rapid City, 200 miles east.   They had been arrested by our Shoal Lake magistrate, who had refused bail.   One was Captain B., a retired Indian Mutiny veteran, the other a much younger man, Mr. J.   The circumstances of their arrest were ludicrous.   A complaint had been made against them for a mere trifle and a warrant issued, but, instead of placing the warrant in the hands of our constables, the magistrate, who had been on bad terms with my predecessor, employed a young and very green settler to carry out the arrest.   On arriving at the home of the accused he spent a pleasant forenoon, and lunched with them at their invitation, not saying a word about his errand until he was leaving, when he turned at the door and said, " Oh, by the way, I have a warrant for your arrest ! "   The Englishmen laughed and refused to believe it, but, as the " special " insisted, B. got his rifle and said, " J., you count one, two, three, and I shall put a bullet through his hat ! "   No sooner said than done, and the terrified special rode for dear life to the magistrate, who, after all, had to employ our constables.   They, as a matter of course, met with no resistance.   The poor fellows were taken from their homesteads to Qu'appelle, where they remained in the guard-room until they knew the names, characteristics and nickname of every officer, man and horse in the force.   Judge Richardson tried them some months later, and, taking into consideration the delay, released them the same day.

Early in the autumn Colonel Macleod resigned the commissionership of the force for the position of stipendiary magistrate.   He was beloved by his officers and men and was a very great loss to the service.   His influence with the Indians was enormous, with whom he was fair dealing and truth personified.   He was succeeded by Lt.-Col. Irvine, assistant commissioner, who was also very popular with the force.

The barracks being finished, we were snug for the winter, and, as the autumn in Canada is the finest season of the year, the trips taken to many parts of the area over which I had supervision were very pleasant. I made many hundreds of miles and visited every important spot. The Indians were now settled on their reserves and preparing for a start at farming the next spring, and the presence of the division had materially assisted in bringing about this state of affairs.

The work of keeping the division in an efficient state meant a great deal more than drills, patrols or treks to the reserves. We were almost self-supporting, herded and slaughtered our own beef, cut and hauled our hay and fuel, repaired our transport, made our sleds for winter travel, etc. " B " division at that time was the only one using the California stock saddle ; the rest had the universal cavalry pattern, which kept the saddlers busy repairing them. Having had experience with both, I alone recommended the stock saddle as best for our purpose, being the most durable, the easiest on horseflesh and the most comfortable, especially for winter. I had ridden mine 6,800 miles in the year 1879–80 in all weathers. It had been used since 1875 and was still in perfect condition, never once having to be repaired. Other saddles were recommended the same year, but the stock saddle was selected and is still in use.

The quarters which I occupied during my stay at Qu'appelle were not palatial. They consisted of a log house roofed with the thatch of the country, and stood on a slope on the north side of the valley in a pretty situation. The floor of poplar boards sloped very much to the south, and a narrow mud fireplace supplied the heat. The kitchen was a lean-to at the back of the cabin. A long narrow wing of round poplar poles lined with rough boards, with some straw stuffed between them and the logs, was my sleeping quarters, a box stove supplying the heat. I slept well in that room in the winter nights, in spite of the fact that the water bucket would freeze to the bottom and the temperature was more than once 30 below zero.

Soon after the New Year an epidemic of smallpox was threatened, and, as that disease had such dire effects amongst the Indians of North America, prompt measures were taken to prevent it from spreading and getting into the camps. Under the North West Territories Ordinance a board of health was convened. Lt.-Col. Macdonald, Mr. W. J. McLean and I were the members. Acting Hospital Steward Holmes was the medical health officer. He had studied medicine for many years and was extremely capable, but as yet had no diploma. There was, however, no qualified surgeon, and we had to do our best. Holmes did remarkably well, visited the threatened localities and quarantined the houses. Orders were posted at every important point and the forks of each trail, warning travellers not to enter houses in the Qu'appelle valley. Holmes, who was usually known in the force as " Doc," vaccinated the Indians on all the reserves, the whites who required it and all the half-breeds in the valley. To perform these duties he had to travel many hundreds of miles, often sleeping out in the snow, with the thermometer indicating many degrees below zero.

When the smallpox scare was over, as he was only paid the 75 cents per diem of a constable, I recommended that he be granted for his services to the Indians an allowance of 10 dollars per month, and, as the division was entitled to a staff-sergeant and he was performing the duties, that he be promoted to the rank of hospital steward, but both of the applications were refused. The smallpox treatment and vaccination had been the least of his services. Hundreds of the Indians, when they came to the district, were in an almost dying condition from the experiences of the previous winter. All these people had been attended and the disease arrested, and the medicines compounded and administered by this useful man. There are some instances of the miscarriage of justice for which it is difficult to find words.

During the winter of 1880-1 I suffered for the first time in my life from snow blindness. I found that the first symptom was the desire to rub one's eyes as if sand or some other irritating substance were beneath the eyelids ; the next sensation was to see the snow a bright yellow. The pain is so severe that the slightest light causes agony ; a handkerchief has to be tied over the eyes and the blinds drawn until the room is in total darkness. I got some medicine and applied tea leaves with no apparent effect, and was sitting wondering what would turn up next when there was a knock at the door and I bade the visitor enter. When he had seated himself he said, " Oh, sir, are you snow blind ? " I answered in the affirmative, and he asked me what I was using, and, when I told him medicine from the hospital and tea leaves, he remarked, " Let me give you an old plain-hunter's remedy. Get a pot of strong black tea made, cover your head with a silk handkerchief, so as to let no steam escape, and look into the kettle." I took his advice, got instantaneous relief and was quite well in a couple of days.

The spring of 1881 opened early, and to prove the capabilities of the soil and give the men some garden vegetables, which up till the present had been almost impossible to obtain at the southern posts, I had five acres of the prairie broken and planted in potatoes, Indian corn, cabbages, tomatoes and, in fact, every vegetable in common use in Canada. All of these came to maturity, the tomatoes ripened on the sod, and the returns of all were astonishing. In addition to this work I made an arrangement with a trader in the vicinity, who had some land, to sow oats for our horses, and, as he had no seed, I loaned him what was required from our store, on condition that he would sell the proceeds to the government for one dollar per bushel and return the seed. This plan answered both parties very well, the settler getting a good price and the force saving the trouble of freighting the oats from the east at an advance of 70 cents per bushel ; the settler was also assisted, and we demonstrated the suitability of the Qu'appelle valley for farming.

One day Sitting Bull arrived at Fort Qu'appelle with about 1,200 of his tribe to have a pow-wow. He began by saying that he expected to meet Major Walsh at Qu'appelle and that he thought the major would obtain for him and his tribe a reservation in Canada, as he did not care to return to the United States. Canada was, he asserted, his country, and the Mela Hoska (Long Knives) had no claim upon him. His friends were the Shaga Lasha (British), and always had been ; the revolution did not give the Mela Hoska the right to govern him and his people.

I told him that the policy of the government was for the Sioux to return to the United States and that it was not at all likely that a reservation would be given to him in Canada. He had long ago thrown in his lot with our neighbours to the south, had accepted a reservation in that country and must return there as soon as possible and receive the benefits which were there for him and his people when they were once more at their agency.

On hearing what I had to say the chief was very much disturbed and in reply reiterated that he had been given to understand that it would not be difficult to obtain a reserve for his people. I replied, however, that it was useless to apply for one, but that a despatch would be sent to the Indian commissioner, who was at Shoal Lake, 160 odd miles east, and he might see him. When the pow-wow was over a messenger was sent to Mr. Dewdney, the Indian commissioner, to let him know that Sitting Bull was with us. He came up and saw him, and arranged to feed his band as far as Wood Mountain, and I provided an escort to go with them and issue the rations as required.

They departed at once, and when they reached Wood Mountain the supplies were exhausted. Sitting Bull went to Inspector A. R. Macdonnell, in command there, and demanded more food, which was refused him. The chief threatened to take it by force, but he was reckoning with the wrong man. Macdonnell told him that he would ration him and his men with bullets. The chief exclaimed, " I am thrown away ! " " No," said Macdonnell, " you are not thrown away ; you are given good advice, which is that if you require food you must return to your own reservation in the United States, where you will be well treated." This was the last of it ; the chief accepted the situation, and the next day accompanied Macdonnell to Poplar River, where he handed over his rifle to Major Brotherton, United States army, in token of surrender, and the remainder of the band went in with Mr. Louis Legare, who supplied carts and food at the expense of the American government.

This surrender ended our troubles with Sitting Bull and his Sioux, and I may say in connection with it that not one word appeared in the official reports of that year to say that Macdonnell had even seen the chief ; and an officer, who was many hundreds of miles away, and Mr. Legare, the trader, who certainly did not supply the Indians for love, were honourably mentioned. The officer was one of the best fellows in the force, and Legare a good citizen, but they had, at the actual surrender, nothing whatever to do with inducing the Sioux to return to their homes in the United States. This honour belongs to Macdonnell.

In the summer I received orders to be ready to supply transport for a tour through the far west, to be undertaken by the Governor General, the Marquess of Lorne, in the months of August and September.

The party arrived at Fort Qu'appelle on August 17, early in the afternoon, and I received the Governor General with a guard of honour drawn up in front of the post where he was to be entertained. Mr. W. J. McLean had met them at the Roman Catholic mission, five miles east, where a number of the early settlers and plain-hunters had assembled, and presented an address of welcome, to which the marquess made a hearty reply.

A large body of Indians had been assembled from the reserves, and on the 18th a great pow-wow was held at the Hudson's Bay Fort, and the Sioux Indians of Standing Buffalo's band from Jumping Deer Creek gave a buffalo dance in honour of the marquess. Each brave had a buffalo head and horns, complete, as a head-dress, the appearance of the party being very weird indeed. The remainder of the Indians, Crees, Chippeways or Saulteaux, and Assiniboines, headed by their chiefs, assembled inside the post, where they were received by the Governor General and delivered eloquent addresses of welcome. Chief O-Soup, a stately Indian, was the most graceful in his delivery, but of course the illiterate interpreters could not give a true idea of the expression of which the chiefs' languages were capable.

On the 19th the marquess left for the west via the Qu'appelle, Touchwood Hills and Carlton trail. A few days after his departure Lt.-Col. Macdonald was informed that he had lost a ring at one of the camp grounds. An Indian was despatched at once to visit the place on the way, and returned in a few days with the ring, which he had found in the long grass where the party had outspanned !

At the Red Deer River a buffalo hunt was held in honour of the marquess. It was the last but one to be held in Canada.

M

The climb at the Red Deer River furnished the party with a good idea of the dry humour so noticeable in the force in those days. One of the four horse teamsters had very soon learned the names of the officers of the staff and had named his horses after four of them. At the very high hill on the south side of the Red Deer the staff walked up to save the teams. One of the horses, now named " The Doctor," after Dr. Sewell, balking and causing the other three to do likewise, the driver exhorted them at the top of his voice, as he laid on the whip, " Pull like a boy, Bagot ! Gid ap, Chater ! Pound the Doctor ! Lay on to him, Jones ! " and so on until the team reached the top. The Governor General and staff were convulsed with laughter as they watched the team until it made the summit. Everywhere the Indians turned out in all their barbaric finery to honour the first Governor General to visit the wild and woolly west. The tour extended beyond the limits of the Dominion, the party going to Fort Shaw, Montana, and thence, with an escort of United States troops, to Helena. From there they returned to Winnipeg by rail.

The distance travelled by the marquess and party to Fort Shaw was 1,229 miles, and my horses, before they got back to Fort Qu'appelle, had treked 1,500 miles. The same year between March and August they had made on other duties a total of 1,434 miles !

The Governor General, before leaving Fort Shaw, made a short address to the escort, in which he referred to the variety of the work of the North West Mounted Police. He said : " Your work is not only that of military men, but you are called upon to perform the important and responsible duties which devolve upon you in your civil capacities. Your officers, in their capacity of magistrates, are called upon to perform even that of diplomacy."

CHAPTER X

Settlers in the west—The land boom—The prodigal son—Recruiting for the force—The construction of the C.P.R.—Regina—" The Pile of Bones "—A game of poker—A speedy trail—The farm Colonies—An amateur rancher—A clever ruse—Work on the C.P.R.—An unsatisfactory N.C.O.—Calgary—Misguided enthusiasm—Trouble with the Blackfeet—General Strange's ranch—Prohibition—Ingenious devices—A brutal murder—Clues—No lynching in Canada—Indian unrest—I am appointed to British Columbia—A prisoner escapes—I am sent to re-arrest him—Crowfoot—Indian hostility—A ticklish position—Firmness succeeds—An amazing acquittal—New Calgary.

DURING the winter of 1881-2 we were kept constantly on the prairie in every direction. The white settlers who were coming into the country knew nothing of the dangers of travel in the wilderness, and would venture out in a garb that was no protection. Many of them thought they knew more than Indians, plain-hunters, Hudson's Bay officials or the Mounted Police, and would take no advice ; bitter experience had to be their teacher. Fortunately, the majority were different and were glad to accept assistance.

Many speculators looking for town sites invaded the country. Their route was from Winnipeg via Fort Ellice and along the Qu'appelle valley. While they had the shelter of the poplars they were all right, but when they struck out from it they suffered much. One party, with a well-known gentleman at their head, established themselves on the surveyed C.P.R. line, 18 miles south of the fort, and, taking up homesteads round a common centre, called the place Troy. It is now Qu'appelle. Others went further east, and many were looking for town sites near the elbow of the South Saskatchewan, a long distance west, near the source of the Qu'appelle. Large numbers of people from the eastern provinces of Canada, inspired by the reports of the Governor General's trip, a full account of which had been published in the eastern papers, had hurried to Winnipeg and started a land boom, which lasted for several months.

In February I obtained leave on private affairs, and started east for Ontario soon afterwards. At Brandon I saw a locomotive for the first time in nine years. I went on as far as Portage la Prairie, 60 miles west of Winnipeg, and found the boom going on there, and I met some men whom I had induced to settle in that fertile region. They were delighted with their success. None had farmed more than 50 acres in Ontario, and now, with their sons on homesteads and their daughters well settled, they, as they said to me, did not have to work. They farmed between them and their sons nearly 2,000 acres each, but did not dignify with the name of work the task of walking round their farms. Nothing was work to them but the severest kind of manual labour.

In Winnipeg lots were selling at, for that time, fabulous prices, and any quarter section in Manitoba, if subdivided into town lots, would realize a handsome fortune for the owner. People were ready to buy anything. The hotels did a roaring trade and the bars made profits of hundreds of dollars a day. Every available space was taken up for sleeping accommodation and the privilege of having a chair or a step on the stairs to sleep on during the night cost a dollar. In the forenoon the speculators were at their writing-tables going through their correspondence ; the city was quiet, though crowded with men. At noon there was the usual hearty luncheon ; at 3 p.m. the fun began, and was kept up until a late hour. Those who had made money were ready to re-invest it, and the real estate offices were crowded with men ready to buy or sell lots.

I took rooms at the Grand Union Hotel and the next day received orders from Ottawa to start a recruiting office. Most of the men who presented themselves were not of the right stuff. I got a few good ones, but I would take none but the best. Towards the end of the winter Inspector Perry, just appointed to the force, came up to relieve me so that I could proceed east.

At Ottawa I was informed that my leave would be very short

owing to the construction of the C.P.R. through the territory and the illness of an officer who was recruiting 200 men in Toronto, as a result of which I might have to take the men west. As things were looking brighter with the sick officer, I went to North Simcoe for a couple of weeks and stayed with my numerous relatives in that part of the country, all of whom treated me as if I had been the prodigal son !

When I returned to Ottawa 13 recruits were enlisted, and I took passage for myself and them by boat from Sarnia to Duluth, Minnesota. My recruits were fine, handsome young men, and were soon great favourites with all on board. The other passengers, not knowing much about the Mounted Police, were surprised that such well-educated men would enlist, and I had to inform them that no other class would be engaged ; such men had been the making of the force and had done much to popularize the service. The party which I had with me had come from the old country and the maritime provinces on purpose to join. Two of them were ex-Life Guardsmen, one was a captain of the Irish militia, whose rank the others never lost sight of, the remainder were college men, and none were under six feet in height.

When I arrived back at Fort Qu'appelle I was appointed acting adjutant of the district and placed in command of the detachments on the line of construction of the C.P.R., and I performed those duties until the railway work ceased for the season. While the summer lasted many visitors came to the valley and settlers began to follow the line, merchants had stores in canvas tents at every new siding, and towns " moved on" until permanent locations such as Regina, Moose Jaw, Swift Current and Maple Creek were found.

While the work was going on the suppression of crime was difficult, but it was successfully accomplished, the force saving the contractors hundreds of thousands of dollars owing to the absence of saloons and the prohibition of intoxicants. There was much smuggling but the sale was kept within bounds and the navvies could not at any time get enough for a spree. The illicit liquor smugglers and gamblers were given the " full benefit of the law."

In August the Canadian Press Association, in an immense

special train, visited the North West Territory and proceeded to the end of the track, which had by that time reached a point 10 miles west of Regina, then merely a canvas town on a bare plain. The party were accompanied by their wives, sons and daughters, and by others interested in the progress of the country. Their visit gave Major Walsh an opportunity to welcome them to the west in the spirited manner peculiar to him.

He paraded a strong troop and, as there was not much time to spare, took us at a fast pace the 18 miles to the siding, which is now the pretty town of Qu'appelle, and concealed us in the woods near the line. When the heavily loaded train came puffing up the grade to the siding we broke cover, the major at our head, and galloped alongside and round it, saluted by the shrieks of the engine, the cheers of the men on board, and the waving of the ladies' handkerchiefs. The train stopped for a few minutes to take water, and the major went on with the party to the last siding west of Regina, which was named Pense, after the president of the Press Association who was on the train.

At Regina the new capital frame houses were already taking the place of the canvas tents. When we arrived there we encamped on the homestead of Mr. George Moffat, on which it was afterwards decided that the headquarters of the N.W.M.P. were to be, and are still. None of the officers liked the site. I suggested another to the comptroller and drove him over to inspect it, but it was a good thing for Saskatchewan and the city that it was not chosen, for it is now occupied by the imposing public buildings of that province, and has the pretty artificial lake where I thought we could have a dam for the water supply, there being nothing but the creek, then known as " The Pile of Bones," to depend upon for the coming winter. The Lieutenant Governor had made up his mind, however, and he decided upon the present location, for which the good citizens of Regina owe him thanks, as well as for the place being chosen as the capital.

On September 13, a short time after the site was chosen, I was sent to Regina to lay out the ground for the portable buildings which were to be our home for a long time to come.

I was to perform all of the magistrate's work and remain in charge of the detachments along the railway as far as Swift Current.

For police protection I placed a strong detachment in the town and, making the men as comfortable as possible, went on with the work of laying out the site and carrying on the rest. There were many loose characters in Regina and the new towns east and west, who had settled down for the winter to make those places lively, and they soon got a taste of our methods of handling such people. Neither the men nor I had a spare moment to ourselves, the former were on the move, coming and going, all the time, and I was on the bench trying cases until far into the night, my court-room being a 16 by 14 marquee, which was also mess-room and sleeping apartment.

We often had visitors during the autumn. Many of them would say, " What a pity the creek is called ' Pile of Bones,' not a pretty name, is it ? " To this remark I always replied, " Wascana is the Sioux name for Pile of Bones, it means the same thing." Of the correctness of the translation I was satisfied, and, as Major Walsh had given the Sioux names of Wapella and Sintaluta to stations further east, I thought it would be a good thing to give one to Pile of Bones, and it is thus that it became Wascana.

There was much secret gambling in Regina, and it was a common thing for half a dozen of the gamblers to be brought before me, but one of these cases had a more amusing side to it than any other that it had been my experience to try. Corporal Stewart, a bright young Trinity College student, who had come to the Mounted Police through the cavalry, was in charge of the town station, and had to keep a sharp lookout on the poker games. The senior partner of the construction company building the C.P.R. had an intense objection to gambling. He had two nephews, brothers, the older, careful and staid, was the paymaster, the younger and livelier was his quartermaster ; he was fond of a game of poker whenever he could indulge in it. They were in Regina on business one dark, wet night, and were to join their uncle on his train west-bound, which was hourly expected. The same evening I was busy writing in my tent near midnight when the younger nephew burst headlong through the door, followed closely by Corporal Stewart, shouting, " For God's sake, Cap, how much is it ? The corporal has just caught me in a poker game and has the pot. Do try me now ! The old man is on the train, and is expected every minute, and if I miss it he will know what has happened, and I shall lose my job. Do try me, Cap ! " By this time the elder brother had entered in a more orderly manner, and with the corporal was standing behind while the younger brother delivered himself of this harangue. When he had finished, the elder said, " I wish you would try him, sir. His uncle will be very angry with him if he hears of this gambling scrape. The amount of the fine matters little, and I should be grateful if you would try him in time to catch his train." These requests had their effect and, when the corporal had laid the charge and sworn to it and the prisoner pleaded guilty, I inflicted the usual fine, which was promptly paid, confiscated " the pot," and the brothers, thanking me for my generosity, made their " best licks " to the station in time to catch the train and escape their uncle's wrath.

This episode has been the subject of a magazine article, which states that I was aroused out of bed to try the case. A Mounted Police officer roused out of bed at midnight ! He might be at 4 a.m., but until the small hours were well on he would be, as I was that night, booted and spurred, ready for the trail. The whole case did not take above ten minutes. The young man often said to me afterwards when he met me, " By Jove, Cap, you did me a good turn then ! "

Late in the autumn Regina became the headquarters of the Mounted Police, but the officers had no mess nor quarters until near Christmas, and the water froze in our bath tubs during the nights. The little dam on the Wascana creek soon gave out and we had to melt snow for men and horses, everyone, no doubt, wondering why such a change was made before we had a permanent water supply. We were accustomed to hardship, however. The winter was very severe, and the officers and men employed in clerical work used to put their ink bottles on the top of the stoves to keep the ink from freezing. Blizzards were very regular in their appearance, and, when duty or pleasure took us to the town or to some neighbour's cabin, we had to be careful lest we should go astray and be on the prairie all night. The whistle of the locomotive at the little station was a very welcome sound on some of those stormy nights.

For a new place there was a good deal of fun going on in Regina. After Christmas the Lieutenant Governor and Mrs. Dewdney entertained a good deal, and parties of civilian friends were with us at balls and parties, and the *Regina Leader*, edited by the brilliant Nicholas Flood Davin, indulged in jokes at our expense. Until March I was the only officer hearing cases, and was kept fairly busy, but about the end of the month I was sent to Winnipeg on recruiting service. I took rooms at the Potter House, then the best hotel in the town, which was full of surveyors and engineers, amongst them the gigantic General Rosser, chief engineer of the C.P.R., who was very interesting to all of us younger men, having been a distinguished cavalry commander during the Civil War in the United States. He was a splendid type of southern gentleman, and was some years later Minister for the United States to Austria-Hungary. Mr. Rodgers, the engineer who had been selected to look for a pass through the Selkirk range of the Rocky Mountains, was there too, and received the necessary information from Walter Moberly, the true discoverer of the pass, who had been exploring in that part of British Columbia in 1871.

Towards spring I met several English travellers, one of them a retired surgeon-major in the British army, who had been visiting one of his nephews, a pupil in a United States farm colony. He gave me an interesting account of the doings of the colonists, who with their polo and horse-racing, which intermingled with their pretended farming, nearly drove the matter-of-fact American farmers in the vicinity to insanity. The pranks of some of those lads were extraordinary, at least the old gentleman thought so. He mentioned his nephew as having gone to a neighbouring town to sell a load of wheat hauled there by a fine span of mules. The youngster did not return for a week, and then calmly accosted the manager with the remark, " I sold the wheat." " Yes," said the manager. " I got —— per bushel." " That's a good price,"

replied the manager. " I sold the mules and wagons for ——
dollars." " Ah, that was a good bargain ! " " I spent the
money ! " " That's all right, I'll charge it up to the old
gentleman ! " meaning this remarkable youth's father in
England. That this story is true I can vouch, and I have
known many quite as strange to happen in the west.

The system so common at that time of sending young
men from the old country to learn farming was very absurd.
Their instructors, although paid to teach, did not care whether
they worked or not ; if they preferred to hang round the
neighbouring villages, it mattered nothing to them ; they were
paid for the lads' board and lodging, and that, with the occasional hour in the rush of seed time and harvest, more than
compensated them. It was also a mistake to send them
out without any experience to start farm or ranch life on the
prairies.

An amusing case came under my observation. A well-known,
in fact famous, professional man sent his son out west with a
good allowance and sufficient capital to make a good start
in cattle-ranching. He wisely hired a practical stockman, who
built his comfortable log house and commodious corrals on the
banks of a pretty stream, while he enjoyed himself in a neighbouring town, assisted in spending his allowance by a number
of young fellows " from home." To encourage his parents
he sent glowing accounts to them of the success of the cattle
venture, and this was so pleasant to hear that the following
summer they decided to visit the young hopeful at his ranch
in the west. This decision filled the embryo rancher with
consternation. He had no cattle yet, and as he had reported
many, what was he to do ? He was soon shown the way ;
he had not yet learned the resourcefulness of the cow puncher,
who had graduated in the Mounted Police and obtained the
rank of corporal, a position not attained in those days without
evidence of a rather remarkable intelligence !

The father and mother arrived and took up their quarters at
the ranch, which was in sight of the snow-capped Rockies. The
next day they were conducted round the corrals in which were
a large number of fine cattle. It is true that they were of
different brands but, as those marks of identification are not in

vogue in the old land, nothing was suspected or noticed. The old gentleman was so pleased with the apparent success of the cattle venture that he increased the allowance of his enterprising son and invited him home for a Christmas visit. This he accepted with alacrity, and, as he now possessed the intimate knowledge of his manager's power of initiative, he made an arrangement by which he was apprised during his stay with his parents that the winter in the west had proved to be so severe that the cattle had died of the cold. This settled ranching for him in Canada, an orange grove came next !

I enlisted many good men in Winnipeg and sent them on to Regina as fast as they were sworn in. One applicant was a splendidly-built man whom I had to refuse on account of his great height. He stood six feet nine inches in his stockings, and was well proportioned, and his travels had led him from England to South America, where he had been employed as a civil engineer. He had first-class testimonials, but he remarked that his great height was a nuisance to him no matter where he went, for people stared at him as he walked the streets and gave him no end of annoyance. On hearing his story I was very sorry that I could not take him, but arranged to do well for him by getting employment for him on the staff of a survey party under a friend of mine. He did excellent work, and the next time I met him he was on his way to England to take possession of a large fortune to which he had fallen heir.

Shortly after this a strike was threatened at Maple Creek on the line of construction, 600 miles west of Winnipeg, and I was ordered to proceed there with all of the available trained men in Regina, while Griesbach took my place on the recruiting station at Winnipeg. The strike ended in a satisfactory way for both parties, and then I was kept busy at magisterial duties, which necessitated travelling along the railway from Medicine Hat[1]

---

[1] The name is a translation of the Blackfoot word " Saamis," given on account of a vision that came to an Indian chief there. Of this there are various versions, but one thing is said to be certain, the chief, whether waking or sleeping, said that he saw an Indian rise out of the Saskatchewan wearing the plumed hat or head-dress of a Medicine Man. Medicine has nothing to do with drugs. It is a charm, a fetish, magic, mystic power, hence the expression, " His medicine is strong," " He is bad medicine," or " It is good medicine." Often in the old days one would hear an Indian droning a weird song, and if one asked what he

to Moose Jaw, and although the work was constant I had not a bad time. I got very well acquainted with the officers of the C.P.R., the train men and other employees, all of whom were very good and most obliging. I took my meals at the section houses or in the cabooses, and slept in the latter or on the prairie. The court-houses were of a primitive character; on several occasions in what is now the prosperous town of Swift Current I tried cases while seated on a Red River cart, with a plank stretched across for the bench, the evidence being taken down on the flap of my despatch bag !

The railway construction of the year 1883 had commenced at Medicine Hat and was under the management of Mr. James Ross, a Highland Scotch engineer. Mr. Donald Grant, a gigantic Canadian Highlander from Glengarry, was in charge of the tracklayers. One always knew how many miles of steel he laid every day by the number of trains which passed to " the end of track." Each of them contained the rails, ties and other materials for one mile of line and there were never less than four passing up every day, and once Mr. Grant beat all previous records by laying eight miles of line between sunrise and sunset. Some years afterwards he beat his remarkable feat by laying ten miles on another railway.

The stations along the C.P.R. from Moose Jaw west were as a rule named after the important persons who travelled on excursion trains to see the line. On one occasion Mr. (now Sir William) van Horne passed up with a train, and, to demonstrate how practical they were, the general superintendent took the lever and Major Walsh worked the brakes, then the old-fashioned kind ; the air brakes, however, had been placed on most trains at that date.

There were new Mounted Police barracks under construction at many points, and Maple Creek, which had taken the place of Fort Walsh, was often visited by the commissioner. Early in June I was at Maple Creek for a few days and saw Big Bear's band going north. They were going to their reserve at Frog

was doing, those who knew would say, " He is making medicine." As already described in a previous chapter the Medicine Men of the tribes initiated the young braves in the Medicine Lodge of the Sun Dance.

Lake and were a bad bunch, " bad medicine " as it were, and should never have been left without at least 100 well-armed and mounted men near them. It would have been useless, however, to ask for this ; it required an Indian rising to open the eyes of the public to such a necessity. The force from the beginning had been kept short-handed for the work to be done ; 500 more men would have saved millions.

I had not been very long back at Medicine Hat when our commissioner arrived on one of his tours and produced a telegram from the Prime Minister, Sir John Macdonald, to the effect that I was to be sent with a strong party of picked men to Rat Portage,[1] now Kenora, where there was trouble between the magistrates of Manitoba and Ontario. The territory was disputed, each province claiming it, and their magistrates were busy attempting to arrest one another instead of taking a sensible view of the situation until the Privy Council should decide the case which was before them.

I took no horses, as all our work would be done on foot, and at Regina was given as N.C.O. a smart-looking young man whom I had rejected at Winnipeg a few years before because he could not produce his parchment discharge papers from the Royal Horse Guards ; he had proceeded to Regina and, after interviewing a young man who knew his history, joined the force and was promoted to corporal in a few days, over the heads, one might say, of more than a hundred well-educated and experienced men. He had alleged to me that he had belonged to the Blues, but had nothing to show for it but a private letter from someone who signed himself as adjutant. He was very well-proportioned and handsome, but not more so than the men over whom he had stepped, and it was fortunate indeed that it did not matter with such men whether I had a N.C.O. or not.

When I arrived in Winnipeg I was met by the Attorney-General, an old friend of mine, and when he saw the smart, athletic men that I had with me he winked and said, " They will do, Steele ! " I was ordered to put my men in barracks at

[1] The name Rat Portage is no more, divided interests brought about a change into a composite word made up of a syllable from each of the three small towns at the head of the Winnipeg.

Fort Osborne, and a few days later Mr. Fred White informed me that as the trouble seemed to have blown over at Rat Portage I need not take the party there unless there were a recurrence of it ; the ordering of the detachment to Winnipeg seemed to have had a deterrent effect. After making my men comfortable in barracks I started a recruiting office and did very well, large numbers of good men coming forward, attracted by the smart bearing, gay uniforms and pleasant manners of my party.

I had not been in Winnipeg a month when the mistake of appointing the N.C.O. was discovered. He deserted one night, leaving some new found friends " in a hole " to the extent of many hundred dollars and taking away his kit.   In his place a very fine and experienced N.C.O. was sent to me, after which all went well.   A few days later I met in town a young man of my acquaintance whom I had first met near Swift Current.   " So the bird has flown ! " he remarked.   " He came to see me before he joined the force and asked me to say nothing about his past history as he wished to join the Mounted Police and, although he had been refused admission when he applied, he was going to try again."   My young friend and he had served in the Blues and they were in Australia together ; the first had bought his discharge and was out there when the other appeared, after deserting from his corps, and joined the Australian Police, but had not been long in them when he deserted, sold his horse and kit and was arrested, fined and imprisoned.   The other was a very good fellow who had committed the grave offence of enlisting in the army.   When he had finished sowing his small stock of wild oats he returned home to Ireland, where his father was a wealthy barrister, in hopes that he would, like the prodigal, be forgiven.   In this he was mistaken, however, for no sooner did he show his face than his father asked him why he had returned, to which he retorted, " I have just come to see what time it is by the town clock, and I thought I would call in."   He has since made good in Canada, and is a welcome guest in every home in his city.

In November I went to Calgary to take temporary command of the district.   I found Lt.-Col. Irvine and one of his staff officers there investigating a somewhat humorous incident.

Several young constables of very short service, who had frustrated the efforts of their comrades to bring to justice some gamblers and toughs, had been given a barrack-room court-martial and, for their lack of *esprit de corps*, were ducked in the Bow, which was full of floating ice at the time, the thermometer indicating fifteen degrees below zero. The victims complained to the C.O., who, after carefully investigating the matter, sentenced the ducked to a term of imprisonment and a heavy fine. Their assailants he placed under arrest for taking the law into their own hands, and telegraphed for the commissioner to investigate the charge against them, which he did on the night after I arrived. As he understood that the ducking was only a misguided display of *esprit de corps*, he dismissed the cases with a caution.

Calgary at this time was a cluster of portable huts and frame houses on the east side of the Elbow River ; where the centre of the city now is, was not then occupied. Some squatters were in possession of it, and these had been bought out by some others, and although the section was odd numbered (15) and under ordinary circumstances would belong to the C.P.R., in this case it did not, at least until their claims went before the courts. The ground was just the same as I saw it in 1878. The Mounted Police barracks were improved a great deal, it is true, and there were a few small frame shops, the Roman Catholic and Methodist mission buildings and a few log cabins of the freighters. The Hudson Bay store still flourished on the east side of the Elbow, and there were also two hotels and two small churches. The Church of England had not yet built a place of worship ; they used our orderly-room on Sunday, and the Rev. (now Archdeacon) Tims used to come up from the mission amongst the Blackfeet and hold services there.

Two days after I took command at Calgary I assigned the magistrate's court to Inspector Dowling, the only officer in the district to assist me, although it covered an area of at least 150 miles square. In addition to this duty he was clerk of the District Court, presided over by Colonel Macleod, the stipendiary magistrate, who had the powers of a Supreme Court judge when associated with a justice of the peace.

When the navvies left for the winter things were fairly quiet as far as the railway was concerned, but there was trouble coming up in another quarter, viz., amongst the Indians and half-breeds along the Saskatchewan; and the Blackfeet, no doubt a fine lot of wild Indians, but unfortunately in some directions looked upon as mild innocents, were giving much annoyance to the stockmen in the cattle country. For this crime there was no excuse; they were fairly well fed, and the reserves were administered by agents who gave them all to which they were entitled.

Early in the winter there were complaints of the Blackfeet killing stock. Small parties of the worst of them would leave the reserve and, secreting themselves in some nook in the vicinity of wood and water, would make stealthy raids on the cattle, and until found and arrested would subsist thus, never taking the trouble to draw their legitimate rations at the agency. When the complaints were made I sent out parties, and the thieves were hunted down and brought to justice. On several occasions General Strange's military colonization ranch suffered loss on account of these marauders. I would go with a strong party, remain at his ranch until near dawn, and then surround Old Sun's camp and capture the thieves before they could take to the woods and prairies. This work was excellent scouting practice for the men, who had learned to take those alert people by surprise, or to get on their trail and track them to their haunts.

On one occasion after these arrests, the agent, at my request, sent for the chief and headmen, and the general and I addressed them, urging them to keep their people honest. These harangues no doubt had a good effect, but a nocturnal visit from the red-coats did much more.

The same old law for the suppression of intoxicating liquor was in force, and proved excellent for the purpose of preserving peace on the railway construction and keeping the Indians from deterioration, but it should not have been forced upon the rest of the community against the will of the majority. It was intended for the prevention of the Indian trade, and our powers under it were so great that we could enter or search any place at any hour of the day or night. The officers and men hated this detestable duty, which gave them much trouble and gleams of unpopularity. We soon learned that compulsion will not make people sober ; it must be brought about by the example of the best people. The prohibitory law made more drunkards than if there had been an open bar and free drinks at every street corner. Liquor was brought into the territories by every conceivable trick. Egg shells were emptied of their contents and alcohol substituted ; tin imitations of the Holy Bible were filled with intoxicants and sold on the trains ; metal kegs filled with alcohol came concealed in the centre of barrels of kerosene, and mince-meat soaked in brandy and peaches prepared in the same manner were common.

We had one brutal murder during the winter. The victim, a fine young fellow, had a store near us, and he was a regular attendant at the Presbyterian church east of the Elbow, and used to see to the lighting of the fires on Sunday and Wednesday evenings. On one of the latter a young man named Francis came to me in a great state of excitement, saying that he had been at the store and found the poor man lying near the desk with his throat cut from ear to ear and the whole place bespattered with blood. I learned from Francis that on that same evening the coloured cook of a neighbouring restaurant had been in the store and disputed in a hostile manner an account which had been rendered to him by the proprietor ; he had even gone behind the counter to give vent to his threats.

On learning this I turned out several parties, mounted and assisted by numerous civilians. They scoured the country until, about midnight, Mr. James Christie, an ex-member of the force, arrested the negro near some Indian lodges about a mile from the barracks, and he was placed in the guard-room, where Kennedy and I went at once and caused him to be examined. We found blood on his right finger nail, but there was very little of it, and a dark oblong stain in his right trousers pocket. We noticed that the right leg of his trousers, being lower than the other, was frozen at the bottom from being in contact with the snow after being wet. The man had overshoes only, without boots, and his stockings were very damp.

The snow round the store, in front and on all sides, as there was no fence, had been trampled over until it would appear

N

impossible to find a trace of any footprints, but at the front window of the store, so close that they could not be obscured by other marks, the tracks of the toes of the overshoes were very distinct, as if the wearer had got as close to the window as possible to see if his victim had returned. From these, in spite of the numerous tracks, the marks were followed for an hour with the greatest care to where they were found distinctly on the right-hand side of the store, where the negro had stood and taken off his overshoes. He had then gone round to the back door in his stockinged feet. These tracks were discerned as far as the inside of the store. There were blood stains on the desk and ledger, blood on the till, and a small twenty-five cent note, called a " shin plaster," was found on the floor. The stockinged feet were with difficulty traced back from the door to where the shoes had been left ; the shoes had been put on again, and the tracks were followed to the trail, the large number of footprints giving much trouble, and at last were traced through deep snow to a hay stack.

The hay stack had been disturbed, as if a hand had been thrust into it, and a search revealed twenty odd dollars in notes which had been held crushed in a bloody hand and pushed into the hay. The tracks were followed back to the trail and along a path through a snowfall, which showed behind the heel of the right foot a semicircle made on the snow by the frozen bottom of the trousers. There were several of these marks, and further on, where the negro had halted for a second or two, a small mark was noticed in the snow, about 30 yards from the trail, as if some article had been thrown into it. We found a razor in its case. The edges of the blade were jagged, as if it had come in contact with bone or some other hard substance ; both razor and case were bloody. Proceeding further the tracks led to an Indian lodge, and from there to where the negro stood when he was arrested the night before, and thence to the guard-room.

The accused was taken out of the cells and led through some snow, and it was seen that the bottom edge of his trousers made the same sort of mark which had been perceived by the trackers. It was fortunate that the tracking was commenced at daylight, for early in the afternoon, soon after it was finished, a chinook came and took off every particle of snow, and no trace was left. The following day Dowling committed the negro for trial, and Colonel Macleod arrived from Fort Macleod next day. I was invited to sit with him at the trial and, as the prisoner had no counsel, Mr. James A. Lougheed, now a senator for the Dominion, was directed to act for him. A strong defence was made, but the evidence was too clear. The jury found the prisoner guilty without leaving the box, and before sentence was delivered by Colonel Macleod he confessed his guilt.

Some weeks later the sentence of the court was carried out, the prisoner marching to the scaffold with a jaunty, military step, keeping time with the escort, and on the scaffold he faced the witnesses to the execution, and stated that drink was the cause of the crime. Dr. Kennedy and I were the official witnesses, and I relate these circumstances for the reason that this was the first execution in the North West Territories of any person other than an Indian, and it was carried out in the barrack square of the Mounted Police.

The murder caused a great deal of excitement, and when it was reported a large mob of citizens, headed by a very decent but excited individual, came to find out what I was going to do about it, and there were threats of lynching the perpetrator if captured. But I said to him, " You lads are all tenderfeet, and have visions before you of taking part in a Neck-tie Social. There never has been a lynching in Canada, nor will there be as long as our force has the police duties to perform, so go away like sensible men, and remember that any attempt at lynching will be bad for those who try it ! " This settled the matter, and from that date he was one of the best friends of the force, always taking a leading part on our behalf. On the night of the execution I was returning to my quarters from the orderly-room, and as I approached the door one of my friends was standing in the passage, and stood gazing over my head, with a look of horror and superstitious dread on his face. I said, " What's the matter ? " and he gasped, " Thank Heaven, it's you ! I thought it was the negro ! "

During the spring of 1884 I got proof that there was trouble before us in the North West Territory. It came about in this

way. My orderly-room sergeant, who understood Cree and
spoke Blackfeet, was on leave for a week-end at High River,
and on his return reported that he had seen a French half-breed
there talking with some Blackfeet Indians, with whom he
seemed to be on very friendly terms, and saying that he had
come from the Judith Basin in Montana with Louis Riel,
and that the Indians had a right to kill the settlers' cattle
if they chose, and that the country belonged to the Indians,
and that the whites should be turned out. He had said much
more, in an undertone, which the sergeant could not catch,
but there was sufficient for me, and I caused information to be
laid against the half-breed, charging him with vagrancy, and
when he appeared in court he admitted that he had come over
with Riel and that he had suggested that the Blackfeet had
a right to kill cattle. The magistrates sentenced him to one
month's imprisonment, and cautioned him that any further
misconduct would be more severely dealt with.

There was nothing heard of the Cree half-breed for some time,
and in April I received orders to hand over the district to
Colonel Herchmer and select from the division a strong party
with me to go to British Columbia, where I was to have sole
charge of the Mounted Police on the line of construction of the
C.P.R. through the Rocky Mountains to where the last spike
would be driven. I had been appointed a commissioner
of police under the Police of Canada Act and a commissioner
of the peace under the Act for the Preservation of Peace on
Public Works.

The whole division volunteered to a man and, to avoid the
dilemma, I selected the best shots with rifle and revolver.
The construction on the mountains began early in April, and
Mr. James Ross returned to the west and made his headquarters
at Laggan, near the summit of the Bow River Pass, where
the end of the track was situated and there was a vast accumu-
lation of material. As soon as the work was well under way
I went to Laggan with a number of the men and posted them
where they were most needed ; it was evident from what I
saw that they had a hard year's work before them. Large
numbers of gamblers, whisky men, in fact almost every
description of criminal, who had been plying their trade on

the Northern Pacific Railway, were wending their way from Sand Point and establishing their dens on every little creek along the line.

The force had to find escorts for the paymaster of the company on his tour to the end of the track to pay the men. Directions were given to use every precaution on all such trips, men were to be sent on in advance to examine any place where a hold-up might be concealed. Two were to be with the paymaster, near the pack ponies with the money, and two more were to be in front and two in rear of it at a safe distance, the whole party arranged so that all could not come under fire at the same time. The N.C.O. was to stay with the paymaster and keep a sharp look-out ; I also gave orders that every man of the tough element was to be under surveillance and his antecedents ascertained.

On my return to Calgary I was holding myself in readiness to depart as soon as I had handed over the district, when Mr. Magnus Begg, Indian agent of the Blackfeet, came to Calgary and reported that the former friendly demeanour of the tribe had changed to one of sulkiness and hostility, and that he was feeling very anxious. I asked him if he had any reason to assign for their altered behaviour, and he replied that a stout half-breed of about thirty years of age was in the camp with Crowfoot, and that ever since his arrival the chiefs and tribe had become sulky. This convinced me that the half-breed was the one from the Judith Basin, who had come over with Riel, and that he was the cause of the change in the behaviour of the Indians, but although I had no great faith in Crowfoot, I could not quite understand his sudden change towards Begg, who had been very kind to him.

There was nothing for it, however, but again to arrest the half-breed, and, as the Blackfeet were holding their Sun Dance, I sent Sergeant Dann and a constable to Gleichen, a station near the camp, to wait there until Begg got a friendly Indian to decoy the half-breed to the station. They arrived soon after dawn, and the half-breed was arrested and held until the train from the east would arrive next morning. In the meantime Lt.-Col. Irvine and Supt. Herchmer arrived for the handing over of the district. Next morning Dann and the constable were bringing their prisoner to Calgary on the morning train, which was making about 30 miles per hour. They were in the mail car with their prisoner handcuffed, and the sergeant was brushing his clothes when the half-breed sprang to his feet, slipped his handcuffs, which were too large, seized Dann's rifle and jumped from the train. Dann and the constable followed, but the former put his knee out of joint, and the half-breed ran at top speed for Crowfoot's camp, or at least in that direction. The constable endeavoured to follow, but his long boots were a handicap when chasing the moccasined half-breed, and he had to turn back.

The train was stopped to pick up Dann and the constable, who, when they arrived in Calgary, reported what had occurred, and I informed Supt. Herchmer and Lt.-Col. Irvine, and was asked by them as a special case to take to the prairie and arrest the half-breed. Herchmer expressed great anxiety to have the arrest made, and seemed to think the behaviour of the Indians serious and the presence of the half-breed in the camp as the cause of the unrest and a bad sign.

I left with two men, one driving a buckboard ; these were constables Walters and Kerr, as I thought it was important to make as little display of force as possible. We scouted east for nearly 40 miles until dark, and then turned into General Strange's ranch, where we were received with the usual hospitality. We waited there until 1 a.m., and then rode to Old Sun's camp, which I found clear of all adults except John L'Hereux, interpreter for the agency, and the Indian who had decoyed the half-breed to Gleichen. There were a lot of lively Indian boys in camp, who, with the usual cheerfulness of their kind, found L'Hereux and the Indians for me.

The interpreter was a man of great experience and equally great timidity. He had lived in the Blackfoot camp for many years, often sharing Crowfoot's lodge, and advising him when any question came up between him and the whites, and seemed to be much in his confidence during the treaty of 1877 at the Blackfoot Crossing. When I told him that he must come with me to get the half-breed at Crowfoot's Sun Dance camp, he showed palpable signs of fear, and I am convinced that he knew what was the matter. I told him that there was no cause for alarm, that Crowfoot and I were good friends, and we were not going to fight, but to make an ordinary arrest. Then, accompanied by him and the Indian, I went with my party to the outskirts of the Sun Dance camp, which was near the Peigan Sand Hills.

It rained in torrents all the time we were there, a fact which I welcomed, as we did a blizzard in winter when on the same sort of errand, for under the circumstances the Indians would not be stirring or wandering about the precincts of the camp as they would in fine weather. As soon as dawn was clear, the friendly Indian pointed out Crowfoot's lodge, and I went there. After telling him I was there I entered with the interpreter, leaving the men outside. The occupants, all men, were seated in a circle round the lodge. They were leading men of the tribe, and Crowfoot sat at the back facing the door, with the half-breed occupying the place of honour on his right. He sat there without a movement or sign, but the moment I entered Crowfoot gazed fiercely at me and showed every indication of hostility.

I spoke firmly to him but in a friendly way, and told the interpreter to say that I had come to bring the half-breed to Calgary, that he had been making mischief, and had to be tried for his offence and must come with me now. I also told the half-breed that he must come at once. He understood English, and I spoke to him in that language, but he showed no sign of moving. All this time L'Hereux was as pale as death, with his knees knocking together in fright, and Crowfoot was speaking with great vehemence, whilst the Indians were expressing approval of what he was saying. I understood him to be speaking in defiance of me, and told the interpreter to tell him I was in earnest and would stand no nonsense. I said to L'Hereux that he was not telling the truth to Crowfoot, that he was temporizing with the chief, and I would not permit it.

He braced up a bit then and told the chief what I said to him. Crowfoot then sprang up and came at me in a hostile manner, but I waved him back, told him not to make an offensive move or it would be the worse for him, and that if the worst came he would be the first to suffer. I spoke sternly, straight at him and moved close to him, and when he stood back I ordered

L'Hereux to open the flap over the entrance or door of the lodge. Holding my right hand on the butt of my revolver, I seized the half-breed, who showed no sign of obeying me, by the back of the shirt collar with my left hand, whirled him round with his back towards me, and dragged him head foremost through the door and had him outside before he had time to resist. I gave him over to Kerr and Walters, who placed him in the buckboard and secured him to the seat. I found the lodge surrounded by hundreds of Indians, all of whom looked sullen and hostile.

When my men seized the prisoner I made the interpreter tell the assembled warriors that they must remember that when the Mounted Police came for an Indian or white, that person had to come, and that anyone who interfered would suffer for it. I told Crowfoot to come out of the tent so that I could speak to him, and that I had to have the half-breed dead or alive, when I was sent for him, and that he, Crowfoot, had behaved badly, although he had always received fair play, that he acted as if he had been treated unjustly, whereas he had received the greatest kindness from the Mounted Police and all of the officers of the Indian Department, and was making a poor return for it, and that I had expected his assistance as the chief of a great tribe. Then I spoke to the other Indians to the effect that anything the half-breed had said to them or the chief was false. I gave them advice, which seemed to have some effect, and then wrote a note to the C.P.R. agent at Gleichen to let Crowfoot have a return ticket to Calgary, saying to the chief, as I handed it to him, " You may go up to Calgary and hear the half-breed tried by Ho-mux-a-stamix (Lt.-Col. Irvine). If you think the prisoner will not be fairly dealt with, then, perhaps, you may explain your conduct in the tent. In future, I should advise you to assist to maintain the law as you promised to do. When you go to Calgary to attend the trial, you will find that you have been harbouring a disturber of the peace."

Whereupon I sent the prisoner away with the men, and when they had cleared the camp I sent by L'Hereux a message to Mr. Begg, the agent, informing him that the half-breed had been sent to Calgary under escort, and that he might be needed at the trial as he had laid the charge. I then followed the men, and when I arrived at Calgary I reported the circumstances to Supt. Herchmer, and the prisoner was lodged in the cells. He was brought before Lt.-Col. Irvine next day. Supt. Herchmer and Crowfoot were present, I was not, nor was I invited or ordered to be. The charge against the half-breed was dismissed !

Lt.-Col. Irvine told me recently that my report never reached him, but Supt. Herchmer most distinctly informed me that he had forwarded it to the commissioner. He said much more that I remember well, and expressed dissatisfaction at the result of the trial. In reply I expressed the opinion to him that Riel having gone to Batoche and the half-breed having come across with him at the same time, and at once fraternized with his hereditary enemies the Blackfeet, had a sinister appearance. Ten months later the truth of this was proved, and, during the rebellion of the following year, had it not been for the active work of the white officials, Colonel Macleod, the agents and police, it is just possible that Crowfoot would have shown his hand. The agent for the Bloods informed me in 1886 that Crowfoot tried to induce Red Crow, the Blood chief, to rebel, but that chief, the best in the Blackfeet Nation, was loyal throughout, and so was North Axe of the Peigans, and all the headmen of those two tribes.

I left Calgary for the Rocky Mountains as soon as possible. A great change had taken place at Calgary during the past few months. The town site had been surveyed on the west side of the Elbow near the police post, taking in the whole of section fifteen ; a railway station was established and, as soon as the authority was granted by the government, nearly all the people on the east bank of the Elbow purchased lots on the west side and moved their portable houses and furniture across. The place had altered almost beyond recognition. Where there had been a bare plain the previous summer, a good start had been made for the present fine city, which covers the hills dominating the pretty valleys of the two rivers.

CHAPTER XI

WHEN, in 1884, the Mounted Police took over the duty of maintaining the law along the line of construction of the C.P.R. in British Columbia, the belt over which we had jurisdiction was only 20 miles wide ; the surveyed line of the railroad was the centre, and the area was proclaimed by the government under the Act for the Preservation of Peace on Public Works. The sale of intoxicating liquor was prohibited, and the difficulties with which we had to contend were that, unless there were a bar in the tent or cabin, no liquor could be seized or confiscated. Persons caught in the act of selling were only liable to a fine of 40 dollars for the first and second offences ; for the third they might be imprisoned, but they got over that by transferring the goodwill of the dive to another, who went on in the same way. Another drawback was that the belt was so narrow that the labourers could go out at any time after they received their month's wages to places outside our belt and spend every dollar in their possession, remaining there for a prolonged spree, thus delaying the progress of the work and causing no end of annoyance to the contractors.

The greatest obstacle in our way was the determination of

the government of British Columbia that the province should not be deprived of its internal revenue. It therefore issued to all comers licences to sell " spirituous and fermented liquors " within the belt already proclaimed under the act. This action gave courage to the liquor men, and many sold who, had they not been granted licences, would not have attempted it.

We had right on our side, however ; the building of the great work must not be retarded. I therefore made up my mind to enforce the laws to the limit, and, no matter how much liquor was distributed and sold throughout our belt, that those who were under its influence in public places or were in any way disorderly should be dealt with in a way that would deter others. I also recommended that the government increase the width of the railway belt to 40 miles, and increase our powers so that the magistrates could punish with imprisonment for the second offence of selling intoxicating liquor. These suggestions were approved and had a good effect. The wholesale and retail stores on the edge of the 20 mile area had to move, and navvies found a 20 mile walk too long for the sake of a spree.

The end of the track at Laggan contained the offices and residences of the principal officials of the company. The latter were situated along the beautiful banks of the Bow. There were several small stores, a few saloons, the post office and boarding-house for the company, and, as our men had been vigilant ever since they were posted, there was not much cause for complaint.

Trains ran regularly, bringing men and materials from the east, but there was small chance of the end of the line being moved on for some months. The difficulties in the vicinity were enormous and would take a considerable time to overcome.

The work was being pushed forward with great vigour to the first crossing of the Columbia River, nearly 70 miles west. This place is now the town and railway divisional point of Donald, named after Lord Strathcona. As it was important that detachments of the force should be placed wherever required, I left Laggan with a strong party the day after I arrived.

We were mounted on exceptional horses and moved along what was called the Tote road, which had been constructed a few weeks earlier to enable the company and the contractors to transport their supplies. These were carried by horse and mule teams ; stores had been established at convenient distances, each presided over by a capable employee. From them the contractors obtained their food, forage, etc., which they hauled with their own teams to their contracts.

The Tote road was exceptionally rough. On the right bank near the Columbia it was cut out of the solid rock for several miles, some hundreds of feet above the river and, except at the Kicking Horse Flats near the Beaverfoot Pass, where the stream spread out into several fordable channels, it was not of sufficient width to admit of teams passing. I placed detachments at all points where large numbers of men were employed, and gave them orders to protect all employed in legitimate occupations.

The Kicking Horse Pass was named by the famous Dr. Hector, who was Captain Palliser's assistant in the exploration of western Canada during the late fifties. He had explored the pass accompanied by a party of Indians, and at one of his camps had the misfortune to be kicked by a wild horse, which he had been attempting to saddle and pack when the brute lashed out furiously, breaking several of the good doctor's ribs and rendering him unconscious. The Indians thought he was dead, and had dug a grave and placed him in it when they saw signs of life and, taking him out of the grave, restored him to consciousness.

The trail along the side of the mountains near Golden was only suitable for pack animals until the Tote road was constructed. It was very dangerous ; at the highest part it was more than a thousand feet above the foaming torrent and bad enough anywhere. One of the most remarkable experiences on it was that of Mr. H. S. Holt, C.E., now of Montreal. He was making his trip over the pack trail from the head of the Kicking Horse to the Columbia. Mr. A. R. Hogg, a prominent engineer, two assistant engineers and two packers composed his party, and he was riding a spirited broncho which he had used on the plains, and which had no experience of mountain trails. When he got to the lower canyon of the Kicking Horse, being the leader of the party, he found the trail very bad ; at one point his horse began slipping on a loose stone, but he managed to dismount and tried to make the brute back up, which she would have done had she been a trained mountain pony. Instead of backing up she started forward and hit Mr. Holt in the chest, knocking him over the side of the canyon, which at that point was perpendicular and about 75 feet from the trail to the river below. In falling he turned a complete somersault, landing on his stomach on the trunk of a dead tree which had been caught in the rocks on the side of the canyon. The distance was afterwards measured, and the tree was found to be $27\frac{1}{2}$ feet below the trail. The horse and the stone on which she slipped, which must have weighed at least 800 pounds, also fell over the cliff, but fortunately fell clear of the tree in which Mr. Holt had lodged, and both fell to the bottom of the canyon.

When the rest of the party came up they lowered to Mr. Holt a lariat, which he tied under his arms, and they pulled him up to the trail. Looking down he saw the horse lying on the rocks below ; thinking her leg was broken and being unable to get down the perpendicular wall of the canyon, he concluded that it was best to shoot her and proceeded to carry his idea into execution. He succeeded in putting five bullets of his revolver into the horse's head without touching a vital spot. The animal then struggled to her feet and fell into the river, which was at that season and all summer a raging torrent, and was carried down about half a mile to the opposite shore.

The next day Mr. Holt sent his packers back to try to recover the saddle and bridle and some papers which were in the saddle bags. They found the horse lying on the rocks with one eye shot out, three ribs broken and one leg almost cut off. As they knew that the animal was a favourite with its owner, they built a shelter of brush over the poor beast and made her as comfortable as possible. When it was reported to Mr. Holt, he sent them back with some oats and gave instructions to them to feed the poor animal and give her a chance to recover, which, wonderful to relate, she did. She was sent to Mr.

Holt's ranch for a year, and when the Alberta Field Force was raised for the suppression of the rebellion I saw a man, who had been employed as a mail carrier in the Rockies, in the ranks of the Alberta Mounted Rifles, riding a one-eyed horse, which he informed me, and so did others, was the animal which went over the canyon with Mr. Holt.

A skittish or shying horse on that trail was an impossible beast. Horses are seldom found to be afraid of a precipice. They fear the rocky wall away from the brink and, if of the shying kind, keep working away from it. After the Tote road was built on that rocky height, some hundreds of feet above the Kicking Horse, some fresh mounts were sent to me from Calgary, and when I received them at Laggan I selected a fine-looking animal to take me to Golden. At the high and precipitous part of the Tote road I met an Italian navvy with his bundle of blankets, and he, as was then the custom, instead of going to the right, planted himself against the wall of rock furthest from the precipice. At the sight of the extraordinary object, my horse, crazed with fright, whirled about, and I just saved myself and the horse by hurling myself on to the road. I kept a strong hold of the reins and head collar and hung on to the animal, whose hindquarters were over the brink, with its body resting on the rocky edge. My companion, who rode a steady horse, ran to my assistance, and with our united efforts we dragged the brute on to the road. Needless to say I had to send the horse back to Calgary with a letter to the effect that if the O.C. there valued our lives he would keep such brutes for the plains as they were of no use in the mountains.

The summer of 1884 on the prairie and in the mountains was very wet ; rain fell nearly every day for at least two months. The wet summer, however, did not in the least retard the work of construction. The men were busy, wet or dry. On one contract the time books, which I was shown, proved that the men averaged more than ten hours per day per month ; some of them had thirteen or fourteen hours per day to their credit, especially in the Swedish camps. If it rained too hard for an hour or two they made up for it when it slackened, and as I rode along I often saw them working in the moonlight, particularly those who had taken the small contracts called station work, where four or five men, generally Swedes, would join together in a small contract where there was no rock.

One thing worth mention was the almost total absence of accidents through the handling of explosives.   There were only two, a clear proof of the care exercised by the contractors, who would never employ any but the most experienced rock foremen.   This is a marked contrast to the construction of other railroads.

The medical department was under Doctors Orton and Brett, who, in spite of the great drawbacks, were successful in keeping down disease, most of which was caused by bad sanitation.   The most common complaint was typhoid, which they called mountain fever, and there were many cases.

On one of my trips to Laggan I met the British Association on its first visit to western Canada.   They had come under the auspices of the C.P.R. and were delighted with the sublime grandeur of the Rocky Mountains and the wild scenery of the Kicking Horse Pass.   Some members of the Association went as far as the terminal in the flats, and one, the proprietor of a Welsh newspaper, walked to the end of the construction, and on his return to the old land wrote many interesting articles. He approved of everything but the severity with which we dealt with road agents, thieves and murderers.   He seemed to prefer that we should manage such gentry according to the methods of orphanages or reformatories.

When the tunnels on Kicking Horse were finished and the end of the track at Golden, I had to see about moving on, and arranged with Mr. Ross to have winter quarters built at Donald, but when they were almost complete it was ascertained that the end of the track would be at Beaver River, and that it would be better to locate my headquarters there for the winter.   Accordingly, a good log building was constructed by the company.   It was very strong, with cells for thirty prisoners, a separate portion for women, a court-room, two rooms for myself, a mess for the staff of the road, excellent quarters for my men, and stables.

On my way back to Golden I strained my ankle owing to

my horse jibbing at a tree and had to lay up from riding, but continued my work on the bench.

One of the most amusing characters on the construction was the sheriff, whose duty it was to collect the poll tax of three dollars each levied on all persons in the district, and in addition to issue licences, etc. His chief amusement was to get a number of friends round him and relate to them some experiences, which made Baron Munchausen's efforts seem puny by comparison. One of them was that when skating on the ice of one of our rivers he was pursued by wolves and, after dodging them for a considerable time, would at last have been obliged to succumb had he not been rescued by two men who were hoeing potatoes on the shore !

After which he related that when in Australia he arrested a man to whose handcuffs he fastened his lariat and led the prisoner beside his horse. On arrival in court the accused complained that he had been ill-treated, the constable having galloped the whole way, taking chasms 20 feet in width by a flying leap ! Our friend protested that he had done nothing of the kind, that he had not noticed anything in the way, but, in spite of all his protests, the magistrate went with him and the prisoner over the route to verify the statement, and, as the sheriff said, " What was the result ? Would you believe it ; I had done it ! "

Early in the autumn, when the Cleveland-Blain contest was at its height, a curious circumstance took place at the Kicking Horse Flats, where there were a few saloons, which resulted in the first homicide, and the only one, which occurred within the jurisdiction of the North West Mounted Police. A large number of American citizens had got together in the tent which a coloured barber used as his shop. Two of them were Irish-Americans, one a big brakesman and the other a small, peppery conductor. The latter, who was a Democrat, got into a heated argument with the barber, who professed Republican principles. While this was going on the brakesman noticed a pistol in the hip pocket of his friend the conductor and, to prevent any shooting, removed it without being perceived and placed it in his own pocket. A short time afterwards the barber became infuriated, drew a razor, made a rush and began slashing at the crowd. Everyone made for the tent door, but the conductor was forced into a corner whence escape was impossible, and the enraged barber made a pass to disembowel him, cutting through his waistcoat and making a hole in his shirt. He closed in to make another stroke when, as quick as a flash, the brakesman thought of the pistol, drew it and " filled him full of holes." He then fled, thinking that he would suffer all sorts of pains and penalties. The constable in the vicinity reported the matter at once, and the brakesman was followed to the north west and brought before me. I investigated the case, which clearly showed that the killing was done in self-defence, and obtained by telegraph from the Attorney-General of British Columbia authority to admit the prisoner to bail.

Soon after this occurrence I heard from a man named Johnston, who had a roadside inn called the Hog Ranche, about 22 miles south of Golden, that a Mr. Baird, in the employ of Eddy-Hammond & Co., of Missoula, Montana, had been murdered 3 miles south of the hotel on the trail to Montana, while on his way to Missoula with 5,000 dollars collected from persons doing business with his firm. On receipt of the report I sent two men in pursuit, Johnston having stated that the murderer must have gone south and that he had sent word to rouse the Indians in that direction. The police ascertained at the hotel that the murdered man had with him the packer and a blacksmith named Manuel Dainard, both very respectable men, and that an attempt had been made to kill all three.

They went to the place and searched for tracks, and found three 45·75 Winchester cartridges behind the upturned root from which the murderer had fired his fatal shot. They also tracked him back to where he had spent the night at a fire in the woods, and from there to where he stood early in the morning on the hill above the hotel, watching the little party making their preparations to start, whence he was tracked back to the pine-root where he posted himself to do the shooting. Another strike from there resulted in finding where he had run after the pack-horse, caught it and cut open the pack, an evidence that he was no packer. The tracks were followed

o

through the ford at Golden, and in it a new Winchester rifle was found ; three shells had been fired and five were in the magazine. The constables reported that Manuel Dainard had stated that the man was unknown to him, but wore a beard, was tall and had a stoop. I sent them on, caused every camp to be visited, wired to the Winnipeg police and to every important point east and south, to the Attorney-General of British Columbia and to our headquarters.

The two constables went as far as the Second Crossing of the Columbia, now Revelstoke, and to rest their horses slept at a camp in the Selkirks, in a tent with a man named Bull Dog Kelly, who was going in the same direction. He was the murderer, but in no way, except as regards height, did Dainard's description tally with his. Kelly disappeared at the Columbia, and for a time we were completely baffled. The finale was not in sight for many months ; but the case was never lost sight of, and large rewards were offered by the government of British Columbia and the firm to which Baird belonged.

I kept my headquarters at Golden until everything was ready at the Beaver, but placed a detachment there under the command of Sergeant Fury, who could easily be depended upon to keep order in the place. After Christmas I transferred my headquarters to the Beaver, which was within a mile of the end of the track.

We had a great deal of trouble with gamblers and toughs of every description, who had concentrated first at Donald, and had built log-houses, saloons and dens of all sorts ; on that account the end of the track was pushed on to the Beaver, where some of the stores, the postal-car, etc., were located. Mr. Ross established the headquarters of the construction staff at Donald in the log-houses which had been built for us, but as there was nothing left as an inducement to the tough element to remain, they moved on to the bridge at the Beaver and located opposite our post. They built saloons, dance-halls and disorderly houses of the cedar logs. Each saloon paid the licence fees demanded by our friend the sheriff.

The people lived by preying upon the navvies who might appear amongst them on pay day and get drunk. The term "rolling" was common, originating in the practice of turning over an incapable man, searching his pockets and appropriating anything which might be found therein. The best thing that could happen to such a man to prevent him from being robbed was to place him in the cells. I know of only three or four who came into court the second or third time ; the reminder and advice seemed to have a salutary effect.

The whisky " dives " were busy, and as Mr. Ross would not permit the trains to bring food for them or any others of the tough element, they had to resort to every kind of dodge and dishonest act to obtain the necessaries of life ; consequently, we were kept more than occupied, and every cell was full. Sleighs left unloaded and unwatched at any siding or camp would be likely to have part of their loads missing in the morning ; a few sub-contractors were tempted to sell part of their supplies, which they could, of course, replace at the company's stores, but the greater quantity was obtained by sneak thieving.

In the evenings the fun began at dances to which the navvies and toughs went, but as half of the police were on patrol the greatest order possible with such a class of men prevailed. When by any chance a fight or riot took place, the cells were filled and I was kept busy all the forenoon disposing of the prisoners, from five to thirty of these appearing every morning, and my afternoons were often occupied in summary trials for petty theft, assault, etc. The town being awake most of the night, we had to be likewise, in case there should be a sudden demand for more assistance, and I must admit that no people in the world earned the title of " night hawk " more honestly than we of the Mounted Police camp at the Beaver. We were rarely to bed before two or three a.m., and were up in the morning between six and seven and breakfasted at eight.

In February the suitability of the Selkirks for a railway by the Rogers Pass was severely tested. Avalanches of the most tremendous weight and power began to roar down the mountain sides. The blasting was partly responsible for this state of things. Glaciers, which had never left their rocky beds above the clouds, under the shocks of the blasting operations broke away and came crashing down, cutting pathways from a quarter to half a mile wide through the forest below. One avalanche, which came at the summit of the pass 20 miles from the Beaver camp, descended 5,000 feet with such velocity that it went across the valley and up on the opposite side for 800 feet.

During the month of February and early in March, 1885, many of the men employed on the construction complained to me that they had not been paid for some time, and that the money was much needed for their homesteads in Manitoba, Minnesota and Dakota. In every case I counselled patience, saying that the money would be forthcoming and all claims settled, but in spite of my advice the complaints at last became serious. Having a thorough knowledge of what was going on, I learned that a strike was on the point of being arranged. When the numbers applying to me increased and the men spoke of striking I again asked them to wait, as there was no sense in worrying when there was a certainty of the money coming to them very shortly. In fact, I did everything in my power to avert a strike, which I feared would lead to rioting and the destruction of property by a large number of ruffians, gamblers and murderers from the Northern Pacific who had left it on the completion of that road. Several of these had been south early in the winter, and but few of them were free from the crimes of robbery or murder in the United States. Amongst them was one who had just returned from a health resort in Arkansas, where it was reported that he had killed three men.

There had been mutterings of rebellion in the North West Territory, which did not surprise me. It was, therefore, plain that, in the event of a strike taking place, I should have no help from that quarter, but I was confident that with the assistance of the railway staff and other well-disposed persons, and with the influence which we had with all classes, I could control the situation. As it was my duty to give warning to all concerned, I told Mr. Ross that a strike was likely to take place at any moment, but I could not convince him of the danger. On my return to camp I telegraphed to the Prime Minister that a strike was imminent on the C.P.R. and that the results might be serious. I then made arrangements with Mr. George Hope Johnston to go up the line and assist in maintaining order, in case I was attacked by the illness which

I felt was coming on.   The next day I was down with fever, and was ordered to stay in bed.

The men struck before I was convalescent, and Mr. Johnston, with Father Fay and several men of the force, went up the line to the west and advised the strikers to be careful to abstain from any lawlessness.   Father Fay had much influence with the men who were on strike, particularly those of his own church, and could be relied on to the fullest extent.   I was on the mend, but very weak, when the Lieutenant Governor of the North West Territories telegraphed me to come out of the mountains with all my men.   I was obliged to reply to the effect that the strike made it impossible.   I did not report my illness, for I was aware that there was no relief for me, the news having come that the rebellion in the north west had broken out and that there had been an engagement at Duck Lake.   My inclinations were the very contrary to what I felt was my duty, but it would have been sheer madness to leave.   Some days later I had an urgent wire from the Mayor of Calgary to this effect :   " For God's sake, come ;   there is danger of an attack by the Blackfeet ! "   I replied :   " Cannot leave ;   telegraph the Lieutenant Governor.'

The navvies had struck work on April 1, and informed the manager of construction that unless paid up at once in full and more regularly in future they would do no more work. They also openly talked of their intention to commit acts of violence upon the staff of the road and destroy property. A deputation of their leaders came to see me, and I managed to sit up in my chair to receive them.   I assured them that they made a great mistake in striking and that, if they committed any act of violence and were not orderly in the strictest sense of the word, I should inflict on the offenders the severest punishment the law would allow me.   They saw the manager of construction, who promised to do the best he could if they would return to their camps.   Some were satisfied with this, and several hundreds returned to their work.   Many remained at the Beaver, however, where a large number of loose characters were ready to urge them to any mischief, and pretended to be waiting for their money.   They were apparently very quiet, but I learned that they had about 300 of their number, most of them armed with revolvers, who were to watch the strikers at the end of the track and prevent them from doing any work, and that they were ordering the tracklayers to strike, the teamsters to leave their teams and the bridgemen, who were Canadians, to stop work.

I had only eight men at the Beaver, as I had sent detachments to the points threatened, and instructed the men to use the strictest measures with any who tried to prevent the work of construction. Amongst the men sent out was a small party from the post under the command of Sergeant Fury, who proceeded to the place where the tracklayers were to work. A train load of them had been sent out but, intimidated by the strikers, had been driven back to the yards. Mr. James Ross then mounted the engine and proceeded to the spot ; when he came to the strikers' position he told the engineer to put on all steam and run past the crowd, which he did, and although several shots were fired no one was hurt. It was fortunate that this happened at the narrow canyon of the Beaver, for the cutting was only the width of the road bed, so that a few men could hold the position against a multitude. The strikers proceeded to follow the train, making a great uproar and firing their revolvers, but the tracklayers started to work at once, and Sergeant Fury drew his party across the canyon to meet the strikers' advance, and upon their arrival stepped to the front and announced that he would shoot anyone crossing the line. The strikers at this made a great noise and started a hostile demonstration, but the determined attitude of the police, and their strong position with both flanks covered, eventually overawed them, and, seeing the futility of further attempts, they gradually broke up and retired to the Beaver, allowing the tracklayers to finish their day's work.

When the sergeant returned and reported the circumstances of the day, I rose as best I could and sat in a camp chair, awaiting the return of Constable Kerr, one of the men who had been in camp all day and had gone to the end of the track for a bottle of medicine ordered for me. Shortly after I had risen Mr. Johnston came in to see how I was and to ask if there were anything that he could do, and a few minutes later Sergeant Fury returned, stating that Constable Kerr on his way back saw a desperate character inciting the strikers to make an attack on the barracks, and that he had attempted, single-handed, to arrest him, but had been overpowered and forced to leave the ground. After hearing what the sergeant had to say I remarked, " It is a pity that he attempted the arrest without sufficient assistance, but as he has done so we must take the man at any cost. It will never do to let him or the remainder of the gang think they can play with us. Take what men you require and arrest him."

Fury went off at once, but after a long interval returned with his jacket torn and other evidences of a struggle about him, saying as he entered, " They took the prisoner from us, sir." I replied, " That is too bad. Take your revolvers and shoot anyone who interferes with the arrest ! " He started off again, and Johnston went to the window and watched the party cross the bridge which connected our barracks with the town and disappear round some buildings. The men were Sergeant Fury, Constables Fane, Craig and Walters. In a few minutes we heard a shot, and Johnston said, " There is one gone to hell, Steele." I went to the window and saw Craig and Walters dragging the accused man across the bridge, the desperado fighting like a fiend, while a woman in scarlet followed them with wild shrieks and curses. Fury and Fane were in the rear, trying to keep off the crowd. I rushed out, calling upon Mr. Johnston to get the Riot Act and come with me. Seizing the Winchester rifle from the constable on guard at the gaol, I ran to the bridge, and as the crowd was on the point of making a rush on to it, I covered them with the rifle and called upon them to halt or I would fire. They answered with curses and cries of " Look at the —— ; his own death-bed makes no difference to him ! " but they halted. In the meantime the prisoner was struggling fiercely with the men who had him, but half-way across Walters raised his huge fist and struck him over the temple, and with Craig trailed him by the collar, as insensible as a rag. As the woman passed screaming, " You red-coated —— ! " I said " Take her in too ! " and went forward over the bridge to the crowd.

By this time Johnston had joined me with the Riot Act,

which he had to get by kicking the orderly-room door open, the key being with Constable Fane, who was busy in the riot, and we stood together before the rioters. Johnston opened the book, and I said, " Listen to this, and keep your hands off your guns, or I will shoot the first man of you who makes a hostile movement." Johnston then read the Riot Act, and when he had finished I said, " You have taken advantage of the fact that a rebellion has broken out in the north west and that I have only a handful of men, but, as desperate diseases require desperate remedies, and both disease and remedy are here, I warn you that if I find more than twelve of you standing together or any large crowd assembled I will open fire upon you and mow you down ! Now disperse at once and behave yourselves ! " By this time a considerable number of engineers, respectable merchants and contractors, all well armed, had assembled at the barracks to back me up. The eight Mounted Police stood at the head of the bridge under Fury with magazines charged, ready to act when needed. Johnston and I remained where we were until the rioters had dispersed and then sent the man whom Fury had wounded to the hospital for treatment from the C.P.R. doctors. Mr. Ross was very kind to him.

Darkness came on soon after that and, as there was danger of an attack on the gaol to rescue the cause of the trouble, I obtained a locomotive from Mr. Ross and sent the prisoner through the woods to the end of track, whence he was taken to my detachment at Palliser, where there were cells to accommodate him. Next morning Beaver and all along the line was as quiet as a country village on Sunday, and as now was the time I caused all who had been ringleaders in the attempt to prevent the arrest to be brought before Mr. Johnston and myself. They pleaded guilty and were fined 100 dollars each, or 6 months' imprisonment with hard labour. After they were sentenced I went by locomotive to Palliser and tried the man there ; he was sentenced to the same punishment. It was several hundreds of miles over the mountains to the nearest gaol in British Columbia, and, the Mounted Police having been ordered to Calgary, it was deemed best to give lighter punishments in hopes that it would be sufficiently deterrent. We were right ; no further trouble occurred. The strike had collapsed, the roughs of the

Beaver, having had a lesson, were quiet. I was much pleased and so were all the contractors, Mr. Ross especially. The conduct of the police was all that could be desired ; there were only eight at the Beaver at the time, and they faced the powerful mob of 700 with as much resolution as if backed by hundreds. On April 7 the labourers were all paid, and I proceeded at once to Calgary, leaving Sergeant Fury in charge to collect the men and horses when everything had been settled. On my way out Mr. Ross wired to me to return if possible, but I was obliged to reply regretting that my orders to go on to Calgary were imperative.

The rebellion in the north west had broken out in March, but trouble had been brewing for many months. The first report on the subject of unrest was made on July 13, 1884, when Supt. Crozier, who was in command of the police in the North Saskatchewan, stated that the half-breeds claimed to have grievances. Louis Riel, who had been the head of the previous outbreak in the Red River settlement, had been asked by them to come to the country from Montana. He had consented, and was now acting as their leader and representative. This disturber had been living at the half-breed settlement of the Judith Basin, in the State of Montana, where he had eked out an existence by acting as a worker to catch votes for a political party in the United States, and was looked upon with little or no respect.

Throughout July, August and September there were reports of meetings of half-breeds and Indians, which Riel addressed. On September 1 a meeting was held at St. Laurent, where a man called Jackson made an inflammatory speech, in which he said that the North West Territory " belonged to the Indians and not to the Dominion of Canada."

In October a Mounted Police post was established at Carlton, and the police of the northern division were increased to 200, distributed between Battleford, Carlton, Prince Albert and Fort Pitt.

On December 23 Supt. Gagnon, who had been placed in command of the force at Carlton on account of his knowledge of the French language and long experience, reported that the half-breeds of St. Laurent and Batoche had held a public meeting to adopt a petition, which had been duly forwarded to Ottawa, and that Riel was pressed to remain amongst them, and had been presented with a house and would be given a purse next month. It also appeared that the chief grievance amongst the half-breeds was that the government would not sanction the way in which they wished to take their homesteads, viz., ten chains front on the Saskatchewan River and a depth of two miles, a system to which they had been accustomed in the Red River settlement. They had in many cases laid out their lots in that way, so as to have a frontage on the river for everyone. No doubt that grievance should have been settled forthwith.

During January reports from several posts indicated " all quiet." The next report was that the agitation seemed to have died a natural death and that Riel had said that he was going to leave the country as he was not recognized by the government as a British subject. This was considered necessary on his part to enable him to fan the flames. The result was that a meeting was held to induce him to stay in the country, to which request he consented.

On March 10 Gagnon telegraphed that the half-breeds were excited and moving about more than usual and that they proposed to prevent supplies going in after the 16th. On the 11th the commissioner received a telegram from Crozier at Carlton, ordering a seven-pounder gun and 25 men to that place from Battleford.

He again telegraphed Colonel Irvine : " Half-breed rebellion liable to break out at any moment. Troops must be largely reinforced. If half-breeds rise the Indians will join them." Colonel Irvine recommended that at least 100 men should be sent at once, and on the 15th telegraphed to the department at Ottawa : " Lieutenant Governor thinks I should go north at once ; roads and rivers will soon break up." In reply he received orders to start for the north with all available men and 20 horses from Calgary.

On the 17th Crozier telegraphed : " Present movements and preparations have quieted matters. No cause for alarm now." There was no likelihood of this apparent security being able to continue, at least Colonel Irvine thought not, and he carried out existing arrangements, his opinion being confirmed by two urgent appeals from Crozier on the 18th for more men, followed on the 19th by the report that the halfbreeds had seized stores at the South Saskatchewan and had made Mr. Lash, the Indian agent, prisoner, besides committing further depredations.

On the 18th Colonel Irvine left Regina with 4 officers, 86 N.C.O.'s and men and 66 horses, all that could be spared, but ridiculously small for the purpose of holding the north.   At the small station on the Salt Plain, where they camped for the night, he received a dispatch from Crozier to the effect that some Indians had already joined the rebels and that others were likely to join them shortly.   Their numbers were estimated at from 200 to 400.

At Humboldt they were joined by Mr. Hayter Reed, assistant Indian commissioner, who remained with Colonel Irvine throughout.   At that point it was learned that about 400 halfbreeds were assembled at Batoche to prevent the police from joining Crozier.

On the 23rd the rebels broke camp, and soon afterwards Colonel Irvine was informed that the mail station at Hoodoo had been sacked by them.   He found that the report was correct.   Everything in the shape of provisions and grain had been looted.   The stage driver had been made prisoner and carried off with his horses.

On the 24th the commissioner and party kept on the Batoche trail for six miles, then turned in a north-easterly direction towards Agnew's Crossing of the South Saskatchewan, thus outflanking the half-breeds at Batoche.   The march was continued in the evening, and Prince Albert was reached about 8 p.m.   In reaching Prince Albert the commissioner felt that the most difficult and arduous part of the object in view, viz., affecting a junction with Crozier's force at Carlton, had been effected in a markedly successful manner.   The plan of the rebels had been to prevent an increase to the force at Carlton by resisting the crossing of the south branch of the Saskatchewan.

Soon after his arrival he received much valuable information from Mr. Thomas Mackay.   He had intended to reach Carlton on March 25, but, on Mr. Mackay's assurance that all was quiet at that post and as his horses had been travelling over a frozen trail for nearly 300 miles, and it was necessary that their shoeing should be attended to, the men's outfit inspected and volunteers engaged to defend the place, Colonel Irvine decided to remain there for the day and keep Crozier informed of his movements and strength by sending a despatch to him giving full particulars.

On the 26th Colonel Irvine left Prince Albert for Carlton, taking with him 83 of his men and 25 volunteers. The services of the latter were offered with a perfect knowledge of the dangers which they had to face, but like loyal and gallant citizens of our country they were ready and anxious to be employed. Colonel Irvine engaged them in order to increase the number of the Mounted Police available for service outside the post, and by prompt action to crush the rebellion at the outset. He knew that if this were not done thousands of Indians would be on the warpath, and it would require a fair-sized army to subdue them. It was not his intention to take the Prince Albert men from their homes for any great length of time, for they would soon be required there with their families, and besides, Prince Albert was an important point and must be guarded. This was made known to the citizens when they were engaged.

During the afternoon Colonel Irvine received the following from Supt. Gagnon : " Supt. Crozier with 100 men started out on Duck Lake trail to help one of our sergeants and small party in difficulty at Mitchell's store. I have 70 men and can hold the fort against odds. Do not expect Crozier to push on further than Duck Lake. Everything is quiet here."

The force was pushed on rapidly on receipt of the despatch, hoping to be in time to avert further trouble, but on top of the hill above Carlton the commissioner received another despatch from Gagnon, which read :   " Crozier exchanged shots with rebels at Duck Lake ; 6 men reported shot, Crozier retreating on Carlton. Everything quiet here, but ready for an emergency."

Colonel Irvine arrived at Carlton in the afternoon of the 26th and there met Crozier, who had just returned from Duck Lake. Early that morning he had sent a party, consisting of a sergeant and 17 constables, with 8 sleighs under Mr. Thomas Mackay of Prince Albert, to secure a quantity of provisions and ammunition from the store of Mr. Mitchell, a trader of Duck Lake. When within 3 miles of Duck Lake, Mr. Mackay, who was riding in front, saw 4 of the Mounted Police scouts falling back, pursued by a large number of half-breeds and Indians, whereupon Mackay rode back to the sleighs, halted them and ordered the men to load their rifles and get ready. Then like a true Mackay he went forward to meet the rebels, who were all well armed and mounted and being rapidly reinforced.

They behaved in a very overbearing and excited manner, demanding the surrender of the party. Mackay refused to surrender and told them in Cree that if they fired, two could play at that game, and all the time Gabriel Dumont and others kept prodding loaded and cocked guns against Mackay's ribs, at the same time threatening to blow out his brains! Two of them jumped on a sleigh belonging to his party and tried to get possession of the team, but the fearless Mackay ordered the driver not to give it up, and all the while the Metis jeered at his small party and called out, " Now, if you are men, come on ! " Mackay then fell back on Carlton, cautioning the rebels not to follow and keeping a sharp look out upon them.

In the meantime a scout had warned Crozier, and on Mackay's return to the fort, Crozier started for Duck Lake with a bronze 7-pounder and 100 officers and men to secure the stores which the first party had not been able to get.

He met the rebels about a mile and a half from Mitchell's store. After half an hour's fighting it was quite evident that the way to Duck Lake could not be forced and that to remain longer on the field against such odds would mean much greater loss, if not annihilation. The attempt to continue the fight was then abandoned, Crozier withdrawing his men in good order to Carlton. Mr. Thomas Mackay was the last man of the rearguard, and on taking a final shot at Dumont, leader of the rebels, he wounded him in the head. This deterred the half-breeds from pursuing the force ; they would not venture without Dumont. We lost 9 killed and 14 wounded, of whom 3 subsequently died.

In connection with the fight at Duck Lake, Colonel Irvine states in his report :

As you will doubtless notice from the substance of my previous remarks, I cannot but consider it a matter of regret that, with the knowledge that both myself and command were within a few miles of and en route to Carlton, Superintendent Crozier should have marched out as he did, particularly in the face of what had transpired earlier in the day. I am led to the belief that this officer's better judgment was overruled by the impetuosity displayed by both the Police and Volunteers. However, once this action had been taken, much confidence, power and prestige were established throughout the rebel ranks, and thus Riel found his hands materially strengthened. In saying this, let me beg you to understand that I do not for a moment lose sight of the steady conduct and most gallant bearing of our officers, non-commissioned officers and men, and the Prince Albert Volunteers, under the most severe fire experienced during the whole campaign.

Even before Colonel Irvine arrived at Carlton he felt assured of the determined opposition which the loyal forces would meet from the Metis, who relied on the blood relationship between them and the Indians to bring the latter over to them as allies.

On Colonel Irvine's arrival a council of war was held to decide upon what action should be taken under the circumstances, and the unanimous opinion was that the safety of the country lay in placing Prince Albert in a tenable position, and it was necessary that the Volunteers should return there to guard their homes, families and property. Colonel Irvine was strongly and justly of this opinion, and it was agreed to, as Prince Albert and the country in the vicinity represented the only white settlement within hundreds of miles. Battleford, a very small one, lay about 140 miles distant, and the next was Fort Qu'appelle. The section south of the white settlement of Prince Albert was already in possession of the rebels, and consisted of their habitations and farms. In view of the opinion of the council it was decided by Colonel Irvine to evacuate Carlton, and the force was scarcely outside the gates when the place was in flames, caused by a fire which had been lighted to warm up a room for the wounded.

No sooner did the news of the Duck Lake fight spread through the land than the people of the whole prairie region were in a state of alarm. The Indians along the North Saskatchewan, already warned by the emissaries of Riel, rose in rebellion, or were ready to do so, according to the turn which events should take. The settlers, missionaries, Indian department employees, telegraph operators and others were either murdered or had to fly for their lives to Mounted Police or Hudson's Bay posts. Prince Albert, Battleford, Fort Saskatchewan and Edmonton were crowded to the limit of their accommodation, and the citizens of every town in the west organized home guards and prepared for defence.

On receipt of the report of the Duck Lake fight troops were hurried to the front. The first ordered were the 90th Winnipeg Rifles and the 13th Winnipeg Field Battery. The difficulty of moving troops from eastern Canada at that time of the year when the lakes were frozen was very great. The C.P.R. along the north shore of Lake Superior had not yet been completed, and long stretches between the sections already constructed had to be passed by the troops along the ice-bound shores of the lake.

In the meantime the presence at Prince Albert of the N.W.M.P. saved that settlement from falling into the hands of the Metis and their fierce allies. The place was the key of the loyal position in that part of the north west, and had it been taken there is no doubt the rebellion would have assumed greater proportions. At one time large numbers of Sioux Indians moved with the intention of making a raid upon it ; but they abandoned the scheme when they saw the trail of the Mounted Police leading to Prince Albert. The loyalty of a large number of Indians and half-breeds was doubtful ; they had to be carefully watched, and eventually the powerful influence of the Mounted Police and loyal citizens of Prince Albert deterred considerable numbers of rebel sympathizers from going over to the enemy. In the meantime General Middleton, with a contingent of troops, arrived in the disturbed area, and Colonel Irvine suggested to him that their forces should combine, but at that time he was under the impression, from the nature of the messages of the G.O.C., that he had only a total strength with him of 350 men, with 1000 following. He also had reason to believe that the attack would take place before the larger force could arrive.

An impression got abroad that the Mounted Police should have attacked at the same time as the troops, but, whether they should have done so or not, they could not have moved without General Middleton's orders, which were to the effect that they were to hold Prince Albert and not join in the attack. Besides, it does not seem to be generally known that the commander of the Mounted Police was in such a position at Prince Albert that he could not know what steps were taken in the east with regard to sending troops into the North West Territory, and it was not until April 16, when Messrs. McDowall and Bedson arrived at Prince Albert by Carrot River, that he was aware that General Middleton had with him a force of 1200 men. Through those gentlemen, the general informed Colonel Irvine, over his own signature, that they were sent to communicate with him. He stated in the message that he intended to attack Batoche on April 18 ; he might be delayed until the 19th, and he also put in a proviso that he might attack earlier. Mr. McDowall stated clearly and positively that General Middleton's orders were that Colonel Irvine was not to attack, but to look for " flying half-breeds." The G.O.C. seemed to be under the impression that the rebels would offer no resistance, but would fly on the approach of his column.

After Messrs. McDowall and Bedson had consulted with Colonel Irvine they saw clearly the importance of the main body of the force remaining at Prince Albert, and they gave him the impression that they would " inform General Middleton accordingly." They left Prince Albert on April 17 with the intention of making for Humboldt and joining General Middleton's column, which they thought would be moving for Batoche. In consequence of this, Colonel Irvine, on April 19, proceeded towards Batoche with a force of 200 mounted men for a distance of 12 miles, sending his scouts well to the front, but he got no information that the G.O.C. was near Batoche, and, none being forthcoming, he very justly concluded that there was delay in the previously contemplated advance of the troops ; ascertaining that none of them were attacking at Batoche, and receiving on the same night a letter from Prince Albert to the effect that it was not unlikely that an attack was contemplated on that place, he very properly decided to return, a step which subsequent events proved to be a wise one to take.

Soon after Messrs. McDowall and Bedson had departed, and when Colonel Irvine had returned with his command to Prince Albert, he learnt from one of his scouts that General Middleton was marching on Clarke's Crossing, and on April 30 Scout Linklater, whom he had previously sent out, returned to Prince Albert, bringing the following letter from General Middleton.

Fish Creek, April 26.

Attacked here on the 24th and after a smart fight drove the enemy back, but lost too many to repeat, so shall make for Hudson's Bay Ferry, where your barges are. Our loss was 6 killed, 4 died since, and 43 wounded. Hear the whole force was opposed to us and believe we have inflicted heavy loss, and have captured a lot of cattle and horses. Our men are in good heart, cannot move at once as the wounded must be sent to the rear. I have ordered Otter to send a regiment to you, if he can spare it, from Battleford, where all is quiet. You may expect me at the Ferry about Thursday, or one of the following days. Have the steamers there to guard the ferry.

Colonel Irvine had, on his own responsibility, anticipated the general's wishes by building scows and posting a guard on the Hudson's Bay Ferry, and on May 3 advised General Middleton that a steamer had left for Hudson's Bay Ferry, South Branch, and that 4 scows and 4 lifeboats were at the Ferry in charge of 2 officers and 31 men. Later Colonel Irvine learned that another change of plans was made and that the other troops would march to Batoche via Gabriel's Crossing and then proceed to the Hudson's Bay Ferry.

This period was the most critical for Prince Albert. The force available for any operations had been much reduced owing to the number of men employed outside. The settlement was $5\frac{1}{2}$ miles in length, and its normal population of 700 had been increased by refugees to more than double that number. There were large quantities of provisions, many valuable

P

buildings and several steamboats, which had been laid up there for the winter. It would therefore seem reasonable that, in the event of the troops receiving a check which would cause delay, there might be an attack made upon the town.

During the whole of the campaign Colonel Irvine's scouts performed valuable services under their daring and capable leader, Mr. Thomas Mackay. They were constantly in touch with General Middleton's force and repeatedly drove back Riel's scouts. Their presence was so dreaded by Riel that he threw up strong entrenchments on the left bank of the South Saskatchewan opposite to Batoche. After the battle at that place Diehl and Armstrong, scouts sent out by Colonel Irvine with dispatches to General Middleton, were two of the three who captured the rebel leader.

The battle of Batoche took place on May 11, and on the 17th of the same month the gallant Prince Albert Volunteers were disbanded, their services being no longer required. It will be seen from this short and absolutely accurate account of the share that Colonel Irvine and his force took in the suppression of the rebellion of 1885 that he and his little force performed the duty under the direct and positive orders of the G.O.C. Yet during the whole of the operations the eastern press teemed with aspersions against Colonel Irvine and his men ; the newspapers containing these were read in the militia camp daily by all ranks. The war correspondents were there who published such stuff as " What is Colonel Irvine doing ? What are the Mounted Police doing ? Why do they not come out and attack Riel ? " Attack him ! with two hundred men, and leave Prince Albert open to rapine and murder ! Such was the tenor of many of the articles ; but in spite of the fact that they were known to headquarters, no effort was made on the part of the officer responsible for Colonel Irvine's movements to disabuse the mind of the public, poisoned as it was by the slanders sent abroad.

CHAPTER XII

ON the outbreak of the rebellion and the removal of the N.W.M.P. from their midst to reinforce Colonel Irvine, the citizens of Calgary were thrown into a dreadful state of alarm, and at their request Major General Strange, who happened to be in the town, organized a troop of scout cavalry and a home guard for the town. Major Hatton, an ex-officer of the Canadian militia, organized a cavalry corps, which was gazetted as the Alberta Mounted Rifles.

Major General Strange, whose ranch adjoined the Blackfeet reservation, in pursuance of his orders from General Middleton, proceeded to take command of the District of Alberta. Orders were sent to Superintendent Cotton, commanding at Fort Macleod, to make arrangements for its defence. Captain Jack Stewart, an ex-officer of militia who owned the Stewart ranch, raised from the cowboys and others in the Macleod country a mounted corps which was gazetted as the Rocky Mountain Rangers, to patrol along the border and towards Medicine Hat. Cotton established dispatch riders at different points between Fort Macleod and Calgary, and, with his Mounted Police patrols, kept in constant touch with the Indians on the Blood and Peigan reserves. Later, at Strange's request, he sent a field gun and a detachment of Mounted Police, under Inspector Perry, to join the column which the general organized to march on Edmonton.

When the organization of this column was commenced the people were found to be in an entirely defenceless state. Not only were settlers in the district without arms, but the cowboys and ranchmen, a class never hitherto without them, had, though surrounded by reserves of well-armed Indians, relied on the protection of our small force and the proximity of the railway.

I arrived at Calgary from the Beaver River early on April 11, and found the inhabitants in a very excited state. Many ladies were at the train with their families, on their way east. I was placed on duty at once, General Strange telegraphing to the Lieutenant Governor for permission to take me with him in command of his mounted troops.

On the 12th the 65th Regiment Mount Royal Rifles, French Canadians from Montreal, arrived by train, under the command of Lt.-Col. J. A. Ouimet, M.P., with Lt.-Col. Hughes, a staff officer of the 6th Military District, as second in command.

At the request of Mr. White, our comptroller, I named Mr. G. H. Johnston as my deputy at the Beaver, and he came to Calgary for instructions to organize " specials."

My appointment to the command of the cavalry and scouts of the Alberta Field Force was confirmed, and I was gazetted major in the Canadian militia. While transport teams were being organized I was directed to raise a mounted corps, which the general did me the honour to name Steele's Scouts.

From all sides messages came in imploring protection. The Indians had risen and destroyed farms in the vicinity of Red Deer, Beaver Lake, Victoria and Saddle Lake. Big Bear's band, whose reserve was at Frog Lake, near Fort Pitt, had massacred nearly all the white men who were employed there, and those spared, as well as the people at Fort Pitt, were reported to be in Big Bear's hands. Ermine Skin's and Bob-tail's bands, whose reserves lay north of Battle River, had plundered the Hudson's Bay Company's stores and the missions, but subsequently repented, through the influence of Father Scollen, who remained with them. The settlers at Red

Deer who came in for help were supplied with rifles and escorted back to their homes.

A few days later the Winnipeg Light Infantry, under Lt.-Col. W. Osborne Smith, C.M.G., arrived and encamped near the barracks.

Before we left for the north to restore the settlers to their homes and bring to justice the Frog Lake murderers, many leading men offered their services to the general, amongst them the Rev. John McDougall, who was one of the best scouts in the west, being as much at home in the canoe, on the trail, or running wild buffalo as he was in the pulpit.   He brought with him four Mountain Stony scouts, and was gladly accepted, the general arranging that he should proceed in advance to Edmonton with his Indians to inform the people there that succour was coming.

On April 19 my Mounted Police, the scouts, and the right wing of the 65th, with transport and fifteen days' supplies, were ready to march.   The left wing of the 65th, under Perry, who had been gazetted major, was to follow with the gun a few marches behind us.   The Winnipeg Light Infantry was to remain at Calgary until the Alberta Mounted Rifles, which had some difficulty with its saddlery, was ready to trek.

On the 20th the first column, under General Strange, pulled out from Calgary.   I was in command of the advance guard, and my force was small for the work.   There were 175 teams and the rest of the force to protect.   Nothing that caution could dictate was neglected.   The start in the morning was like a circus.   The horses, with few exceptions, had seldom been ridden, and bucked whenever mounted, until two or three days had gentled them. This little performance interested the men from Montreal as they gazed at the gyrations of the cow-puncher soldiers and Mounted Police.

The scouting of the men the whole way and at all times was excellent and the discipline the very best.   The cowboy has no superior in the world, and in spite of his free life he takes to the order of military experience as if he were born to it.   The Mounted Police and the scouts were, of course, British subjects, but there were in the ranks several American cowpunchers and broncho busters, first-class men, ready for hard work, good-tempered and obedient.

On the 25th we reached the Red Deer, 90 miles from Calgary. The stream was much swollen and rising rapidly. The following day the 65th was sent across the river to scout the dense woods and to cover the passage. The ford was so deep that the waggon boxes of the transport had to be raised on the bolsters to prevent the supplies from getting wet, and several carts were swept away and recovered with difficulty.

At the Blind Man's River, 8 miles further on, General Strange received a dispatch from the Rev. John McDougall, who had arrived at Edmonton with his scouts, to the effect that the place was safe. He approved the general's projected movement to the eastward along the North Saskatchewan to restore the settlers to their homes. Many of them had taken to the woods for refuge from the Indians, and were likely to die of starvation. This movement had already been thought out, and it had been ascertained that scows could be built to transport the gun, infantry and supplies down the river. As I had been over that part of the country before and knew the trails and the settlements, he called me to his tent to discuss the route. After further consideration he sent orders to Mr. McDougall to construct the scows and boats to transport the troops and supplies to Fort Pitt.

On the evening before we arrived at the Battle River the Rev. George Mackay, a brother of Mr. Thomas Mackay, of Prince Albert, came into camp, having ridden 200 miles from Fort Macleod to join the column and offer his services in any capacity. Brave as a lion, an excellent horseman, a good shot and speaking Cree fluently, he was just the man for the cavalry, to whom the general very kindly attached him as chaplain !

At the Battle River we were joined by Fathers Lacombe and Scollen, well known to many of us, who had been busy with the Indians to induce them to keep the peace. We also had confirmation of the report that the Indians of Bobtail's and Ermine Skin's bands had plundered the Hudson's Bay Company's stores. Those chiefs were with the priests, but the general refused to shake hands with them ; they had had for years an unsavoury reputation, and he warned them that on the conduct of themselves and their bands their future treatment would depend. They were a most forbidding pair, and their bands the most depraved in the north west. Even in the days when the buffalo were plentiful the majority of them preferred to loiter about the posts on the frontier rather than make an honest livelihood. They were " coffeecoolers " of the worst type.

We arrived at Edmonton on May 1 and were met by Major Griesbach, my old comrade, who was in command at Fort Saskatchewan, where he had under his protection the whole of the Beaver Lake refugees. My three brothers, Richard, Godfrey and James, were at Edmonton, and were sworn in as scouts. The Home Guard there did much to calm the fears of the people from the settlement who, on hearing of the massacres and murders, had taken refuge in Edmonton, which at that time was a very small place but of great promise. The company was disbanded the day after the arrival of General Strange's column and the men returned to work on their farms in the vicinity.

On the morning of the 6th I moved east by the old Edmonton-Pitt-Carlton trail, with 110 Steele's Scouts under Captain Oswald, 25 Mounted Police under Lieut. J. A. Coryell, two companies of the 65th under Captain Prevost, and a large waggon train of supplies in charge of Mr. John Colman, late of the N.W.M.P. We were the advance and flank guards of the river column which was to be moved by scow down the Saskatchewan.

Before the general left Edmonton he was given a great deal of unnecessary trouble which caused delay to the advance. Objections were made to him by a senior officer to the effect that the construction of the boats was faulty, that the power of resistance of the flour sacks, the only means available for the protection of the men in the boats, should be tested, and finally a request was made to condemn a large proportion of the ammunition issued to the troops. This sort of thing was straight obstruction, and was met by General Strange in a characteristic manner. He ordered a board to assemble and take the evidence of experienced Hudson's Bay Company navigators and boat builders, the penetration of the flour sacks was left to hostile bullets, and those who objected to the quality of the ammunition were advised to reserve their fire for short ranges. The boats were reported fit for service, and the troops held in readiness to embark.

One night the 65th, according to orders, had tied up their scows for the night and were resting, when one of their sentries gave the alarm of Indians! No more was necessary for the corps. They were under arms in a moment and, led by their gallant commander, charged up the heights with loud cheers and swept the prairie with a shower of bullets. Five of my scouts who were out had to lie down in a deep hollow, where there was cover for themselves and their horses, until it was discovered that the sentry's Indians were young poplars waving in the wind!

The first news of the rising had been received by Inspector Dickens from Mr. Rae, the Indian agent at Battleford, 90 miles east of Pitt. It was to the effect that the country was in a state of rebellion, and that the Indians were much excited, but that he had hopes that Dickens and sub-agent Quinn would endeavour to prevent Big Bear and his people from going to Battleford. On receipt of the report Dickens at once advised Quinn to come in if he considered that there was serious danger, and offered to reinforce him if he could not leave. Quinn replied at once that the Indians at Frog Lake were perfectly quiet, and that he was confident that he could keep them there by feeding them well and treating them kindly; but, as the presence of the detachment of Mounted Police might excite them, he would send Corporal Sleigh and party to the fort.

The corporal and his men arrived on April 2 and reported to Dickens that the white people at Frog Lake had at first decided that they would go to Fort Pitt, but Quinn and Farm-Instructor Delaney were determined to remain at their posts, and the others had made up their minds to stay with them. Corporal Sleigh at first refused to leave without the white women, but Quinn insisted that he should leave without them, and gave the corporal a letter to Dickens, explaining why the Mounted Police left and asserting that the Indians were quiet.

Sergeant Martin had been at Onion Lake the same day and

found the Indians excited, firing their rifles and yelling, and they told him that they had been informed that 2,000 soldiers were coming to kill them, but the sergeant told them to keep quiet as there was no danger whatever. This had the effect of calming them for a time. On the 2nd Sergeant Roby, who had been at Onion Lake, reported to Inspector Dickens that the Indians were talking of something which had taken place at Frog Lake, and that Mr. Simpson, of the Hudson's Bay Company, on his way there with freight, had hurried on there hoping to be in time to prevent mischief. Inspector Dickens had redoubled his guard but, although he had the letter of the agent at Battleford, he had little faith in the rumours of Indian war talk. Mr. Quinn had promised to send a messenger in the event of anything serious, but in the afternoon Mr. and Mrs. Mann with their children came in from Onion Lake, the Indians there having informed them that all the white people at Frog Lake had been murdered and that they must fly for their lives, as the Indians had risen and were going to kill all the whites in the country.

On receipt of this news preparations were made at Fort Pitt to receive an attack, the windows and doors of the dwellings and store-houses were barricaded and loop-holes made in the walls. It would have been impossible, however, to have held the post in the night time, for it covered so much ground and had so many combustibles, such as hay and firewood, that it could have been set on fire at any time. It would have required at least 200 well-armed men to defend it, but Dickens prepared to hold out to the last. On April 4 Henry Quinn, a relative of the agent, arrived at the fort and reported that he and the remainder of the white people at Frog Lake had been made prisoners by the Indians and were being taken to camp when he broke away on hearing them say that all the white men would be killed.

He was hotly pursued for a considerable distance, and had with difficulty succeeded in making his escape. The same day the Rev. Mr. and Mrs. Quinney were escorted into Fort Pitt by four of the Onion Lake Indians, and later, John Saskatchewan, a well-known plain-hunter and guide, arrived there with a letter to Dickens, advising him to proceed to Battleford by the north trail. This he refused to do as he had not enough transport and the Indians could easily overtake them travelling slowly, as they would have to do with the women and children, and if attacked in the open they would have to protect them and would be worse off than if they were in the Hudson's Bay post. The civilians were of the same opinion, and, as matters were getting very serious, Dickens wrote to Battleford, asking for 50 men, as under the present circumstances it was impossible to move.

No reply was received to this letter, the bearer having been intercepted, but for all that there was no excuse for leaving the people in Fort Pitt in such a terrible plight. Battleford was perfectly safe and could not only have defended itself but have spared more than 50 men to assist those in distress. It was reported later that 50 N.C.O.'s and men had volunteered to proceed to the relief of Fort Pitt, but were not permitted to go.

In the meantime Dickens continued to strengthen the post, and a scow was being built by the carpenters of the Hudson's Bay Company, when on April 13 a large body of Indians appeared on the rising ground to the north of the post. They had with them as prisoners Cameron, Halpin and Dufresne, of the Hudson's Bay Company. The latter was sent to the fort with a flag of truce. He brought letters from Mr. Halpin, in which he stated that Big Bear demanded the surrender of the arms and ammunition. This offer was, of course, contemptuously refused, and shortly after this Mr. W. J. McLean, believing the Indians to be a peace party, went out to interview the chief, and the latter agreed to keep them quiet that night. But next morning he sent a demand that the Mounted Police leave the place at once. Dickens refused all overtures and would not permit the Indians to approach the fort.

Later on in the day Mr. McLean went out again and was taken prisoner, and constables Cowan and Loasby and Special Constable Quinn, who had been out to ascertain what had occurred at Frog Lake, came upon the Indians, who lay between them and the fort. Young Cowan, a fiery, hot-headed lad, in charge of the party, decided to ride through them. Quinn would not agree to this, and turned back to find his way round.

Cowan and his horse were shot, and the Indians rushed forward and drove muskrat spears into the poor fellow's body, tearing them out again to increase his torture.[1] Loasby's horse was shot under him, but he got up and ran towards the fort, the Indians pursuing him for a considerable distance, until he was struck down wounded, and feigned death, while the redskins took his belt, bandolier and ammunition. By that time the men in the fort had opened fire, compelling them to retreat, while Loasby, under the cover of their rifles, staggered into the fort.

Shortly after this incident darkness came on, and with it a message from Mr. McLean directing his family to join him. The remainder of the civilians prepared to depart with them and surrender to Big Bear, whereupon Dickens, finding that their minds were made up, decided that it was now his duty to see to the safety of his men, who had remained at their post for the protection of the people. He caused the spare arms to be destroyed, collected the food and ammunition and, under cover of darkness, embarked his detachment on the scow. Mrs. McLean did not leave the post until the last man was on board, knowing that it was unlikely that any of the Indians would come to the fort until she went to the camp. The party eventually arrived safely at Battleford.

While these events were transpiring Quinn had gone round to the Saskatchewan, moved along in the shelter of the cut bank until the fort was between him and the Indians, and galloped into it to find to his horror that it was in their possession. He was seized and would have been put to death, had he not said that he was a friend of Mr. McLean, who had done a good turn to the leader when he was in a scrape some years previously. This saved his life, and he was conducted to the camp and placed with the prisoners, amongst whom were Interpreter Pritchard, of the Frog Lake reserve, and the two white ladies from there, Mrs. Gowanlock and Mrs. Delaney, whose husbands had been put to death. They owed their lives to Mr. Pritchard, who, seeing them in the possession

---

[1] On our arrival at Fort Pitt we discovered poor Cowan's remains ; the body had been mutilated by scalping and cutting out the heart, which was found impaled on a stick close by. His horse's remains were found lying near the corpse.

of one of the Indians, gave him a couple of horses for them. This purchase of the ladies is explained by the custom of the Indians in war, which gives them the right to the captive, to dispose of him or her as he pleases.

The day after our arrival before the ruins of Fort Pitt, I sent scouts across the river and to the north and east of our bivouac. Whitford found a heavy trail in the direction of Onion Lake, but there was only the trace of a cart and the print of a white woman's shoe, which had no doubt been picked up by some squaw and appropriated to her use. In the forenoon, when looking round for traces of the direction taken by the hostiles, I found Miss Amelia McLean's first letter to her mother from St. John's Ladies' College at Winnipeg. Mrs. McLean had shown it to me in 1880, and I recognized it at once.

On the afternoon of the 26th Big Bear's trail to the north was found, and I was directed to proceed in pursuit to locate the whereabouts of the enemy. I was ready to start when the general told me that the scouts at headquarters and several gentlemen who were attached to the force were of the opinion that the hostiles had crossed the Saskatchewan and gone south to join Poundmaker, the prominent Cree chief, who had been on the warpath near Battleford early in the spring. I assured him that the south side had been carefully scouted by my best men and a cart trail and the track of a woman's shoe were all that was to be found there, and there was no sign of a large number of the enemy except to the north, where there was a heavy trail going east. The general agreed, and I trekked north, taking with me 2 officers and 90 mounted men. About midnight a Chippeway scout, named Beatty, was brought to me, saying, " Beatty smells Indians and has cold feet ! "

Soon afterwards I halted on the high bank of the Saskatchewan, and to the westward, about 3 miles away, I saw the camp fires of General Strange's column. As it was time to halt, I passed the word to Coryell to keep a sharp look out, and went down the hill with Sergeant Butlin and Corporal McLelland to find a place where I could bivouac without danger of the horses being stampeded. Captains Oswald and Wright followed, and I had just found a suitable bivouac and remarked,

" This is just the thing ! " when an Indian, lying in the grass to my right front, sprang to his feet, fired two shots at us in rapid succession, and ran across my front towards a horse tied to a tree to the left. I turned to fire, but Corporal McLelland, close on my left, was between us, and at 60 yards dropped the red man. When the Indian fired at me I saw another sitting on his horse about 30 yards off, and the moment the Indian discharged his rifle we were in the midst of a yelling, whooping band ; rifles and pistols cracked, while the lurid remarks of Butlin and McLelland could be heard a mile away. The hot flashes of the Winchesters of the Indians almost singed our faces, and several times we had to pause lest we should shoot one another. This lasted a minute, when the Indians departed with headlong speed to the eastward, exchanging shots with my rear party as they passed by. As no more Indians were to be seen, we concluded that this was a party that had been watching the fires of the column with the intention of stampeding the horses as soon as the camp was in darkness.

Soon after daylight I continued east along the Indian trail. At one of their bivouacs I counted where 187 camp fires had quite recently been.

Whitford went to the front, and I had not long to wait for intelligence. He had not been gone more than half an hour when I heard Indian yells and saw him, at the head of his scouts, riding for dear life, followed by a large band of yelling braves, and more could be seen in the hills behind him. I pushed forward some men to cover his retreat, and extended the remainder, dismounted, ready to receive them if necessary, but as soon as the savages caught sight of us they halted at a respectful distance and galloped away. Whitford explained that the scouts had kept together to a place at the hills, where they intended to extend, when he heard a horse stamp as if annoyed by mosquitoes, and his attention was further attracted by hearing an Indian say, " Wait, wait, let them come a little further." Whitford halted and then said in a low tone, " Shall we fight or fall back ? " and the answer was, " Let us draw them ; to fight is no good. We were not sent here for that." Whitford turned at once and came back at the fastest pace until he got to us, followed by the band of yelling Crees.

Shortly afterwards General Strange appeared with the infantry, a small party of Hatton's corps and the 9-pounder gun. The infantry had been placed in waggons to save time, and the 65th Rifles went down the river on the flat boats so as to be ready to land when required. A company of the regiment had been left to fortify and protect what remained of Fort Pitt, and guard the large quantity of stores and camp equipment left there. On reaching me the waggons were formed into a corral under Captain Wright; the drivers, being armed, were able to take care of the transport. When that was arranged the march was resumed. About 2 miles further on the scouts reported the enemy to be holding the wooded hills in front, and the general extended the force and advanced to the attack. No sooner was the movement begun than a fine-looking band of Indians appeared on the summit of a large round butte, about 1,500 yards distant. They were galloping in a circle to warn their camp, their excellent horsemanship and wild appearance making a remarkable picture as they were silhouetted against the blue sky. Directly they were sighted General Strange gave them a shot from the 9-pounder; the first fell short, the next swept the butte, the shrapnel tearing up the grass and gravel a second after the wild horsemen disappeared from the summit. The advance was continued and the position carried. The 65th, on hearing the firing, left their boats and dinners behind them and joined us. Owing to the density of the woods the gun had to keep on the Indian trail. The scouts were far to the front before dark and could be seen moving up the slopes of Frenchman's Knoll, which had changed since I last saw it in 1876 from bare prairie to fairly thick woods. Scout Patton, one of the Edmonton men, was very far forward and obtained a good view of the ridge behind which the Indians were posted. The force was corralled for the night, and great precautions were taken. My scouts were out to the front about a mile; the advanced post, under Patton, could see the glow of some fires amongst the trees along the ridge.

At daybreak next morning the woods were again reconnoitred and the force advanced, the Mounted Police and scouts in front on foot. About half-past six the enemy's position was

located on a thickly-wooded ridge about 600 yards distant
across the valley of the Red Deer. The general ordered me to
turn the enemy's right. The gun came into action with
shrapnel, but soon after I was informed that the force was to
retire out of the woods and I was to cover the movement. The
gun had kept up a rapid fire and no doubt had a good effect,
but no Indians were seen on the ridge. The reason for our
retirement was that a report came in from Hatton's corps to
the effect that the hostiles were turning that flank, and there
appeared to be nothing for it but to get clear of the woods.
The correctness of the report was doubtful. When the force
was clear of the woods it was halted and the situation was discussed. The general decided that the proper thing to do was
to attack the rifle pits on the right and drive the Indians out,
but before giving any orders he had a talk with two senior
officers, and later summoned me. It was clear that his plan
was not received as cheerfully as it merited, and the force
retired to Fort Pitt.

On the 31st we moved out again and on the following day
we found the rifle pits unoccupied. The position proved,
upon careful examination, to be even stronger than anticipated,
300 rifle pits were counted, 200 along the front and 100 in
reserve. Several were large enough to shelter a dozen men,
and many were proof against shells. There was much plunder,
which could not have been carried off ; a great deal of it
very valuable, furs looted from the Hudson's Bay stores at
Pitt and Frog Lake.

Seven trails were found, which eventually led into two,
and these were followed until at daybreak Big Bear's line
of retreat was discovered. In the afternoon the infantry
were busy collecting the waggons, carts, flour, bacon, tools
and furs which had been left behind. The whole of this
was placed in charge of an officer and party of men, to be
restored to the original owners or credited to them, and it
was estimated that there was many thousands of dollars'
worth of loot recovered.

In the night the scouts reported that Mr. and Mrs. Quinney,
Messrs. Halpin, Cameron and Dufresne were in the forest,
having been left behind by Big Bear, and Major Dale with a

few of my scouts brought them into camp. When the Indian trail was reported to me I had only 20 of the Mounted Police, 20 of my scouts, and 22 of the Alberta Mounted Rifles available ; but, as it was important to rescue the remainder of the captives and capture the Frog Lake murderers, I was directed to follow the hostiles.

We could not wait for either the pack-animals or pack-saddles. The supply of ammunition was small, but there was no help for it, as no time was to be lost, and when I was ready to move I had with me Major Hatton, Capt. Oswald, Lieut. Coryell and 62 N.C.O.'s and men. Just as I was moving off the brigade-major ordered Hatton to return at once, and the poor fellow actually wept and broke his hunting crop to pieces on the horn of his stock saddle. General Strange informed me as I moved off that General Middleton had landed, and would be sure to send his mounted troops in support.

At lunch time we were in touch with the enemy's scouts. I pushed forward and charged across an open piece of meadow that lay between us and the Indians, as there was no way round. When we were almost across the Indians fired and wounded one man, but we pushed on gaily. When I was about 50 yards in the woods I heard behind me a fierce war whoop and turned, expecting to see an Indian, but it was our friend, Canon Mackay, who, like the majority of western men and boys brought up among Indians, could utter a war whoop which would make Sitting Bull turn green with envy ! His eyes were blazing as he hurried along uttering his fierce yells. He was dressed in a pea jacket, felt hat and moccasins, his pantaloons were tied with strings round the ankles, and he was obviously full of fight. Further examination of the woods proved, however, that there had been only a small party of scouts, and I hurried on in hopes that they had gone into the forest to the left, so that I could get so far ahead that they could not give warning to Big Bear before I caught sight of him.

The next day the enemy were reported in sight. From a long ridge we saw before us a large and very beautiful lake with many pretty bays ; a long point jutted out from the east side of it, and might be an island ; it was densely wooded to the water's edge. Along the west shore a dry swamp of spruce and tamarac extended, and a semicircular range of hills, bounding a small prairie below us, came round to where we lay. The woods near us being dense the trail could not be seen, but on the side of the lake next the prairie an Indian lodge stood, and in the ford which separated the point or island several Indians were crossing. I suspected that they were a decoy and that there was an ambush along the trail in the woods below us, but, as the proper thing to do was to ask the Indians to surrender, I was about to get the canon to call out in Cree that the war was over, that the remainder of the Indians and half-breeds were defeated and prisoners, that as we were a strong force it was useless for them to continue their retreat, and if they came in only the Indians who had been ringleaders or concerned in the murder of the whites would have to stand trial.

The canon had scarcely got ready to hail them when a party of Indians opened fire upon us, prematurely, I think. Their fire was a signal for us to attack, and we rushed to the front with Indian yells and rolled up the ambuscade which lay along the trail. We drove the Indians out of the swamp on the right front and across the little prairie. They posted themselves under the shelter of the hills opposite to us and again opened fire, their bullets tearing the bark off the trees round my trumpeter, Chabot, and myself. Chabot offered me his rifle to fire at the red men, who seemed to be making fine practice, but I told him to go ahead as I had something else to do, and a few minutes later I heard an Indian chief leading his men with yells of encouragement round the hills to my left front, and to meet the attack sent the men on my left up the hill. They went up in fine style, led by Coryell, Sergeant-Major Fury and Sergeant Macdonell.

On the crest of the hill Fury was wounded and rolled down the steep declivity, whereupon the canon, who had been very forward in using his rifle, ran to his assistance. The remainder, however, rushed on with spirit and, meeting the Indians in the forest, pressed them back with a sharp fire to the ford. My centre men now dashed across the open at the party under the

Q

hill, driving them out of there ; the whole were then forced across the ford, and from there kept up a sharp fire. As we were short of ammunition I deemed it useless to reply, and ordered " Cease Fire " to sound. Accompanied by the canon, I ascended the highest hill commanding the ford, hoisted a white flag and hailed the Indians, who on seeing it ceased fire.

The canon told them what I had intended to say before the fight commenced. He had a splendid deep voice, and every word was distinctly heard by the Indians, who listened attentively, all save one, who kept up a steady fire, causing us to shift our positions each time he obtained the range ; he was an exceptional shot and armed with a good rifle. One of the Mounted Police was standing with his back against a tree. As he had broad shoulders, the Indian could see them project, and placed a bullet just behind the centre of his back but, fortunately, it did not come through.

After hearing what I had to say, the Indians made no reply ; there seemed to be no one to take the lead. A few called out that they would not surrender, and in the meantime, as there was no sign of General Middleton, not even a scout, and more men would be needed to turn the position by the other side of the lake, I caused a count to be made and found that I had only one day's rations and 15 rounds of ammunition per man. Only two men had been wounded, but their hurts were very severe. The worst of the situation was that there was no sign of the promised support which should have been with me early in the day. No one had been sent to ascertain what had become of the little band of 65 men sent in pursuit of 500 desperate and blood-thirsty Indian braves who held in captivity white men, women and children !

Having called once more upon the Indians to surrender, without result, I caused the wounded to be carried along in the best way possible, and withdrew to the top of the ridge from which I had advanced to the attack. I then sent to General Middleton my report, which covered every important point required to enable him to follow the Indians.

As soon as Butlin had gone off with it I left a small party under a N.C.O. to watch the ford and any move of the Indians, and fell back a few miles with the wounded men. The party on the ridge opened fire several times on people whom they took to be Indians, but were no doubt mistaken. Later on I learned that W. J. McLean and Simpson had come forward to surrender the Indians to me, the fight having demoralized the band. This was one of the chances of a lifetime which one misses !

I bivouacked in the woods about 3 miles from the lake, and on June 4 continued the retirement, expecting to meet the troops at any moment, but none appeared. The next day Sergeant Butlin returned with the information that he had delivered my report to General Middleton in person at two o'clock the day I sent him. He had found the troops a few miles in the woods and had been questioned by the G.O.C. as to the trail, but had no message for me ! The column was now only 7 or 8 miles from me trying to make pack saddles, and that remarkable vehicle called a travois had also come into the calculations of the transport officer ; the troops were mounted and had Gatling guns.

Next morning General Middleton and his A.D.C. appeared, and I gave full particulars as to the best way to proceed. The general then ordered me to rejoin General Strange's columns, but changed his mind and decided to take me with him.

The force arrived at Loon Lake on the second day, and halted on the hill which overlooked the scene of the fight. After examining the ground we crossed to the opposite side and discovered some newly-made graves, which the general caused to be opened to ascertain if any of the remains were those of the captives. There were trails in several directions from there, one of them led south-east and was no doubt that of Big Bear's Crees escaping to the United States. From the camp a good view of the large and beautiful lake was obtained ; few white men had seen it until Big Bear's band arrived with their captives. No exploration of that part of the Great Lone Land had ever been made.

The same afternoon two scouts who had crossed the little narrows reported that they had seen the dead body of a squaw who had hanged herself on account of being lame and unable to keep up with the rest of the people. They stated that there was a muskeg on the far side of where she was found, and, as it was important that it should be examined, I crossed the narrows.

From there I went on with the scouts to the muskeg they had reported, which, upon careful examination, I found to be a swamp with a solid bottom 2 feet below the surface. The two scouts crossed without any trouble, as the Indian men, women, captives and children had already done, their trail being quite distinct. It was quite practicable for the mounted troops, but not for the Gatlings. There were indications that the Indians were not very far away.

The remainder of the force crossed the narrows, excepting, of course, the Gatling guns and a small escort. It has been said that the muskeg was impassable, but this statement is incorrect. It may by some have been considered impracticable, but this contention is absurd in the face of the fact that delicate women and children had been able to traverse it a few days previously. The staff, however, would not listen to any representations made by members of the Mounted Police, nor to the evidence of their own senses, but leaned on those who had no experience to guide them, with the usual results.

The official report states that the whereabouts of Big Bear were still uncertain ! Well might it be, for that wily chieftain was well on his way to Carlton, where he was captured on July 2 by Sergeant Smart and another man of the Mounted Police.

On the afternoon of the 15th General Middleton had a pow-wow with some of the Chippewayans, who, it is said, went unwillingly with Big Bear. This was sheer nonsense, mere romance. Father Le Goff was present. He had done his best to make his Indians keep the peace, but until they came under the fire of Strange's rifles they were keen enough to break the law. After the pow-wow two of them were sent down the river in search of Big Bear. The next day a pet fox, said to belong to the McLean family, was found, and one of the staff, in real earnest, remarked, " Ah, we have something tangible at last ! " This was the same officer who remarked to one of the transport officers that he had been conversing with some of the drivers and had found them to be " quite intelligent " ! To which that irrepressible joker replied, " If I find any of them possessed of any such quality, out he goes ! They have their orders pasted inside the crowns of their hats, and that is all that is required." Whereupon he was reported to be mad.

On our return to Fort Pitt I called on Mr. McLean and asked him about his captivity. He stated that when he went out the second time from Fort Pitt to Big Bear's camp on the hill he was detained a prisoner. When Constable Cowan was murdered, he was covered by the rifle of Wandering Spirit, the chief of the Frog Lake miscreants, and, on pain of instant death, compelled to ask his family to leave the fort and join him, accompanied by the rest of the whites who had taken refuge there.

Some time after Dickens and his detachment of Mounted Police had left the post, Big Bear's band, the Wood Crees and Chippewayans, departed for the position near Frenchman's Butte and entrenched themselves, and when they saw General Strange's column arrive at Fort Pitt Big Bear sent out a party to stampede the horses. This band was joined by 30 more, and were the same with whom I came in contact when I left Pitt on Big Bear's trail.

When General Strange attacked the Indians at Frenchman's Butte there were more than 500 Indian warriors in the rifle pits. He and the captives were some distance off under guard. The Indians had the range of all the positions and kept up a steady fire, until the gunners found the true range and killed several in the pits. A retreat of the Indians was the next move, but, with the exception of a few scattered bands, they went north after Big Bear, taking the McLeans and Simpson and Fitzpatrick with them.

After the attack at Loon Lake Big Bear's band broke up, and the squaws of the Plain Crees threatened to butcher the captives, but the Wood Crees protected them. The Plain Indians went south-east, except a few of the murderers, who went north with the Wood Crees. The latter took the captives with them, but before any move was made McLean and Simpson were sent by the Indians to surrender them to me, and they went to the ford to hoist the white flag and proclaim the fact, but when they approached, the fire from my scouts on the hill was so hot that they could not show themselves and were forced to retreat into the woods.

On the day following the Wood Crees and their captives crossed the narrows and muskeg and went on to Beaver River, suffering much hardship en route, crossed it and halted about 10 miles further on, not far from Lac des Isles, where they held several councils. Mr. McLean addressed the Indians through an interpreter and explained to them that, as long as they held him and the other captives, the troops would be kept in the field in pursuit of them, and as it was impossible for them to make a living they would eventually die of starvation, and it would be better for them to release himself and his fellow prisoners at once.

During these councils the Indian women used to go near enough to hear what was said, and, influenced by Mr. McLean's remarks to the chiefs, upbraided them for their obstinacy. Before long all but Dressy Man, the wretch who had taken the leading part in the murder of Constable Cowan, were willing to release the captives, and eventually he was persuaded to let them depart. When this was arranged they left for the south. At the Beaver River they fortunately met a party of friendly Indians and were ferried across in their canoes. At the muskeg, where General Middleton had retired, they found some tins of canned corned beef which had been left there by the troops. These were a welcome change from the rancid pork upon which they had been forced to exist. At Loon Lake they were met by Mr. Bedson, Mr. Hayter Reed and George Ham, with supplies of food and clothing, and the trail from there having dried and been much improved since they had passed over it, they were soon at Fort Pitt.

The whole of the force except those on the lines of communication having concentrated at Pitt, there was a little delay waiting for the boats to take them down the river.

Before the column broke up Major General Strange issued farewell orders, in which every unit was remembered, and Major General Middleton in his dispatch stated : " I have already sent to the Comptroller of the N.W.M.P. the names of those officers of that corps who came under my personal command whom I desire to mention as having done excellent work during the campaign, and to whom my thanks are greatly due, in Lt.-Col. Herchmer, Major Steele, Major Perry, Inspector White Fraser."

Major General Strange mentioned me in his dispatches thus : " Major Steele and his cavalry were the eyes, ears and feelers of the force, and their spirited pursuit of Big Bear crowned with success the long and weary march which they had protected and, to a certain extent, guided.   The Rev. John McDougall and Canon Mackay, from their large and intimate knowledge of the country, were usefully connected with the force."

General Strange also recommended me to General Middleton for the C.M.G. in these words : " I have the honour to submit for your favourable consideration the name of Major Samuel Steele, Superintendent of N.W.M. Police, who commanded the cavalry of the Alberta Field Force under my command during the late campaign.   I need not detail to you the eminent services he rendered, as already mentioned in my dispatches, as well as in that forwarded by him when sent forward by me with my cavalry in pursuit of Big Bear's band, also the details of organization he carried out in raising scouts under my command.   I beg respectfully to submit that he has earned the distinction of a C.M.G., usually bestowed for military services to the Empire in connection with the Colonies."

It did not matter, however, who was mentioned in dispatches, no one but the G.O.C. received any reward.   He was voted in parliament the sum of 20,000 dollars and was knighted ; but there was nothing for General Strange after all his hard work. He had saved Alberta, had rescued the captives who had been in Big Bear's hands, not one shot had been fired against the chief or his murderous tribe and their allies, the Wood Crees, except by Strange's men, and he should certainly have been granted the K.C.M.G.   It is not too late now, however, and it is hoped that steps will be taken to do him justice

I left Fort Pitt on July 3 and, having been informed that some of the teamsters who were ahead of me on the route to Edmonton intended to loot Saddle Lake Indian reserves and take the farm implements, I sent Sergeant Parker, of the Mounted Police, ahead with a party to prevent it. He was in the nick of time ; many of them had their teams loaded up with machinery and other articles, which Parker compelled them to restore before they left. This action saved the government the loss of several thousand dollars' worth of property. One of my men, however, on the march to Pitt, had accidentally damaged a set of weighing scales. Of this the Indian department took due notice, but not of the action taken to save their property. Such is life !

We arrived in Calgary on the evening of the 18th. The Mayor and the Council and a large concourse of citizens met us and presented us with an address of welcome. The reception was enthusiastic, and everyone did his best to make our stay agreeable. On the 19th I received a telegram from Mr. White, congratulating me on being promoted ; Major Perry also was gazetted, but it was some weeks before any more names appeared. As soon as my men were paid off, the citizens of Calgary gave us a banquet and presented me with a valuable diamond ring.

Shortly afterwards I went to Winnipeg for ten days. A few days later, on my return from the Winnipeg races to the hotel, the young constable who was with me came to me in a great hurry to say that he had seen the ruffian " Bull Dog Kelly " on the train coming from the races, and he had asked him if I had a warrant for his arrest. He had replied that he knew of none, and had scarcely spoken when Kelly jumped off the train near the station and disappeared.

On hearing this it struck me that Kelly was the man who had murdered Mr. Baird the year before, and I reported this to Murray, of the Winnipeg Police, who had been informed by me of the murder and the large rewards offered for the arrest of the murderer, and he came to the same conclusion as myself, that Kelly was the man. Accompanied by Sergeant McRae, until two years ago chief of the force, Murray went in pursuit of Kelly. Taking the train to Crookston, Dakota, they found him in one of the hotels. Stealing cautiously up to his bedroom they hurled themselves against the door, bursting it open and securing their man. Had they undertaken the arrest in any other way there would have been some shooting ! They then lodged their prisoner in gaol in Crookston to await an investigation, and I hurried back to the Rocky Mountains to have the case worked up. When I arrived there I found that Dainard, who had known all the time but was afraid to speak, was now ready to swear that " Bull Dog Kelly " had fired the fatal shot. What an amount of trouble we should have been saved had he spoken out at the time !

The evidence was damning and conclusive but, although the commissioner reported in favour of extradition, the authorities at Washington would not sign the papers, and Kelly was released, but was again arrested in Minneapolis and brought before another commissioner, with the same result. The Attorney General, or his deputy, from Victoria, B.C., was there watching the case for Canada, but as the proceedings had already cost many thousands of dollars it was not deemed wise to do any more. The murdered man was an honourable American citizen ; the murderer was an American. We had done our duty according to our traditions of justice, and there was nothing to be done but abandon the case. Kelly died a violent death the following year. His right name was McNaughton, and during the trials he was encouraged by the fact that the desperado who had inspired the crime was present with a large amount of money supplied by the criminal class in Chicago and the members of a secret organization noted for its hatred of everything British.

I now returned to British Columbia and resumed my duties as the Dominion commissioner of police. The saloons, gambling houses and dives for the ruination of the navvies were, as before, in spite of the Peace Preservation Act, licensed to sell intoxicants. The government of British Columbia still held that the province should not be deprived of its revenue through the enforcement of a Dominion act of parliament, and fees must be collected, the rum seller take care of himself, the dram drinker take his chances, regardless of the consequences to his morals.

The B.C. stipendiary had been after the " specials " employed by the Dominion when I was away on the prairie, and made a particular point to designate them as North West

Mounted Police, which he well knew they were not. He corresponded regularly with the B.C. papers and did his utmost to bring discredit upon Mr. Johnston and his men, who had at best a hard uphill fight against the lawless element, supported as they were by this mistaken policy of the worthy gold commissioner and stipendiary magistrate. Some of the worst characters on the American continent had congregated in this place. Road agents and confidence men had to be watched, and it was marvellous that there were no murders or hold-ups. To prevent this we had to be constantly on the watch, and the Mounted Police court was full of cases from 9 a.m. until dark.

Before I arrived an unpleasantness occurred between the Dominion magistrate and his hard-headed countryman " frae the borders " through one of the Dominion special constables having arrested a man in the act of bringing in a cargo of intoxicating liquor by pack train. The prisoner complained to the magistrate of B.C., who at once issued a warrant for the special, charging him with highway robbery. The B.C. constable, who was deputed to execute it, was himself arrested for assaulting the constable in the execution of his duty and sentenced to seven days' imprisonment. The B.C. magistrate then issued a warrant for the arrest of the Dominion magistrate, swore in a large number of specials, and, when he appeared on the streets, had him seized and brought before him for preliminary hearing and released him on bail for a large amount. It would not have been safe to have attempted the arrest in any other way, for the assaulting party would have found that the stronghold on the hill contained as determined men as the ancestors of its chief, who, when they were asked in the midst of their revelry, after one of their famous raids on the innocent people of Cumberland, the following question, " Are there nae Christians in this hoose ? " replied, " Na, na, only Johnstons and Jardines ! " Be that as it may, however, the arrest was made, the prisoner was bailed, and Colonel Macleod, fresh from his valuable work in keeping the Blackfeet Nation quiet during the rebellion, appeared to " clear up the situation."

When he arrived I called upon him, introduced the two magistrates to him, and he sized them up in no time. The accused appeared in court, and eloquent and feeling addresses caused the disputants to shed tears over the fact that " twa chiels frae the borders " should have such a " fa' oot." They were soon reconciled over a glass of hot Scotch and a pipe, and the gallant and tactful Colonel Macleod departed, well pleased with the success of his mission.

Soon after peace was restored I was again at the first crossing, when my friend the sheriff wired me from the Roger's Pass, " Please arrest —— for interfering with an officer in the execution of his duty." I replied : " Report the circumstances to the non-com. in charge at the summit." I heard no more of this for at least a month, and then when I met the sheriff I said : " What about that case of yours at the summit ? " His eye gleamed with satisfaction and he answered : " It was just this way. I went into a restaurant and ordered a dozen hard-boiled eggs. There was a man sitting opposite to me, and he began to help himself to my eggs. I hit him on the nose ; we had a desperate fight, and I got him into the wood-box (a box for fuel) and, would you believe it, he tore the side out with his teeth ! "

From this time on I was able to utilize the valuable services of Mr. Johnston, who had done such good work during my absence. Mr. James Ross had given him a very high character, and he was very busy in court until the railway was completed. In November the line was ready for the last spike, and Mr. James Ross arranged for an excursion to Victoria, B.C. The principal directors in Canada who could spare the time and the leading men of the staff arrived from the east by a special train, passing through Revelstoke on the morning of November 7, picking up several of us who had the privilege of proceeding with them. There were two well-filled trains of excursionists, and when they arrived at the place, Mr. Donald Smith seized the heavy sledge hammer provided for the occasion and with vigorous strokes drove the spike which united the great Dominion from ocean to ocean.

Amongst those present were Mr. James Ross, manager of construction, Mr. W. C. van Horne, manager of the C.P.R., Mr. Sandford Fleming, Mr. James A. Dickey, Dominion government engineer, Mr. John M. Egan, superintendent of the lines west of Fort William, Mr. John McTavish, land commissioner for the company, and many others.

The trains now continued on their way, passing over the last laid rails at the place which is now named Craigellachie, the significant motto of the Clan Grant, and speeded on their way to the Pacific. Jim Dickey and I, after we arrived at Kamloops, changed to the private car of the manager of the traffic on Mr. Onderdonk's section of the line. Dickey knew him well, which was sufficient to ensure a warm welcome, and the train rushed along at the rate of 57 miles an hour, roaring in and out of the numerous tunnels, our short car whirling round the sharp curves like the tail of a kite, the sensation being such that when dinner was served Dickey, the manager and I were the only men in the car who were not suffering from train sickness. I think this was one of the wildest rides by rail that any of us had taken, and was, to say the least of it, dangerous, for had the train left the rails it would have plunged down a precipice a couple of hundred feet into the wild waters of the Fraser. The next morning when the train rushed out of one of the tunnels a hand-car loaded with section men was seen on the trestle bridge in front ; the navvies jumped off and clung to the sides of the bridge, in the nick of time to save their lives and see their car hurled through the air to the torrent below.

Many years have passed since that memorable ride, and to-day one whirls through the mountains in the most modern and palatial observation cars, but the recollection of that journey to the coast on the first train through is far sweeter to me than any trips taken since. It was the exultant moment of pioneer work, and we were all pioneers on that excursion.

When we arrived at Burrard Inlet the steamer *Olympia* was ready at the dock, and all went on board. She then steamed round the shore of Cold Harbour and English Bay, soundings being taken, which proved to be most satisfactory to the directors, and the location of what is now the fine city of Vancouver was chosen. The vessel was forthwith headed for Victoria, where the magnates of the railway were received with enthusiasm, and a few very pleasant days were spent, all being delighted with the situation of the city, and of one mind that a prettier place for the capital of the province could not be

ALL THAT REMAINS OF OLD FORT GARRY

FORT EDMONTON, WINTER

FORT SASKATCHEWAN

RED CROW, HEAD CHIEF OF THE BLACKFEET NATION, 1895

CHIEF BIG BEAR, OF THE PLAIN CREES, 1885

LT.-COL. JAMES FARQUHARSON MACLEOD, C.M.G.

ON THE BOW RIVER

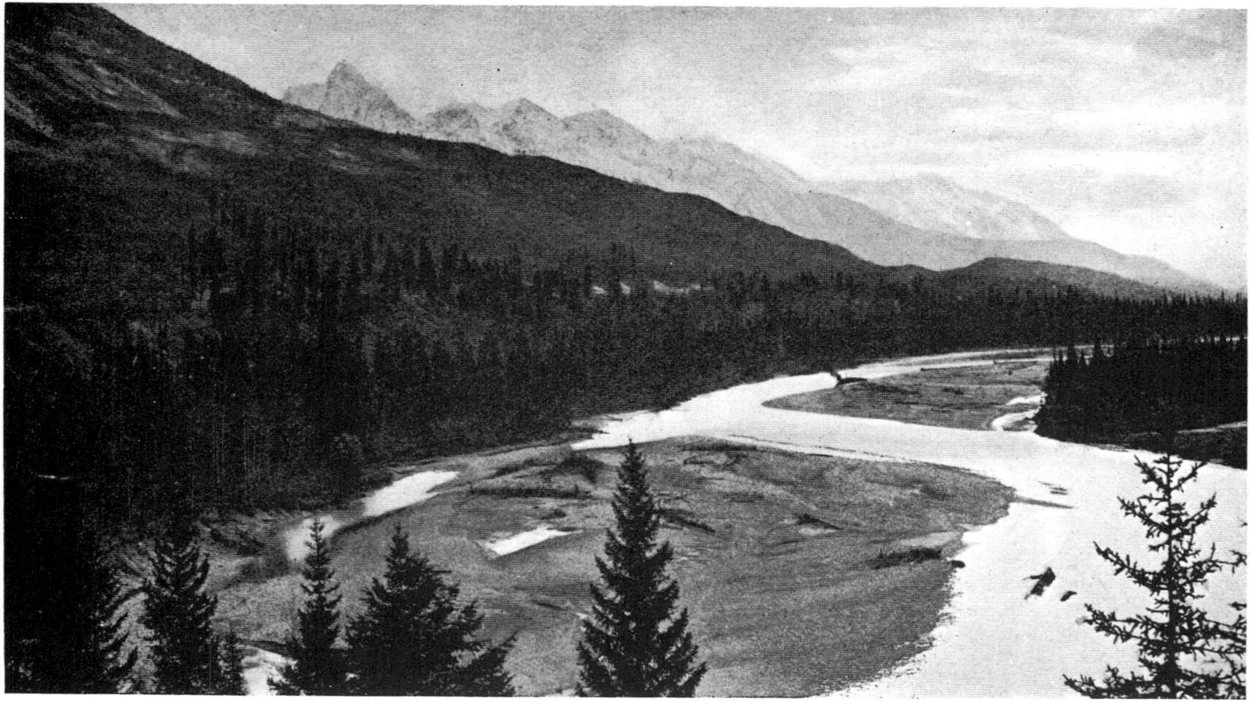

KICKING HORSE FLATS

PIONEERS OF EDMONTON

YOUNG BLOOD SQUAWS AND CHILDREN IN MACLEOD DISTRICT

N.W.M.P. ARTIZANS, MACLEOD

CALGARY INDIANS

DYEA TRAIL CANYON, 1898

Colonel Steele   Miss Scott   Captain Staines   Mrs. Staines
Captain Burstall

GROUP TAKEN AT MIDNIGHT AT THE YUKON POLICE BARRACKS, DAWSON, JUNE, 1899

LORD AND LADY STRATHCONA AND THE OFFICERS OF STRATHCONA'S HORSE

From a photograph lent by Mrs. William Ogilvie

selected. We saw everything, took jaunts round the inlets, visited the Chinese quarter and attended the theatre, in which about one thousand Chinese expressed their satisfaction with the play and music by maintaining solemn silence throughout.

When it was time to return eastward we boarded the *Olympia* and were given a delightful trip up the beautiful Fraser to Yale, where we took the train for Donald. After a short stay there to put our affairs in order, engineers, contractors and Mounted Police left the mountains in two huge trains.

When our train emerged from the Bow River Pass, and we again saw before us the magnificent expanse of prairie, with the beautiful sparkling Bow meandering to the eastward, pleasure beamed on every countenance, and was given vent to in cheers of delight, one stalwart engineer shouting at the top of his voice, " Hurrah ! Civilization at last ! "

I was very sorry to leave all the kind friends we had made. The force was popular with all good citizens. Mr. James Ross, when he bade them farewell, paid my men a high compliment, and among other things said that they could count on him as a friend, always ready to do them a good turn. This he has repeatedly done, and all have appreciated his kindness. With reference to him personally, I know he was regarded by the leading contractors as the ablest manager of construction they had ever known, and his place in Canada will be difficult to fill

CHAPTER XIII

IT was getting late in the year when we got back to the
plains. We were not sorry to leave the mountains.
All seemed to feel free once more; there were no lofty
peaks to dominate them, to make them feel their
insignificance. The weather was cold with snow on the ground ;
but when we arrived at the South Saskatchewan, 22 miles
from Swift Current, I found the ice too thin to cross with safety.
That we should not be delayed, I had to make a bridge by
placing a layer of hay of the width required, pouring water on
it until it froze, and repeating this until it was thick and
strong.

At the "Sixty Mile Bush," the first point of woods on the
north side of the plain, we met the deputy sheriff, I. W. Gibson,
Reynolds, Indian agent, and an amateur hangman, the man
who had volunteered to operate upon Big Bear's Indians. He
was a very respectable citizen, but more than willing to hang
any of the rebels in revenge for the severe and cruel treatment
he had received at Fort Garry when he was a captive of Riel,
in 1869-70. These officials had been at Battleford in connection with the trial and execution of the Frog Lake fiends.
The murderers had been tried by Judge Rouleau and a jury

of six, found guilty and hanged. We spent the night at the " Sixty Mile Bush," and two days later were in Battleford barracks, where all received a hearty welcome.

The force at Battleford consisted of " D " and " K " divisions, in all about 225 men, under Major Crozier, who had recently been promoted to assistant commissioner. I was at once placed in command of " D " division. The majority of the men had been enlisted during the rebellion to bring the force up to 1000, double its former strength, and had been sent hurriedly to Battleford to garrison the place, the Indians, although disarmed, being still in an unsettled state and the inhabitants nervous. Just before Christmas Crozier left for Regina, and the command of the Mounted Police in the district was entrusted to me.

We had to pay constant visits to the Indian reserves. The red men were in a bad humour. They had no arms but we had to see that they could not get any, and regular patrols were kept going amongst them. There was no Indian agent when I took command, and steps had to be taken to select one for that important post. After some persuasion the Venerable Archdeacon John Mackay consented to take the position. The negotiations were made by and through me. The clergy of all other denominations were interviewed and the matter discussed at considerable length, with the fortunate result that they expressed themselves well satisfied with the appointment. It was popular with all classes and creeds, for the archdeacon was genial and broadminded, and soon brought his red charges into a proper frame of mind.

Early in the winter an amusing test of discipline occurred. The majority of our men were recruits of less than six months' service, only partially trained, and I noticed that very few of them attended their churches. There had been no parades for the purpose, the parson of the Church of England having objected to them. Our regulations were very clear on the subject, but only five men attended the morning service of his church, and they were in the choir, when there should have been at least 100. I decided that I would not order church parades if I found all ranks attending the morning services regularly, and, to make it easy for them, I gave orders that there would be no noon stable parade on the Sundays. It was cold weather, the horses would not drink until late in the morning and could be fed by the stable orderlies at noon.

I naturally expected something from this arrangement, and the next Sunday went to church, confident that there would be a large turn-out. I was disappointed, however, on seeing that the number had only increased to seven! This settled the matter. Orders were given for all hands to parade and march to their respective places of worship. This filled one side of the Church of England, but the young fellows boycotted the plate when it was passed round for the offertory. After this had occurred several times the parson's church-warden, the late Mr. Robert Wylde, an ex-member of the force, made up his mind that they should contribute, and, when the time came, he proceeded with the plate in his left hand to take up the collection. On approaching the first of the obstinate troopers he made the motion of pointing a revolver at him with his right hand as if to hold him up! This ended the boycott; all were on the broad grin, and the civilians of the congregation were almost convulsed as the men groped in their pockets for silver.

The rebellion had left a great many persons, particularly the loyal half-breeds, in poor circumstances, and I received orders to select the sufferers from the rebellion, regardless of the part taken in the " unpleasantness," and give them something to do to keep the wolf from the door. As new barracks would have to be built in the spring I obtained authority to employ the sufferers at hauling lumber from Prince Albert, the nearest place where any could be obtained. The distance by train was about 150 miles, but the men were very glad to get the work, as it not only provided them and their families with enough to maintain them for the winter, but left a comfortable margin for food and seed grain for the following summer.

The resignation of Lt.-Col. Irvine, our commissioner, came as a great shock to all who knew him. He was a great favourite throughout the west, a hard-working, conscientious officer who had served his country faithfully for many years. He was still in the prime of life, and for my part I could see no reason why he should retire, particularly after the good work that he had done during the rebellion.

He was succeeded in the command of the force by Lt.-Col. Herchmer, whose lines fell in much more pleasant places than those of any of his predecessors. He found the force doubled in strength, the Canadian Pacific Railway completed ; and the rebellion had taught the people that there must be no penny-wise policy after this. He had a well trained and highly disciplined corps to carry out the duties assigned to it, and was able to do much for the benefit of the settlers and others who required advice or protection.

In the spring of 1886 the settlers who had taken refuge in Battleford on the outbreak of the rebellion and had remained there during the winter were escorted to their homes, and from that time on they were frequently visited and reports were made of their situation. Complaints were attended to at once. I also introduced mileage returns of the distances travelled by our horses on duty, a system which was afterwards adopted throughout the force, and gave a perfect knowledge of the work done. These visits to the settlers restored their confidence and were kept up throughout the country until the people became so numerous that it would be impossible to carry it on without a large increase in the force.

During April I received the new Mounted Infantry book with orders to introduce it at once. It was very unpopular, a wretched substitute for our first-class single rank drill, which was good enough for Stuart and Sheridan. When we had adapted it to suit our purposes the father of the work would not have recognized his child. It could not have been intended for a corps of first-class horsemen, and was superseded ere long to suit circumstances. When spring opened the recruits of the past year were put through a long and useful course of training, and, as no one in the N.W.M.P. would be promoted unless he were thoroughly trained in all exercises, I kept them at it until there was no part of it that they could not do well. The divisions at squadron and regimental drill could take their high jumps in line or column of troops. They could swim their horses across any river with ease, and find their way either in winter or summer without guide or compass

R

to any place for hundreds of miles round.   Mounted sports of every kind, tent-pegging, etc., were encouraged and well performed.

In June the medals for the Battleford Rifles came and were presented to them in the town, and I paraded my men in review order, dismounted, to be present to do them honour.   The company had behaved well during the rebellion and deserved all we could give them.   The N.W.M.P. had not yet received medals, and, when the gift was approved, it was delayed until 1888, three years after the war !   Even then only those who had been in an engagement were permitted to receive them. Scouting parties, in which men of the corps were under fire and several killed, were dealt with as if they had not been in action !   The military officers and men who had served in any capacity in connection with the campaign very justly received medals within the year, and why the N.W.M.P., who held important posts, kept the Blackfeet in check, and prevented sympathizers in the United States from crossing the international boundary, should have been deprived of the medal it is difficult to understand.

Towards the end of August I was reinforced, and in September my division was transferred to the south west.   My orders were to march on September 1 for Fort Macleod, 365 miles across the north west part of the Great Plain.   Our route was trackless and, as the season was very dry, water was hard to find.   We arrived at Fort Macleod on the thirteenth day from Battleford, and encamped on the banks of Willow Creek, going into barracks next morning with every horse on the bit and not a sign of the march on any of them.

The official records of the winter of 1886-7 proved it to be the coldest that we had experienced.   The thermometer at the barracks indicated 50 below zero ;   snow covered the ground to the depth of 3½ feet ;   the chinook seldom visited us, and then only long enough to thaw the surface and was followed by severe frost, which formed a hard crust on the snow, through which the cattle could not penetrate to the grass.   The ranchers, with a few exceptions, had trusted to luck and failed to stack enough hay to tide them over the severe weather ;   the horses being able to paw did, as usual, very well, but the losses of the cattlemen were very severe, and at one time it appeared as if all their stock would die of starvation.

On January 7, the barracks at Lethbridge being ready for occupation, I transferred my headquarters there, and eventually had the whole of the division with me. The new buildings were the best and most comfortable that I had occupied for many a day. As soon as I had time to look about me I noticed that a great change had come over that part of the territory since the days when the buffalo roamed. One would never have believed that only eight or nine years had elapsed since the vast herds were grazing over the spot on which 2,000 inhabitants of the town were making things lively, or that seventeen years previously a battle had been fought between wild Indians on the opposite bank of the river. There was a narrow gauge railroad connecting the town with Dunmore junction on the C.P.R., 110 miles east. The great coal deposits had been opened, and trains of cars pulled out daily with several hundred tons, and other signs of civilization were to be seen on all sides. In spite of all this, its newness made the surroundings unattractive. The people were kindly and hospitable, however, and many of the pioneers were there ; but it was neither one thing nor the other, for it had none of the charms of the wilderness nor yet of the great city.

We had the detestable prohibitory liquor law to enforce, an insult to a free people. Our powers under it were so great, in fact so outrageous, that no self-respecting member of the corps, unless directly ordered, cared to exert them to the full extent. We were expected, on the slightest grounds of suspicion, to enter any habitation without a warrant, at any hour of the day or night, and search for intoxicants ; no privacy need be respected. Yet, owing to the pressure of a lot of fanatics who neither knew nor cared to understand the situation, parliament would not repeal the law and let the white people speak for themselves. This state of affairs continued for some years, despite the fact that the judges quashed nearly every conviction which was brought before them on appeal.

The winter continued severe until March ; trains on the narrow gauge railway, irreverently nicknamed " The Turkey Trail " by the driver of the Macleod coach, were often snowed up for several days at a stretch, and had to be dug out by gangs of men or snow ploughs. This did not cause any cessation of our work, however. The old routine or hard winter trips went on all the same throughout the force all over the territory, but the settlers on the ranches in stormy weather remained in their homes in comparative comfort, while the Mounted Police and cowpunchers were out in all weathers.

In Lethbridge there had as yet been no time to build curling or skating rinks, but the citizens enjoyed their spare evenings all the same. Hospitality reigned supreme, and consisted mostly of card parties and dances ; the latter were public. Young and old went in for a good time, and were soon well acquainted. The picturesque caller-off, such as we had at Macleod and other parts of the territory, was not so much in evidence, however ; quadrilles were fewer and round dances the favourites.

At last the country was visited by a welcome chinook, which saved the stockmen from much loss. It was the first of any consequence that winter, all others had lasted but a short time, with the result that the snow was not melted and more harm than good had followed. This one was so remarkable that it is worth while to describe it.

One night during the first week in March I was one of a whist party at the quarters of Mr. C. A. McGrath and Dr. Mewburn. The thermometer indicated 30 below zero, and the fires had to be kept going until the stove was almost red hot. At eleven o'clock the temperature began to rise, and at midnight it had gone up 75, and continued rising. I left about that time and, as I went up the street, going east, I heard the roaring of the chinook as it surged from the mountains. It finally overtook me, accompanied by clouds of drifting snow, sending me ahead of it to the barracks, the blizzard so thick that I could scarcely see the lights of the guard-room. Next morning every particle of snow was gone and every hollow was full of water. By noon the wind had dried all shallow pools, and by six o'clock in the evening the dust was flying along the trails over many thousands of square miles. Every large coulee was a huge river, caused by the enormous quantity of melted snow.   The wind had the velocity of a hurricane, and continued for many days.

On May 20 I received orders to hold myself in readiness to proceed to Kootenay district, taking with me Inspectors Wood and Huot and 75 N.C.O.'s and constables of my division. One officer and the remainder of my men were to be left in the Lethbridge district and transferred to Supt. Macdonnell's division, which had been ordered south from Battleford to relieve me.

The duty for which we were detailed was to restore order amongst the Indians of the Kootenay district, then almost inaccessible, there being no way in during the winter, except on snowshoes, and during the summer only by pack trail.   The settlers in the district were very few in number and uneasy on account of Chief Isadore, of the Kootenay tribe, having, with part of his band, broken open the gaol at Wild Horse Creek, an old mining camp, and released Kapula, one of their men who had been arrested, charged with the murder, in 1884, of two white placer miners at Deadman's Creek on the Wild Horse-Golden trail.   Isadore then ordered Provincial Constable Anderson, who had made the arrest, and the Hon. F. Aylmer out of the district, forbidding them to return.   The latter was a prominent engineer and land surveyor, who had been at work in pursuit of his profession.

This action caused the scattered settlers and prospectors much alarm, and they applied to the authorities for help.   Isadore and his Indians had other grievances, one of which was the sale of the lands on Joseph Prairie, a beautiful spot in the foot-hills, 12 miles west of Galbraith's Ferry, which had been occupied by them and their progenitors for several generations past.   It had been purchased from the government of British Columbia by Galbraith Bros., who afterwards sold it to Colonel James Baker, late of the British army, a brother of Sir Samuel and Valentine Baker Pasha.   The Galbraiths had left the Indians in undisturbed possession of their land, and there was no trouble until some time after the sale, when Colonel Baker ordered Isadore to vacate it.   This he flatly refused to do, and there was no organized power in British Columbia at the time to enforce his compliance with the colonel's wishes.

These difficulties were brought to the notice of the government, and in January, 1887, Lt.-Col. Herchmer was sent into the district to investigate and report upon the state of affairs. He went in from the west through the Moyea Pass on snowshoes, and obtained a great deal of useful information from the leading people.

The Indians of that region were the Shuswaps, of the Upper Columbia Lakes, and the Upper and Lower Kootenays. The former lived on their reserve under their quiet chief Mathias. The Upper Kootenays, a fine class of Indian of good physique, objected to living on the reserves set aside for them ; they preferred to roam the valleys and mountains at will, as they had always done, hunting, fishing, raising horses and cattle, of which they had a large number, as they were horse Indians, and used to cross the Rocky Mountains in the days of the buffalo to hunt and trade. The Lower Kootenay Indians were located along that river from where it re-entered Canada to its outlet on the Columbia, but they recognized no boundary line and mixed with their relatives in the United States. They had very few horses or cattle and were known as canoe Indians, who lived by fishing and trapping.

Before it was quite decided that the N.W.M.P. should be employed in the Kootenay district, a commission, consisting of A. W. Vowell, Esq., gold commissioner and stipendiary magistrate of the district, Dr. Powell, general superintendent of Indians for British Columbia, and Lt.-Col. Herchmer, visited Wild Horse Creek in June. After several interviews with Isadore, they induced him to hand over Kapula to the authorities. Lt.-Col. Herchmer ascertained also from other sources that the Kootenays had several hundred fighting men well armed and supplied with ammunition. They had also 500 head of cattle and 2,000 horses of very good quality.

On the 10th I received orders to entrain at once on the narrow gauge railway and proceed to Swift Current, on account of alarming rumours which had been circulated from there. The cars being very small, we had to take the waggons apart to load. When I was ready to depart the citizens came to see us off and presented us with an address.

We detrained at Dunmore next morning and transferred

to the C.P.R., which brought us to Swift Current early on the 13th, and on the 14th I met Lt.-Col. Herchmer on the train there, and was informed that reports had been made of an intended rising of the half-breeds, and that patrols would have to go out. I sent them north and south, made personal investigation, and soon learned that rumours of a rising had emanated from the fertile brains of some of the merchants who were anxious to see a division of the N.W.M.P. stationed at Swift Current. I had found considerable numbers of poor half-breeds, the once happy plain-hunters, making a precarious livelihood by collecting buffalo bones for the sugar refineries and bone dust factories of the United States, but they were perfectly harmless and would never have thought of rebellion even if suggested to them.

Persons must often wonder why there are so few buffalo bones on the plains where those animals roamed in such vast numbers. The answer is that they have been gathered ; many thousands of tons have been collected and sent away, leaving very few to tell the traveller that the bison were once in millions on our prairies. There are now some herds in the Peace River country under the protection of our Mounted Police, and several hundreds, which are rapidly increasing, were purchased some years ago by the government of the Dominion. These, if properly cared for, will increase so rapidly that many people now living may see thousands distributed throughout the Dominion. The possibility of this should not be lost sight of by those responsible for their preservation.

As soon as I had reported the true state of affairs I was ordered to Regina, where I arrived on the 22nd. After a short stay to talk over Kootenay matters with the commissioner, I returned to Swift Current and left with my division for Golden, B.C. It was made up to full strength at Dunmore by men and horses from Lethbridge, and I arrived at Golden on the 28th and went into camp on the south bank of the Kicking Horse The next day Lt.-Col. Herchmer came to see us and left by the east-bound train in the evening.

We left again on July 18, and on the 30th we arrived at Six Mile Creek, where it had been suggested that I should make my permanent camp. A careful examination of the locality, however, proved it to be in every way unsuitable. I inspected the vicinity of Four Mile Creek with the same result. The same afternoon Colonel Baker called upon me to welcome the division to the district. On seeing the situation he expressed surprise that it had been chosen as a site for our quarters when there were so many excellent places to be found round Galbraith's Ferry and south on Fenwick's Flat on the Kootenay River, 20 miles east of Six Mile Creek.

Next day, according to our arrangement, Huot and I accompanied Fenwick to Galbraith's, where we found him, his sister and brother-in-law, Mr. and Mrs. Clark, at home, and were heartily welcomed. We crossed Wild Horse Creek, at that time much disturbed by Dave Griffith's hydraulic giant, which was at work about 5 miles up stream at the Old Town, as the old mining camp was called, and went to inspect Fenwick's Flat, but one glance showed that it would not answer our purpose.

I asked Galbraith for permission to build on a point of land which was in the angle formed by the confluence of the Wild Horse Creek and the Kootenay. He very kindly gave me a lease of the ground for as long as we should require it for the modest sum of one dollar. The spot was an ideal one. It commanded the trails to Tobacco Plains, the Crow's Nest Pass, Moyea, and the Columbia Lakes, and was the most central situation from which to communicate with the Indians and give protection to the whites.

I returned to Six Mile Creek the same evening, and next morning, Monday, August 1, moved the division down to the ferry. Before dismounting the men, I clearly explained to them on parade the duty which we had to perform and the line of conduct which we should pursue in our relations with both whites and Indians, so as to gain their respect and confidence. After our camp was pitched all hands were told off to their tasks, one party cutting and hauling logs for our winter quarters. I arranged for a summer mail service by dispatch riders to Sam's Landing, where it would meet the boat, and purchased a pack train of 24 fine ponies and three Kayuse, with aparejos and other equipment complete. This train proved to be a good investment, earning its value every month, costing nothing for forage, and teaching many men the art of packing.

As soon as I had got settled in camp I sent for Isadore, and directed him to bring in Kapula and another Indian named Isadore who was suspected of being an accomplice.

Five days later they were brought before me at Wild Horse Creek lock-up, where they remained for eight days to give the witnesses for the prosecution time to appear. There was not, however, sufficient evidence to send them to trial, and they were accordingly dismissed, and I sent them home with food for the journey. Isadore was present during the whole of the proceedings and followed the evidence with keen interest. I was pleased with the bearing of the Indians, both accused and witnesses. They showed great intelligence, and it was clear that they knew nothing of the murder, which was probably committed by some loose character frequenting the trails.

After the investigation Isadore came to see me. He had been informed by the white men and Chinese that we had come to Kootenay with hostile intentions towards the Indians. I told him, however, that we were in the district to maintain the laws of the Great Mother, and that both whites and Indians would receive just treatment and would be equally severely punished if they deserved it. The effect of this interview was a marked improvement in the demeanour of the Indians. With few exceptions, however, the whites remained in fear of them for some months.

A great change was now coming over the Kootenay district. A waggon-road was under construction from Golden. Patrols were sent out and travellers, assured of protection, visited the district. The work of building the barracks proceeded, and soon we had an excellent camp. Meat and vegetables were purchased from the Indians, and a new era of confidence spread over the place.

On September 22 three commissioners, the Hon. Mr. Vernon, minister of lands and works in the province, Dr. Powell, and Mr. O'Reilly, superintendent of Indian reserves and lands for British Columbia, came into the district to make an inspection of the Indian reserves and, if necessary, allot more land. The majority of the Indians, however, were away at the time, and the commissioners were unable to meet them as they could not wait. I was instructed to acquaint Isadore and his Indians with their decision.

The part of Joseph Prairie occupied by the chief had to be restored to Colonel Baker and, as I expected, Isadore objected, saying that he had occupied the land before the whites came. I told him that Dr. Powell would be responsible in full for the payment of his claim for improvements. He replied that he would vacate the land only if he were paid at once. On my telling him that this was a reflection upon the word of the commissioners, he launched forth into an eloquent account of the wrongs of his people, and I could get from him no direct answer. Eventually I persuaded him to appoint an arbitrator, which we accordingly did, and the matter was more or less amicably settled. We on our part dug him an irrigation ditch, and later an industrial school was opened, and now every Kootenay can read and write, and many of them have learned trades under the supervision of the Indian agents and their missionary at St. Eugène.

During the whole time, over 12 months, that we were in Kootenay district, there was not a case of theft nor one of drunkenness brought to our notice. Crime was rare amongst the Indians, and it was the opinion of the best whites that the Kootenays were very good. They often packed large quantities of liquor into the district for white merchants and carried whisky from the stores for white men, but none of them were known to meddle with any that was placed in their charge, and Isadore was the most influential chief I have known. Crowfoot, the Blackfoot chief, or Red Crow, dare not, in the height of their power, have exercised the discipline that Isadore did.

When Christmas came the Indians, as was their custom, rode in a body to St. Eugène mission, where they took up their quarters in their log houses, and for a whole week attended the church services. In the intervals, Isadore and his four sheriffs seized all who had been guilty of any offence, such as gambling, drunkenness or theft. They were tied down on a robe, hands and feet secured by rawhide thongs to stakes placed in the ground, and soundly flogged, regardless of age or sex. By some means or other the chief knew the culprits, but, in spite of that fact, and the consequences of their folly, they never failed to appear at the church to take their medicine. At Easter the same ceremonies were followed, when they assembled to perform the Easter duty.

In the spring Messrs. McVittie, land surveyors and engineers, surveyed the Indian reserves, and while they were at work Isadore complained that the reserves were too small and that he had been promised larger ones. There was no way of disproving this statement ; no treaty had been made as in the North West Territory ; no records of what he had been promised were recorded with his signature upon them, so that there was nothing for it but to induce him to be satisfied. One thing was certain, the Indian agent was an upright and talented man, who would, if anything, be too good to the Indians, and he was ably supported by Father Cocola, the missionary who had relieved Father Fouquet, in charge of St. Eugène. He was a Corsican of high family, and did much to create a good feeling between the Indians and whites.

The work on the irrigation ditch was commenced in May, the industrial school was under construction, irrigation was carried out on the gardens near the mission, and everything looked rosy with regard to the Indians, when more food for annoyance was found. Colonel Baker, who had been in Victoria all winter at his legislative duties, returned on May 24 and found several newly-constructed camps and corrals on the land which had been vacated by Chief Isadore, and informed me that the Indians had been trespassing.

As soon as I heard of it I arranged for Inspector Wood to proceed there with the interpreter. They saw the sheds and corrals which had been built, and the Indians were ordered to come to barracks and explain to me the reasons for the trespass. They arrived the same evening and stated that Mr. Hyde Baker had given them permission to stay there for the summer, and I received a letter from the colonel to the effect that he did not like to be hard on the Indians, and that they might stay there for the year. I informed them of his wishes, and they went away, apparently satisfied, but it was evident that they were under the orders of their chief and would not have moved without his permission except by force. This did not end the matter, for on the 29th Colonel Baker complained that Chief Isadore, who had been absent when Wood visited the Indian camp, had been insolent to him when he volunteered to show him the boundaries of his estate, and accused him of taking all the land in the country. As it appeared to me that serious trouble might result, I requested Chief Isadore to come to the post and asked Colonel Baker to come also, so that the matter could be cleared up. They arrived on the 31st and met in the office of Mr. Michael Phillips, the Indian agent. I had wanted him to settle the whole matter, but he refused, so I had to take it up myself.

Colonel Baker made a clear statement of what had occurred, and I demanded from the chief an explanation of his conduct. He admitted having been insolent to the colonel, but that he meant no harm. That gentleman had appeared angry and had ordered him to leave in a couple of days. This was merely an excuse on the part of the chief, who knew well that he had provoked the colonel by his language.

I warned the chief that his conduct would lead him and his tribe into trouble if persisted in. Colonel Baker, I said, was one of their best friends, and by acting as he did the chief was going contrary to the wishes of the Great Mother, whose desire was that her children of all colours should live together in peace. When I had finished speaking Isadore arose and shook hands with Colonel Baker, saying that he would never again trespass on his land, a promise which has been faithfully kept.

On June 16 I received definite orders to move to Fort Macleod in July. The training was completed before the end of June, and I arranged to have our annual sports at Four Mile Creek, and invited all the inhabitants of the district, white and red, to take part in them, with the object of enhancing the friendly feeling which was growing between the white people and the Indians. A large subscription list for prizes and refreshments was made up amongst us, and Mr. Galbraith put his name down for a large amount. Marquees were pitched under the trees, and an ample supply of food and refreshments provided so that no one need go home hungry, and anyone who came a long distance and wished to rest in camp for the night was welcome to do so.

The sports began on July 2, and I opened them just before noon by a march past Colonel Baker, so as to impress Isadore. The colonel did not care to do it but, as I felt that it would place him in an important position with the Indians, he consented, and all of the movements of a cavalry squad were performed before him, at all paces, and the whole of the visitors joined the Mounted Police in three hearty cheers for the Queen. After luncheon the sports commenced, whites and Indians taking part in all events. Colonel Baker was appointed referee, Mr. Galbraith and Mr. Norris, collector of customs, the judges, and I acted as starter. The Indians proved themselves to be very athletic and entered heartily into the sports. In the sprinting our men were first and the redskins a close second. At the long distances the latter shone, and at wrestling on horseback they surpassed anything I have yet seen. Our men did not compete, as it would not have been wise on account of the position they occupied in the country ; a few of the civilians did, but though they were first-class horsemen they were hurled from their saddles by the Indians, whose powerful limbs gripped their horses as if in a vice. In the mile race an Indian won on a buckskin, which traversed the course in one minute and fifty seconds, timed by two stop watches, remarkable speed for a pony. I weighed the rider, Maiyuke, after the race as he stood in his moccasins, the Indian tipping the scale at 197 pounds !

The sports were a great success, everyone was pleased, and in the evening Isadore assembled his Indians and came to say farewell at the head of his tribe. I received him on some rising ground, accompanied by Colonel Baker, Mr. Galbraith, Mr. Norris and other leading white men. The chief addressed me on behalf of himself and his people, speaking in the highest terms of the manly and moral behaviour of the men of the division, and adding that when we came into the district the Indians did not know us, and very naturally were in doubt, but all had changed, and he hoped that when we returned to the North West Territory we would look back with kind feelings towards them. When we arrived the white men and Indians in the district had mutual distrust, but that had disappeared, never to return, chiefly owing to the good advice given to the Indians by the officers of the force and the kindly and honourable behaviour of the men. He added that if in future there were any cause for complaint, instead of taking the law into their own hands, they would visit Fort Macleod to obtain advice from the Great Mother's red-coats.

After the pow-wow Isadore and his tribe, men, women and children, filed past me, shaking hands in farewell. This was the last of the Indian question in Kootenay, but on July 5 I received a letter from Mr. Michael Phillips to the effect that there was some danger of the American Indians of the Tobacco Plains, U.S.A., causing trouble amongst ours, who objected to their presence, as it was reported that the United States government intended to remove them from their reservations on account of murders which had been committed by them the previous autumn. On receipt of the letter I cancelled the order for the march out of Kootenay and requested Mr. Phillips to accompany Inspector Wood to the scene and, if necessary, to cross the boundary line and visit the United States' officers. They made a fast ride and found that there was nothing in it. Some of the American Indians had murdered three white men and had been lynched by the friends of the victims, but the remainder were not to be moved off their reserves.

On August 7 we started for Fort Macleod. We went by the Crow's Nest Pass, and, in my report to the commissioner on the doings of the year, I laid particular stress upon the value of the coal lands in the pass, its suitability as a railway route, and the lightness of the work in comparison with that of the Kicking Horse Pass. Everything I had seen I described as clearly as possible, and what I stated has since been proved to be correct. The great coal lands, remarkable for their extent and value, have been developed, employing thousands of men, mostly foreigners, who make large wages and strike on the slightest excuse or by command of foreigners, regardless of the suffering of the British subjects who people the Dominion. Such a state of affairs should not be permitted. The Canadians own the coal lands and should see that with such an enormous area, larger than the British Isles, they should not be forced, on account of those strikes, to turn to the United States coal miners for relief.

The commissioner in his report for that year stated :

Having reported upon all which I consider interesting to you, I will specially call your attention to the extremely able manner in which Supt. Steele managed matters in the Kootenay district, B.C., and which I think will be found to have a lasting impression on the Indians of that country, and I propose with your permission, as soon as the Crow's Nest Pass is clear of snow, next June, to send a patrol into Kootenay for a few weeks. The satisfactory passage of " D " division through that part of the north west reflects the greatest credit upon Supt. Steele and all ranks of his command, and my inspection of that division, a short time after their arrival at Macleod, gave me the most intense satisfaction.

He added, concerning the whole of the N.W.M.P. :

The force is well drilled, but from the numerous and different avocations in which the men are employed, although individually drilled men, they naturally require some days together before they are in a condition to do justice to themselves on parade. The general public are unaware of our multifarious duties and, when we make mistakes as police proper, they make no allowance for our qualifications. I may be allowed to name a few of the different things we do for ourselves outside of ordinary duties and patrols. We are trained soldiers, both mounted and dismounted, and every division understands its drill ; we do our own carpenter work, painting, alterations of clothing, blacksmithing, most of our freighting and teaming, plough when required, extinguish prairie fires, act as customs and quarantine officers, do most of our waggon repairing, mend all and make a great deal of our saddlery and harness, act as gaolers and keepers of the insane for weeks at a stretch, and there is not a division that cannot go into any country and erect complete barracks either of logs or frame. " D " division, under Supt. Steele, erected first-class barracks at Kootenay, B.C., last year, the division being completely housed before winter set in. In physique we are second to no force in existence ; our men are well set up, young, active, good-looking, stout and tall, and we have very few men who cannot ride day in and day out for 50 miles. Only first-class men can stand 5 years in the force.

After the inspection, the division was mentioned in General Orders, and our comptroller informed me later that Sir John A. Macdonald, G.C.B., Premier of the Dominion and Superintendent General of Indian affairs, was well pleased with my report of the work done in the Kootenay district, and of the Crow's Nest Pass.

On December 8, 1888, I was placed in command of the Macleod district, one of the most attractive, interesting and romantic in the territory, and the only one, except headquarters, containing two divisions, squadrons in a military sense. Wood and Macdonnell commanded them. Both were hard-working, loyal officers, great favourites throughout the country, and better comrades could not be desired. Each division was organized into four sub-divisions, which were equivalent to troops, the district into four sub-districts, commanded by inspectors, the sub-district into sections in charge of a N.C.O. or senior constable. The section contained within its area several townships, 6 miles square. Lists were kept of the settlers, all of whom were visited by patrols, to ascertain if they had any complaints. Each post had the necessary drill, law and brand books, and the men were catechized monthly as to their knowledge of their duties and tested at their drill.

The increase of the force in 1885 had been a good thing, for we were able to keep a watch on the criminal element in a way which was impossible with a smaller force. At the present time, when large numbers of people are pouring into the country, it is as important as in the wildest and most unsettled days to give in every part of our western territories perfect protection for settlers. They are entitled to it, but no undisciplined, ill-trained force can provide it. The " gunman " laughs at such, but there is terror in his heart when he finds that the men of a well-disciplined force with good traditions are on his trail. No man in such a force will hesitate to risk his life ; discipline, self-respect and *esprit de corps* compel him to face numbers without hesitation.

In the eighties and nineties the settlers were fewer and had no near neighbours, which made the visits of our patrols possible and important. Each settler was visited by the Mounted Police, and signed the patrol slip, with remarks thereon as to whether he or she had any complaints. If there were any they were attended to at once, and weekly reports of circumstances and actions taken were forwarded through the proper channel to district headquarters, with copies of diaries of all officers, N.C.O.'s and constables, and extracts were submitted in the commandant's monthly report to the commissioner.

The N.W.M.P. had, in 1888, arrived at a very high state of efficiency, not only as police, but as soldiers. The training throughout was the best, the men a fine class, good-looking and well-educated. On joining headquarters they had a steady grind at military and police instruction, and lectures on every part of their duties were given ; they were then distributed to fill up the vacancies in the districts ; the commandants, during the whole of their future career in the force were responsible for their efficiency. The mounted infantry book had been gauged at its real value, which was small, and the true system for mounted rifles resurrected. We were soon far in advance of the time in everything that goes to make good scouts, soldiers and police. A careful watch was kept that we should excel in horsemanship, which had to be of the very best. No fault was overlooked ; the riding-school was before every careless rider. Firing from the saddle with revolver and carbine was part of the instruction.

The divisions of the force were in a position to take the field complete with transport in less than half an hour at any time of the day or night, and the smaller parties, so often required in an emergency, were obliged to be in the saddle, ready for the prairie, in fifteen minutes from the time they were roused from their slumbers.

The Macleod district and those contiguous were at that time the home of the stockman, and very little farming in the true sense was done. The horses and cattle roamed at will, a great temptation to the horse and cattle thief. This necessitated constant vigilance. The patrols were obligatory night and day, no matter how severe the weather might be, rain or shine, frost

s

or snow. The Bloods and Peigans, two of the strongest tribes, were on their reserves in the centre of the district. They were, as a rule, well-behaved, but the young bucks were always ready for war with their hereditary enemies, the Crows and Gros Ventres, to the south of the border, or for any other mischief. Although well fed they would turn out at night and raid the ranches for cattle and horses ; the former they would kill for food ; the latter they would run off to the United States to trade with the receiver of stolen stock, who would in turn sell them to travellers who were going south, just as they sold horses stolen in the south to persons who were on their way north, thus reducing the chances of detection.

In the prevention of these crimes the patrols on night duty along the borders of the Indian reserves frequently came in contact with the Indians, and were obliged to make their arrests at the pistol's point. Conflicts occasionally occurred, but such episodes had to be made light of and kept as quiet as possible, lest the settlers be alarmed and rumours of a disturbing nature be circulated throughout the country. The Indian war of 1885 had made the people very nervous, and the slightest rumour caused many to see Indian risings every spring when the grass was good.

Apart from the Indians the cattle ranchers had enemies to their prosperity who were far more dangerous because they were their own neighbours. These settled on homesteads in the centre of the leases, and did their best to make up small herds at the expense of the large concerns. They were a curse to the cattle industry. Fortunately many were caught and punished, but their detection was difficult.

Prairie fires gave us much trouble. They were a great danger to the stock interests. The grass became very dry, in fact turned into hay on the ground in August, and was as nutritious as when it was green, but it would ignite as easily as tinder, and many hard rides had to be made to detect the wilful or foolishly negligent persons who were responsible. The moment smoke or any sign of fire was noticed the policeman who saw it had to proceed to the spot and others in the party had to turn out every male settler, man or boy, within ten miles to extinguish it. Waggons loaded with barrels of water and empty sacks were soon going at full speed to the fire ; mounted men with damp sacks tied to their saddles rode furiously in that direction ; ploughs were brought to run lines of fire-guards to cut off the area in flames. When the grass was short the fires were extinguished by beating out the flames with the wet sacks. Sometimes I had a hundred men out for several days at a time ; everything had to be set aside for this. All the officers and men of my two divisions were fire guardians under the laws of the territory, and many civilians held the same office. The fines were heavy, the informant being entitled to half, a provision in the law which caused at least one rather amusing episode.

Our hay contractor generally cut the hay after it had turned brown. One of his men, when smoking, set the prairie on fire where they were working, whereupon the contractor rode at full speed towards Pincher Creek village, where there was a magistrate. On his way he met a Mounted Policeman riding hard towards the fire and, as he galloped by, called out, " One of those men of mine has started a fire ; all the hay will be burned ; for the Lord's sake turn out as many as you can to put it out. I'm after—— ! "

The policeman rode on, and men were turned out and the fire extinguished before he returned. He had been to the magistrate, before whom he laid an information against himself for causing the fire through his hired men, was fined 100 dollars, paid the amount promptly, then cleared half as informant, thus saving 50 dollars. When he returned to camp he had the laugh on the other fellows.

One morning we had a little example of our share in the prevention of fires spreading. A cowboy rode up to the orderly-room and reported that prairie fires were raging along the northern part of the Porcupine Hills. He looked as if he had ridden hard, and said that the stockmen and their neighbours had been fighting the fires for a couple of days and nights and were exhausted. As there was need of immediate help I sent Sergeant Joyce, a very hard-riding and capable N.C.O., with 50 mounted men to the scene of the fire, some 35 miles distant. They found everyone in a state of exhaustion, but, starting work at once, with the assistance of a few of the ranchers who were able to carry on, they extinguished the fire after 6 hours' strenuous toil, and were back at Macleod within 24 hours, none the worse for their trip and their 70 mile ride.

In some places where the grass was long and the wind high, nothing could stop it. The fire travelled faster than a horse. On one occasion a rancher was followed by a fire of that sort and had to start another ahead to save himself from being overtaken, resting on the burnt ground until the pursuing fire had passed on both sides. He followed the flames to his ranch, expecting to find it in ruins, but, to his intense relief, found his stacks and home safe, and the Mounted Policemen of the neighbouring detachment seated on the wood-pile, blackened and panting from their efforts.

These experiences were all in the day's work with us ; the main thing was to see that the settler was protected and that the work be so well done that he did not need to take part in a "neck-tie social," as they had to do in a neighbouring State in 1884, when at least 40 enterprising fellows who had annexed their neighbours' horses were hanged, without the intervention of judge or jury. Amongst them was a young man who was travelling south from Canada and who on his way stopped for the night at a road house, where he met a number of men dressed in the cowpuncher's garb. They invited him to a meal, of which he partook, and all had settled down for a night's rest when the house was surrounded by the vigilantes, and all hands taken out and hanged. The young fellow protested his innocence, and was backed up by his supper mates, who stated that he did not belong to their gang, but it was no use, he was strung up with the rest. Another innocent man was a freighter from Canada who had once been a sergeant in the force and who, with several others, was lynched through the treachery of a British subject.

None of these things could take place in Canada or, in fact, in the Empire, but we had at one time the men for it if it had been permitted. They had been driven out, however, or had a trip " over the road " to the penitentiary. They were a desperate lot, fearing nothing and ready to face death at any time, regardless of the lack of preparation. One of them after he went across was hired by a rancher near Sun

River, Montana, and, after serving him for some time, took it into his head, in the absence of the proprietor, to murder the mistress of the house and the manager. Two children who were there escaped to the brush along the creek and finally warned some neighbours of the occurrence. The sheriff was sent for, but, after arresting the murderer, he was forced to give him up to the enraged citizens, who brought the miscreant in a waggon to a convenient tree and drove under a branch. When the rope was properly adjusted, the murderer, anxious to have the work over as soon as possible, called out, " Are you all set ? " " Yes, all set ! " was the reply. " Then, drive on, you—— ! " he called out. The whip was applied to the team and the wretch left dangling in mid air.

CHAPTER XIV

WHEN I took over command of the Macleod district the Sun Dance, which I have already described, was still a strong and baneful feature of Indian life, particularly with the Blood tribe, the most war-like of the western Indians. It kept the red man from becoming civilized, and the mischief was enhanced by the practice of the older men of " counting their coups," *i.e.*, relating to the assembled warriors their real or imaginary feats of valour in war. This conduct encouraged the rising and recently initiated braves to commit crimes, such as horse and cattle stealing and raids upon their hereditary enemies, the American Indians.

In 1889 one of these expeditions was led by Prairie Chicken Old Man, an active and daring young Blood Indian. It was first reported to me on April 30 that a party of 15 Blood Indians had left for the Crow reservation on the Big Horn River, in the United States. The names of the Indians were obtained and retained for further use. On the 22nd I had received a telegram from Mr. R. S. Tingley, of Big Sandy, Montana, to the effect that our Indians were stealing horses in that neighbourhood, and asking me to take action in the matter. My outposts were warned to keep a sharp look out for their return in case they should escape notice. Later on I had another telegram from Mr. Tingley, stating that the Bloods had stolen 17 horses from him, and I sent an officer and all available N.C.O.'s and men to intercept the Indians, and notified the districts to the east and all outposts.

On May 7 I received a telegram from R. B. Harrison, Helena, Montana, that the Bloods had stolen 40 horses belonging to the Crows. I also received a telegram from Colonel Otis, U.S. army, who was commanding at Fort Assiniboine, to the effect that nine Bloods had passed through the Bear Paw Mountains near there with stolen horses belonging to the Crows in their possession. Several rumours also came in to the effect that the party was under Prairie Chicken Old Man and that they were all killed by the Gros Ventres. On the 16th the outpost scouts captured The Bee, one of the raiders, and sent him into barracks. On the 18th Hind Gun, Young Pine and The Scout gave themselves up to the Indian agent, and were confined in the guard-room at Macleod.

The day after he was arrested, Young Pine confessed to me, when he was arraigned in the orderly-room, that the party consisted of five Bloods and one South Peigan, and that on the Big Horn, over 300 miles from Macleod, they stole and drove off from near the Crow agency about 100 head of horses most of which were not in good condition and had to be dropped along the trail. When they were returning on the second day from the Crow agency they were surprised by a large party of Gros Ventres, who commenced shooting at them, and they were pursued by the Gros Ventres into the Bear Paw Mountains. They kept on, returning the fire, and in their efforts to break through for Canada they met two Indians on the trail in front of them, pursued them and killed one of them, an Assiniboine. The Scout took his horse and Prairie Chicken Old Man his scalp. A party of American cavalry tried to head them off, and in their efforts to escape they were obliged to leave most of the stolen horses with the Gros Ventres. However, they arrived at the Blood reserve with five of the stolen horses and one that they found straying.

A month later the Indian commissioner was at Macleod and had an interview with the Indians already captured, and they were released to come up for trial when required. Later another member of the marauding party came and gave himself up to me, and, as the others had been released and no charge had been laid against him, I allowed him to go, giving him a severe " telling off " for his misconduct.

This raid was a fair sample of the daring character of the Blood Indian braves, and of the annoyance that the younger ones were in the habit of giving us and, in this case, the authorities on the south side of the border. Their crimes should have been severely punished as soon as the witnesses could be obtained, which would have been easy enough, but it appears to me now, as it did then, that the civilization of the Bloods was not eagerly sought after by the worthy persons responsible for it.

The Sun Dance, the chief cause of much mischief, commenced that year, and a horse thief, named Calf Robe, had taken refuge there, believing it to be a sanctuary. Staff-Sergeant C. Hilliard reported to me that Calf Robe had levelled his rifle at one of the constables a few days previously when he made an attempt to arrest him for his crime. I was determined that we must have no further trouble with refugees at the Sun Dance, and ordered him to proceed there and arrest the horse thief, taking with him a sufficient number of men for the purpose. The task no doubt required great tact and courage, but Hilliard and his men were well fitted for it.

They found Calf Robe in the medicine lodge, and attempted to take him, but in vain ; several hundred armed warriors fell upon the police, overpowering them and turning their prisoner loose. He was seized by the three and another attempt was made to drag him forth. The men were often on the ground in their struggle with the Indians, dozens of rifles were pointed at their heads as they lay on the ground hanging on to their prisoner, or when trying to bring him away, and at the last he was torn from them and, protected by over 200 howling braves, galloped off. It is a wonder there was no bloodshed, and there most certainly would have been if the police had lost their heads and tried to draw their revolvers. Their cool and resolute conduct was worthy of all praise.

On his return to Stand Off, Hilliard reported his failure to make the arrest, and early next day I ordered Inspector Wood to proceed to Stand Off with a small party, and held the remainder of the men in barracks ready to support him if necessary. My orders were to Red Crow, through him, to bring in Calf Robe and all of the ringleaders in the interference with the three police; if he did not bring them in, I should take out a party strong enough for the purpose. Wood acted with his usual tact and skill, and returned the next day with five Indians, whom he confined in the guard-room. The chief came with them and expressed his regret at the occurrence.

The Indians were brought before Inspector Wood and myself for their preliminary trial, the Indian agent appearing in their defence, and, after the witnesses had been heard, were committed for trial before the supreme court. The Indian agent and Red Crow went bail for them. The legality of the arrest was questioned, and there was much correspondence, but my action was supported in every particular by Sir John Thompson, Minister of Justice, who held that we could arrest an Indian at any time or place. They were wards and we were officers of the Crown, therefore there was no chance of a miscarriage of justice.

On September 9 I received instructions from headquarters to provide a travelling escort and transport to meet the Governor General, Lady Stanley, and several of their friends, with a number of staff officers, who were making a tour of the southern part of the territory and British Columbia.

The party came to Lethbridge by rail and were met there by the escort on October 11. They left for the Blood agency on Belly River, where they arrived at noon, and halted for luncheon and to receive an address from the chiefs of the tribe. I met them there with two strong sub-divisions. When I arrived I formed them facing the ground on which the Indian ceremonies were to be performed. The Indians had assembled in large numbers, and when the Governor General and party arrived there the chiefs were presented. Red Crow, the fine old chief of the Bloods, came first, of course, and, after this part of the ceremony was over and the usual speeches made, the Indian warriors who had assembled gave a mounted war dance. This was really an illustration of what they would do in war, such as riding into the camp of an enemy and stampeding his horses. The braves were beautifully decorated, plumed and painted, and all were well mounted and in high spirits. Our horses were so accustomed to the weird sights and sounds of the old Indian camps which they had so often to visit, and of the prairie on which they were bred, and to the practice given them in the force by waving blankets and shooting over their heads at the annual training, that they did not pay the slightest attention to what followed.

The Indians formed up some hundreds of yards in front of us, and the Governor General's party were on the verandah of the agency. When his turn came, each centaur rode at full speed towards us, rolled up in his blanket like a ball, both feet coiled up under him on the saddle, and when he was close enough, suddenly unrolled himself and, standing erect on his horse, spread the blanket to the full extent of his arms like the wings of a bat, coming at us with wild yells, flapping it as he passed at a gallop round the flanks of my party. Others came waving the blanket in one hand and firing their rifles as they approached with their wild war whoops. Many galloped in, firing as they advanced, or rode by yelling and shaking their rifles at us as if in defiance, but there was not a tremor amongst our horses, and I judged that the Indians were quite disappointed at the failure of their efforts.

The visitors enjoyed the proceedings, as they did their subsequent visit to the Cochrane ranch, where Mr. W. Cochrane turned out his cowboys and gave the party a fine display of ranch work, roping and branding steers " as were steers," not the miserable in-bred lot that one sees at the stampedes and other exhibitions throughout the country to-day. Each of the animals would weigh several hundred pounds more than the Texan variety, and was much stronger. When they came for a man " bull dogging " was of no avail.

In January, 1890, I went on leave to eastern Canada to be married, and owing to the importance of the district I was relieved by the assistant commissioner of the force.

The winter traffic on the C.P.R. in those days was not heavy. After I reached Dunmore the only passengers with me in the Pullman were Sir John Lister Kaye and a young man from Vancouver. We were delayed for a day at Biscotasing, a small place on the north shore of Lake Superior, and found the weather extremely cold. There was no dining-car with us at the time, but through the kindness of the agent we received very good meals, which only cost us 15 cents as a tip to the cook for his trouble.

When I arrived at Montreal the city was in the throes of a blizzard. I stayed there for a day or two, and then went to the village of Vaudreuil, in the county of that name, and on January 15 was married to Miss Marie Elizabeth Harwood, the eldest daughter of Mr. Robert Harwood, M.P., a seigneur of the county and maternal grandson of Michel Gaspard Chartier de Lotbinière, the last Marquis de Lotbinière, a direct descendant of Allan Carter, a Scottish officer who as a youth accompanied Margaret of Scotland to France when she went to that country to marry the Dauphin. He was afterwards ennobled as Marquis de Lotbinière, and the family has for many generations been closely identified with the history of Canada.

After our marriage we visited New York and other places in the United States, and were received with great hospitality. We saw everything of note in greater New York. The fire department turned out 60 engines for us, and we saw many of the precincts (divisions) of the police of the city, and I met the principal officers of that remarkable force. As we drove round on our visit the sergeants and inspectors said, " Yes, Major, we own this city, we can handle any riot ourselves, and we have great influence." I could see quite plainly that they had ; the force was well paid and well equipped.

After a month south of the border we returned to Vaudreuil, and visited several of the leading cities, a very pleasant winter being spent. On one of my visits to Ottawa, Mr. White, our comptroller, stated that Sir John Macdonald wished me to report at his office. Sir John gave a skip as he entered the ante-room, where a number of people were waiting to see him, poked one of them in the ribs with his cane, followed it up with a joke, and asked me to go into his office. When we were seated he said that there was a bill for the Calgary-Edmonton Railway before the House, the line to run from Macleod through Calgary to Edmonton, and he wished me to tell him all about the country and to give an opinion as to the route to be taken. I informed him that the line was much needed and that the country through which it would pass was very fertile and would fill up with settlers as soon as there were facilities for transportation, which there were not at that time. He expressed himself pleased with what I told him, and the bill was rushed through the same afternoon and surveys commenced the following summer. That was the first and last interview that I had with Sir John, sad to say; he was not to be very long at the head of the force after that, although to all appearance he might have had a great many years before him, he was so active and bright. After a very pleasant time in the east, my wife and I left Vaudreuil in May and arrived at Macleod on the 14th, where our friends gave us a very warm welcome.

The district was now beginning to be known as Southern Alberta, although it had not yet arrived at the dignity of a province, and had only one member in the House of Commons and one senator. There was an impression abroad that the district was unfit for anything but stock-raising, and our friends the horse and cattle ranchers did their best to strengthen the idea, now happily exploded. The Mormon settlement at Cardston, or Lee's Creek, had done much to demonstrate that the district was one of the best in the north west, but until they were firmly established on their farms the majority of the people in the country round imported their butter, eggs and vegetables. Even the large ranchers who owned thousands of cows used tinned milk, and even tinned vegetables. There were other farmers besides the Latter Day Saints, but they were few and far between, and had no appreciable effect on the supply of farm products.

Our situation was better, every detachment had a small garden and was supplied with seeds. They were loaned cows by the larger ranchers, and there was ample space on which to pasture them, and facilities for keeping fowls. After the

Mormons were started we were able to get much from them, and to the towns of Lethbridge and Macleod they were and still are a god-send. The head of the Mormon settlement was Mr. Card, after whom it was named. Mrs. Card was a daughter of Brigham Young, the prophet, who led them on their great trek to Great Salt Lake, and established them so firmly there that for many years they were the most influential community in Utah. Card and his wife, " Aunt Zina," as she was called in the community, did much to direct their people on the way to prosperity. The new settlers of their faith were assisted in every way. Much land was purchased and the extent increased as soon as they could afford it, and their system of locating in a village and carrying on their farming operations from there was an excellent plan, suiting the prairie country extremely well.

The Mormons worked their farms from a common centre, which admitted of their having their gardens, houses, corrals, stores, halls, assembly-rooms, churches, shops and schools within easy reach of all, thus giving them advantages impossible for those who reside on their homesteads. The women and children are always within call if assistance is required should the man of the house be away. We found the Mormons a hospitable people, but they had the reputation of being over sharp in their business dealings. I saw much of them in my frequent visits to the sub-districts, and my wife and I often stayed overnight at the Cards. Parties of ladies and gentlemen came with us sometimes, and much enjoyed the trips ; they were received in so kindly a manner. Strange to say I found the Mormon women-folk the strongest supporters of polygamy. Brilliant lawyers and able financiers who were with me had all they could do to hold their own in arguments with the leading lady of the settlement.

At this time they were under close surveillance, detectives being in their midst, and finally, on reports which I furnished, the criminal code was amended to meet the circumstances. The social customs of the Mormons were different from those which existed amongst the " Gentiles," as they called those outside of their faith. Their dances were opened with prayer ; the master of the ceremonies, standing at the upper end of the hall or room, raised his hand enjoining silence, and, still holding it aloft, called upon God to bless the proceedings of the evening. If any Gentiles were present the Mormons were permitted to have two round dances out of respect to the visitors, but amongst themselves these were not allowed, only quadrilles were permitted and that fiend, the caller-off, was present in all his glory.

At Macleod and throughout the district, although the life was strenuous, there was no lack of amusements or sports. During the summer quadrille and tennis parties, polo and golf were frequent, and, when transport could be spared, the guests to the barrack dances with their visiting friends in town were driven to and from them. There were few halls in the little town to accommodate a large ball or party, and to help the people a wing of the barracks was thrown open to the St. George's, St. Andrew's and St. Patrick's Societies for their annual balls.

Our annual ball was given during the winter, all ranks subscribing sufficient to make it a success, and, no matter what ball it was, the billiard and reception-rooms, etc., were thrown open, and as the dance went merrily on a smoking concert was held in the recreation room, where cigars and soft drinks were dispensed to the non-dancing men. The sitting-out rooms were furnished by the married officers and men. Robes and fur rugs decorated the floors and comfortable seats were provided. These parties usually numbered several hundred. The whole countryside was invited, and many came very long distances in their spring waggons, often 30 or 40 miles, but they did not mind that. As it was not always convenient to leave the numerous babies at home, they were stowed away comfortably in the houses of their friends in town. At parties held in the country the youngsters were often seen a dozen at a time tucked up in one of the beds; so close together and so mixed up would they be before morning that it was difficult to know one from the other. More than once practical jokers changed the babies, and it was very difficult for the almost distracted mothers to know " which from which."

During the summer there were race meetings on a very good

course and, at intervals between races, roping the wild steer, riding the broncho and other events peculiar to a great stock country were indulged in. The competitors in these events had often come from a long distance and were past-masters at the games, sometimes champions of the great stock regions south of the line and in our own country from the ranches in the vicinity. The racers were brought in from distant parts of the country, but as a rule that sport was not first-class. The Blood and Peigan Indians with their squaws attended, accompanied by their ponies, papooses and dogs. These were in evidence every day and evinced a keen interest in all that was going on. Horse races were arranged for the Indians, both men and boys, for the red men were real sports and rode to win; Jerry Potts was always the starter, and decided many disputes. He was a leader amongst them, and remained so until the day of his death.

In the roping contests the wild steers were run out. These were not the light Texan variety, but the huge animals of the ranches of the districts of southern Alberta, and as savage as any. When they had passed the line about 100 feet the cowboy on his well-trained pony followed at full speed. His horse kept its eye on the lasso until it fell over the steer's head, then came to a dead stop with all four feet planted to receive the strain. The sudden shock caused the steer to go heels over head and fall on the broad of its back, the cow pony still keeping the rope taut by hanging back until the rider had time to dismount, hog tie the steer, throw off the rope and mount his horse, which had stood watching every move during the operation.

The bucking contests were no circus affairs, the horses were perfectly wild, at least five years old, and had never been ridden, saddled or handled. The horsemanship had to be of the very best. Man and horse often came to the ground together and were up again with the rider still in his place. There were very few casualties, however, although it is really wonderful that no one was hurt.

Amongst the most extraordinary feats of horsemanship that we had the good fortune to witness was one by Mr. Charles Sharples, of the Winder ranch. He had brought some horses to Macleod to sell to the Mounted Police, and had them in a livery stable near the Old Man's River, where there was a perpendicular bank about 40 feet in height. He started out to show one of them to the commissioner at the barracks, but the brute bucked fiercely towards the cut-bank, sidling and fighting against its rider until at last there seemed to be nothing for it but to go over the brink, side on. Sharples would have none of that, however. He turned the brute sharply towards the precipice, gave it the spur and went out into space. Everyone in the vicinity, and there were many, rushed to the bank to see what had become of the bold horseman, and were surprised to see him still firm in the saddle, with the horse swimming towards the opposite bank, none the worse for his wild leap.

Often we drove to the Glengarry ranch, a most attractive spot in a valley of the Porcupine Hills, 35 miles north of Macleod. The managing director, Mr. Allen Bean Macdonald, and his charming wife and family did their utmost to make our visits agreeable by taking us for jaunts over the hills to the best fishing pools of the numerous pretty trout streams which meander through that favoured region. In the evenings after dinner the men of the ranch, several of whom could speak Gaelic and English, or, as they laughingly said, " the two talks," came to the house and, to Mrs. Macdonald's inspiring music, danced Scotch Reels, the Highland Fling, etc., until the approach of the small hours warned them that there was another day's work before them. Several of the cowboys on the ranch were brought from Mr. Macdonald's county of Glengarry, a very Highland Scotch corner of Ontario, and under his careful instruction developed into that useful person the Canadian cowboy. Not confining themselves to the mere handling of the cattle, these men could do any useful work, evidence of which was to be seen on all sides, in that neatness so attractive on a well-managed ranch or farm.

In 1892 my wife took a trip east for the summer. The Calgary and Edmonton railway was under construction, but was not completed until the autumn. In the interval Supt. A. R. Macdonnell had three guests at his home, and, when I started off on the last round of all the posts before sending in my annual report, I invited them and Mr. and Mrs. D. W. Davis to come with me, and all gladly accepted.

When we started off Mrs. Davis and Mrs. C., Macdonnell's niece, were in the back seat, and Mr. Davis and I sat facing them with our backs to the horses. The driver, Constable J. Macdonald, had two new horses in the team, and as they were almost exactly like the others a mistake was made and they were put in the wheel. This we discovered to our cost when we arrived at the top of Spicer's Hill, a very steep and high declivity by which we had to approach the Kootenay or Waterton River. There was a sharp turn at the foot of the hill, where a barbed wire fence ran across in front of us, a bad thing to face. When the team commenced to descend the breeching came against the young horses and they sprang forward, starting the leaders, and off we went at the utmost speed of the team, all believing that we stood a fair chance of this being our last journey. " D. W." and Mrs. Davis sat as if a runaway on the highest and worst hill in the district was an ordinary recreation. Mrs. C., in very natural terror, clung to Mrs. Davis, whose calm demeanour and soothing manner towards her companion in trouble was one of the finest things in the way of genuine pluck that I have seen. The driver, one of the best in the country I should think, handled his team with great skill, swinging it round the corner clear of the wire fence and keeping on at a fast gallop until he brought it up exhausted at the ford. We changed the wheelers next morning and I cautioned Macdonald to avoid another mistake, and in the evening, when we halted at Stand Off, he looked over the numbers on the horses' hoofs to make sure that it could not happen again.

The following night we halted at our post at Cardston, and next morning headed our teams for the detachment at Boundary Creek, near the foot of Chief Mountain. Our trail led along the high bench of Lee's Creek, on its way to the foothills, and a few miles up we came to a long hill leading across the creek by a narrow bridge without a parapet. On both sides there was a drop of about 10 feet to boulders and dry gravel below. Along the trail to our left a strong barbed wire fence confined it, and to our right there was a steep hill, a couple of hundred

T

feet in height, along the side of which our trail descended so that there were really two hills, one in front and the other on the right. No sooner did the team arrive at the top of the first hill than, the breeching touching the wheelers, the team sprang madly down the hill, and to all appearance there seemed to be but little hope of avoiding a fatal accident, had not Macdonald, powerful in the arms and with his wits about him, wheeled his horses, faced the hill on the right and drawn them up exhausted at the top, a narrow escape for us. There was no chance of another for the same reason, however, for out came poor Macdonald's notebook to take down the numbers of his horses.

The next adventure with Macdonald and his team was a few years later, when he drove my wife and myself south. The rivers had been at flood a short time previous to this, and with those mountain streams it is a common thing for the fords to disappear, and years afterwards for others to take their places. There are regular changes, the high water washing away the banks, one season on the right, the next on the left, the river gradually cutting down further and making the valley deeper. On this trip, as there was no sign of a change to the true ford, we drove in, to find in a few seconds that our horses were swimming boldly across as if it were their accustomed work. The waggon floated, but the box filled with water, and my wife and the two children had to get on top of the seat. Fortunately the waggon was the old sensible broad gauge, the only one fit for fords and side hills, or it would have upset, and no doubt, in spite of all one could do, someone would have found a watery grave. As it was, it tipped now one way, now the other, as the wheels struck boulders, and bumped along at a great rate. My wife showed no sign of fear, and the children, of course, did not know what it all meant. At last, by dint of good swimming by the team, we were brought safely to land some hundreds of yards below, and were soon dry and comfortable in the quarters at Stand Off.

Christmas was a jolly time in the west in those days and is still, and was kept in the best style at all Mounted Police posts. Dinner was always in the evening, and this was the occasion when the N.C.O.'s and men invited their bachelor friends to accept their hospitality in return for their many kindnesses during the year at their ranches and homes. They spared no expense to make the occasion all that could be desired, and, as is customary all over the Empire, the officers, headed by the C.O., visited the mess-rooms to see the decorations and wish their men a merry Christmas and a happy New Year.

During these years at Macleod the changes in the territory were assuming greater proportions. Large numbers of useful settlers were coming in ; every day during the summer their prairie schooners, as their covered waggons are called, were to be seen on the trail through the district from the United States to the north country. A customs post had been established at St. Mary's in the south to meet the vastly increasing travel. Farm delegates from the old country travelled all over the west in the four-horse waggons of the force, and were entertained at our posts and at the homes of the stockmen. Many farmers from the eastern provinces of the Dominion and the New England states came to spy out the land and select homesteads for themselves and their neighbours. They would return in the spring with large parties of their friends, and were soon comfortably settled.

The Calgary and Edmonton Railway, a useful line extending for 300 miles from Macleod in the south through Calgary to Edmonton in the north, was completed early in the autumn of 1892.

On September 5, 1894, Canada suffered a great loss in the death of that noble character, Lt.-Col. James Farquharson Macleod, C.M.G., a judge of the Supreme Court of the North West Territories. As a soldier, a judge and a gentleman he had few equals. From the time he arrived, in everything for the well-being of the people of the North West Territory his hand was to be seen. No one was jealous of him ; he was the admired of all, and kind to a fault. He had been transferred to Calgary some time before his death, and was much missed in Macleod. He was a near relative of the chief of the great clan whose name he bore, and his father, Captain Martin Macleod, had settled at Oak Ridges in the township of Whitchurch, county of York, Ontario. His son James was educated at Upper Canada College, Toronto, and at Queen's University, Kingston, and after graduating he studied law and was called to the bar of Upper Canada. On war being imminent with the United States owing to the Trent affair, he served on the frontier until the trouble was over. Later, when Fenian raids were threatened, he was again at the front, and in 1870 he was brigade-major on the Red River expedition. In 1873 he was appointed to the N.W.M.P., eventually becoming commissioner of the force, which he maintained at a high state of efficiency until he resigned in 1880, to take up the appointment of stipendiary magistrate of the territory.

In 1877 he was one of the commissioners for making the great treaty with the Blackfeet and other Indians at "The Ridge under the Water," as the Indians called the Blackfeet crossing. In 1885 he was the principal factor in maintaining peace amongst the Blackfeet, who looked upon him almost with adoration, justly regarding him as the personification of truth and honour. In 1887 he was appointed to the newly-organized Supreme Court of the North West Territories, and was one of its judges until the day of his death. From 1876 until the legislative assembly was complete many years later, he was *ex officio* a member of the council for the government of the territories and initiated much useful legislation.

On July 14 our remarkable interpreter, guide and scout, Jerry Potts, died of consumption, after 22 years of faithful service. He was the man who had trained the best scouts in the force, and, in the earlier days when the prairie was a trackless waste, there were very few trips or expeditions of importance that were not guided by him or the men to whom he had taught the craft of the plains. As scout and guide I have never met his equal ; he had none in either the north west or the states to the south. Many such men have been described in story and their feats related round many a camp fire, but none whom I have known or of whom I have read equalled him. In the heat of summer or in the depth of winter, in rain, storm or shine, with him as guide one was certain that one would arrive safely at the destination. It did not matter whether he had been over or in that part of the country before, it was all the same to Potts, although he never looked at compass or map.

Potts' influence with the Blackfeet tribes was such that his presence on many occasions prevented bloodshed. The Mounted Police and Indians knew his character for tact and pluck and believed that he would stay with his party to the last moment no matter how serious the situation might be. In his dealings with the red men he was a master of finesse, a most important quality in all who deal with those keen children of nature. It was a great pleasure to know Potts, for his conduct was always that of a gentleman, and he possessed most of the virtues and few of the faults of the races whose blood coursed through his veins. As an interpreter he was the most reliable that we ever had, being truthful and clear. In explaining to the courts and the members of the force he had a clear-cut but terse way of his own, one might say, boiling it down to the finest point needed, and to the Indians the remarks of the white officials were explained so accurately that there could be no shadow of doubt in their minds. It would take a large volume to describe even a small part of the usefulness of this man, his record being worthy of a place in the archives of the country which he served so well.

During the autumn of 1896 the N.W.M.P., the settlers and the Indians of the district were engaged in the most remarkable and difficult of man hunts that has taken place in the west. It began on October 13 and was kept up without intermission until November 12, and for the whole month at least 100 officers and men of the force, many cowboys, stockmen and settlers, with the addition of the two Indian agents and at least 75 Blood and Peigan Indians, were riding hard in pursuit of, and on the look out to capture, by every stratagem that the white or red man's brain could devise, a Blood Indian, whose pluck and endurance were a wonderful example of what the greatest of natural soldiers is capable of, when put to the test.

The hero of this chase was Bad Young Man, or Dried Meat, who had been nicknamed Charcoal by some of the white men who were employed as issuers of rations at the Blood agency. He was at least the equal if not the superior in character and prowess of the ideal Indian of Fenimore Cooper's novels, and for some years before we met the Bloods was spoken of by them as one of their most remarkable young warriors, a hero in their eyes from every point of view.   In those days he rarely slept in his camp, was generally on the warpath or on horse stealing expeditions against the hereditary enemies of his tribe, a restless brave who for a long time hated the whites. To many he seemed to be a myth, but when we came into the wilderness we found him only too much alive.   He had given us much trouble, but as time went on our just treatment had the effect of making him friendly, and for several years he had been well behaved.

In 1896 Mr. James Wilson was the agent in charge of the Bloods, and Mr. Harry Nash of the Peigans ; both were able and self-denying officers of their department.   On October 13 it was reported that a Blood Indian named Medicine Pipe Stem had been found dead in a cattle shed on the Cochrane ranch, and I sent the coroner, Mr. W. S. Anderton, to the scene.   I also sent a dispatch to Inspector Jarvis, who was at Big Bend, directing him to proceed at once to the reserve and investigate, and later on the same day it was reported that some unknown person had made an attempt to murder Mr. Macneil, the farm instructor of the Blood reservation, and that Little Pine, one of the braves who had been on the horse stealing expedition to the Crow Agency in 1889, had informed the Indian agent of the Bloods that Charcoal had been to his lodge and confessed to him that he had killed Medicine Pipe Stem and that he had tried to kill Macneil.   Little Pine wished to arrest Charcoal, but, although himself one of the pluckiest of men, he would not venture to do so without assistance, and he went to get some of his friends to help him, but on his return Charcoal had gone, accompanied by his family, which consisted of four squaws and two children.

When I received this information all the detachments were warned, and Inspector Jarvis, Sergeant Hilliard with our men, our Indian scouts and other Indians were sent in pursuit. At the inquest a verdict of wilful murder was returned, and I issued a warrant for the arrest of Charcoal.

At Big Bend, soon after my arrival, a settler named Henderson came to the post and reported that while he was loading timber in the woods a few miles distant an Indian had stolen his overcoat. He gave chase, but could not overtake the thief. The description of the Indian agreed with that of Charcoal, and I sent Jarvis and his party to the place at once to institute a search at dawn. Mr. Henderson volunteered to assist.

On reaching the woods the police took off their hats and boots, so that they could move without noise, and in this manner proceeded five miles. They located the murderer's lodge in a valley below them, where the pines were very thick and the mountains towered above it to a great height, whilst the undergrowth was very dense. The spot was approached with caution, but, very unfortunately, when the party were quite close to the lodge the cracking of a dried branch alarmed the fugitive, who at once left his tent and fired several shots at them. The police and Indians fired a couple of rounds, but had to cease lest they might kill the women and children.

The murderer then dodged into the dense brush, followed by two of the squaws and a lad, leaving behind him the other two and one child, the tent, several ponies and a considerable stock of provisions, sufficient to support the Indians for at least two months. The pine forest where the lodge was concealed was about 500 acres in extent, and was surrounded at once. Inspector Davidson had already arrived at the west end of it and had extended his men so as to prevent the murderer from penetrating farther into the mountains. Jarvis distributed his party round the remainder of the forest, and it seemed as if the escape of the Indian during daylight was cut off. It was arranged by both officers that the men should be careful to prevent escape during the night, patrols being kept moving, a long chain of Blood Indians and police. It was also intended that a careful search would be made in the brush at dawn, and all hands were notified of the hour it would commence. The chain of sentries were cautioned not to fire into the woods lest they might harm their comrades. Previous to this Inspector Davidson, finding that his horses were in the way while he was moving about on foot, sent them to Mr. R. Bright's ranch, six miles distant, and put them in the stable for the night, but when he sent a man at daylight to feed them, they had been stolen. Trailers were then sent to the ranch, which was unoccupied at the time, and they came to the conclusion that the horses had been taken back to the timber. I did not believe that this could be so, and my idea proved to be correct, when later in the day I received a dispatch from Inspector Sanders informing me that Charcoal had been seen at La Grandeur's ranch on the Old Man's River, about 45 miles from the place where he was last seen, and that Davidson's horses had been stabled. Thus the murderer, from the time he stole through the chain round the woods, had covered 6 miles to Bright's ranch on foot and from there 50 mounted.

As soon as I heard this I sent a message to Mr. James Wilson for 30 reliable Blood Indians to reinforce me, and to Inspector Sanders at Macleod for more of our men with arms and ammunition for the Bloods, and, as the weather was getting cold, ordered warm underclothing and blankets for all.

Charcoal was first seen at La Grandeur's early on the morning after he had left Bright's ranch. He had entered the house when only the lady was present, helped himself to food without remark and had departed. Mrs. La Grandeur then informed the police, who, after searching the woods in the valley of Old Man's River, struck the trail and, following it, found Davidson's horses, but the moccasined fugitive left no traces on the hard, dry ground.

When I heard of this I rode to La Grandeur's ranch. During the night I was roused by a report that a Peigan Indian named Commodore had been fired upon by an Indian supposed to be Charcoal, who was trying to steal his horse, which was tied near the house. The woods in the vicinity were searched, but without success.

Charcoal's boy, who had escaped with him, was arrested in the Peigan camp, and informed the agent that his father and two squaws were in the Porcupine Hills several miles north west, where they had gone from La Grandeur's, and that Charcoal had visited the Peigan camp the previous night with the boy behind him, for the purpose of stealing a horse, and had concealed him in the bush, but was not long away when the lad heard a shot and thought that Charcoal had been killed, and he ran away in fright to where he was found.

After a great deal of persuasion the boy was induced to show the way to the murderer's hiding-place ; two Indians in their ordinary garb were sent with him, and some more Indians and our men were sent after them to assist when the fugitive was found. Shortly after they left I learned that Long Mane, a half-brother of Charcoal, had supplied him with clothing. I caused him to be arrested, so that he could do no more mischief. The next morning the parties returned to the agency with news that the Indian had seen them coming and had been able to escape into the woods.

Day after day the search continued, and on the 28th Bear's Back Bone, a brother of Charcoal, was arrested for assisting him to escape. The other brothers and some female relatives had gone to the Mormon settlement, 30 miles distant, to trade, and as Left Hand, another brother, who was with them, had been aiding the murderer, he also was arrested, and with him 22 other relatives were brought to the barracks, where they were confined in the guard-room for aiding in Charcoal's escape. Left Hand was naturally anxious to obtain his release, and Mr. James Wilson, the Blood Indian agent, informed me that he had a great deal of influence with him and that he thought that if he were released he would assist in obtaining information as to the fugitive's whereabouts, and inform me or perhaps induce Charcoal to surrender. I had no belief that the Indian would give himself up, but was under the impression that if I could get reliable information as to his whereabouts the capture might be affected. I therefore released Left Hand on the 5th on condition that he would arrest him by the 10th, or if he could not do so he was to let the police know when he visited the reserve.

I then sent for Inspector Jarvis, who was at Stand Off, and on his arrival I had an interview in his presence with Left Hand and Bear's Back Bone, and made them understand that if Charcoal could not be arrested the brothers should at least disarm him, for I was certain that we should never get the murderer until at least one of his pursuers had been killed, and I had carefully warned every person engaged in the pursuit that while the Indian had fire-arms no chances were to be taken with him.

The Indians promised to assist, and I told Left Hand that if they did not keep their word they would be charged with aiding and abetting the fugitive, and that their relatives, who were in the guard-room, would be brought to trial on the same charge. He seemed so deeply impressed with what I had to say that I felt some confidence in his promise. I also arranged at the same time that five Indians should watch the cabins of Charcoal's relatives.

At 5 a.m. on November 2 I received a dispatch from Corporal Armer, who was in charge of the police detachment at the Mormon settlement, to the effect that when he was on his way to lock the stable the evening before he was fired at and slightly wounded by some person who was hiding behind the water trough in the yard. The bullet fired at the corporal was of the same calibre as those fired at Medicine Pipe Stem and Mr. Macneil. Armer had a lantern in his hand at the time, and it was ascertained that he was only eleven yards off when the Indian fired at him, no doubt missing on account of the glare of the light. The constable came out when he heard the shot, but the assailant had disappeared in the darkness.

Three and a half miles up Lee's Creek a Mrs. Lamb, whose husband had been away from home, had heard some person gallop furiously along the trail which passed close by the house. She knew from the rate that the horseman travelled that it was not her husband, and she was very much alarmed. She heard a noise in the store-room behind the house as if some person were pulling things about, and on going there in the morning she found that a quantity of food had been stolen.

From that house the party, with Scout Green Grass, a remarkable trailer, followed the track of the fugitive. It led in the direction of the pine wood at the head of the Belly River, where he was first seen on October 17, but the trail was lost on the hard ground and could not be taken up again. It was at last ascertained that Charcoal had turned suddenly from his north west course to the north east, and, after a hard ride of about 50 miles to the lower Blood agency, the same morning left his horse near there, " played out," and lassoing another

went across the Peigan reserve to the Porcupine Hills. I
organized a pack outfit to follow every clue until the murderer
was run down and captured.

Charcoal was seen at Beaver Creek and immediately pursued
by Sergeant Wilde and a party. He was again sighted near
Thibaudeau's ranch on the north fork of the Kootenay. He
was riding one horse barebacked and the other, which he led
alongside, was saddled and had provisions strapped upon it.
He paid no attention to his pursuers at first, but when they
began to push as fast as possible through the deep snow, he
changed horses, turning the unsaddled one loose. The murderer
could be seen with his carbine across the saddle in front of him
and looking over his shoulder occasionally as he rode along.
Sergeant Wilde, whose horse was above the average, closed
up rapidly, leaving his men far behind.

A Mr. Brotton, who was riding a fiery young horse and round-
ing up cattle, was within 50 yards when Wilde closed up on
the murderer, and he saw Wilde place his carbine across the
front of his body and reach over to take hold of the Indian,
who wheeled sharply round and fired. The sergeant fell, and
the murderer rode on about 20 yards, turned and rode back
to where Wilde's body lay, dismounted and fired another
shot into the murdered man's remains. He then raised
his hat over his head, gave a fierce war whoop of defiance
at all in sight, mounted Wilde's horse, took his carbine and
galloped off.

Shortly after this one of the scouts, a Blood Indian named
Many Tail Feathers Around His Neck, came up on foot ahead
of the rest, and Mr. Brotton, who was himself unarmed, offered
him his horse, but, as it was almost unbroken and very nervous,
it would not let him mount. He therefore mounted the murderer's horse and continued the pursuit alone, Charcoal and
he disappearing in the gathering gloom. Scout Holloway and
the Peigan, when they came up, carried the sergeant's remains
into Thibaudeau's ranch, whence they were taken to Pincher
Creek the following day and an inquest held. The verdict
was wilful murder against Charcoal.

On receipt of the sad news of poor Wilde's death I sent
Inspector Sanders and a strong party to join in the chase,

and meanwhile Many Tail Feathers Around His Neck continued the pursuit during the night. A party from Pincher Creek, under John Herron, followed the Indian's trail and caught up Many Tail Feathers.

They trailed the murderer to the Rocky Mountains at the head of one of the ranches of the north fork of the Kootenay, where Herron espied the Indian fugitive standing in the woods behind his horse with his rifle levelled upon the party over the saddle. Thibaudeau and Many Tail Feathers were with Herron, the others some distance in advance on the trail. Charcoal had doubled on it and was waiting for them to pass.

On seeing him Many Tail Feathers called upon Charcoal to surrender, and fired upon him, but missed. The remainder of Mr. Herron's party, hearing the firing, galloped back to his assistance, but by that time the murderer had disappeared in the woods. The party then divided and guarded the woods, while the scout and Hugh Leaper searched them. This was continued until after dark, without success, when they found that Charcoal had started for the reserve, and four of the men followed his trail.

In the meantime, after Herron's men had driven him from his refuge, the fugitive rode 55 miles as the crow flies to take shelter on the Blood reserve, but as he had to pass round high hills, lakes and sloughs, the distance could not have been less than 70 miles. When he arrived at the reserve he went to the house occupied by Left Hand and Bear's Back Bone, to whom I have already referred as having promised to assist me in arresting him, and knocked at the door, which the Indians opened and asked him to come in. He gazed sternly at them and said, " You have betrayed me," and after standing at the door for a moment he returned to where his horse was waiting, and was on the point of mounting when Left Hand, who had followed him out, seized him and called upon Bear's Back Bone to assist, and after a severe struggle they succeeded in securing him.

After they had taken Charcoal into the house and quieted him by giving him a smoke, they proceeded to search him, and then noticed a flow of blood from him, which, upon ex-

amination, proved to have been made by an awl which the
prisoner had in his possession, and he would have bled to death
had they not perceived the blood. After binding up his wounds
Left Hand sent for Sergeant Macleod, who was in the vicinity
with his party as had been arranged, and Charcoal was taken
to Stand Off until he was able to move, and on November 14
he was confined in the guard-room at Fort Macleod.

On the same day Sergeant Wilde's remains were interred in
the cemetery there. He was one of the finest men who had
served in the Mounted Police, faithful, true and brave, useful
in every capacity. The citizens of Pincher Creek erected a
monument to his memory. Poor Wilde had two large and
faithful hounds always on guard where he was, and when the
pall-bearers were entering his room at Pincher Creek to remove
his remains, one of the animals would let no one approach and
had to be shot.

Bad Young Man, alias Dried Meat, alias Charcoal, during
the time he was a fugitive never left the Macleod district,
although he might easily have escaped to the United States.
He knew, no doubt, that he would eventually be captured,
but was determined to leave a name which would not soon be
forgotten, and in this he certainly succeeded. His craft and
endurance were remarkable, and excited such admiration that,
had he not killed Sergeant Wilde, he would not have been
likely to suffer the death penalty, proof having been produced
at the trial that he had so much justification in killing Medicine
Pipe Stem that no doubt the jury would have returned a
verdict of manslaughter only.

During the pursuit of this Indian many wild and unfounded
reports were circulated by the eastern press to the effect that
the settlers were alarmed on account of my arming the Indians
to assist in his capture. One of these was that I had as many
as 200 armed with repeating rifles. This was all nonsense.
Only 75 Indians were employed, and these not all at one time.
When they were fatigued through want of sleep and hard
riding, their moccasins torn and their clothing worn to rags,
they were relieved and others chosen to take their places.
They preferred to work under the officers and N.C.O.'s of the
force. The kind treatment which they had always received

from us, the careful management of their tribes for some years previously and the kindness of the agents had gained the confidence of the majority, consequently they cheerfully assisted me.

Their tracking and picking up of the trail were all that could be desired, in many cases marvellous, for it must be remembered that there were thousands of horses roaming over the district ; consequently it was covered with their tracks, making it difficult to know which was which. Amongst the best were Green Grass and Many Tail Feathers Around His Neck. The whites who worked with them formed a high opinion of their loyalty and skill, and the settlers, far from being uneasy, were well pleased that I had established a precedent in the west of arming the Indians and obtaining their assistance in the pursuit, all being alarmed lest Bad Young Man might commit some outrage. Even the Indians who were not engaged in the chase, with few exceptions, bolted and barred their doors and windows, and were ready to give their redoubtable tribesman a warm reception. Charcoal was found guilty of murder and hanged in due course. He died like a true warrior, singing his death song all the way to the scaffold.

1897 was the year of the Diamond Jubilee, and there were great rejoicings throughout the Empire. Strong contingents of troops assembled in London to do honour to the occasion, and a good troop of the N.W.M.P. was sent to take part, under the command of Major Perry. These were given a hearty reception in the Old Land. Several were selected from the Macleod district ; all were anxious to go and take part, but of course the number had to be limited and every district given a share. I sent with mine the horse which poor Sergeant Wilde was riding when he was murdered, and Sir Wilfred Laurier presented it to the regiment in which he had last served. The men of the contingent were granted two months' leave, and had a right royal time in the Old Country.

In 1897 the Crow's Nest branch of the C.P.R., from Lethbridge through the Rocky Mountains to Revelstoke on the main line, was under construction, and my district furnished the officers and men to maintain order on the British Columbia portion of the work, Inspectors Sanders and Jarvis being in charge. Their troubles were reduced, however, by the departure from British Columbia and the coast states of the majority of the lawless element. The rush for the Klondyke commenced in the autumn, and the hold-up men went after the prospectors, as shall be seen in my next chapter.

CHAPTER XV

IN 1894 a complaint was received by the government from a prominent trading and transportation company at Forty Mile Creek in the Yukon Territory to the effect that miners and prospectors working on the creeks on the American side were giving them much annoyance by taking the law into their own hands. Supt. Constantine, an officer of wide experience, was sent out to investigate, and in consequence of his report it was decided that he, with Inspector Strickland, Assistant-Surgeon Wills and 20 N.C.O.'s and men should be stationed in the territory. The party was accompanied by Mr. D. W. Davis, who had been appointed collector of customs for the Yukon Territory. The route taken was by ocean vessel to the mouth of the Yukon, and thence by steamer up the stream for nearly 2,000 miles to their destination at Forty Mile Creek. The party was soon in comfortable quarters, built, as usual, by themselves.

As this was the first effort on the part of the government to establish its authority in the Yukon Territory, which was still part of the North West Territory, I shall give a short sketch of the situation. Supt. Constantine was appointed magistrate and recorder of claims. Inspector Strickland, a very active officer, was as much at home in the sawmill or running the logs down the river, as an example to his men, as studying the art of war at the Royal Military College or scouring the plains of the north west. Dr. Wills was an indispensable man, the only surgeon in a region as large as France. Mr. D. W. Davis was a pioneer of long standing, and had been 10 years a member of the House of Commons.

Before the first year had passed over their heads the force was popular with the very men whom it had been sent to keep in order, and everything went smoothly. The comparative quiet of the place did not last long, for in August, 1896, a great discovery of placer gold was made on Bonanza Creek, a tributary of the Klondyke, properly the Tronduick or Tronduck, a river which joined the Yukon about 50 miles above Fort Constantine, the name given to the new post. Everyone who could reach it rushed to the spot. Men left their old claims and, with a blanket, an axe and a small supply of " grub," prospected the new creek, staked and registered their claims. The news created great excitement throughout the civilized world, and the great gold rush began, in consequence of which reinforcements and supplies were sent into the Yukon for the Mounted Police.

The supplies were pushed across the Chilkoot Pass as fast as possible ; a cabin was built at Lake Bennett, Inspector Harper was posted there, and the men of the force whipsawed the lumber out of the green logs of spruce and fir and constructed the boats as fast as the boards were ready for them.

The difficulties of the situation were at their height on September 28. The Skagway trail to Lake Bennett via the White Pass had been exploited by that interesting individual, the company promoter, who had reported how easy it was to get to the Klondyke if people would take the Skagway trail. It was far otherwise, but, attracted by the statement and the ill-advised chatter of the persons coming out from the gold-fields, men from all parts of the world were going that way to the new El Dorado.

From Seattle and other points in the south every crazy craft which had been condemned was brought into use again and put on the Skagway route, each of them on arrival unloading hundreds of passengers, large quantities of supplies, mules and

U

horses for packing. The result was that the trail was soon jammed and further progress wellnigh impossible. Rain fell in torrents for several weeks, making the trails knee deep in mud; oats and hay became scarce, horses and mules to the number of 3,000 died from ill-usage and starvation, choking the trail with their carcases, and many men became discouraged and returned home.

When Strickland arrived at Lake Bennett, Inspector Harper had completed four boats and had already departed for Dawson, the new town at the mouth of the Klondyke. Head winds detained Strickland until October 1, when he left for Tagish, the customs post at the foot of the lake of that name, which he reached after five days' hard pulling against head winds. He built quarters for his men and settled them down to their hard winter's work.

On October 8 the Hon. Clifford Sifton arrived at Skagway accompanied by a large staff of officials, including Major Walsh, late of the Mounted Police, recently appointed commissioner of the Yukon Territory, Mr. Justice McGuire, of the Supreme Court of the North West Territory, Mr. King, chief astronomer, Mr. Ogilvie, F.R.G.S., Mr. Fred Wade, legal adviser, and Inspector Wood, a large party of Mounted Police, dog drivers, 100 train dogs and a considerable quantity of stores. Mr. William Ogilvie was an able surveyor and explorer, who had been employed on the survey of the Alaskan boundary and, when required, in surveying mining claims. Judge McGuire, Mr. Wade and others left for Dawson by the Chilkoot Pass. Major Walsh followed a few days later, but was detained by an ice jam. At that time seventeen prospectors were frozen in at Little Salmon and others a few miles lower down, which testifies to the severity of the weather.

On January 7 Inspector Robert Belcher arrived at Skagway with reinforcements, and Wood left him in charge there and started for Big Salmon, where Major Walsh was camped, taking with him 22 men, 9 dog drivers and 43 pack horses. At Lake Bennett he organized three parties to haul freight to Tagish and La Barge, to be taken on by the boats in the spring. The trip was a hard one, storms raged continuously, the snow was very deep, almost smothering the pack horses, and the temperature remained in the forties below zero. At Lake La Barge Wood met Major Walsh returning. He had started for Dawson, but the report of an American Relief Expedition with food for the Americans who were alleged to be starving at that place caused him to return.

When the great rush to the Klondyke began I had no idea that I should be called upon to serve, nor as a matter of fact had many others whose experiences have been related. On January 29, 1898, I was directed to hand over my district to Supt. Deane and proceed to Vancouver by the first train. There I should receive further instructions from Ottawa. I left Macleod next morning, leaving my wife and children in the barracks to be quartered there until my return. At Vancouver I found Supt. Perry, who was on duty in B.C. After we had opened our orders he took passage for Skagway and I followed on the 6th as arranged, on board the *Thistle*, a small but well-commanded, seaworthy craft, in which, owing to the rush, I had great difficulty in securing a berth.

The boat had formerly been employed on the Alaskan fur seal trade and was filled to her utmost capacity with stalwart men in black mackinaw suits bound for the Klondyke. My berth was one of three situated above the screw, in a little cabin which had a strong odour of ancient cheese. The berths were so small that it was with the greatest difficulty that we could remain in them when the boat pitched in the heavy seas which she encountered during the voyage.

The master of the vessel and his pilot were natives of Newfoundland, skilled in navigating the icy seas in the whaling and sealing industries, and no better sailors than they are can be found. The food was coarse but well served, and, as there were more than 200 to feed in the little vessel, only 120 feet in length, the tables were crowded all day, only one-sixth of the passengers being seated at one time. Fortunately for our trio the master gave us places with him and the pilot in a sheltered nook on the lower deck.

The weather during the voyage of 1,100 miles was very severe ; snowstorms and hurricanes raged, and the seas, as we crossed Queen Charlotte Sound and Dixon Entrance, tossed our little craft as if it were a cockleshell. The other parts of the route being studded with rocky islands and no light-houses having as yet been provided, we were often roused during the night by the whistle sounding for echoes to enable the navigators to ascertain the proximity of rocky shores. Occasionally the boat would stop, and then back away from some danger discovered in that way. These were made plain to us in daylight, as we passed the remains of vessels wedged on the rocks, a fact which caused all hands to thank their stars that they were travelling under the guidance of expert navigators. We were also certain that our vessel was seaworthy, the hull and boilers having been inspected by competent men, which was not always the case with the boats of our neighbours to the south, where, owing to the harvest of dollars in view, any old hulk was brought into requisition and put on the Klondyke route. The boiler of one of those death-traps was in such a bad state that when the ship struck a reef the shock caused it to burst and the vessel blew up ; none of the crew or passengers were saved.

On the way up we touched at Wrangel, a mean and squalid spot, with the usual number of gambling dens and other low dives, frequented by very tough-looking characters, but there were numbers of fine men on their way to the goldfields by the Stickeen and Teslin Lake route. Juneau was our next port of call. The town is on the mainland and was supported by the mines in the district, the famous Treadwell, on an island opposite, being one of the largest in the world. It was simply a mass of ore, which was taken out as if from a quarry, and was discovered by Pete Deville, a Frenchman of good family, who told me himself that he sold it for 700 dollars ! Such is the way of the prospectors, others reap the benefit of their toil and misery.

We arrived at Skagway on February 14. The thermometer read 30 below zero when we landed, and we struggled along the quay against a biting blast which came roaring down the White Pass, searching us to the bone, an earnest of pleasures to come. The town of Skagway when we arrived had about 5,000 inhabitants. We had an office in the town, established for the purpose of forwarding supplies and drafts of men to their stations in the Yukon, as well as for giving advice to persons of all nationalities. It was the means of preventing disaster to many venturesome prospectors.

I found the office with the assistance of my friend, Mr. D. Stewart, of Glengarry, Canada. There was no officer of the force there, Inspector Wood having gone to Big Salmon to meet the commissioner of the Yukon, and Perry having left for Lake Bennett as soon as he arrived on the 10th. He was expected back any day, and returned on the 16th, having organized two strong parties of the force, and posted them on the Chilkoot and White Passes, with Inspectors Belcher and Strickland in command, to establish customs offices on the true boundary and guard the passes. Each station was provisioned for six months, had machine guns and an ample supply of ammunition. The men were housed in tents, and a cabin was under construction on each summit, which was to be the customs house and quarters for the officer in command.

After his return Perry had to wait until we were certain that the customs posts were in working order and the flag hoisted, so that he could report it on his arrival at Vancouver. To make sure of that I left on the tug-boat for Dyea and the Chilkoot. The weather had been very stormy since the 15th, and when I boarded the boat, accompanied by Constable Skirving, who had come with me from Macleod, we found the wretched craft coated with six inches of ice from stem to stern and the thermometer several degrees below zero. At Dyea when we were landing on the ice-covered wharf several lost their footing and fell into the sea. Their clothes soon froze solid, and they had to be hurried to shelter lest they should be severely frostbitten.

When I landed I took rooms at the hotel, and had the pleasure of dining with Major Rucker, of the United States army, and two of his officers, who were in charge of a large quantity of provisions for American citizens, who were alleged to be starving at Dawson and other parts of the Yukon. Shortly after daylight I left on foot with some teams in the employ of a transportation company, which was engaged hauling supplies and in building an aerial tramway over the summit. As we proceeded up the pass we faced a wind so cutting that we had often to make a rush for the shelter of a tree, or walk in a crouching position behind the tailboard of the sleighs for a few minutes' respite. We saw no people moving on the trail, they were afraid to venture out in the storm, in fact it was useless to do so, for no one could work in such a wind ; even the horses had the greatest difficulty in making headway against it.

We arrived about noon at the stables of the company, half-way up the pass, and, as it was wellnigh impossible to go on, we halted there for the night of the 22nd and were given shelter, food and a hearty welcome from the jolly old prospector in charge. The employees and ourselves slept in the stables on beds of straw made up in the vacant stalls to protect us from the intense cold.

We were off again early next morning with serviceable directions as to our course. The storm was still at its height, but many men had ventured out of Sheep Camp, a tent town of several thousand people which we passed early, and we overtook many staggering blindly along, with heavy loads on their backs, some of them off the trail and groping for it with their feet. These we assisted to find it, or they would most likely have fallen into the numerous holes along the trail.

When we arrived at the foot of the steep ascent from a point called The Scales to the summit, the storm made it impossible for us to find the lifeline which had been placed to guide the people up the steps cut in the ice which covered that part of the ascent, and we turned back to the camp of the men who were constructing the tramway. It was difficult to find, and we had almost given up the search when Skirving called out, " Here it is, sir ! " and there I found a tunnel which led into a huge snow drift which covered two large tents. One was occupied by the civil engineers, the other by the labourers, cooks, etc., of the company, and two men were busy shovelling the snow out of the tunnel to prevent the occupants of the tents from being suffocated. We were hospitably received by the engineers, who made us feel quite at home and offered us quarters for as long as we cared to stay. They were a very jolly lot of men, both British and American, who had worked at their professions all over the civilized world. Their tent, on account of the quantity of snow covering it, was comfortable, very little fuel being used.

Next morning the storm was still raging. Shortly after I had wired to Supt. Perry the cause of the delay, Corporal Pringle came down the mountain from Belcher's camp on the summit and reported that they were ready for work, and I sent him back with orders to Belcher to begin collecting next day, February 25. After wiring Perry to that effect and that I was returning to Dyea, I started on the back trail next morning, after the flag was hoisted on the summit, sending my baggage on to Bennett, where I was to have my headquarters.

On our way down to Dyea the weather had changed for the better, and many thousands of men were on the trail, packing their supplies to the summit, or in caches near The Scales at the foot of the big hill. The work of these men was very severe, each one having to bring into the Yukon district at least 1,150 pounds of solid food besides tents, cooking utensils, prospectors' and carpenters' tools, or he would not be permitted to enter the country. Money was of little use to him, it could purchase nothing, and starvation was certain if no food were brought in. This order given by the commissioner of the territory was one of the wisest given in the Yukon, and was the means of preventing much trouble and privation ; needless to say it was strictly enforced.

At Dyea I met Perry, and together we returned to Skagway in a small sailing boat. The weather, although not stormy, was very cold, and as the tide was out we were obliged to wade through the pools on the shore in our moccasins. When we embarked we were soaked to the middle of the thigh, and our clothes were like boards. When I arrived at the office, papers had to be got ready for Perry to take back to Vancouver, and of course I had no time to change my clothing, the result being that next morning I had contracted a severe attack of bronchitis, which lasted for several weeks. Perry left on the afternoon we arrived from Dyea, and I was at work letting contracts for the transportation of supplies to the foot of Lake La Barge, where the boats were being built to take them down the river in the spring. Wood had returned from the interior on the 25th, and was soon up to his eyes in work.

The town of Skagway at this period of its existence was about the roughest place in the world. The population increased every day ; gambling hells, dance halls and variety theatres were in full swing. " Soapy " Smith, a " bad man," and his gang of about 150 ruffians, ran the town and did what they pleased ; almost the only persons safe from them were the members of our force. Robbery and murder were daily occurrences ; many people came there with money, and next morning had not enough to get a meal, having been robbed or cheated out of their last cent. Shots were exchanged on the streets in broad daylight, and enraged Klondykers pursued the scoundrels of Soapy Smith's gang to get even with them. At night the crash of bands, shouts of " Murder ! " cries for help mingled with the cracked voices of the singers in the variety halls ; and the wily " box rushers " (variety actresses) cheated the tenderfeet and unwary travellers, inducing them to stand treat, twenty-five per cent. of the cost of which went into their pockets. In the dance hall the girl with the straw-coloured hair tripped the light fantastic at a dollar a set, and in the White Pass above the town the shell game expert plied his trade, and occasionally some poor fellow was found lying lifeless on his sled where he had sat down to rest, the powder marks on his back and his pockets inside out.

The town of Dyea at the entrance of the Chilkoot Pass resembled Skagway in many respects, but the worst features were to be found further up at Sheep Camp. Many thousands of men and some women were encamped there, most of them engaged in packing their supplies over the summit, all anxious to get to the head waters of the Yukon to build their boats for the passage down. Neither law nor order prevailed, honest persons had no protection from the gangs of rascals who plied their nefarious trade. Might was right ; murder, robbery and petty theft were common occurrences. The shell game was there likewise, the operators could be met with on every turn of the trail, pushing the business to the utmost limit so as not to lose the golden opportunity which could not be found on the other side-of the pass, where life and property were safe.

During the few weeks that I was detained in Skagway an incident occurred which will give an idea of the state of affairs in that place. One Sunday morning Wood and I were roused from our slumbers on the floor of our cabin, which answered the purpose of office, bedroom, sitting-room, etc., by the cries, curses and shouts of a gang who were having a pistol fight round us. Bullets came through the thin boards, but the circumstance was such a common event that we did not even rise from our beds. Wood jocularly suggested that we should get up and take a hand in the scrap, but that was all. The pursued left for some other part of the town, followed by the others, who were most likely men who had been robbed by some of Soapy Smith's gang and were trying to " get even."

A description of the box rushing business may well be given here. In the variety theatres, the upper part of which consisted of rows of boxes for the theatregoers, the actresses in the intervals rushed up to the boxes and, by all sorts of wiles, induced the occupants to " treat," or rang the bell themselves, receiving a small ticket from the waiter, which on presentation at the bar entitled them to receive twenty-five per cent. of the money paid for drinks. These girls were under the protection of the most villainous set of men that I have ever seen. One of our contractors, a soft young man, engaged in transporting goods to Lake Bennett, visited their resorts, and before the wretched man had left he had paid 750 dollars for one box of cigars, 3000 for drinks, and was alleged to owe another 1000, which the proprietor had the assurance to ask our party to collect for him. I told him that it was fortunate for him that he was not in the Yukon, where he would get his deserts if he came across the summit.

It would be difficult to describe the hardships gone through by the Mounted Police stationed on the passes. The camp on the Chilkoot, under Inspector Belcher, was pitched on the summit, where it is bounded by high mountains. A wooden cabin was erected in a couple of days ; the place where it was in the pass was only about 100 yards wide. Below the summit, on the Canadian side, was Crater Lake, named after an extinct volcano. On its icy surface the men were forced to encamp when they arrived. On the night of February 18 the water rose in the lake to the depth of six inches. Blankets and bedding were wet, the temperature below zero in the blizzard. The tents could not be moved, and the sleds had to be taken into them to enable the men to keep above the water at night.

The storm blew for days with great violence, but on the 21st had abated sufficiently to admit of the tents being moved to the top of the hill, where, although the cold was intense, it was better than in the water-covered ice of Crater Lake.

The nearest firewood was 7 miles away, and the man sent for it often returned badly frost-bitten. Belcher, collecting customs, performing military as well as police duty on the summits, lived in the shack, which had all the discomforts of a shower bath. Snow fell so thickly and constantly that everything was damp and papers became mildewed. From February 25 to March 3 the weather was dry and cold, but on that date another terrific storm began and continued almost uninterrupted until May 1! This storm reached its height on Saturday, the 3rd, when the snow buried the cabin and all the tents on the summit, the snowfall for the day being 6 feet on the level.

On the White Pass the tents at first had to be pitched on the ice, no timber for cabins or firewood being nearer than 12 miles. Logs were cut at the nearest bush and hauled by horses. Blizzards raged as on the Chilkoot for 10 days, and there was great danger of losing men. On February 27 the Union Jack was hoisted and the collection of customs began. The guard was posted in the most commanding position, and men were told off in reliefs to examine the goods during the day, and at night to shovel the snow from the door of the customs cabin lest the occupants should be smothered. The great rush began on March 3, and poor Strickland, overworked and suffering from bronchitis, struggled along in charge, loyally and ably assisted by his men. An immense amount of work was done on both passes, and thousands of dollars were collected every day on account of the goods having been purchased outside the Dominion. Had the miners outfitted themselves at Victoria or Vancouver they would have saved themselves a large amount of money. On the 20th I received from Regina a reinforcement of 20 men under Inspector Cartwright. As Drs. Grant and Runnels had just reported that Inspector Strickland, like myself, was suffering from a severe attack of bronchitis, which threatened to become chronic if he were not immediately relieved, I left Wood up to the eyes, as usual, in all sorts of work, and departed on March 25 for Lake Bennett, accompanied by Inspector Cartwright and Mr. Dan Stewart. We rode pack horses hired for the occasion, as there were no others, and had a most uncomfortable but interesting ride up the pass. There were many thousands of people on the trail, hauling their supplies. The gamblers and shell game ruffians were busy taking what they could out of the numerous tenderfeet who were on their way in. Like the majority of their kind, they thought they " knew it all," until they found themselves minus most of their dollars and, realizing the situation, began to fire their ill-aimed revolvers at the expert, who occasionally got impatient at the fusillade and returned the fire with fatal effect. At nearly all the places men in the mackinaw garb of the goldseekers were to be seen " boosting," that is encouraging the unwary to take a hand in the game. These and their accomplices were members of Soapy Smith's gang, and amongst them, employed in the same way, were others who were a disgrace to an honourable profession.

Honour among thieves had no place with these people. The week previous one of them on his way down the Chilkoot to Dyea, with 900 dollars in his pocket, the proceeds of his day's work, sat down to rest. He wore spectacles, and, as he gazed pensively at the snow, one of his own sort came along, poked his " gun " under his cap peak, demanding, " Cough up your pile, or I'll blow your specs off ! " He coughed up both pile and pistol, and was told to " git," which he made haste to do.

When I arrived at the post I found Strickland no better, so I put Cartwright in command, and sent Strickland to Tagish, where the clear, dry atmosphere soon restored him to health. I remained with the White Pass detachment until the 27th, when Cartwright was well started at his work. While there I noticed the difference in the demeanour of the people of all nationalities when they arrived under the protection of our force. There was no danger of Soapy Smith or his gang ; they dared not show their faces in the Yukon. The " gun," the slang name for a revolver or pistol of any description, was put in the sack or valise, and everyone went about his business with as strong a sense of security as if he were in the most law-abiding part of the globe.

The day after I arrived a Klondyker named Pat Galvin called at the office. As he had walked all the way from Skagway that morning and was tired, I gave him a drink. He then inquired my name, and was surprised when I told him that I had seen him in the United States, and that he was favourably known to the force. He thereupon informed me that he was a partner of Mr. John Brothers, who had once served under me at Fort Macleod and had gone to the Yukon with Constantine, taking part later in the stampede to Bonanza and other creeks. Afterwards, when his time was out, he took his discharge, and had, in conjunction with Pat Galvin, done very well. The latter had just returned from negotiating the sale of their claims for a large sum, and was on his way " inside " to see about it. Before leaving he asked for the names of the officers who were working under me on the Upper Yukon, and started for Lake Bennett. I left next day, and halted for the night at Macaulay's ranch, and next morning early started off on the old pack horse. The day was mild, the snow falling thickly, and the trail was crowded with men moving backward and forward from one cache to another, carrying their loads by stages. The snow was many feet in depth, not less than seven or eight anywhere, and the ancient and experienced plug that I rode, accustomed to having a wide load on his back, would dodge to one side whenever we met anyone, so that he could pass, and his imaginary load would not touch him and bury both of us in the snow up to his withers. On one hill he turned a somersault and rolled over on top of me, with the horn of the stock, saddle planted firmly on my chest. I hung on to it, however, and found myself in my place when the brute regained his feet.

About noon I arrived at the lake and called on Commissioner Walsh, who was encamped on one of the foothills above it. The situation was certainly unique, and not likely to be repeated on this earth again. The place was busy but orderly, about 7,000 men were encamped in the immediate vicinity, and across the river the sound of axes, hammers and whipsaws was incessant, making the place seem like one of the large shipyards in the days of wooden walls. East and west of us, from the foot of the Chilkoot and White Passes to Tagish, nearly 60 miles east, every available nook or flat was crowded with tents. The mountains towered to 5,000 feet north and south of these stretches of lake and river. To the west lay Lake Lindeman, several miles in length ; to the east Lake Bennett stretched for 11 miles to where it narrows at Caribou Crossing, the channel which connects it with Nares Lake, which at its lower end joins Tagish, a magnificent stretch. The lakes and rivers were all frozen over.

The post at Lake Bennett was well situated for our purposes, being at the head of navigation on the Yukon, and where the trails from both passes unite. During the great rush, which was now at its height, strange sights met the eye. An old woman in male attire, breeches, mackinaw coat, moccasins, and whip in hand was driving four goats hauling a sled, which contained part of a stock-in-trade for a laundry which she purposed starting in Dawson. She had lost her husband and children, but, full of pluck, she hoped to do well on the Klondyke. Another common sight was that of active men, for no others need be there, holding the gee pole of their sleds, which had sails set if the wind were fair, and their dog or dogs hitched up beside them, trotting along, their tails wagging with the enjoyment of being in the same team as their masters. Pack-trains came in for us every day, the loads being transhipped from Bennett to the foot of Lake La Barge.

From the time I arrived at Lake Bennett until the opening of navigation, except for short intervals for exercise and meals, I could not leave my office, which was also my quarters. It was a small room at one end of the log building in which the whole force lived. The furniture consisted of my wooden trestle bed in one corner, a rough table of boards which answered for my desk under the six-panelled frost covered window, another on the left of it at which my capable young clerk, Corporal Tennant, worked from 9 a.m. until midnight, a cylindrical sheet-iron stove and a few home-made wooden chairs. In the next room the N.C.O.'s and men were quartered, and when they had finished their meals and gone to work I had mine cooked and served on the same table. Captain Rant, late of a British cavalry regiment, and Mr. Godson, a customs officer on my staff, messed with me, and occasionally I had welcome visits from friends and brother officers who were constantly on the move to and fro, on duty. Captain Rant was the stipendiary magistrate for the part of British Columbia in which Lake Bennett was situated, and was very tactful in all his dealings.

My work began at 4 or 5 a.m. each day, and at 9 I breakfasted, a strenuous life indeed. At 10 I commenced interviews with Klondykers, who came all day and far into the night, asking advice and assistance in connection with every imaginable phase of their lives. Sometimes they should have gone to Captain Rant, but it made no difference, the matter, according to the custom in the force, was put right for them, notwithstanding how roughly they may have accosted us, which made them eventually as polite as ourselves, confirming what has been said, that the contact with the pioneer civilizes the coarse mannered.

We had to settle disputes between men who had known one another for years, had been educated at the same schools, but still did not really know one another, nor the true test of friendship. Some were hard, inconsiderate beings. Many would quarrel about some petty trifle connected with their work and arrange to dissolve partnership, and ask us to see a fair division of the property. This course was seldom necessary, however, a few words of advice usually had the effect of restoring them to good humour, and all would go well. All sorts and conditions appeared to consult us as to what they could or should do, and amongst them were men who had been doctors, lawyers, clergymen, soldiers and engineers, and women in tights—by far the most convenient dress for them—all hurrying along the trails to the new Bonanza.

Deaths were brought to our notice occasionally, and then we took hold, acted as administrators, kept a careful count of everything in possession of the deceased, disposed of the effects to the best advantage, except watches and trinkets which might be prized by the next-of-kin and mailed them to the proper address, with letters, clear statements and last messages. The addresses were not difficult to obtain, for one of the first things I caused to be done after I arrived at Lake Bennett was to have every boat, scow and canoe numbered, and the number painted on it as soon as it was ready to launch, and these particulars, with the names and addresses of every man, woman and child, the names and addresses of their next-of-kin, and the number of their boat, were recorded at Bennett and Tagish in books kept for the purpose. The number of the boats and the names of the crews and passengers were kept, so that in the event of a boat being wrecked, or a person missing from it, or anyone being overtaken by death, or any other calamity, we should be able to get and give a clear account of everything. These entries entailed a great deal of work, which was well performed at Bennett by my customs officer, Mr. John Godson, and at Tagish by Inspector Strickland.

A number of petty cases came before me, but I sent them to Captain Rant for trial, for although all the Mounted Police officers were magistrates of British Columbia, we never dealt with such matters when there was an available magistrate outside the force. This was most satisfactory and avoided all friction, not that there would have been any when the B.C. stipendiary was such a capable and even-tempered man as our friend Captain Rant.

One day a lady and gentleman arrived on their wedding tour ! They came by the White Pass and had sent their baggage ahead of them to Lake Bennett by pack-train, keeping only a small valise and no change of clothing with them, an unwise proceeding, as was afterwards proved, when they broke through the ice on one of the creeks on our side of the border line. The bride, being soaked to the skin, had to accept the hospitality of the N.C.O. in charge, who placed his tent and wardrobe at the disposal of the young couple. As they could not dry their clothes, there was nothing for the lady to do but to ride into Bennett in scarlet jacket and yellow striped pantaloons.

During my stay I had many callers, and no two alike. One was Mr. Jack Dalton, a leading trader in the vicinity of Haines Mission and the Chilkoot Pass, where he had a post. His adventures would fill several volumes of romance, although he was still comparatively young. He had been in the western territories of the United States in the days when a man had to be " healed " (armed) if he had any property to protect, and he had learned to shoot in self-defence. One of his feats was to gallop along in the pass and shoot the pine knots for recreation. His visit to me was to take the contract for the supply of our men who were to be posted in the Chilkoot Pass on his trail, and a good contractor he proved to be, always giving the men more than their allowance. When he was with me several ladies and gentlemen dined with us, and were charmed with his manner and conversation, little knowing the serious trials through which the handsome young American had passed, or the number of times he had been compelled to defend his life at the expense of his assailant.

Another interesting visitor was Captain Jack Crawford, the poet-scout, who had been through the American Civil War, had fought Indians, prospected, knew Wild Bill, the splendid frontiersman, who, as a reward for his services, was made U.S. Marshal of a new territory after the war. Wild Bill had a partner who was married, and one day he had to visit some of their properties, and, as it was likely that the trip would be prolonged, he asked Wild Bill to call upon his wife and children, who lived five miles out of town on the lonely plain, and see how they were. He started for the purpose one afternoon with six rounds in his revolver. On the way he shot a prairie chicken, and when he arrived at the house he sat and chatted with his partner's wife. While doing so, he noticed an octagon barrelled rifle hanging over the fireplace, and this he examined casually, finding it loaded. Presently the lady of the house said, " ——'s gang passed here a while ago, and they will be coming back soon, and if they see your horse at the door they will come in and murder you ! " Wild Bill did not reply to her remark, but continued the conversation. In a few minutes they heard galloping horses, and a man called out, " Bully for Wild Bill ! We've got him at last ! " The gang hurriedly dismounted and made for the door, pistols in hand. Wild Bill seized the rifle from above the mantelpiece, killed the first five with his revolver and a sixth with the rifle, brained two with the barrel, and in a desperate struggle dispatched the last two with his bowie knife, ten men dead, and he not disabled. The lady of the house during the fierce conflict lay under the bed in the next room with her children, almost paralyzed with fear.

Once in the course of his duty Wild Bill was insulted by a

gun man, and a duel was arranged. The men were to be armed with pistols, stand back to back and, at a given word, walk 50 paces, turn and fire. His opponent stepped about 47, then treacherously turned round and fired at Wild Bill, whose back was still towards him. He missed him, and Wild Bill, wheeling quickly, shot him dead, then facing the mob, all of whom were friends of the gun man, backed towards his horse, mounted and rode off. Every one of the crowd would have shot him had he dared, but to carry his hand to his gun meant certain death.

A few years later he was with Crawford, and in one of the hotels of that wild and woolly region he was accosted by a desperado whom he had brought before the courts, and was covered by two revolvers, the fellow saying : " I have you now, you —— ; you are my meat ! " To this Bill calmly replied that it was in the performance of his duty as U.S. Marshal, and seemed to be talking coaxingly to the ruffian, when all at once, without a symptom of warning, he uttered a wild yell and sprang into the air. This so startled the desperado that the revolvers were both fired without effect, and Wild Bill shot him dead.

During the Civil War Wild Bill was in the northern army as a scout, and sometimes as a spy. On one of the latter occasions he was in the ranks of a southern regiment a few hours before a battle, and one of the sergeants on the outpost challenged anyone in it to ride as close to the northern ranks as he. Wild Bill accepted the challenge, and they rode together to within 50 yards of a strong body of the enemy, and were still approaching, when Wild Bill was recognized, and a northern soldier foolishly called out in astonishment, " It's Wild Bill ! " whereupon the sergeant turned and fired at his companion and galloped off. Bill could have shot him but, as it would not have been a fair deal, he refrained, calling, " Go it, sergeant, go it ! " and then joined the picket of his side, as he thought it would be unwise to return to the southern troops.

Before the ice left I was visited by my two good friends, Major Woodside and Dr. Good, the former a jovial editor who had visited me at Macleod, the latter a leading specialist of Winnipeg. Both were on their way inside to see what

w

the country was like, and, fortunately for that part of the world, prolonged their sojourn. The managers of the Banks of British North America and Commerce came in with their staff, and Mr. Wills, of the latter, gave me the custody of two million dollars in bank notes, which I was obliged to stow under my cot for safety, as there was no better place.

An interesting female personality at Lake Bennett all winter was a young girl from California, who was known best by the name of a coast city to which was tacked on her Christian name, Belle. She was a waitress at a log restaurant, where she was earning money to take her inside. Near the place there were several men in an improvised hospital, suffering from pneumonia, bronchitis and pleurisy, brought on by dreadful exposure. Belle had much to do in the restaurant, but she nevertheless found time to help the doctor, cheer the sick and give them their medicine and food. This caused her to be looked upon with kindly and respectful regard by all with whom she came in contact. In this self-sacrifice she was not alone. Dr. Grant, a clergyman as well as physician, treated hundreds of sick without remuneration. Our force owes him a heavy debt of gratitude for the way he saved our men. More than half of those at the summit and Lake Bennett had pneumonia, but were so well treated that we lost none. I have never seen men in such a dangerous state, and it seemed impossible that they could recover, yet they were pulled through. Another case of pluck and self-sacrifice came to my notice. Dr. Sugden, who was on his way in to dig gold, was called upon as a last resort to go down on the ice of the Yukon to treat a woman who was at death's door. There was no other doctor near, so he started off cheerfully on foot, diagnosed and treated the case, which was very serious, and, to save her life, placed her on a hand sled and hauled her with his own hands the 100 miles to safety and shelter.

On April 26 I received a report from Inspector Belcher, in command on the Chilkoot summit, that a storm which had been raging for a week had reached its height and had buried his cabin and the Klondykers' caches of supplies on the summit. Six feet of snow fell that day, and the quantity there had already attained sixty feet on the level ! At seven o'clock next morning there was a lull, and large numbers of men began packing their supplies and outfits up the mountain to the summit, which they had been prevented from doing for many days owing to the tempestuous state of the weather.

While a number of them were on the summit the storm increased in violence, and, knowing how difficult it would be for them to descend the mountain and return to Sheep Camp, and that they could not remain on the summit and live, they began to descend to The Scales, a place near the foot. They managed to reach a point half a mile below the mountain, but were caught there by a tremendous avalanche, which buried sixty-three of them. Fifty-three perished ; the rest were dug out with difficulty. Two women who had been rescued from a smaller slide at The Scales, the same day, were buried in the larger ; one of these was again rescued, the other being killed. The next morning the manager of the Chilkoot Tramway Company reported that nineteen of their men had perished in the same slide. Amongst them were several of the kindly young engineers who had given shelter to Constable Skirving and myself when we went up the Chilkoot Pass. All the bodies were dug out but two, which Belcher stated were found in the spring. Although towards the end of April, it was to all appearances the depth of winter.

When the avalanche was reported to me I requested Belcher to send a party to the scene to be present when the bodies were exhumed, and, although the accident occurred in the United States, to render all assistance possible, to organize a committee of good American citizens to see that the property of the dead was taken care of, and make a point of looking after the interests of British subjects, what property they had on them, and the names and addresses of all. This work was well done. A committee collected the effects of the deceased Americans and was assisted by Belcher in checking over any property which happened to be cached on our side of the border, and, on the assurance of Belcher that the men composing the committee were trustworthy and had proper authority to act, I allowed them to take possession of the goods on British soil which belonged to the dead. Belcher saw that the affairs of the unfortunate people were in honest hands. A list of all the deceased persons was obtained and sent to the comptroller at Ottawa and a duplicate list, giving full particulars, to Perry at Vancouver. I also wrote to the next-of-kin of all persons killed or injured, no matter where their homes might be.

It was indeed a fortunate thing that the weather was so stormy at the time of the accident, or the trail would have been covered with people and many hundreds, perhaps thousands, would have been buried under the snow. Truly the Chilkoot summit was a dreadful place on which to spend the winter. It was bad enough to live there, but to carry out the responsible duties which the police had to perform was a tremendous task. The hardships and difficulties were beyond description. Great care had to be exercised lest there should be any attempts to evade the payment of duties. The severe storms and intense cold, the large amount of snow and the small space on the summit of the passes, especially the Chilkoot, compelled the officers in command to hurry the people on as fast as possible, lest they should be caught in the blizzards, which meant certain death. As careful an examination as could be performed was made of the goods, but had it been made as strictly as it might have been in a good warehouse or in a better climate or season, large quantities of valuable goods would have been destroyed and a blockade on the summits, followed by much suffering, would have been the result. The work was simplified, however, by the desire of the travellers to push on out of the storm centre.

On April 12 I received another reinforcement, Inspector Jarvis arriving at Skagway from Calgary with 18 men, and on the 14th he was sent with his party to establish a post on the Dalton trail in the Chilkoot Pass, to collect customs and to protect the numerous persons who were going in that way to prospect. Excellent log quarters were built, and a large supply of everything needed was packed in as arranged with Mr. Jack Dalton. There was great difficulty in penetrating the pass ; the river was rising fast, the snow was six feet in depth and the roar of the avalanches could be heard on all sides. The Chilkoot and its tributaries were difficult ; they are great salmon streams, and when the snow has gone the run begins, and it is impossible to cross on horseback without killing many of the fish.

On May 3, the ice being still firm, Major Walsh and staff left for Dawson. The American Relief Expedition, which he had expected to meet, had been cancelled, as there were no starving people to feed. Prices had been high, but Constantine and his officers had arranged for supplies to be treated in such a way that everyone got his share, and no corner in them had been permitted. In the early part of 1897 some speculators had bought up a quantity of provisions, and the report came out that there would not be sufficient. Eggs, which were imported during the winter by dog trains, were 18 dollars per dozen, and oysters were 25 dollars per tin, but there was plenty of plain food, abundance of work and a meal ready for anyone who chose to visit the shanties of the hospitable miners on Dominion, Eldorado and Bonanza. The ice left the Yukon at Dawson on May 8 and the river at Lake La Barge was clear on the 9th. It left Tagish Lake on the 28th, and the rush from Bennett and other points began on the 29th, when it became general all the way down the river.

The first boat arrived from Lake La Barge at Dawson on the 13th of the same month, and the heaviest of the work of forwarding supplies and attending to the wants of the people passing into the Yukon via Skagway being over, Inspector Wood came to Bennett and the pay office was established there. At Tagish, on May 11, Strickland was informed that two prospectors, Meehan and Fox, had been attacked on the McClintock River by Indians; Meehan had been killed outright, and Fox severely wounded. Strickland immediately dispatched Dr. Barre to render surgical assistance, and at the same time Corporal Rudd and a party were ordered to run down and capture the murderers. After a chase of two weeks, through deep snow in an unknown country, Rudd and his men succeeded in securing the four Indians concerned in the murder and brought them in irons to Tagish, where Inspector Strickland, in his capacity as a magistrate, held the usual preliminary investigation, committed them and sent them to be tried at Dawson by Judge McGuire and a jury. The murdered man and Fox had been prospecting 12 miles up the McClintock and were drifting down the river in their canoe when the Indians, in hopes of getting their outfits, fired a volley at them from the shore ; Meehan was killed, but Fox, who was only wounded, lay in the bottom of the canoe, feigning death, until he drifted out of sight of the Indians, and finally landed and found his way to the nearest police post.

At Lake Bennett the Queen's birthday was loyally observed and everyone was busy at the games which we had arranged. The tug-of-war was the great event ; there were Scotch, Nova Scotian, American and Australian teams competing, selected from the most powerful of the many strong men who were encamped along the shores of Lakes Lindeman and Bennett, but in the final the lithe, active Mounted Police got the best of it. When they lined up for the last pull it was thought that they might be defeated ; the anchor man of the opposing team stood 6 feet 7 inches in his stockings and weighed about 250 pounds of hard muscle and bone ; none of the team was less than 200. Captain Rant was one of the judges, but, true to his cloth, could not help throwing his hat into the air when the red-coats won the event.

On May 29, the lake being clear of ice, the wonderful exodus of boats began. I went up the hill behind the office to see the start, and at one time counted over 800 boats under sail on the 11½ miles of Lake Bennett. I had arranged to go down to Miles Canyon and the White Horse Rapids to super-intend their passage, and went down the lake on the little iron steamer *Kilbourne*, accompanied by several friends. The afternoon was very fine, a light and fair breeze blowing, and the sight, I suppose, the most remarkable of its kind. During the 50 odd miles of our trip we were not at any time more than 200 feet away from a boat, scow or canoe. Opposite the lower end of Windy Arm, a howling pass from the south, something went wrong with the machinery, which compelled us to turn back to repair damages. We were off again early next morning, however, and in the afternoon arrived at Miles Canyon, a deep and dangerous gorge with perpendicular cliffs of granite, which no one could climb, and a current which ran like a mill race. The water, being closely confined, worked up into a ridge in the centre, which made the passage by small craft doubly dangerous. The canyon was named after the distinguished General Miles by Lieutenant Schwatka, who, when he passed there years before, did not know that it was in British territory, and gave the names of his countrymen to the majority of the physical features, such as Lindeman, Bennett, Miles Canyon. No one objects, of course, least of all military men, all of whom in the English speaking world admire General Miles and Bennett, but for whose enterprise we should never have known Stanley so well.

Before the canyon are the dangerous White Horse Rapids, named after a Finn who was drowned there, whom the Indians called White Horse on account of his flaxen hair and great strength. I found several thousand boats tied up at the head of the canyon. I had a detachment there, consisting of Corporal Dixon, a clever swift water man, and several constables. A Mr. Macaulay had a tramway, which extended across the portage, and was about 5 miles in length. The carriages were hauled by horses and were on grooved wheels to fit the poles which answered for rails. There were several store-houses, the Mounted Police log cabin and several tents, occupied at night by Macaulay's men and half a dozen river men and sailors, who were engaged in taking boats through the canyon and rapids. The tramway was used by the steamers, which were gathering there with loads of goods for Dawson. It was unfortunate that an accident had happened to the little steamboat the previous day, for when I arrived I learned that some of the people who got there before me had started to run the canyon and rapids, regardless of consequences, with the natural result that about 150 boats and outfits had been lost and smashed to pieces on the rocks and 10 men drowned. Our detachment had rescued several women and children who had been in the boats. It was remarkable that more people were not drowned.

This state of affairs decided me to take action against a recurrence of such accidents, and I requested the people to assemble so that I could speak to them, and said :

There are many of your countrymen who have said that the Mounted Police make the laws as they go along, and I am going to do so now for your own good, therefore the directions that I give shall be carried out strictly, and they are these :—
Corporal Dixon, who thoroughly understands this work, will

be in charge here and be responsible to me for the proper management of the passage of the canyon and White Horse Rapids. No women or children will be taken in the boats. If they are strong enough to come to the Klondyke they can walk the 5 miles of grassy bank to the foot of the White Horse, and there is no danger for them here. No boat will be permitted to go through the canyon until the corporal is satisfied that it has sufficient free board to enable it to ride the waves in safety. No boat will be allowed to pass with human beings in it unless it is steered by competent men, and of that the corporal will be judge. There will be a number of pilots selected, whose names will be on the roll in the Mounted Police barracks here, and when a crew needs a man to steer them through the canyon to the foot of the rapids, pilots will be taken in turn from that list. In the event of the men not being able to pay, the corporal will be permitted to arrange that the boats are run without charge. The rate now charged, 5 dollars, for each boat, seems to be reasonable.

They all seemed satisfied with the arrangement, and when they got through, I know they were, for many thousands of boats were taken through after that without one being lost.

The following day I returned to Bennett. There were many more boats on the way. Strange and motley were these craft ; large scows with oxen, cows, horses and dogs on board, well-built skiffs, clumsy, oblong tubs, little better than ordinary boxes ; light and serviceable Peterboro' canoes, were met. Before I arrived at Bennett, we had seen almost the last of the great rush on " the trail of '98." More than 30,000 persons, everyone of whom had received assistance or advice, had passed down the Yukon. Over 150,000 dollars in duty and fees had been collected, more than thirty million pounds of solid food, sufficient to feed an army corps for a year, had been inspected and checked over by us. We had seen that the sick were cared for, had buried the dead, administered their estates to the satisfaction of their kin, had brought on our own supplies and means of transport, had built our own quarters and administered the laws of Canada without one well-founded complaint against us. Only three homicides had taken place, none of them preventable, a record which should and, I believe, did give satisfaction to the government of the Dominion.

On June 9, the trails being fairly safe, I dispatched Wood to Victoria with about 150,000 dollars in gold and notes. This was a dangerous and important duty when one considers the class of persons who were still to be found in Skagway and Dyea. The party was escorted as far as the Chilkoot summit, but beyond that Wood preferred to take his chance with sufficient men to carry the loads of gold, etc., which were packed in the ordinary Mounted Police kit bags. It had been quietly circulated that Wood was on transfer to the north west prairies, and was taking his baggage and boatmen only. After a very anxious time he reached Dyea, crossed the bay in a small boat and on one occasion had to threaten to fire on a row boat full of men, who appeared determined to run them down and were only kept at a distance by the threat of shooting. On arriving at the wharf it was found to be crowded by a bad looking crowd of men, who jostled the escort and no doubt would have robbed Wood and his little party had not the captain of the C.P.R. boat *Tartar*, who had been previously warned, sent a heavily armed escort of sailors, all R.N.R. men, to meet them. He had likewise posted a strong party on the hurricane deck of the ship, covering the pier with their rifles. Soapy Smith was there, but, seeing the precautions taken, merely smiled at Wood and invited him to stop over in Skagway for a day or two ! The rest of the way was easy, the party deposited the treasure in the bank at Victoria, and as Major Perry had gone to Ottawa on duty Wood remained at Vancouver until his return.

On July 30, when we were ready to hand over the customs posts to that department, Mr. Clute, the inspector, arrived and placed several young clerks in charge, but it was still necessary that escorts should remain to support them, otherwise there is no doubt that they would have a bad time, although there were but few people coming in except merchants with supplies of goods for the diggings. The customs having been handed over, summer camps were placed and sites selected for the winter quarters in the passes. An iniquitous practice was instituted by the United States officials in

Skagway of sending escorts with all parties who had Canadian goods in bond. These unlucky people, although they had only about 19 miles to go, and no place where they could hide or sell the goods en route, were forced to pay five dollars a day, and, as they had to pack their goods and it took some days to do that, the expense was ruinous. The American customs officer endeavoured to force them to take escorts as far as Bennett, 25 miles inside British territory, but as soon as I heard of it, I gave orders that the escorts could come no farther than the summits of the pass. There is no doubt that the American government knew nothing of this, which was nothing less than extortion.

The weather was delightful during the summer of '98, and the daylight lasted so long for six weeks that photographs could be taken at midnight. Many persons of note came into the country for pleasure or profit and went as far as Dawson, a few going even further, and returning home from the mouth of the Yukon by sea. Steamboats had begun to run regularly on the Yukon early in the summer, some on the upper river, others below the rapids to Dawson. The majority of the latter were built during the winter near Bennett or Tagish, and were run through Miles Canyon and the White Horse Rapids by Corporal Dixon.

The mails were escorted by our men by trail to Bennett and thence to Dawson, the return to Bennett being by boat. The same men had often large quantities of gold dust under their escort on the return trip from Dawson. I went often to the White Horse Rapids and was present when the steamers were run through, but had only one trip down on a steamer, the only one which was not piloted by Corporal Dixon. We were rushing through the canyon in good style, piloted by a friend of the owner, who had not asked Dixon to take the boat. The bright genius lost his head, and in consequence the boat struck the wall of the canyon with great force. A lively American waitress who stood on the bulwarks on the side narrowly escaped death by being crushed against the rocks, as she hung on to the upper deck to view the scenery of the canyon. I was on the upper deck, and had scarcely warned her to get inside, when the vessel struck with such force that everyone was thrown on the deck by the shock and every loose thing was scattered about. The boat took in water rapidly, and to save her from sinking she steamed at full speed, passing through the White Horse Rapids in a few minutes, and was beached some distance below in the nick of time. Every steamer but this one was steered so skilfully through the rapids that one would scarcely have known that there were any difficulties in the way.

When the last steamer had passed through I returned to Bennett. I met there a young English lady who represented a leading paper in the old country. She had pluckily walked over the summit and was on her way to Dawson. When I saw her safely on board steamer, I directed our men who were on mail escort to see to her comfort and protection, and did everything possible to facilitate her progress. On her return Inspector Belcher, who happened to be in Bennett on that day, escorted her on her way to the sea by the Chilkoot. This, of course, in the great west, on either side of the line in those days, was unnecessary, but now that we have become civilized it is quite another thing. Women and children require escorts just as in the east, unless, of course, they get clear of steamboats or railways. On her return to the old land she wrote much of her experiences and gave lectures in London, which were very interesting. She is now Lady Lugard, and has seen much since then, in a very different climate from the cool and invigorating Yukon.

Amongst my pilots on the White Horse route was a bright, young English doctor, who had been at one time a midshipman and had seen a good deal of hard work on a whaler. He had taken up the work at the rapids with considerable success, and called on me one evening at Bennett on his way out to Skagway. I suggested that he remain " inside " until he could leave for good and all, as a trip to Skagway was far from advisable. He laughed at my advice, saying that he would take care, but the next time I saw him he had two very palpable black eyes, about the possession of which I inquired, and learned that when at Skagway he went into a variety hall for a glass of beer. This had no doubt been drugged, for it made him stagger about the bar and against a big member of

Soapy Smith's gang, who jumped upon him at once, knocked him down and relieved him of his pocket-book. Dazed and disordered he found himself downstairs and outdoors, where he was accosted by a gigantic and forbidding member of the same gang, who said to him, " What's the matter, doctor ? " When informed of the trouble, he said, " Come up with me ! " and led our friend upstairs. On his assailant being pointed out, he proceeded to administer to him a severe thrashing, went through his pockets, restored the doctor's wealth and, taking charge of that young gentleman, saw him snugly ensconced in bed at the only respectable hotel in the place. To the doctor the conduct of his protector was quite inexplicable, but when he learnt next morning that the man had been a typhoid patient of his during the previous autumn, he realized that he owed it to gratitude.

CHAPTER XVI

O N July 7, the government did me the honour of
appointing me one of the members of the council of
the Yukon Territory, which had by a recent act of
parliament been separated from the North West
Territory. I was also put in command of the N.W.M.P. in
the Yukon Territory and British Columbia, promoted to
Lieutenant Colonel, and given the thanks of the Governor
General in Council for the work done since I came to the
north. I was also much gratified by the promotion of
Inspector Wood to a majority and the rank of superintendent.

Later on in the same month I heard of the discovery of gold
near Atlin Lake, B.C. Several prospectors had gone there
in the winter over the ice of Tagish Lake, and, crossing the
divide between it and Atlin, found gold on Pine Creek, on the
opposite side of the lake. Under the impression that the find
was in the Yukon Territory, they staked their claims in
accordance with the Yukon mining laws and recorded them
with Inspector Strickland at Tagish. Having doubts of the
accuracy of their contention I sent Strickland to Atlin Lake
by canoe to ascertain if possible its true position.

Shortly after his departure I noticed signs of a stampede
to the lake being organized, and, fearing that there would be

some confusion and difficulty for both the Dominion and provincial governments, I set off on the *Kilbourne* with Captain Rant, who would have to administer the laws of the province if the diggings proved to be in British Columbia, and an escort of the force, and steamed up the Tagish Lake.

At the mouth of the Toochi Creek we met Strickland returning in his canoe. He had been to Pine Creek and was under the impression that it was in the Yukon Territory. We continued our way, however, and 70 miles from Tagish reached Atlin Creek. The stream was so swift that the *Kilbourne*, in spite of all the steam we could crowd on, could not pass up, and we were obliged to land and walk over the portage to Atlin Lake. After a careful study of the situation and consultation with Rant, I came to the conclusion that we were well within the boundary of British Columbia. On my return to Lake Bennett, at the request of Captain Rant, I sent Sergeant Davis and Constable Woodhouse to Atlin to establish a post and maintain order, for as the mining claims had been staked and recorded under the laws of the Yukon, which permitted a much larger area than the regulations of British Columbia, there was danger of a conflict unless some of the force were posted there. A recorder was sent with them by Captain Rant, and matters were soon amicably settled.

A short time after the clean-up of the claims in the Dawson district, Pat Galvin returned on his way to " the outside " with a good stock of bank drafts which he had received in exchange for the gold dust cleaned up from his claims. I then learned why, when on his way in during March, he had obtained the names of the officers from me, for the kind-hearted Irishman handed over to me for each one of them a beautiful gold nugget with the name of the recipient pasted securely thereon. Needless to say they were all delighted with the keepsake.

On August 14, Major Walsh arrived from Dawson, accompanied by his secretary, Mr. Patullo, and informed me that he had resigned and was on his way home, and that his successor was to be Mr. William Ogilvie. On the 30th the new commissioner and staff arrived at Lake Bennett, escorted by Major Wood. He halted at Bennett until September 1, whilst I arranged the organization of the force in the Yukon. Wood was placed in command of the force on the Upper Yukon, from Five Fingers rapids to the south, and, as there was no officer of the rank of superintendent at Dawson, I decided to take immediate command of that division and district as well as of the force in the country. Wood's headquarters were to be at Tagish, and Inspectors Primrose and Jarvis were ordered to join him with some of their men and horses. I left Dr. Fraser at the Dalton trail post, as he was a justice of the peace and one was needed there. This organization lasted as long as I was in the country.

I left Bennett on September 1 with the commissioner. The trip down the Yukon was very pleasant, although autumn was drawing near, and the journey was much enlivened by the stories with which the commissioner beguiled the time. He was a perfect mimic, and his yarns would have filled a large book. He was indeed a delightful companion, a true friend and an upright, self-denying officer of the government. The scenery along the route was very beautiful, the banks of the river well wooded with a luxuriant growth of fir, spruce and birch; the cut banks were many and thickly covered with swallow's nests, built against the clay, and all along the shore a streak of white volcanic ash showed itself in proof of the character of the mountains in the vicinity. The commissioner knew every foot of the course of the great river, and as we steamed onwards sites were selected for Mounted Police posts, which as soon as I arrived at Dawson I was to establish, in addition to those which we had already built and occupied during the past summer and winter.

We touched at Selkirk, the new post of the Yukon Field Force, a provisional battalion of the permanent soldiers of Canada, which had been sent into the Yukon during the summer. The barracks were situated on the site of and named after the Hudson's Bay post, which had been established there by that remarkable pioneer of the company, the late Chief Factor Campbell, who, accompanied by several officers of the company, had discovered the upper waters of the Yukon in the early forties and, judging that the country was a good one for trade, went all the way to Fort Garry on snowshoes to report the result of his observations. What would most snowshoe tramps of our clubs look like beside that wonderful one of 2,300 miles!

The company had approved of Mr. Campbell's suggestions, and he returned to the Yukon in 1852, and built the post which he named after that pioneer of the western settlement of Canada, the famous Lord Selkirk, whose name will endure in this country as long as the world lasts. When Mr. Campbell built his post, the Indians of the coast, an extremely bad lot at best, were enjoying a trade with those of the interior, and the presence of the company's post gave them much annoyance, and Mr. Campbell, expecting an attack from them, kept his friendly Indians round him for some time, but was obliged at last to let them go out to hunt. The coast Indians, learning that he was to a certain extent defenceless, attacked the post early one morning when he was alone, burnt the place and turned him adrift in the woods without food or any means of subsistence. Nothing daunted, however, he made a raft of drift wood, bound together with withes, which he cut with his jack knife, and floated down the Yukon for about 100 miles, to where he found a camp of his own Indians. After a rest of a few days he found his way across the Rocky Mountains, eventually reporting himself at Fort Garry.

We arrived at Dawson on September 5 and took up our quarters in the post. A look round the place next day revealed the fact that there was not sufficient gaol accommodation to enable me to carry on the duties of such a big district, containing such a large number of " bad men." I had 34 new cells, quartermaster's stores, hospital and offices built of squared logs and sawed shingles. At the same time I sent Inspector Harper up the river by the steamer *Canadian* with a party of men provided with building materials and a year's supply of provisions for the posts which I gave him orders to construct at the places selected on the way down. He made a good job of this, and every place was provided with men, rations, dog-trains, food for the animals, and canoes, so that, when the ice should go in the spring, the men could navigate the Yukon and its tributaries. I obtained authority to reserve from 10 to 40 acres of land round each of the posts, so that we could keep trespassers and others from building too close. Care was taken, however, that we did not encroach on established locations.

Among other things I discovered that the work of the force in Dawson could not be carried on with our present strength. Guards had to be provided for the banks and escorts to oversee the work of the prisoners. I therefore requisitioned the commissioner of the Yukon for a reinforcement of 50 N.C.O.'s and men of Lt.-Col. Evans' force.

This I considered, under the circumstances, a moderate request, for to have the duties conducted in a thoroughly efficient manner Dawson needed a garrison of at least 100 N.C.O.'s and men, that is, a force equal to a full division of the Mounted Police.

This letter met with a prompt response from the commissioner. Lt.-Col. Evans was consulted as to the barrack accommodation he would require and arrangements for rationing his men, but later on it was found that the work was so hard that more men would be needed, and I requested that 20 should be sent down to reinforce them. Captain Burstall and Captain Ogilvie, of the Royal Canadian Artillery, arrived in October with 9 N.C.O.'s and 41 men. The next detachment came on January 3. A short time after the arrival of the Yukon Field Force company a fire broke out in Dawson, and had it not been for the Mounted Police and troops the place would have been destroyed. As it was, two large blocks were laid in ashes.

Dawson was far from attractive in any way, and most unhealthy. It was built on a frozen swamp which had been navigable the previous spring owing to a flood which submerged the place for some weeks, the people going about from one spot to another in canoes. It had partially dried up, but its last state was worse than the first. Sixteen thousand persons had been encamped on the ground before moving up the creeks to prospect ; there had been no attempt at sanitation or organization. The hospitals, Saint Mary's and Good Samaritan, had been put in order by the Rev. Dr. Grant and Drs. Thompson and Good and other capable doctors in the town, and they, with the half-dozen small private hospitals,

x

were filled to their utmost capacity. The majority of the patients were suffering from typhoid and scurvy. Our hospital was full of typhoid patients ; these were in two small log buildings in the barrack square, but fortunately some young ladies of the Victorian Order of Nurses came down from Selkirk, where they had been with the Yukon Field Force, and helped Dr. Thompson, our assistant surgeon, out of his difficulties, by their kindly and strict attention to the sick.

The expense of maintaining the sick was very great. Champagne was 20 dollars a bottle, it had been 45 ; milk was a dollar a tin, eggs at least 5 dollars a dozen. No expenditure could be spared to restore the sick to health, and, to perfect the sanitation, I recommended the formation of a board of health, under the provisions of the North West Territories Ordinance, and Dr. Thompson was appointed medical health officer for the town and inspector for the Lower Yukon district. The council met and appointed me chairman of the board, which consisted of three members, including Dr. Thompson. When he went on leave Dr. Good took his place. A sanitary inspector was appointed for the city, and a thorough investigation was made to ascertain the state of the place. This was carried out to the fullest extent and everything done to remove all causes of illness.

In addition to these duties the medical health officer had to relieve numbers of people who had no means ; the worst of these had to be sent to hospital at a big expenditure to the Yukon government and the country. Those who did not go into hospital were visited by the doctor in their cabins within a radius of two miles from the town, others had to be called upon at the barracks. It was now quite clear that the Klondyke was no place for any but those with the most powerful and sound constitutions. No finer men could be found in any country than those of the rush of 1897–8, but large numbers of them succumbed to the climate and the great hardships attendant on residence in the Yukon. The council was taxed to the utmost in caring for all who applied for relief.

When Mr. Ogilvie arrived at Dawson he was supposed to have to his credit sufficient funds to meet all emergencies, in fact to manage the territorial government for a year, but he was disappointed to find that, owing to the enormous prices, the funds lasted only a few weeks, and he did not know where to turn for more, as there was no vote to cover the necessary expenditure.   The place was, however, full of loose characters who had come into the country to prey upon the respectable but, as a rule, simple and unsuspicious miners, and I dealt with them with the utmost severity.   The heavy fines furnished a large and useful fund, which in a few months amounted to many thousands of dollars, every cent of which was devoted to the patients in the fever-crowded hospitals.   A board of licence commissioners was formed, of which I was the chairman, the members being Mr. Wills, manager of the Bank of Commerce, Mr. Davis, collector of customs, and Inspector Belcher, secretary.   All saloons, dance-halls, wayside inns and other places where intoxicating liquor was sold had to pay for licences to carry on their business.   We were all too busy to hold our meetings in the day time ; 10 p.m. was our usual hour, and our services were given free, for we wanted to be sure that the work of our country was the best that Canadians could give.   The only charges against the fund were for stationery and postage, and before winter was over we had collected about 90,000 dollars, the cost of which to the public was only 75 dollars !

During this time our good commissioner, too pure-minded, one would almost suppose, for such a situation where so many were " on the make " regardless of consequences either in this world or in the next, was on a bed of thorns in his fight against graft, which he had to keep up from start to finish.   I gave him the strongest support in my power, which was a great deal, for I had with me the officers and men of our splendid force, and the approval of at least nine-tenths of the people in the district.   In all parts of the civilized world the already high reputation of the force was enhanced by the work done in the Yukon, which was performed by all with the sole object of being a credit to our country.

We had great support from Judge Dugas, who made Dawson a hot place for evildoers, and we had the fine services of our brothers-in-arms of the Yukon Field Force, particularly those who shared our trials in Dawson.   On their return to the east they must have felt as if roused from a horrible nightmare. Order was brought out of chaos eventually, however, but before this desirable state of affairs came about the amount of work done and hardships undergone by the officers and men of the force were beyond belief.   As for myself, my waking hours were at least nineteen.   I retired to rest about 2 a.m. or later, rose at six, was out of doors at seven, walked five miles for exercise between that hour and eight, two and a half miles up the Klondyke on the ice and back over the mountain, visited every institution under me each day, sat on boards and committees until midnight, attended to the routine of the Yukon command without an adjutant, saw every prisoner daily, and was in the town station at midnight to see how things were going.

In July I had been notified that the mails, which up to that date had been carried and forwarded by the police, were in future to be brought in by a man from Seattle, Washington, who had the contract for the United States mail to Alaska. Ours continued to arrive at the coast, but, although the contract was for a fortnightly service, there was no sign of the contractor or his men, consequently, for the convenience of the public, I continued to send letters all the summer in charge of a N.C.O. or constable of the force.   This had given Dawson a system of mail service two or three times a month, until the close of navigation on the Yukon.   It turned out afterwards that the contractor had sublet his contract, and, as he had paid no more attention to it, no mails came through unless we undertook to bring them in.   This state of affairs after the close of navigation was serious, and to save the situation I suggested to the commissioner of the Yukon that, as there were about 40,000 persons without mail communication, our force should carry on the service by dog trains, for I knew that our men would respond with alacrity, no matter how difficult the task might be.   The duty belonged to another department, but, as always, they were ready to stop a gap, and I arranged to send the mails out from Dawson on the first and fifteenth of the month and to bring in any that were ready, until navigation opened.

The first mail went out on November 15, in charge of Corporal Richardson and Constable Bell. I gave them orders to shorten the trail by cutting across the bends and points along the river, and to obtain the assistance of the detachments all the way to the coast to make the route practicable for the parties to follow. They were to change dogs at every post as they went along and make all possible speed. This mail was very important, consisting as it did of the official returns and annual reports, bank reports, and drafts from the banks for large as well as small amounts. When Richardson arrived at the 8 mile cabin near the Hootalinqua river, 190 miles from Dawson, to change dogs, he was on the point of going ashore with the outfit when the ice, which was at least a foot in thickness, on account of some rise of water up-stream, suddenly rose and broke up in pieces, sweeping the two men and their load down the river together. The mail was a total loss, but Richardson and his comrade saved themselves by seizing hold of the branch of a tree and hanging on for dear life until helped out by their companions on the shore. The dogs had been sent up to the cabin to be exchanged for others before the ice broke up. As soon as they had dried their clothing, the corporal sent Bell back to Dawson to report to Major Wood. From Tagish he went to Skagway with a dispatch reporting the accident and returned to Dawson with a description of the trail along the river, making the distance, 600 miles, in 12 days, on foot.

The next mail went out on December 1, taking the duplicated drafts and reports. Now that the trail was well known and the trees blazed across the points, I arranged that for the remainder of the winter men and dogs should be relieved every 30 miles, the distance separating our posts. The mail was to be kept going and coming, night and day, the changes of men and dogs to be made in 20 minutes. All attempts made by others during the winter to send out mails were failures. The Arctic Express Company's agent started one off on December 8, but the effort had to be given up at our Stewart River post, where Corporal Greene took charge of it and sent it on with his dog train.

I sent the next mail out from the post office on December 15, and from then on from 500 to 700 pounds of letters were carried each way, the men making their best efforts to beat past records, the 600 miles being frequently covered in seven days. Nine days was the slowest. A dog train of Major Woods' used to make the 57 miles from Tagish post to Bennett in seven hours, the driver, on account of the speed, being forced to sit on the top of the load, or he would have been left on the trail. The dogs were the well-known Labrador breed, very fierce, and they had the remarkable reputation of having at one time killed and devoured their driver. One of the fastest stages was by the constable at Indian River, who used to make his 30 miles in 4½ hours, running behind his team all the way, pretty good proof of the condition of our Yukon men. In addition to this work of bringing the mail in and out, the men at the 20 posts along the Yukon assisted everyone who required help and attended to all police duties.

Quarters and food were provided for all officers of the two forces and other government officials going and coming to and from the " outside." Frequently the men helped on such of the latter as required it by our dog teams, thus being obliged to put a greater strain on themselves and the dogs, and as a rule these persons were grateful, but not always. Sometimes people were found in lonely cabins lying almost at the point of death, through exposure or scurvy. These unfortunates were picked up and given the most kindly attention until placed in hospitals or nursed back to health in the Mounted Police huts. Many whose circumstances compelled them to leave the Yukon for the " outside," and perhaps had no means, were fed and lodged as they passed out along the icy trail. These were expected to do an hour's good chopping in return for the work done for them. Several of the criminal class, driven to the last extremity, but against whom there was no charge, found their way out in this manner, a very good thing for the country. They had made Skagway and Dyea as bad as could be, but found Dawson very different, the strict watch kept upon them making it wellnigh impossible for them to commit crime and escape detection.

The majority of the people in the country were orderly and many were refined and well-educated persons, but there were considerable numbers of foreigners who, although doing well and given the protection of the best laws in the world, had not the decency to abstain from abusing the form of government of the country which gave them the privilege of digging out its gold without receiving any appreciable benefit.   Canada had but few of her sons in the Yukon ; four-fifths of the people were foreigners, and the royalty on the gold did not pay the expenses of the government of the territory or of the protection afforded.   Some of the people objected to Royalty in general, did not like monarchs, and would speak slightingly of ours.   One of those was an actor in the theatres in Dawson, and when his conduct was reported by the sergeant he was given an opportunity to say he would sin no more or take his ticket for the outside.   This had the desired effect.

We had in our cells a white man and some Indians awaiting execution.   As All Saints' Day was a religious holiday and festival, Mr. Justice Dugas decided that the executions, which were set for that date, could not take effect, and he reprieved the condemned men until he could hear from Ottawa. As he had only arrived at the decision late on the night of October 31, the news did not become known until late on the morning of November 1.   There was at that time in Dawson an enterprising young lady who represented a leading Toronto daily.   As she wished to make a " scoop," she wrote out a full and complete description of the execution and sent it off by the mail going out that morning.   When she heard of the postponement she came to me in tears, imploring me to help her in her difficulty.   The mail had to be overtaken, and, as it was several hours on the way to the coast, there was no time to be lost. A dog train was secured, and after a fast run of 30 miles the offending report was captured and brought back for future use, much to the relief of the distressed damsel.   The men were executed on the following August 4.

Christmas passed off in a very lively manner, but, despite the large quantities of liquor consumed, there was no trouble. The days were now very short, one might say that there was no daylight.   For 27 days of January the sun was not seen and lamps were lighted all day.   The escorts for the prisoners had no sinecure, for there were as yet no walls to prevent escapes, and lanterns had to be carried, but, in spite of these drawbacks, and although there were about 50 prisoners to guard while at work out of doors sawing wood, there were no escapes. One man made a bolt, and started for the town so as to escape the rifles of the escort, who could not fire lest any of the people might be struck by a bullet, and he finally took to the ice of the river, but was recaptured about 10 miles down on his way to Alaska.

It was not with darkness alone that we had to contend. We had the intensely cold weather of the Yukon, always during the winter about 30 below zero at noon and often 60 to 70 below at night, but it did not deter anyone from going about his usual work. During my walks for exercise I do not remember a morning in which the trail to the creeks was not well crowded with men, and often healthy, active women and girls were met.

The quantities of firewood consumed in barracks and government offices were enormous. Fires had to be kept up all night except in my quarters, and the absence of it was for self-preservation, for, had my stove caught fire, I should not have been able to escape, as it was between me and the door. I preferred to have the water bucket frozen to the bottom every night. This was a regular occurrence, although my fire did not go out until about 3 a.m., and was replenished and lighted at 6. One can form some idea of the amount of wood consumed when I say that the Mounted Police and government used nearly 1000 cords, equal to a pile of fuel almost 8,000 feet long, 4 feet high and 4 feet wide, all of which was sawn into stove lengths by the prisoners ! They hated the " wood pile," if possible, more than they did their escorts. That wood pile was the talk of the town, and kept 50 or more of the toughs of Dawson busy every day.

These prisoners were under the supervision of my provost, Corporal Tweedy, one of the best N.C.O.'s that I have known. He is now an officer in the South African Constabulary, and has been for several years an authority there on all police matters. He was a terror to all evildoers and, no matter how they boasted of what they " would do to him," one glance of his keen eyes or a grip of his well-skilled hand was sufficient.

I used to see them every morning in and out of their cells, and have never known prisoners kept in a better state of discipline. The Yukon Field Force guarded them during the day in turn with our men, and also furnished guards for the banks, while Sergeant Wilson had charge of the town police, and with his 12 men made Dawson safe for anyone during all hours of the day and night. The men were not put on a beat, that would not do in such a place; they had to be everywhere to keep an eye on all resorts, and none of the criminal class could make sure of going anywhere in town without meeting one of them.

The criminal class were much the same as one saw in Skagway and Dyea when the rush was on. Many had committed murders in other lands, had held up trains and stage-coaches, committed burglary and safe-blowing, or were diamond thieves, but they could not display themselves openly. No Soapy Smith could have lived in the Yukon. Our detectives, who were only known to myself, obtained the names and former history of the criminals. They were under our eyes all the time, no mining camp on the creeks was unprotected, and when a crime was committed the delinquent was soon on the " wood pile " or in gaol awaiting trial. These were not the only people who needed watching; there were others, wolves in sheep's clothing, who cheated the decent miner of his hard-earned claims, and had to be disciplined. Compared to them the " road agent," gallant and bold, the Dick Turpin of America, was a gentleman. Many a sleepless night poor Mr. Ogilvie spent, thinking of what ought to be done with these unworthy creatures. The commissioner's years in the Klondyke, while holding his high office, were one long nightmare.

The council passed many useful ordinances; we were not tied down by foolish precedent, the situation was before us and had to be faced. Nothing was omitted that was for the good of the community. The hotels and other houses of entertainment along the trails had to provide suitable accommodation, and, on account of the dangers of typhoid, they were obliged to serve chilled boiled water to all who preferred it. The sale of intoxicants to children and their employment in saloons and variety halls was prohibited. The gambling houses were left as we found them, wide open but closely watched, lest there should be any cheating, and those seductive gentry well knew that there was no money in sharp games. There were worse men in the world than the gamblers of the Klondyke. Some of them were the most charitable of men, always ready with money to help the sick or assist a mission, and one often thought what a pity it was to see such naturally fine characters making their living in that manner. Sam B. was one of these, he had a large place and made much money, but the sick or poor never went to him in vain.

In the winter I took several trips to the creeks. The sight was a remarkable one, the ground being frozen to the depth, in some places, of 200 feet, the frost of the ice age, not of the present. The miners had to thaw out the ground with large fires of fir or pine wood until they had, after many scrapings and burnings, reached bed rock, and then had to drift along its surface to enable them to scrape up the gold. This operation was dangerous to inexperienced persons, and several, who had no idea of the strength of the fumes of the charcoal, went into the drifts too soon after the fire had been extinguished, and were taken out unconscious or dead.

All the way up the valleys the air was full of dense choking smoke. The spectacle was one which is not likely to be seen again on this earth. There had been steam machines invented which thawed the gravel and hoisted it to the surface, but they had not yet come into general use. They were, however, much sought after on account of the absence of danger.

These visits to the creeks were frequently made by the officers of both corps, who always received the greatest kindness from the hospitable miners. A remarkable change had come over the majority of the latter since they arrived in the territory ; there were few disputes now, and our official intercourse was pleasant. Apart from the amusements provided by professionals, few were indulged in except by those who led sedentary lives ; there was, notwithstanding, some hockey and ski-ing, the latter by the Norwegians, who were obliged to kill time. These taught many the best way to come down hills without breaking their necks.

The Mounted Police had no time for such recreation, being

obliged to take the trail on inspection tours or be in the office. One of them was paymaster, quartermaster, a justice of the peace and, when necessary, superintendent of construction of buildings ; one was sheriff and police magistrate, others were in charge of posts on the creeks where goldmining was being done, or out inspecting the posts. Every officer was a magistrate, with the powers of two justices of the peace. In addition to the duties I have mentioned I attended the meetings of the council, and at the end of the month had huge stacks of cheques, vouchers and returns to be signed, so that payments could be made. The whole of the government officers and their employees had to be supplied through us, which made the quartermaster's work very heavy.

In addition to these duties there were many interviews with persons on all sorts of subjects, and letters to be answered from all parts of the world, inquiries about relations from whom the writers had not heard.

Every evening numbers of persons dropped in, often as late as midnight, to see me or to have a chat with others who came every night. Frequently I was unable to be present, but it did not matter ; they could get on very well until I returned. The party was always cosmopolitan. English, Scotch, Irish, Canadians, Jews, Americans, Norseman, Danes, Poles, Germans, doctors, lawyers, engineers, soldiers and sailors were amongst the visitors, and discussed the affairs of the territory and the outside, the amount of pay dirt in their claims, their troubles and intentions, until about 2 a.m., when they usually retired to rest, and in winter I was in my sleeping bag by 3 a.m.

The spring of 1899 brought with it much severe work for the garrison at Dawson, but the tough element had departed ; at least very few of them remained when spring opened. The city required cleaning up and draining, and the council gave full authority and let contracts to make drains and improve the water supply. Dr. Thompson had left early, and Dr. Good took his place as medical health officer. His duties were multifarious ; there was much to be done, and he was determined there should not be another epidemic of typhoid. None occurred ; the doctor was everywhere ; he inspected the water supply and the food, and prosecuted those who were guilty of keeping supplies of bad quality. He visited the numerous steamers and small boats, inspected all supplies on board, and saw the sheep and cattle before they were slaughtered, displaying remarkable veterinary knowledge.

As he said himself with the usual merry twinkle in his eye, he " led a useful and active life," which resulted in reducing the numbers of sick to one-tenth of what there had been the previous year. There were, however, many cases of scurvy coming in from the creeks ; on several occasions people were carried in on the backs of our men, though often heavier than the men who were performing this work of charity out of real kindness of heart. The poor sufferers would be found in their cabins, far from help, and when the patrols found them they were brought in to Dr. Grant's Good Samaritan hospital for treatment. That good clergyman was an authority on the disease, and had gone to much trouble to get at the root of it. He was unremitting in his attention to the sick, often coming to the council to press them to do even more than was within their power.

Amongst the citizens of Dawson was a certain " Colonel." His countrymen had given him the rank unsolicited, and as the boy said, " He came when called ' Colonel.' " On one occasion, at a banquet given in honour of Mr. Ogilvie, the health of the colonel was drunk. In his reply he said, " I wish to explain how it is that I hold the rank of ' Colonel,' which you always give me in this town, and why I have that title instead of that of ' Judge,' which was the only alternative ! It is thus : I was in New York many years ago, and met at one of the clubs three colonels ; one was from the regular army, another had served with the Confederate forces during the Civil War, the third was a Kentuckian. In the course of conversation the second, who was a Virginian, said to the latter, ' What regiment did you command in the war, sir ? ' ' Nevah commanded any regiment in the wah, suh, natural bawn colonel, suh ! ' and that is what I am—a natural born colonel ! "

When the warm spring sun began to melt the snow I suggested in writing that the royalty on the gold could be collected with greater advantage to the country than formerly if the officers and men of the force were employed as when they collected the customs in 1898. The commissioner approved of this offer, which was not to cost the country any extra outlay, and I posted officers and men on all the creeks which were being worked, Bonanza, Eldorado, Dominion, Hunker, Gold Run, and a few of less note. As it was very difficult to find out from the miners how much gold they had taken out, and to prevent us from being imposed upon, I directed the officers to take the cubic measurement of all dumps of gold bearing gravel and take an average by panning out in different parts of them, so as to find an approximate average of the yield and give us a fair idea of how much royalty we might expect. This plan was just to both parties and answered very well, the royalty being far in excess of what it would have been had the former methods been permitted. The gold output of the Klondyke that year was very great. From some of the claims it was enormous. One young man, for his winter's work, obtained 1,950 pounds avoirdupois of gold dust, valued at 400,000 dollars, ten per cent. of which went to the government in royalty.

Almost all gold, particularly the large yields, was escorted to the banks by a constable of the Mounted Police and some of Captain Burstall's men, under a N.C.O. It was then weighed, and the royalty deducted and paid over to the government. After the gold was received in the banks it was made into ingots, and I sent escorts with it to wherever the bank manager wished, which was always Seattle, Washington, U.S.A.

The escorts, always from the N.W.M.P., had more gold in their charge, and under more difficult circumstances, than any men who have performed such duty in any country in the world. Four men took at least five tons of ingots down the Yukon each trip, 2,000 miles of the stream through a wilderness by steamer to the ocean, then transferred it to a sea-going vessel of very little importance, and finally delivered it at the bank in Seattle, another 2,000 miles distant, and this was always done without a hitch in the arrangements. The men performing this duty were serving for the sum of one dollar twenty-five cents per day. The banks usually made them a small present, but had they employed specials it is highly improbable that the work would have been done so well, and it would have cost at least 500 dollars per man employed, and even then it is doubtful if the gold would in every case have gone through safely to its destination.

The summer of 1899 in the Yukon, like its predecessor, was delightful. There was very little rain, and for at least six weeks of the season there was no darkness. We had no regular office hours. They extended to past midnight, but we were ready at any hour between 7 a.m. and 2 a.m. the following morning, when it was expected that we would be permitted to rest. The circumstances were such that we had to be up and doing at least eighteen hours of the day.

During the spring several government officials, amongst them two of the council, went to Ottawa on leave, and many changes were reported to be on the tapis. In August the officers and men of the Yukon Field Force, stationed in Dawson, were transferred to eastern Canada. We were very sorry indeed to see them depart, for they were generous comrades and good soldiers, and had been of great assistance to us. Little did I think that in a couple of months the majority of them would be on their way to South Africa, and that we should serve side by side with them in fighting for the Empire.

Early in September I was relieved by the representative of Supt. Perry. Many of the leading persons came to ask me if I would remain in command if an arrangement could be made. To these gentlemen I replied that on no account would any influence induce me to remain unless I were ordered, and even then it would be much against my will. In spite of all I said, I learned after I arrived in Montreal that the population, as a body, desired that I should be sent back to the Yukon. Inspector Primrose came and took over the division at Dawson and the command of the Lower Yukon until Major Perry should arrive to assume command.

I wished to leave the territory as quietly as possible, but despite all I could do the report leaked out and, quite without my knowledge or desire, steps were taken to give me a grand send-off. I was glad to leave the territory, for my time, almost two years, was the most trying that has ever fallen to the lot of a member of the N.W.M.P. I had done my best, which the whole of the people of Canada who knew anything of what I was obliged to do admitted was a great deal. The late Mr. Ogilvie, one of the truest and best of men, got the benefit of my long and varied experience. I stood up for the credit of Canada and the honour of the force to which I belonged, and it is no idle boast to say that at no time in its history did the police show to better advantage than during the trying years of 1898-9, when I commanded its fine officers and men on the Yukon. I left the force in the highest possible state of efficiency, and had the support and approval of our splendid comptroller and assistant-comptroller in Ottawa, Lt.-Col. White and Mr. L. Fortescue. I could say too that, although I had perhaps half a dozen enemies from an officer's point of view, I had on my side every honest man of the thousands in the Yukon, and my foes had not a single supporter. They went to Dawson " on the make," and dragged the good name of Canada in the mire, and they were my enemies because, through my influence and support of the commissioner, their efforts to bring the force down with them failed.

Shortly after I received orders to leave for the east, Judge Dugas, Lt.-Col. Evans and several prominent men came in the evening to bid me an informal farewell.

On September 26 I took passage on one of the steamers for White Horse Rapids. I was surprised to find that many thousands of people had assembled from the creeks and every part of Dawson to give me a parting cheer. Every wharf, steamboat and point of vantage was packed with people. Many personal friends came on deck to shake hands, amongst them the commissioner, the judge, Major Woodside, Mr. Boyle and others, and a committee presented me with an address and testimonial. When the boat threw off her lines and started up the river, steamers whistled, and the people cheered and waved hats and handkerchiefs until we passed out of sight.

The captain of our steamer was a smart fellow, and one day he gave us an illustration of his expedients. He had arrived at a rapid by moonlight, and did not care to be bothered by putting out a line. The rapid had only an abrupt rise of about two feet, and the pilot gave orders that on the first sound of the whistle all were to run aft, and thus raise the bow of the boat over the step, and when she was half-way up with full steam on, the next whistle summoned the two hundred passengers to the front to balance the vessel like a see-saw. The wheel made a terrible row when it cleared the water and whirled round in the air, but there was way enough to admit of her passing up in the novel manner and proceeding on her voyage.

Among my fellow passengers was a pretty woman, who had left her husband and children in New York while she took her annual flying trip to Dawson to collect the revenue from the claims of which she had become possessed through promises of marriage to various foolish fellows with whom she had agreed to be united if they made some shares over to her. When the papers were duly drawn up and signed, however, she played the game on others, who were kept on the string in the same way. Her share in the " wash up " of 1899 amounted to more than 30,000 dollars, and on this trip she could be seen at the saloon tables the centre of a poker game, which went on every day of our trip up the river as soon as the tables were cleared after meals.

We stopped at a very crudely managed hotel in Skagway. The place had changed, and there was no more rush, in fact the place looked dull after what we had known of it on our way inside. Soapy Smith had been given his quietus during the previous summer. The ruffianism of him and his gang had come to such a pass that no respectable citizen could mention Soapy's accomplices in an uncomplimentary way without the danger of being murdered. To put a stop to that state of affairs a young mining engineer with a couple of friends went down to the pier one dark night to talk over ways and means of putting an end to the lawlessness of the town, and the engineer stood guard at the narrow part of the pier and the others went to one of the storehouses to concoct their plan.

Soapy Smith was somewhat intoxicated that night, and hearing what was in the air took a Winchester repeating rifle and went to the wharf to kill the lot. When he saw the engineer he called upon him to stand aside and, when he refused, fired point blank, mortally wounding the young man, who, as he was falling, killed Soapy with a shot from his revolver. The other men rushed out at them and alarmed the town, and the people, hearing that Soapy Smith was dead, seized every one of his gang and took them to a clump of trees to hang them, when the troops interfered and took them in charge. Photographs were taken of them before they were sent to Sitka for trial, and amongst them was the marshal, whose duty it was to keep order in the place.

Eventually I reached Montreal, where I met my wife and family. My wife had suffered much inconvenience since I left for the Yukon. The children had been ill several times and the house in quarantine. It had first been decided that she should join me in the Klondyke, but, as my stay there was not to be more than two years at the longest, we decided that it would be better for her to go to Montreal, where she would be within easy reach of her relatives and mine.

At Montreal theatres, parties, concerts, etc., were all the go, but war was in the air, and the feeling in the city was intense, and was, of course, increased by the sailing of the first contingent a few days after I arrived ; but there was at that time no talk of any other.

CHAPTER XVII

TWO months after the first Canadian contingent had
sailed for South Africa I heard that it was likely
that a mounted corps would be sent to the war.
As the Mounted Police might form part of the contingent I should stand a good chance of being accepted if I
wished to volunteer. I placed my name on the list, and in a
few days was told to report at Ottawa. When I was presented
to the G.O.C. he informed me that the Canadian government
had directed him to raise, for special service in South Africa, a
four squadron regiment of mounted riflemen.

He intended to give the command to an officer who was
already in South Africa. I was offered the appointment of
second in command. I was to organize the regiment in every
particular, except with regard to recommending the officers,
and take it to the theatre of war. Three of the squadrons
were to be commanded by officers of the permanent force, and
the fourth by an officer of the N.W.M.P. Inspectors were to be
offered lieutenancies and the quartermaster's billet, whilst
the permanent force would provide the adjutant, and the

transport officer would come from the west. Half of the N.C.O.'s and men would be taken from the permanent force and the militia cavalry, and the remainder from the Mounted Police and stock ranches.

I decided that the arrangement would be unfair to the N.W.M.P., which was more than double the strength of the permanent cavalry, and had for many years been highly trained in all that goes to make a first-class mounted rifle corps. I felt, too, that in such a mixed regiment I should be only a fifth wheel to the coach, so I declined the offer.

I was recalled the next day and informed that two regiments of two squadrons each were to be formed, one in the east and the other in the west. They were subsequently styled respectively the Royal Canadian Dragoons and the 1st Canadian Mounted Rifles. I was to be offered the command of the western regiment, which I accepted. Having been gazetted, I was on the point of proceeding west to organize the corps, when of my own accord and for reasons of my own I gave up the command and was appointed second. Lt.-Col. Herchmer was appointed to command the corps, and I proceeded west to assist in the organization. I visited Medicine Hat, Calgary and Macleod, to inspect the men and horses, both of which were of first-class quality. The men were expert horsemen and good shots, several were experienced scouts. The staff and the majority of the officers and N.C.O.'s were members of the Mounted Police. Half of the men also were from the force, and the remainder of all ranks were trained military men, and the owners and employees of the horse and cattle ranches of the North West Territory.

When the organization was completed we proceeded to Winnipeg, the city of hospitality, and from thence on to Ottawa, where Lady Minto presented us with guidons.

I went on to Halifax, and had been there only two days when Sir Frederick Borden, minister of militia, telegraphed for me to return to Ottawa to raise and command a corps of mounted riflemen for Lord Strathcona, who was sending a regiment to South Africa at his own expense. I was to be allowed to take with me any officers and men of the Mounted Police who had volunteered for the service and could be spared from their duties, and I could have the services of the remainder to recruit the corps.

One squadron was to be raised in Manitoba, another in the North West Territory, and the third in British Columbia ; the whole of the saddlery, clothing, transport waggons, and many other articles of equipment had to be manufactured. The horses had to be purchased at the very worst time of the year, and were to be cow-horses, that is, animals trained in round-up and all range work. Recruits were not wanting ; one could have got thousands of the best men in Canada. I had an offer from six hundred first-class Arizona stockmen. They were prepared to supply their own arms, pay for any class of rifle that I desired, furnish their own horses, spare and riding, if I would take them for Strathcona's Horse. I had, of course, to decline, but it was clear proof of what the Empire can expect in time of trouble. One could have had the assistance of thousands of the finest horsemen in the United States.

The recruiting was completed on February 8, and was most satisfactory. On the 14th we reached Ottawa, and were quartered in Lansdowne Park Exhibition Ground. The regiment was cheered at every station en route. On March 6 I paraded the regiment for the inspection of the Governor General. Our space was limited, and the snow, being above the horses' knees, prevented me from doing more than march past in sections of fours, but the corps looked well.

The corps was at last complete and ready to move at a moment's notice, all the result of one month's work. During these strenuous days I had much encouragement from Lord Strathcona, who wrote me several kindly letters, impressing upon me that I was to spare no expense in providing for the comfort of the men and the efficiency of the regiment. I could say that in every respect I had carried out his wishes to the fullest extent and with due regard to economy, and, thanks to his liberality and the active assistance I received from all concerned, I am sure it would have been impossible to find a better equipped corps in the world.

We were banqueted on March 12 at the Windsor Hall. Many of the leading citizens of Montreal were present, every regiment in the garrison was strongly represented, and

the galleries were filled with ladies. The mayor was in the
chair, supported by the Chief Justice, Sir Alexander Lacoste,
Principal Peterson of McGill University, Archbishop Bruchesi,
and others. All made speeches extolling the munificence of
Lord Strathcona in sending the regiment to fight for the Empire,
and the mayor duly proposed the corps. During the progress
of the banquet my brother-in-law, Mr. C. A. Harwood, K.C.,
placed my two little girls on the table beside me, each of them
holding out to me bashfully a pretty bouquet of flowers. The
mayor, in the goodness of his heart, not knowing they were
my daughters, and to make sure that I should do the right thing,
said, " Kiss them, Colonel, kiss the little dears ! " which, of
course, I did, to the satisfaction of the assembly, who cheered
heartily. In the main hall our little boy was passed from
hand to hand till his poor mother was in fear lest she would
lose him in the crowd.

When the banquet was over we marched to Bonaventure
Station, where our train had been transferred, and had great
difficulty in getting through a crowd of at least 30,000 which
had assembled there.

At Campbellton, New Brunswick, a large crowd was gathered,
and we were presented with a beautiful silk standard. Later
in the day another silk flag was bestowed upon us by the
citizens of Monckton, accompanied by an address.

On March 17 we embarked upon the Elder Dempster SS.
Monterey at Halifax. Our marching out state was 28 officers,
512 other ranks, and 599 horses.

Shortly after we had embarked I received from Lord Strathcona by cable the following message, which when published
on board was received with hearty cheers in every part of the
ship :

Very sorry cannot see my force embark. Have transmitted
Dr. Borden gracious message I have received from Her Majesty,
which he will publicly convey to you and the men under your
command. Have also asked him to express my best wishes
to you all, and that you have a pleasant voyage, every success,
and a safe return. Appointments of all officers gazetted ;
they will receive their commissions from the Queen. Hope
to forward them to reach you at Cape Town, where you will

find letter on your arrival. Report yourself to the General Officer Commanding Cape Town.

Strathcona.

The arrangements on board for the comfort of all ranks were excellent, yet our voyage was far from satisfactory. No sooner did we get out into the open sea than, in spite of the fact that it could not be called rough, the vessel rolled heavily, a motion which she kept up on the slightest excuse for the greater part of the trip. After a few days one of the horses developed pneumonia, and from day to day many went to feed the sharks. The greatest care was taken, but it was of little avail, the disease had to run its course, and it was a pitiful sight to see so many exceptionally fine animals thrown overboard.

On April 10 we arrived and anchored in Table Bay. On the 12th I had letters from Lord Strathcona, all containing useful advice. He sent out 150 field glasses and wire cutters, whilst money was placed to my credit to purchase lassoes, extra tea and tobacco. On the 13th I called on Sir Alfred (now Viscount) Milner, the High Commissioner, at Government House.

All our transport arrangements were soon made, and we could have left for the front at once had it not been for a telegram which I received on the 14th, and which read as follows :

From the Field Marshal, Commanding-in-Chief, Bloemfontein.

The officer commanding Strathcona's Horse not to be disappointed at not being brought here. There is important work for his corps to do for which I have specially selected it.

A further annoyance for me was a request made by a general officer friend of ours, who was at Bloemfontein, for volunteers from Strathcona's Horse to join a scout corps for the advance of Lord Roberts. One of his scouts wrote to some of my men, asking them " on the quiet " to volunteer, but they, like good soldiers, informed me of it. I called for volunteers, but none appeared ; however, I paraded the men and told them that as no one had volunteered I wished to tell them that I was pleased that none would leave the regiment. I also said that in any case I was determined that we should not separate.

We were raised by Lord Strathcona for special service as a unit, and not to be broken into detached parties.

On June 1 we sailed from Cape Town for Kosi Bay, in Amatonga Land. Just before we left I received my sealed orders. At the mouth of Kosi Bay we found H.M.S. *Doris*, the flagship of Admiral Sir R. Harris, commander-in-chief on the Cape station, H.M.S. *Monarch*, and a small cruiser. The coast to the north of where the Kosi River runs into the little narrow bay is low and sandy, and from a strip about 300 yards in width the land rises abruptly and is steep and rugged, covered with thick, low, scrubby bushes. The cruiser had run a line about 500 yards north to mark the landing place; the surf was 25 feet wide or thereabouts, but not difficult. Preparations were made to lower the horses and swim them to land as soon as the man who was to meet us appeared on the shore.

My orders were that on account of contraband of war being smuggled through Portuguese territory by the Delagoa Bay railway, I was to land at Kosi Bay and proceed with one squadron to the railway bridge over the Komati River and blow it up. Captain Livingstone, R.E., and his brother officer, Lieutenant Walker, were to perform the engineering feat. The scheme had been objected to by more than one distinguished officer on the score of its being impracticable, but the authorities had decided that the attempt should be made. Mr. Roger Casement,[1] who knew the natives, was to accompany me.

Extreme secrecy was necessary. The essence of the plan was surprise, and it could only be effected by landing at Kosi Bay, a lonely spot. The Lebomba Mountains, which had to be crossed, were bad, and it was therefore decided that the party to destroy the bridge should not exceed 200. Pack animals only could be taken. It was understood that if we had the good fortune to blow up the bridge we should not be strong enough to hold the place or to prevent it from being repaired; for this a stronger force would be necessary. In consequence the majority of Strathcona's Horse with guns and mule waggons was to move to Eshowe in Zululand, as if

---

[1] He has since been noted as the exposer of the dreadful rubber atrocities in Central Africa and Peru.

moving to cover General Buller's flank along the western border of Zululand, and while they were at Eshowe they were to collect supplies for the whole force for several weeks. Whilst they were doing this, my party was to land at Kosi Bay and make for the bridge as fast as possible. The ship was then to return to Durban and advise the rest of the regiment that they were to start at once in support, taking the coast road through Zululand to Lebomba, and by that time the bridge would be blown up.

The next day I learned that a ship had been sent to Delagoa Bay and had returned with the bad news that tidings of the plan had got into the hands of the Boers, that the garrison at the bridge had been strengthened, and that 500 of the enemy had been posted on each flank of our route.[1] On receipt of this intelligence, which the admiral had good reason to believe, and as there was no sign of the appearance of the guide who was to have met us at the bay, he called off the expedition and we sailed for Durban the same afternoon. The abandonment of the expedition had a most disheartening effect on the men, and the naval force regretted the loss of the practice in landing the horses on such a difficult coast.

I next received orders to proceed to Eshowe, in Zululand, as soon as possible and make an attempt from there to reach the Komati and destroy the bridge. The orders to join General Buller had been countermanded.

We reached Eshowe, and the same evening we were ready to make a rapid move north to the bridge, but to the intense chagrin of every officer and man in the corps, I received by wire orders to return to Durban by road, and from there proceed to Zandspruit, on the border of the Transvaal, to join General Buller's force. I was sorry that the attempt was abandoned, for it would have been successful.

On June 20 we joined General Buller's army at Zandspruit. It was dark before I arrived there, and the hundreds of bivouac

[1] Several years later, when in the South African Constabulary, I went to Komati Poort on a tour of inspection, and I learned that the guard on the bridge at this time consisted of, at most, 150 men. It seems incredible that the circumstance was not known to our people in Delagoa Bay. It is good proof of the ability of the Boers to spread false news to deceive their enemy.

fires were a cheerful sight. On the following day the brigade, under Lord Dundonald, which I had been ordered to join, marched early.[1]

While we were on the march Sir Redvers Buller rode up with his staff and passed in and out through our troops, which were in column, and expressed himself very much pleased. He said : " I know Lord Strathcona very well ; when I was in Winnipeg on the Red River expedition of 1870, it was arranged with him that I should go west to distribute the proclamation ; but it turned out that I was required with my regiment, and Butler went instead, a very good thing too ; for he wrote a very good book describing his journey, which I could not have done." Sir Redvers' manner was delightful. He spoke of Canada and the pleasant time he spent in the country when he was a young officer of the 60th King's Royal Rifles, and when he saw my general service ribbon he spoke of the Red River expedition and his experiences at that time.

The next day we entered Standerton unopposed, welcomed by large numbers of British people, who waved handkerchiefs and hats, calling out, " Welcome, Canadians ! " Before we arrived a loud explosion was heard, and a cloud of black smoke arose, which was explained when we entered the town and saw the ruins of the railway bridge which the enemy had blown up. There was also a large quantity of railway stores in flames ; as several of the railway officials had participated in this wanton destruction, they were made prisoners of war.

The names I mention must not always be assumed to be those of towns or villages, as every farm in the Transvaal and Orange Free State was named and numbered. They are very large, generally 6 or 7 miles square, and are shown on the maps with numbers and recorded. There are many of the same name, and they are described thus : Oliphantsfontein No. 10 ; Krokodilpoort No. 50, and so on. When the voortrekkers came into the country they laid out the farms to suit themselves by riding as straight as possible for an hour at the usual tripping pace—single-footing or racking, we call it—

[1] It was composed of Composite Regiment, South African Light Horse, A Battery, R.H. Artillery, Engineer Troop, Strathcona's Horse, Thorneycroft's M.I.

then turning at right angles to the course and again at the end of another hour, until a square of about 6 miles had been described. Marks were placed at the corners, and the house and kraals were erected as near as possible to the water supply furnished by some spruit or fontein, then trees were planted and an effort made to beautify the place.

On the 12th we bivouacked at Witpoort, and on the following day I sent Major Sangmeister out to the right with a troop to cover that flank ; but the clear atmosphere of that region, although he had resided at Heidelberg for some time previously, caused him to miscalculate the distance ordered, and he went out too far, and before there was time to warn him, he approached One Tree Hill, a high kopje which rises abruptly from the plain. He saw some of the enemy on top of it and without hesitation charged them at the head of the troop, receiving a heavy fire at close range, and was captured with seven of the men by the strong commando which was posted on the summit. Two of the men were severely wounded and several horses shot. An ambulance was sent for the wounded men and brought them into camp in the afternoon.

During the following night the plucky major sent in a report by a Kaffir to Lord Dundonald, giving him full particulars of the strength of the enemy. The remainder of the brigade in the meantime came in contact with the Boers in a strongly prepared position across the ravine. I got within a short distance and opened fire, and the brigade pursued them until dark, inflicting severe loss. Our casualties would have been nil, but for the misfortune of poor Sangmeister.

At Waterval Lieutenant Adamson, with 38 men and 40 horses, reported to me as a reinforcement from Canada. They had been sent by Lord Strathcona to fill up casualties, and were a very good lot. I posted them to the regiment at once, keeping them in a troop under Adamson.

I learned at Heidelberg that there was a possibility of the regiment being retained for work on the line of communication. As such was not to our taste I wrote to our brigadier, pointing out that the corps was not raised by Lord Strathcona for work on the line of communication but as advanced scouts and with the advance, as that class of troops had been specially requested at the time of organization, and that there would be great disappointment throughout the corps, and no doubt at home, unless we were kept with the advance of the army.   The letter produced the desired effect, the corps being kept well to the front during the remainder of its service in the field.

Poor Sergeant Parker, an ex-captain in the Essex and prominent in the Kootenay district, B.C., was killed near Waterval Bridge.   Some Boers had sent in word to the officer in command that they would surrender to a troop if it went out to receive their submission, and White-Fraser was sent to meet them, as they had stated that they did not care to come in to lay down their arms.

White-Fraser, a capable officer in the field, proceeded with caution, and it is well that he had no faith in the proposals of the enemy, for as soon as he approached the place the troop came under a hot fire at long range from about twice its number or more posted in kraals and sheltered by kopjes.   He continued his advance until there was a certainty that treachery was intended, and then fell back slowly, keeping well to the front of his men and nearer the enemy.   Sergeant Parker and one of the privates, however, when well out to the flank, were fired upon by a strong party of the enemy concealed in a kraal not more than 25 yards from them.   The Boers called upon Parker to surrender, but he replied defiantly and was shot dead.   The wounded private had to be left on the field, but was picked up by a farmer and kept in the house until medical assistance was sent.   As he could not be moved he remained there until my arrival, when I sent out an escort to bring him in from the Boer farm, but the poor fellow died of his wounds before he could be moved.

At Paardekop the men of the west had an opportunity of showing what they could do besides soldiering.   A band of 500 horses fresh from Natal broke out of one of the kraals through a gate which had been left open, and were soon careering wildly across the veldt.   We had to turn out and lasso at least half of them, the remainder being rounded up in the usual way.   In return for this service, which could not have been performed had we not been equipped with lassoes and stock saddles, I was given the first pick of the remounts,

50 of which I required. I thanked my stars that on my recommendation the regiment had been provided with stock saddles and lassoes. They very often came in useful later on, in capturing wild horses found on the veldt and in dragging others out of bogs or sloughs, for all one had to do in this latter case was to throw the rope over the mired animal's head, take a turn round the horn of the saddle, and drag the animal out by the neck, not a hard task, for as soon as the brute felt the strain he made desperate efforts to keep up with his captor and plunged forward on each yank of the rope until on dry land.

On August 5 I dined with Sir Redvers Buller and his staff. Sir Redvers had always kept in touch with Canada, and talked a great deal of his experiences there. He was possessed of the dry humour of a Mark Twain, keeping the table merry during the meal and drawing everyone else out. It was evident to me that he was held in great esteem and was a favourite with everyone.

The story of the South African War has been told many times over, and I do not propose to do more than string together some incidents and events that appear to me to be of peculiar interest. We saw much fighting, and I think proved that from the Dominion came as good fighting men as ever played at the great game of war.

When searching a house that displayed a white flag the system in the 3rd Mounted Brigade was to make good the ground on all sides with the flankers and advance, so that no enemy could escape. The support would then search the house. By taking this precaution there were no white flag incidents. Very often the white flags were put up with no sinister intent ; every house in sight placed them, no doubt they were raised sometimes by the women for their protection, and very naturally, as the kraals round the farm-houses were strong stone fences behind which the retiring Boers took cover and opened fire on any of their foes who approached. On one occasion a young cavalry officer with a party of his regiment was reported to have gone straight to a house from which a white flag was displayed, and talked to the occupants, women and children, for the purpose, it was stated, of getting information. When they were on the point of riding away, every saddle was emptied, several of the men being killed outright and the remainder wounded, some mortally, the fire being directed from an adjoining kraal.

Early one morning as the regiment passed out of the bivouac at Vogelsluitspruit to its position on the left of the column we met Sir Redvers Buller and his staff. In response to my salute, and " Good morning, sir," he greeted me heartily, saying, " We shall have hot work to-day, Steele ! " It was a pleasure to serve that gallant man, a jovial, cool-headed soldier, the perfect type of the best of his race, always where he was wanted, always cheery. That day's action at Bergendal Farm was a great credit to Sir Redvers Buller, who had planned the battle and was reported in dispatches by the Commander-in-Chief as having handled the operations with great skill.

On one occasion at Machadodorp, as we halted to water the horses at a long ditch, we observed some stragglers from another corps, fellows who ought to have been under fire ; but at that moment they came under that of the tongues of some Boer women of the farm below the hill. There were pigs and fowls about, which these enterprising troopers were carrying off, while the women, young and old, were busy screaming all sorts of things at the " verdommed Rooineks," and belabouring them with broom handles and mops. The victims of the assault rent the air with their shrieks of laughter, the pigs and fowls joining in the chorus. This entertainment was still going on when, a few minutes later, we galloped to the front and threw ourselves, dismounted, under cover to the left rear of the Chestnut battery, which came forward at a gallop and was soon busy with the enemy's Long Toms posted on the heights of the Drakensberg, where they had been for most of the day. Thus comedy and tragedy were being enacted at one and the same time.

One day the provost-marshal of Lyndenberg called at my bivouac, and we had a pleasant chat, during which he said, " I am told you have been informed that I stated on the day the column entered Machadodorp that your men had looted in that town." I replied, " Yes, I was so informed, and reported to Lord Dundonald that immediately after the 3rd Mounted Brigade carried the town I had reassembled the corps in the square, and that I saw every man fall in, and that no looting had been done." To this he answered that if anyone had stated that he had spoken in that way of the regiment he told an untruth, for he had not made any such statement nor had he any grounds for it. There was " no regiment in the army more free from any kind of irregularity than Strathcona's Horse."

Having taken a prominent part in the Battle of Lyndenberg, we were still at Spitzkop on the 22nd, and the convoy returned from Nelspruit with supplies. Their march was through a malarial tract of country, and they had found the remains of several of the field guns which had been destroyed by the Boers who had retreated before us on the 13th and broken away in that direction. The usual daily summary of news stated that President Kruger had sailed for Holland from Lourenço Marques, resigning the Presidency to Vice-President Schalk Burger. There were also erroneous reports to the effect that General Botha had been forced to resign owing to ill-health, and that many of the enemy had thrown down their arms and retreated into Portuguese territory.

Lord Dundonald had interesting interviews with some of the brigade on the subject of looting. Certain enterprising young Colonials had turned down the brims of their felt hats and put dints in the crowns to make them look like the Canadian hats, but it was not successful, the saddles gave them away, as we had the California stock saddle, which could not be imitated in a hurry. There were no complaints against our men and very few against others, for woe betide the marauder who got into the hands of our chief ! General Buller's orders on the subject of looting and damaging property were very strict and well carried out ; as Lord Dundonald tersely stated, " It is not war to loot the poor people or to burn their homes."

Frequently, when we bivouacked, I ordered that no fires should be lighted, as it was not worth while having the corps under fire and having men and horses damaged for a cup of tea. Camp fires would spring up everywhere else, and, as they made an excellent mark for the enemy, fire would be opened upon the column, but no shells fell amongst us. Once when shells, all shrapnel of course, were falling, Major Belcher and I were smoking with our backs against an anthill, and we heard an A.S.C. man say, " I've been looking for a blasted ' funk-hole ' all night and can't find one ! " a remark which caused us much amusement, as the young man was roaming about without the faintest desire for shelter !

On October 8, in the valley west of Helvetia, we met General French's column returning from Barberton, and marched with it for some distance. While halted outside Machadodorp to let the transport pass on, I was ordered by Sir Redvers Buller to move in quickly for him to say good-bye to us before he left for England that night. When I arrived on the ground I formed the regiment on foot and, with the officers at their posts, received him with a general salute. Sir Redvers then addressed us as follows : " I have never served with a nobler, braver or more serviceable body of men. It shall be my privilege when I meet my friend, Lord Strathcona, to tell him what a magnificent body of men bear his name."

At Machadodorp I learned on October 9 that we were to accompany General French's column to Standerton, and the next day received orders, much to my regret, that the 3rd Mounted Brigade was to be broken up here. I instructed the quartermaster to prepare statements of stores issued to the regiment from time to time, and lost or missing through active operations, these to be submitted to a board of officers so as to have them struck off the books. However, on the 11th, we were directed to move by rail to Pretoria, and, at the request of Lord Dundonald, who wished to say good-bye, I paraded the regiment. He stated that he was very proud of Strathcona's Horse, and from the time the regiment joined the brigade under his command it had covered a great deal of ground and had undertaken and successfully carried out many dangerous duties. At the conclusion of his address we gave him three hearty cheers. He was a very great favourite with all ranks and respected for his fine soldierly qualities. Although the work was hard, everyone of us enjoyed it, and, from the time we joined the Natal army until Sir Redvers Buller and Lord Dundonald departed, I can assert that our experience was delightful and valuable. We received nothing but kindness from our gallant commanding officers, their brilliant and capable staff, and from the whole of our comrades, not only of the 3rd Mounted Brigade, but from all the Natal army which was now broken up and its component parts sent to other columns.

On the 12th I handed over our horses to General French's cavalry, the major in charge of the party stating, as well he might, that they were the best that he had seen in the country. The animals from Canada did not enjoy the change, and several of them bucked so badly that I had, at the request of the remount officer, to send some of the men over to remind them that they had to behave themselves. These horses had not bucked for months, yet, strange as it may seem, no sooner did they change masters than many of them began their old tricks.

We reached Pretoria on October 14. I took a room at the Grand Hotel for myself and staff to work up back correspondence and prepare for more work. Two days later I was ordered by the Commander-in-Chief to prepare for further service in the field. On the 20th I was sent for by Lord Kitchener, Chief of Staff, and given orders to march to Germiston by the Johannesburg road, leaving at 2 p.m., after Lord Roberts had inspected the regiment. The Commander-in-Chief, however, was indisposed, and did not inspect us, a great disappointment ; but Lord Kitchener came out of the headquarters, and when he stated that Lord Roberts could not appear, he inspected us and expressed himself pleased with the regiment.

At Germiston we entrained for Wilverdiend, whence with other troops we were to march under Colonel Hicks to relieve Major General Barton's column, which was out of ammunition and being pressed by General de Wet at Frederickstadt. None of us had ever met before, but it made no difference, we were all of the same sort. In giving us our orders he told me that he was giving Strathcona's Horse the danger point, and that I had to protect the left front, left flank and left rear. The enemy had been reported in considerable strength on the left of the long range of rugged kopjes called the Gatsrand.

The firing was heavy, but the march of the column was not checked or interrupted, and we reached Frederickstadt with the welcome ammunition and assistance. Major General Barton at once attacked the enemy, who was occupying a deep donga, which extended for some distance about 600 yards from our position. A heavy fire was opened upon him, and the Royal Welsh Fusiliers, Imperial Light Horse and Scots Guards attacked, scattering the enemy, who suffered severe loss in killed, wounded and prisoners. Our column remained in reserve during the action. The enemy had his dismounted men too far from their horses, with the result that our infantry, in prime condition, closed with them, and many were bayoneted. While the action was in progress Colonel Hicks came and thanked me for the way the regiment did its work on the way down.

Our subsequent operations were very satisfactory, and included the capture of 600 head of cattle and a very large number of sheep, which were carried into Frederickstadt. On November 10 I received the following from Major General Barton :

I cannot speak too highly of the practical and effective manner in which the duty assigned to your splendid corps was carried out by yourself and all under your command yesterday, and I have specially mentioned this in my report to the Field Marshal Commanding-in-Chief. I only regret that circumstances prevented my supporting your movements by advancing further with the main body. The capture of the stock is most satisfactory. I regret the casualty of one man missing and one wounded.

Private Reed, who had been captured in the Buffeldorn Pass, escaped from the enemy during the night and appeared in our lines in the morning. The Boers, after posting their scouts, had a dance in the farm-house where he was, and while it was in progress Reed was placed in a chair in charge of one of the guard, who sat before him and made himself comfortable with his Mauser between his knees. Reed feigned sleep, and very soon his captor, overcome by fatigue and the heat of the room, was deep in slumber. The door being open to admit the cool breeze, the prisoner seized his chance, stole out into the night, and was soon on his way to rejoin the regiment. He made a clear and highly intelligent report, giving full parti-

z

culars of the strength of the Boers and the quantity of ammunition in their possession, which I submitted to the general.

Private Stewart, one of the special scouts, had an opportunity one day of showing his courage and determination. He met two of the enemy at a farm-house and was covered by their Mausers. He dismounted and threw down his rifle, but the Boer nearest to him levelled his weapon to shoot him. He was not quick enough, however, and before he could fire Stewart's trusty revolver dropped him at about 50 yards. The other fired at the same time, wounding him in the chest, but seeing some of our scouts galloped off.

At Klerksdorp I got a touch of ptomaine poisoning and on the return march to Potchefstroom was obliged to ride in our ambulance, and when we arrived at Potchefstroom I was very ill, but did not go on the sick list. Near our bivouac there lived the family of one of the Boer quartermasters, and my always active batman, Private Kerr, the son of my old and tried comrade, Jack Kerr, City Clerk of Perth, Ontario, obtained a room for me from the lady of the house. I shall never forget her kindness and that of her daughters, whose husbands were also in the field. I have never felt worse in my life ; but there was nothing that those kind people could do that was left undone to bring me back to health. Their behaviour gave me a good impression of the character of the people against whom we were at war.

One of our duties at Potchefstroom was that of moving Boer families into the town from their farms on the river. The work was not pleasant, the lamentations of the women and children having a depressing effect upon us ; but it was better for them to be brought in and cared for than to be left out at the farms suffering from want of food. A heavy thunderstorm overtook the squadron while it was employed in that way, and when the women and children arrived they were wearing the khaki jackets of Strathcona's Horse to protect them from the heavy rain. A number of soldiers, natives, children and transport animals were killed by lightning in the town and in our bivouac, but none of the regiment was struck. The first detachment of the South African Constabulary arrived there under Colonel Edwards, who was to command A Division, 2,500 strong.

While at Frederickstadt the previous month I had been offered and promised to take command of B Division if, when the service of Lord Strathcona's Horse terminated, Sir Wilfred Laurier would permit me to be seconded for service in South Africa, at the end of the war. At that time we were under the impression that it would be concluded very soon.

Soon afterwards Lieutenant Snider came into the bivouac with a convoy of supplies from Smithfield. He had had a good deal of difficulty fighting his way through, but by marching at night he averaged twenty miles per diem. At de Wetsdorp he found a number of dead who had not been properly buried, and set his Kaffir drivers to put the graves in proper order. His trip, in spite of considerable discomfort and responsibility, was not without its amusing features.

He had, on one occasion, a train of two thousand oxen. The officer in command of the escort was a young captain of a celebrated regiment, who did not know much about the peculiarities of ox transport, and one day when they had outspanned and the oxen were lying at rest after feeding, he got impatient and said, " It's time to move on, Snider ; you must inspan ! " to which the latter replied, " We cannot inspan yet ; the oxen will get sour stomachs if we do. They must chew their cud." " Their cud ! What in h—— is that ? " Snider told him, and he was satisfied to let them carry out that useful operation.

There were many splendid instances of Canadian pluck during the long months of the war. One day at Clocolan two of the men, Corporal Macdonnell and Private Ingram, both sons of good western stock, were sent to cover a ridge at a considerable distance from the remainder of the men. They ascended it and at the top came face to face with eight Boers, who had come up the other side. They dismounted and opened fire with their revolvers, while the Boers followed suit with their rifles. Three of the enemy were killed and two wounded. Poor Ingram, a first-class man, was killed, and Corporal Macdonell was shot through the body, but walked four miles to Clocolan.

Christmas Day found us at Clocolan resting while the horses grazed. Reveille was at half-past four, and the men were given permission to collect some fruit and other articles. We patrolled the vicinity, and cossack posts remained out as usual, and a small issue of rum was authorized. The Irish Yeomanry gave a smoking concert in their lines, and all hands had a very pleasant time. The yeomanry and the regiment got on very well, and when poor Ingram was buried they sent a wreath for his grave and attended the funeral. On the headquarters staff we were in luck, the kind Scotch lady at the drift having supplied us with turkey, plum pudding and a bottle of Cape wine to drink to " absent friends." After dinner some of us smoked ; we were, however, reduced to the black twist of the country, and the experience of the first who tested it was sufficient warning for the remainder, and we decided to do without for the present.

The regiment was now within a month of one year embodied, and, as it was the general impression that the war was almost at an end, it was recommended that the corps be permitted to return to Canada, for the majority had come away from the ranches in the west at considerable expense. On January 11 when at Viljoen's Drift, I received a telegram from our depot officer to the effect that we were to embark for Canada. The corps had been five weeks without time for a change of under-clothing, nor had anyone of us heard a word of news from any quarter.

The next day we lay at Elandsfontein, and I had the pleasure of a call from Major General Baden-Powell and Major Bird-wood, and I called upon Major General Barton, who had several of us to dine with him. On Sunday, the 14th, I paraded the regiment and informed them that Lord Strathcona had arranged for them to return to Canada via England, and that I expected that, while in London and elsewhere, they would prove themselves to be as well behaved in peace as in war, a credit to their country.

On the 15th I received orders to entrain for the Cape. Prior to our doing so, Lord Kitchener, Commander-in-Chief in South Africa, arrived to say farewell to the regiment. The corps received him in line, and, after the usual salute, the Commander-in-Chief, accompanied by Major General Barton and the staffs of both, addressed us. He thanked us for our services and stated that we had marched through nearly every part of the Transvaal and Orange River Colony, that he had never heard anything but good of the corps, and that we should be greatly pleased if he told us of the number of letters he had received from generals all over the country asking for Strathcona's Horse.

The regiment arrived at Cape Town on January 20, embarked at once on the *Lake Erie*, and sailed on the following day. All hands were refitted with new clothing from head to foot, and new hats were sent out by Lord Strathcona, and the men were trimmed up to the usual smartness.

There were many lying reports circulated to the effect that the regiment behaved badly at Cape Town when waiting there to embark. One officer from another Dominion wrote to a paper in that country stating that, badly though his own regiment had behaved at Cape Town when waiting to embark, they could not hold a candle to Strathcona's Horse, the misbehaviour of which was the worst he had yet seen! As a matter of fact, *the regiment marched direct from the train to the ship!* Another Ananias put an article in the papers which circulated over the civilized world to the effect that when some Boers fired upon a party of the regiment from a house which showed the white flag, they prepared to lynch them, and did so, and, when a staff officer interfered, threatened to lynch him! This is sheer nonsense. There may have been men in South Africa who would have done this, but they were not in Strathcona's Horse! Proof of the conduct of the regiment under all circumstances is to be had in the report of the evidence of officers of the British army who appeared before Lord Esher's commission on the conduct of the war in South Africa.

After a very pleasant voyage the *Lake Erie* arrived in the Thames, but too late for the tide. We had a visit from Mr. Joseph Colmer, C.M.G., secretary to Lord Strathcona, the High Commissioner for Canada. He came on board to welcome us and gave me an idea of the programme which was to be carried out after we landed. I received the following telegram from Lord Strathcona:

Just a message to wish you a hearty welcome. Hope you have all had a pleasant voyage. Informed steamer would land regiment this morning Royal Albert Docks at eight o'clock. Was there to meet you but found steamer delayed. Hope we shall meet some time to-morrow. Colmer going down to see you this afternoon.

(Signed)   Strathcona.

On February 14 the regiment disembarked at the Royal Albert Docks and proceeded to Kensington Barracks, where, later in the day, we were met by Lord Strathcona, who welcomed us heartily. There were present with Lord Strathcona, Lady Strathcona, the Hon. Mrs. Howard (now Lady Strathcona), Dr. Howard, Mr. and Mrs. Joseph Colmer, with many personal friends. When the ceremony was over one half of the regiment was quartered in Kensington Barracks ; the regimental staff and half of the squadron officers in the Royal Palace Hotel, Kensington, and the remainder at St. John's Wood Barracks. The accommodation was all that could be desired. At the Royal Palace Hotel, mess-room, ante-room, the best bedrooms and an orderly-room with telephone were provided. During the parade several photographs of the corps were taken at Lord Strathcona's request. Lord and Lady Strathcona and I formed one group.

On February 15 I marched the corps to Buckingham Palace and formed up inside the grounds, which were kept by the King's company of the Grenadier Guards. The snow had already been swept off, but there was scarcely sufficient space for the regiment on parade. It was made to answer the purpose, however, and the ceremony was concluded without a hitch. On the terrace of the Palace the King and Queen were present, attended by a large number of ladies and gentlemen. The Duke and Duchess of Connaught, the Duke and Duchess of Argyll, the Duke of Cambridge, with the Duke and Duchess of Abercorn, Earl Roberts, Lord Strathcona, Sir Evelyn Wood, Sir Redvers Buller and many others, were there. His Majesty presented each officer and man with the South African war medal, the first issued to any troops, as the decoration had only just been struck. When this was done His Majesty presented the regiment with the King's colours, and said to us : " It was the intention of my late mother to present you with this colour. I do so now, and ask you to guard it in her name and mine." He then handed the colour to me, and I in turn placed it in Lieutenant Leckie's hands. His Majesty then presented me with the Victorian Order; the regiment presented arms and His Majesty addressed us as follows :

Colonel Steele, officers, non-commissioned officers and privates, I welcome you to these shores on your return from active service in South Africa. I know it would have been the ardent wish of my beloved mother, our revered Queen, to have welcomed you also, but that was not to be, but be assured, she deeply appreciated the services you have rendered, as I do.

It has given me great satisfaction to inspect you to-day, and to have presented you with your war medals, and also with the King's colours. I feel sure in confiding this colour to you, Colonel Steele, and to those under you, that you will always defend it and will do your duty as you have done during the past year in South Africa, and will do so on all future occasions.

I am glad that Lord Strathcona is here to-day, as it is owing to him that this magnificent force has been equipped and sent out. I can only hope that your short sojourn in England will be agreeable to you and that you will return safely to your friends and relatives.

Be assured that neither I nor the British nation will ever forget the valuable service you have rendered in South Africa.

I replied on behalf of the regiment, and the regiment then marched past his Majesty and returned to Kensington Barracks, and was formed up and addressed by Lord Strathcona. Photographs were taken of the corps, and it was then dismissed for the day, and Captain Mackie and I had the honour of lunching with Her Royal Highness the Princess Louise and the Duke of Argyll. General Strange, our old friend of the far west, Miss Strange, Colonel Chater and Mr. Hulme were present.

On Saturday, the 16th, by express command of His Majesty, I proceeded to Buckingham Palace with three of the privates of the regiment who, on account of being on baggage guard, were not able to attend the ceremony the previous day. The hour was 9 a.m., and punctually to the moment His Majesty appeared in the brilliant uniform of a Field Marshal and surrounded by many officers in full dress, a gay contrast to our sombre garb. We were then ushered into his presence, and I presented the men to him in turn by name. When he had pinned the medals on their breasts he shook hands with each of them and wished them long life and happiness. They were self-possessed and soldierlike, and no doubt felt the great honour paid to them in being specially ordered to appear to receive their medals, a mark of consideration so characteristic of our late great and good King. The ceremony over, we were permitted to depart, and from that time until the regiment left London I had little time to spare except for the regiment.

The officers and men had a splendid time, and I did not neglect the opportunities given me. I was never in bed before 3 a.m. and was up at 6. Moir, the orderly-room sergeant, was invaluable and almost sleepless, for he never retired before me. Many whom I had met in the west in the earlier days and who resided in England called, among them Major General Sir Ivor Herbert. Major (now Brigadier General) Paget of " A " battery, R.H.A., asked the officers down to the west of England to have a few days with the hounds, a delightful act of courtesy which indicated how we stood with " A " battery. The Royal Artillery mess at Woolwich invited us down to lunch, and as many as possible went and received the most kindly attention from the gallant gunners. The men were invited out and asked to accept the hospitality of some of the most influential people in the city.

On February 17 the majority of the officers and men attended church. I lunched with Lord and Lady Strathcona. The next day the theatres and all places of amusement and interest were thrown open to the officers and men. Splendid arrangements were made to show the N.C.O.'s and men the sights of the greatest city in the world, an opportunity few of them had experienced before. Guides from the Household regiments and brakes containing 25 men each were provided for their use. The late Marquess of Hertford, whose son served in " C " squadron, invited the whole of his comrades to dinner, including, of course, the officers of " C," and they had a delightful evening under his hospitable roof.

Lord Strathcona gave a magnificent banquet, modestly called a luncheon, to the officers, N.C.O.'s and privates of the corps. Many leading personages were present, including the

Earls of Derby and Aberdeen, ex-Governors General of Canada, the Earl of Dundonald, Major General Laurie, M.P., Major General Hutton, and many other officers of the army, prominent Colonial statesmen and gentlemen interested in the Dominion and other oversea portions of the Empire. Lord Strathcona, surrounded by his guests, received each officer, N.C.O. and private at the entrance of the banqueting hall. The fine physique and hardy appearance of the regiment was freely commented on. When I saw the men at the tables I felt that any country would be proud of them.

Lord Strathcona proposed the health of the regiment, coupled with my name, and I responded. Several toasts were drunk, that of Lord Strathcona producing the wildest enthusiasm, the officers and men springing to their feet and making the roof echo with their ardent cheering. The names of Sir Redvers Buller and Lord Dundonald, who, in the absence of Lord Roberts, took his place on Lord Strathcona's left, were also heartily received, the men rising to their feet to honour them. When the banquet broke up the men went on their round of sightseeing.

On the 19th Majors Belcher and Jarvis, Captains Howard, Mackie, Cartwright and I had the honour of dining with the Duke and Duchess of Abercorn. Major General MacKinnon was amongst the military men who dined, and he gave me much pleasure by saying that the admirable bearing of the men of the regiment " was the talk of the clubs." During the evening a number of young officers of the Household troops came in to add to the brightness of the scene, one of them a son of the house. The Duke and Duchess took a great interest in the war and in matters connected with Canada and other parts of the Empire.

On February 21 several of us dined with Mr. St. John Brodrick (now Viscount Midleton), Secretary of State for War, at his home. Amongst the guests were Earl Roberts, Commander-in-Chief, the Earl of Derby, Lord Strathcona, Mr. Joseph Chamberlain, Sir James Willcocks, the successful leader of the latest Ashantee Expedition, and Mr. Winston Churchill, now First Lord of the Admiralty. The evening was very pleasant, and I had the pleasure of a long and interesting conversation with Mr. Joseph Chamberlain. We had a most agreeable time indeed, and the next day, the last we were to spend in London, Lord Strathcona gave a splendid banquet to the officers of the regiment, all of whom were present. Lord Strathcona received all the guests in the great drawing-room of the Savoy Hotel, and presented me to them when they had greeted him. I had the place of honour on his right, Earl Roberts, the Lord Mayor of London, Lord Lansdowne, Secretary of State for Foreign Affairs, Mr. Joseph Chamberlain, Sir Redvers Buller, Lord William Seymour, Sir James Ferguson, and about thirty other gentlemen were present. The Rev. John Macdougall, our old friend from the far west, was there, too, and said grace. An enjoyable evening was spent, and I responded for the regiment, and proposed the health of the Commander-in-Chief.

This, our last, night will never be forgotten by Strathcona's Horse. The splendid hospitality we had received, the uniform kindness of all whom we met, Lord Strathcona's goodness to all ranks, had overwhelmed us to such an extent that we felt we were utterly undeserving of it all. When I returned to the hotel there was so much to do that it was useless to think of sleep. Next morning at 7.30 the regiment entrained for Liverpool; Lord Strathcona, the Earl of Dundonald and many friends of theirs and ours came to see us off. After a splendid reception there we sailed for Halifax, N.S. This was the first time for years that I felt the need of a rest, and I took full advantage of it.

We had a very bad voyage, and, when we arrived at Halifax, thirteen days from Liverpool and six days overdue, we found that there had been great anxiety on the part of our relatives and friends. We were in port on the night of March 8, and everything was got ready to enable us to proceed to our homes without loss of time. On the following morning Mr. (now Sir Frederick) Taylor, Inspector of the Bank of Montreal, and Lieutenant Ketchen, assisted by our paymaster, who produced the vouchers, proceeded, by order of Lord Strathcona, to pay the regiment for the full period of its service the difference between the Imperial Cavalry pay and that of the North West Mounted Police, which was much higher; a bonus was also given to each officer, Lord Strathcona treating all with the greatest liberality. This came as a surprise, for all thought that he had been more than generous already. Many ladies and gentlemen came on board, amongst them my dear wife, who had been, with our three young children, a prey to very great anxiety, as the ship was so long overdue.

We left by special train for Montreal. The journey was an ovation ; we were welcomed at every station en route, and the the first night at Monckton I was presented with an address by the citizens who had assembled in a great crowd to welcome us back, and the ladies presented me with a handsome travelling bag, which had been subscribed for in small sums so as to enable as many as possible to participate in the presentation.

I remained one day in Montreal, and on the 13th proceeded to Ottawa and called upon the Governor General and Sir Frederick Borden. With the former I talked over commissions for a few of the officers and men who were willing to join the South African Constabulary, a large contingent of which had been raised and was at that date stationed in the Exhibition Buildings. There were very few vacancies, but I sent in some names.

When I called on the minister of militia he informed me that it had been the intention of the government to make Strathcona's Horse a part of the permanent force, which it is now, but there was no hope for that at present, which was reason for me to prefer to return to South Africa. While in Ottawa *The London Gazette* appeared, granting many officers and men of the regiment special decorations. The C.B. was given to me ; the C.M.G. to Majors Belcher and Jarvis ; the D.S.O. to Captains Mackie and Cartwright and to Lieutenants Christie and Leckie ; and many N.C.O.'s and men were granted the medal for distinguished conduct in the field. The officers of the regiment were given their honorary ranks in the British army for life. *The Canadian Gazette* promoted Lt.-Cols. Otter, Drury, Lessard, Evans and myself to Brevet-Colonels, dated May 17.

After I had finished the work in connection with Strathcona's Horse I applied to Sir Wilfrid Laurier for leave to proceed to South Africa and take up the appointment of Substantive

Colonel on the staff of the South African Constabulary, which I had been granted by Sir Alfred Milner, on the recommendation of Major General Baden-Powell, and he very kindly consented. Sir Frederick Borden also was so good as to second me to the constabulary for five years, and placed me on the reserve of the Canadian forces. I was to have sailed with the Canadian contingent for the S.A.C., but was not quite ready, and had to get a month's leave from the Inspector General in South Africa.

I cannot close this chapter without placing on record my appreciation of the honour conferred upon me by Lord Strathcona in putting me in command of the regiment, and my gratitude to Sir Frederick Borden for his kindness under all circumstances, and I can say without hesitation that all ranks under me did their utmost to prove that they were worthy soldiers of the Dominion and this great Empire of ours.

CHAPTER XVIII

HAVING made the necessary arrangements for leave of absence from the N.W.M.P. I sailed in the *Australasian* for Liverpool, accompanied by Captain Alexander Boyd, of the 10th Grenadiers of Toronto, who had been appointed to a captaincy in my division of the South African Constabulary, and Messrs. Bartram and Kerr, who were going out to join that force.

When we arrived in London, Boyd and I called on Lord Strathcona, and during our stay in town received the greatest kindness from him. He went with us to obtain passages from the War Office, where it was somewhat difficult to get the officers to understand that, as we were commissioned officers of a force which was paid by the British Government and were going out to the war, we were entitled to our passages by military transports. From the War Office back and forth to the Colonial Office we went, but Lord Strathcona eventually put matters right, and it was arranged that we should sail on the transport *Makool*, the same ship which had taken Strathcona's Horse to Kosi Bay.

I spent a week-end at Knebworth House, with Lord and Lady Strathcona, and met there Dr. and the Hon. Mrs. Howard (now Lady Strathcona) and several Canadians of prominence.

I returned to London with Lord Strathcona, and, as the transport was not ready to sail, I left next morning for Abergavenny, Monmouthshire, where I was met by my kind and still active cousin, Dr. Samuel Steel, then in his eighty-first year, and his charming wife and daughter. I enjoyed three days there, and the evening of my arrival there was a great gathering of the family at Dr. Steel's. We had much pleasant talk about the various changes in the family when my father and his five brothers went into the two great services. Dr. Sam was the son of my uncle William. The birthplace of the family was Coleford, Gloucestershire, where it had come from the north, and the name has been in the course of time spelled Stele, Stiel, Steell, Steel and, lastly, Steele. My father spelled his the latter way, on account of his first commission being written with the final " e " by mistake, and never altered it.

During my three days there I saw the tree my father planted in 1831, when he left for Canada to carve out new homes for himself and his family of six, my half-brothers and sisters, all of whom died at good old ages, one of them, not long since, at ninety-three. While at Abergavenny I was shown over the beautiful country, and saw much of the doctor's son, William, who is colonel commanding one of the battalions of the South Wales Borderers, and Mr. Henry C. Steel, of Blaenavon, where he and his ancestors have been in charge of the coal mines and lands attached to the great steel works there for the past hundred years.

Early in June we sailed for the Cape. There were several officers on board who had been wounded in the early stages of the war and, having recovered, were on their way out to take part in the second phase. Two of them, a captain of the Royal Welsh Fusiliers and a captain of the Seaforth Highlanders, had been shot through the brain, but were none the worse for the mishap. I made the acquaintance of many of the passengers, all of whom were much interested in Canada, but had heard little or nothing about it until the Canadian contingents had taken part in the war. I had found this lack of knowledge of Canada and other parts of the Empire very general in the old country amongst all but those who were financially interested ; in fact, many seemed to think that Canada was under an alien flag. Indeed, I have been told that, when in 1897 the Canadian contingents were banqueted in London, the Stars and Stripes were entwined with the Union Jack round the room, and when the kind hosts were asked why, the reply was, " In honour of the Canadian visitors ! " Happily, and in a large measure owing to the patriotic behaviour of the Dominions and colonies overseas, they are better known now in the old land.

We arrived at Las Palmas on July 10, and while we were coaling the sergeant-major of the detachment of the Post Office corps which was on board and my batman were placed at the gangway to prevent the stokers who were on short leave from bringing intoxicants on board when they returned. A short time afterwards my man came up to the saloon deck and complained to me that the stokers had fallen upon him and the sergeant-major on their return to the ship and knocked them down in the coal dust. The batman's appearance was proof of the truth of his story, and, as I was only a passenger, I sent him to the officer of the day. I was within a few feet of him when he made his report, and saw the ten stokers come up the companionway. As the batman related his story of the assault one of them called him a liar, whereupon he threw himself fiercely upon the crowd and thrashed them soundly, throwing them to the orlop deck, while the captain, a lively Irishman and fond of a fight, looked on with keen enjoyment.

We reached the Cape after an uneventful voyage and immediately proceeded to Johannesburg. The day after our arrival, Boyd and I lunched with Colonel Nicholson, chief staff officer of the S.A.C. We then left for the dynamite factory at Modderfontein, several miles north.

Modderfontein was the temporary headquarters of the S.A.C. and the depots for the reserve and " B " division of the force, and at the station I was met by my senior staff officer, Major Cantan, of the Duke of Cornwall's Light Infantry, and Lieutenant Hildyard, the staff adjutant of my division, and de Havilland, also on my staff.

The S.A.C. had been called into existence by Earl Roberts' proclamation, and was organized and trained as a military as well as a civil corps. Major General Baden-Powell had been directed to draw up a scheme for the organization of the force to police the Transvaal and Orange River Colony, and to be prepared to take over the duties by June, 1901, under the orders of Lord Milner, High Commissioner for South Africa. At that time peace was supposed to be at hand, and 6,000 officers, N.C.O.'s and men were thought to be sufficient. The Commander-in-Chief agreed to hand over to the force a proportion of the officers, N.C.O.'s and men up to 20 per cent. of each corps, to form it, and to equip it complete with horses, saddlery, arms and transport, in fact everything that it would require to carry on its duties, including medical treatment of sick or wounded at the military hospitals.[1]

In December, 1900, it was found necessary to increase the force to 10,000, and early in 1901 a reserve division was organized. From the time that the constabulary came into existence until the end of the war, it was unable to perform any police duties and was employed as a military force under the Commander-in-Chief and constantly engaged in field operations and on the block-house lines. Some block-houses were built where they could guard the concentration camps where the Boer women and children were maintained by the British government to save them from the ever-present danger of starvation on the veldt. While I am on that subject, which has been a burning question, the British government, the army, and all connected with the management of the camps having been abused for the way they were conducted, I can state, from a personal knowledge of facts, that the people were indeed fortunate to be in camp. They were under the supervision of kind and capable officers, doctors and nurses ; they had their own schools and school teachers ; they were well sheltered in good tents and they were well fed.

---

[1] The corps was first organized into four divisions. There were to be three divisions in the Transvaal, and one in the Orange River Colony, all divided into troops, consisting of one captain, one lieutenant, and 100 N.C.O.'s and men, but as hostilities showed no signs of ceasing the army was unable to carry out the proposed agreement, and consequently the Inspector General established recruiting offices in England, Cape Colony and Natal, and arranged for a contingent of about 1,300 N.C.O.'s and men, with their own officers, from Canada.

The Canadian contingent, which had sailed before I left, was distributed throughout the three divisions of the Orange River Colony and eastern and western Transvaal ; none were at present posted to " B " division, which was under my command. It had been intended that they should be divided amongst the men of the other troops, but when they were raised the recruiting officer gave them the impression that they would be in one division by themselves, under me, and when the men heard that they were not, they showed such signs of discontent that I recommended to the Inspector General that they be kept in distinct troops, and he very kindly permitted that arrangement. The impression has been circulated that they were all Canadians by birth, but such was not the case ; at least half of many of the troops were originally from the old land, and had joined to have a look-in at the war.

I took over command of Modderfontein and my division the day after I arrived. It consisted of six troops, well commanded by officers of experience. Several were stationed west of Modderfontein, and, having made myself acquainted with my surroundings and pushed on the organization and instruction, I left two days later to inspect my outposts.

With few exceptions every officer in the S.A.C. had served in other fields or had been through the experiences of the previous years of the Boer War. The majority were seconded from the army or colonial corps, and the rank and file were highly intelligent, stalwart and, usually, well educated. The greater number had enlisted in the expectation that the force would be permanent, and many had hoped that commissions would be within their reach.

As the Inspector General was in England, the divisional commandants of the force had to take their orders for work in the field from Lord Kitchener, commanding the forces in South Africa. I reported to him at Pretoria. After a look over the maps he ordered me to keep pushing my troops north and west along the Rustenburg road to clear the country beyond the Magaliesberg range. The interview was pleasant, and I found the Commander-in-Chief, as I expected, keen, business-like and clear in his instructions.

The chain of posts as far as Rustenburg had been placed

on the 13th, and, all being in order in Pretoria, I left for the Rustenburg line, where my headquarters were to be. The post had been placed in a good state of defence. An isolated mountain, called Wolhuter's Kop, was my signal station, in charge of an officer, and was in communication by helio and lamp with all my troops for at least 40 miles, and with several infantry posts also, including the Suffolks, West Riding and Lincolns, who were stationed along the Magaliesberg in touch with Pretoria. That part of the Transvaal was a favourite resort for small active commandoes of the enemy, placed there to make raids upon columns of transport and on the lines of communication, by going south through the neks in the Magaliesberg to cut the Krugersdorp-Klerksdorp line, or turning their attention east to blow up the Pretoria-Pietersburg railway.

After an ineffectual attempt to get a suitable house for the staff in Pretoria, I reported to Lord Kitchener in the usual way, and when I brought the matter to his personal notice I was assigned the residence of the late president of the Transvaal as quarters for my officers, and Mr. Eloff's house next door as offices. There was good stabling, a carriage house, which contained the state coach, Mrs. Kruger's phaeton and a covered carriage for private use. Mr. Kruger's trek waggon stood in the back yard, just as it had been left after his last trek to the low veldt.

The house was a long low building in the Dutch colonial style, and contained a large reception-room, a dining-room, a lady's boudoir and several bedrooms, one of which had been occupied by Mr. Kruger, and was protected by strong steel shutters inside, which were closed at night and secured by an iron bar. In front of the house the usual stoep extended, and at the entrance from the street Barney Barnato's marble lions reclined, facing the passage to the stoep. In the large reception-room there were several curios, amongst them the first shell fired at Spion Kop, which had been duly inscribed and presented to the president by some enthusiastic admirer.

When Major General Baden-Powell returned to the country he made a tour of the division, accompanied by Majors Steuart and Kearsley, and inspected every troop. The Inspector

General was a great favourite in the corps, a good disciplinarian, kindly and patient. A proof of the latter quality I saw at Naauwpoort, where one of the officers produced a gramophone to amuse the company, and kept the wretched records going from dark until nearly midnight, gazing the while on the party with a smile of intense satisfaction, but not a word from the general, nor any one else, until we nearly dropped asleep from sheer exhaustion !

In the middle of May, when there were signs of peace. When negotiations were opened, several of the Boer delegates were passed through my lines under a flag of truce.

From this time, there being no great necessity for my presence with the main body of the division, I left it under the command of Major Steuart, who had been transferred to me as second in command, and went into Pretoria to prepare for our future employment both as peace officers and as soldiers. The depot was very strong in numbers and augmented a short time after peace was proclaimed by Canadian and Australian troops, and one of Boers who had fought all through the war. When the latter came I had them paraded and gave them words of encouragement, which seemed to please them. The depot was very busy, at first under Captain Trew and later under Captain Hilliam, late of the R.C.M. Rifles, who had been strongly recommended to the Inspector General by Colonel (now Major General) Rimington, for whose column he had served as leader of the scouts. He was one of the best instructors that I have known, and his varied service in the 17th Lancers and the N.W.M.P. had fitted him well for the command of the depot.

When things were as I wished at the depot every troop officer took a course in the duties of paymaster and quartermaster under the officers of the division at the head of those departments, and the men, after passing their recruits' course, were sent in large parties to work for a few weeks with the Pretoria blue police, so that if need be they could work in the small towns, which were the seats of the resident magistrates, and were to be the headquarters of S.A.C. districts. I had Dutch instructors employed and classes of 50 men were taught the language as we went along, orders being given that they were to be practised in it at stables and other duties, so that if need be they could work amongst the Boer farmers without an interpreter.

To encourage the large number of well educated men in the corps the Inspector General had arranged that there should be promotion from the ranks to commissions in the force. The first men who came in to be examined were not in every case fairly selected, and some who were not N.C.O.'s were sent to the depot on the recommendation of some friend who was exercising that curse, social influence, ten times worse than political influence. I put a stop to this, however, by ordering that no one under the rank of sergeant, and promoted on his merits, would be recommended, and when they came in I gave them a severe test before I permitted them to come up for examination, and those who failed were retained at the depot under instruction until they proved to be efficient in every respect.

While peace was being arranged in Pretoria the Boer generals who represented their country were at the local hotels, and created a very favourable impression, being soldier-like men, with pleasant manners. The most distinguished were Generals Botha, de la Rey and de Wet, all of whom had great influence with their fellow countrymen. They had opposed the war in the first instance, but when it was forced upon them, like true patriots, they fought to the end, and made the best terms possible.

In May the Inspector General gave orders that the four divisional commandants should send to him a daily diary of events and suggestions which they might choose to make for the good of the force. This method worked well, and its good effects were soon evident in the increasing efficiency of the corps, which at that time was the strongest mounted police force in the world, its parade state totalling at least 10,500 men.

The thumb-mark system of identification was brought into the S.A.C. during May, and everything done to make the corps at least as modern as any other. The present head of the Metropolitan Police was in Johannesburg and the head and leader of that system, which had been brought to perfection under him.

On May 24, 1902, a vast concourse of people assembled in

Church Square, Pretoria, to hear peace proclaimed, but as it did not come off they left, very much disappointed. The treaty of peace was, however, signed on May 24, and on June 1 the clergy of the city informed their congregations of the good news.

On the 29th I completed in my office a list of the Boers and other burghers of the Transvaal Colony and registered them. The same was done throughout the S.A.C., I believe, and was a great help to us for the remainder of our service in South Africa. This information had been obtained from the archives of the Dutch Republics. The northern or " B " Division of the Transvaal was placed under my command. Although it contained the homes of a large number of farmers, it had within its limits more Kaffirs than all the rest of the two colonies. Many hundreds of thousands were scattered about the numerous kraals, and were a decided menace to the whites who had returned to their homes, for they had a large quantity of arms and ammunition. These had to be taken from them at an early date, or we should be faced by serious consequences. As soon as I learned the true state of affairs, I recommended that the natives be disarmed, even if the government had to compensate them for the loss of their rifles and other fire-arms, and the question was seriously taken up.

Before Lord Kitchener left for England he addressed us. He said that he had never seen finer men on parade, nor more gallant ones in the field, under circumstances requiring fortitude and self-denial. Though we had lost many men during the campaign, the force had always been ready when wanted. He also gave much sound advice as to the future conduct of the force towards those who had been recently in arms against us, but were for the future to be our friends and fellow subjects of His Majesty.

Peace having been now assured, the government had a very important and difficult task before them in the repatriation of our new fellow subjects, the restoration of the theatre of war to its normal state and the improvement of the two colonies by the building of roads, the establishment of schools, the improvement of the railways and of every other public service.

The new law department appointed resident magistrates for every magisterial district. The system was peculiar, quite different from any other part of the British Empire, and, with a strong and capable police force, likely to cause friction between the resident magistrates and the district commandants. The resident magistrates, who had been long in the colonies, or were born in them or were lawyers by profession, got on very well with us from the first, but in cases where they were military officers and senior in rank to the S.A.C. commandants there was very often a great deal of misunderstanding. Sometimes there were faults on both sides, but not often on the side of the S.A.C., for the reason that from the first the officers studied the laws, ordinances and regulations, and were in most cases quite fit for the bench themselves. The law department refused for a long time to make our officers, or any other persons, justices of the peace with power to try petty cases, such as breaches of the masters' and servants' ordinances, etc., giving as a reason that an officer should not try cases in which his own men give evidence. At the same time, many of the resident magistrates tried to interfere with the S.A.C. officers and do the police work themselves !

The magistrates personally were very agreeable men, and, as time went on, almost all learned that the S.A.C. were their best friends, and at the same time quite capable of managing the police work and the many other duties assigned to them without interference. But it was many a day with some of them before they came to the conclusion that, after all, as magistrates, they were not in command of the police. We had a few regulations which had applied to the old regime in other colonies when the magistrate would interfere with everything, inspect the men's quarters, the cells, etc., as if they were in command of a regiment, ask for men to act as mere servants, so that the police were looked down upon, but the S.A.C. soon put an end to such ; in fact we did not permit such a course on the part of the resident magistrates. Our men were highly respectable, the officers from the military services and the colonies, and the Inspector General would not permit them to be treated in a way that would lower their self-respect. The force had not been doing duty amongst the Boers and other persons in the cities and towns for more than six months before they were looked up to as a credit to the races to which they belonged.

We had not been out at our posts very long and we were busy at our multifarious duties when it became evident that, as in the early days of settlement and government under a council in the North West and Yukon Territories of Canada, it was necessary that the constabulary should be represented on the council, and in one of my daily letters to the Inspector General I suggested that the force should have a place at the council board. In reply he offered to recommend me for it, but I pointed out that it was his place, not mine, and that the chief staff officer should be there also; the suggestion was adopted, to the great advantage of the public service.

A short time after my troops were placed it was reported that the Kaffirs, as I expected, were not at all friendly to the Boers, and showed themselves very impudent in demeanour towards them. They had formed an impression that, as we had fought with the burghers, we were hostile to them. I gave orders to my troop commanders and senior captains at the district headquarters that they were to insist upon the natives treating the Dutch people with respect, as formerly; ex-Commandant Beyers had reported that armed natives were interfering with Boers who were returning to their farms, and he thought that the S.A.C. had no orders. I relieved his mind, however, and issued further instructions to the force that it was their duty to protect all persons in their legitimate occupations, and that, to do so with effect, they must act at once in all cases where there was any danger of a breach of the peace, and were not, on any account, to wait for orders from any central authority. They were to exercise judgment, promptitude and tact.

Shortly after this a number of native constables, mostly Zulus, were engaged, and, as the other Kaffirs were in considerable dread of them owing to their reputation for courage and strength, they were a great assistance to the force in every division. Every detachment, no matter how small, had one or more attached to it, and, as they made good use of them, it was not long before all causes for complaint were removed.

This did not admit of any slackening off, however, for the Kaffirs, particularly those who had been treated too familiarly by the whites attached to the army, were prone to be insolent, and even commit, as they did a short time after repatriation of the Boers, very serious crimes, some of which, apart from murder, were punishable with death.

Rinderpest was reported amongst the transport oxen at Piet Potgieter's Rust on July 16, and from that date the department of agriculture, the South African Constabulary and magistrates had a very difficult task to keep alive the herds of cattle and make the Boer farmers understand the seriousness of the situation. This was soon followed by tick fever, another disease fatal to stock and very difficult to eradicate. It eventually came to such a pass that the infected areas had to be fenced to keep them apart from the sections where the cattle were still sound, and, as the government gave compensation to owners, it was not an uncommon offence for the farmers to trek into the infected areas so that their cattle would catch the disease in order to have the animal paid for. Passes had to be given to go in certain directions, and, instead of proceeding according to the pass, they would be found going in opposite directions, and when caught would feign ignorance of the purport of their pass.

The tick fever would never have found its way into the country had the advice of our veterinary surgeon been taken. Captain James Irvine Smith reported that the cattle which were being imported from the Portuguese side were diseased, but the other veterinary surgeons, none of whom were in our service, declared that his diagnosis was wrong, with the natural result that the country was soon overwhelmed with diseased stock. Great experts had to be sent for eventually, and reported that Captain Smith was right, and that had his advice been taken the country would have been saved from enormous loss.

When the cattle diseases were known the men of the S.A.C. assisted the farmers in every way by showing them how to prevent the spread of it amongst their cattle. As Professor Theiller, a bacteriologist and pupil of the great Koch, lived in Pretoria, I took advantage of his presence to send a number of my men to learn from him all about the diseases, and the veterinary surgeons took charge of them, and they were divided amongst the districts, but this did not happen until after 1902.

On July 18 reports came to me which were sent on to head-quarters to the effect that at least 50 per cent. of the Kaffirs had rifles and other fire-arms, and I again suggested that the natives in my division should be disarmed at once if peace were to be maintained. The same day Captain Pomeroy, for the same reason, took the rifles from several of the Kaffirs. This was brought to the notice of the government by the Inspector General, and early disarming and compensation for their rifles was promised.

I made my first round of the troops in the north on the last week of the same month, accompanied by Captain de Havilland, and inspected all troops on the way to Zoutpansberg. I found the Boer families hospitable and cheerful. As it was reported that diseased cattle were being brought into the Zoutpansberg from Rhodesia in the most reckless manner, I ordered patrols north to the Limpopo to stop them, and a station was placed on the main trail from the north where the road crossed that river. I found also that there were attempts to meddle with the duties of my officers and men, and directed that they must not permit it and must be firm on all points.

On my way I found that we were put to great annoyance by having to bring Kaffir and other prisoners many miles, to the great inconvenience of ourselves and witnesses, and I reported to the Inspector General that it was important that the government should appoint our senior officers justices of the peace, with powers to try cases, as in other parts of the British dominions. After several complaints of our troubles bringing witnesses and petty cases sometimes 60 or 70 miles before the resident magistrates, the Inspector General and I went to the law department. It was no use at that time, the officials were unaccustomed to such methods, but later they were obliged to comply with modern ideas and have some consideration for the farmers.

There was much trouble with regard to cattle imported in a state of disease, and Captain Jarvis complained that the

Rhodesian authorities had again given passes to a Boer to bring 42 diseased oxen into the Transvaal. These animals had tick fever and were quarantined immediately. I again wired orders that, pass or no pass, all cattle on the move from Rhodesia were to be turned back from the Limpopo, and officers were not to wait for orders on matters of such vital importance ; they must keep their patrols for the protection of the stock interests on the move. I also reported to the department of agriculture, and asked that we be given full powers to act in all cases such as those, and received orders to act on my own judgment, and I delegated the same to all of my officers that they were to do likewise.

On August 16 arrangements were made to send a party of Boer delegates and their wives to visit the overseas dominions of His Majesty. Canada, Australia, New Zealand and, of course, England were visited, but the season of the year did not suit Canada at all ; the harvest was over when they arrived, but they saw much to interest them. Judging from their report they were well satisfied, but I fear they learnt very little except the enormous extent of the Empire. The move was a good one, nevertheless, and the delegates could not but have been impressed with the kindly way in which they were received everywhere.

The Kaffirs had got it into their heads that as the Boers had been defeated the whole of the land in the Transvaal belonged to the natives, and we were constantly getting reports of strained relations between Boers and Kaffirs. Up to date no steps had been taken to disarm the natives, although there was great danger of outrages being committed on the unarmed whites. About this time I had to forward a report of high officials exasperating the Boer farmers by alluding in an offensive way to the late war.

On August 19 I went north to accompany the Inspector General on a tour of inspection of the posts in the Zoutpansberg. With him was Captain Kearsley, his aide-de-camp, and they came on to Pietersburg the same day.

Next morning we trekked east to Haenertsburg, 43 miles from Pietersburg, and the Inspector General went over the troop next morning. In the afternoon we rode back to

Pietersburg, a most uncomfortable ride for me, as I had bronchitis, a very sore throat, and my face was swollen to twice its natural size. Moreover, my horse turned a somersault and rolled over me, giving me quite a severe wrench, the effects of which I felt for several days.

At 5 p.m. the following day we left for Spelonkin, Captain Jarvis' post at Fort Edward, 72 miles north east on the road to the Limpopo and Rhodesia. It was a fine, cool night, and at 10.30 we had made the 42 miles to Dwaar's River, where there was a detachment of Jarvis' No. 14 troop. It was quite dark when we arrived there, but no sooner did we dismount than I saw that the ways of the North West Mounted Police prevailed there to a considerable extent. Our horses were taken to shelter at once, and the men busied themselves making tea and preparing food for us, and the Inspector General, a man after their own hearts, was soon talking game and sport to a gigantic British Columbian, who was a noted shot. When going round with the corporal I found that he was the son of Mr. James Audy, an officer of the Hudson's Bay Company, and had served a short time in the N.W.M.P.

Fort Edward, which we reached next morning, had been constructed during the war under the direction of a Royal Engineer officer, and was in a good state of defence. The situation was pretty, on rising ground above a large spruit of fresh water, and across the spruit there was a fine farm, owned by a family of Scotch descent, named Cooksley. Mr. Cooksley, when bathing in the spruit some years before, had been seized around the chest by a young python, but had held his own until his wife and a Kaffir boy came to his rescue ; they took hold of the reptile's tail and unwound it, and the three killed the snake.

Iguanas were plentiful in the neighbourhood, and one of the officers was startled by one jumping on to his chest as he sat drying himself after bathing. As he had never seen one before, he took it to be a young crocodile, and there was a laugh at his expense, in which he very heartily joined, when he had recovered from the sudden start which it gave him.

On the slopes of the Zoutpansberg there was a settlement of mulattoes called the Buys (pronounced Base) Boers, who were named so after a voortrekker, who had led a commando there in the early days. As there were no Europeans they took Kaffir wives, and located themselves in that rather favoured region. Reports had been made in Pietersburg to the effect that these people were on bad terms with the Dutch and natives, but I ascertained that there was no truth in it, and I was told that they were kindly, well-disposed persons.

Lieutenant Welstead's post, in the north of the Zoutpansberg, was a difficult one ; the Kaffirs were in large numbers and well armed, and the lions were so bold that fires had to be kept going all night to keep them at a distance.

I returned to Pretoria next day, having been travelling when suffering from bronchitis, sore throat and much swollen face, and had been in torture the whole time I was out. There was no help for it in the S.A.C., however ; I had to keep going until I recovered in the ordinary course.

No hay had ever been cut in any part of the Transvaal, and there was no bedding for the horses. Most of the forage had to be brought from overseas. I therefore obtained mowing machines, and we made hay as in western Canada and salted it in the stacks. The horses were soon in better condition, as there was ample for bedding as well, and during the whole time I was in South Africa our horses, although they did very hard, constant work, were admired by everyone who saw them. The grass in that country is not by any means as nutritious as it is on the prairies of western Canada. It becomes brown and useless with the first frost ; ours, of course, dries into hay on the ground in August, and is almost as good as when it is fresh and green.

The ordinance respecting the disarming of the Kaffirs came into our hands at the end of August. The first important disarming took place on September 22, and by October 8 19,740 guns and rifles and a considerable quantity of ammunition had been surrendered to my division alone. In this work the Native Commissioner had been escorted and protected by the S.A.C., and the good work went on until every gun and rifle in the possession of the natives had been handed in, destroyed, and paid for, leaving the Kaffir powerless for mischief against black or white.

The policing of the border next the Portuguese possessions was the most difficult. The country was what is called the low veldt, very unhealthy in the summer or rainy season. Horse sickness, fever, ague and other diseases peculiar to a hot climate prevailed, and the heat was very great, the maximum at midnight in several places being about 125 degrees Fahrenheit. White people almost invariably suffered from malaria, and after being there for a few years, if they live that length of time, are often very severely attacked when they return to the high, healthy veldt.

Such being the country which had to be policed along the eastern border, detachments were placed on the high ground. I would not station them in the low country, but occasional patrols with Kaffir police were made by an officer and N.C.O. in the summer, and in the winter parties went over the ground, and maps were made by officers of the division, with the result that the patrolling was efficiently done and we had very little fever.

By October 15 the S.A.C. had been distributed to suit the circumstances, and inspecting officers found the men very good. There were, indeed, people holding high office in some of the districts who thought we were too soldier-like, but they had evidently failed to observe that every successful police force in the world has a military style, is drilled, obeys orders, and is invariably commanded by men who are soldiers in everything but the name. One of those who worried about this was a military officer himself, and when asked for a case of neglect of duty on account of the force being military in manner, could produce none. With the majority of resident magistrates the officers and men became favourites, and eventually, in spite of much opposition, the officers, as in the N.W.M.P., were appointed justices of the peace, and proved the value of the system. But before this became law reams of foolscap had been written, forwarding the complaints of the Boer farmers, who had to travel many miles to attend petty court cases as prosecutors or witnesses, and of the officers of the force, who had to send their men 30 or 40 miles mounted, escorting Kaffirs who were on foot, and perhaps only guilty of a trifling offence, which could have been tried nearer home. When the change came about the country had much to thank Lord Milner for, in the alteration to common-sense methods.

In connection with our work I may say that we seldom had the support of the law department. Even the magistrates disapproved of the way some of its officials looked upon the officers and men, without whom they would have been of little use themselves, but with the other departments we were on the best of terms, and helped them as much as we did the legal branch in every way possible.

When the proper time came we took the census; every man, woman and child of the white population, except in the cities of Johannesburg and Pretoria, where we had no jurisdiction, was known to us, and there was not a Kaffir kraal, or chief, nor a burgher before the war who was not on the rolls and his character and opinions known to us. As I said to a friend of mine who was a resident magistrate, and had done duty in one of the districts as a staff officer and objected to our placing the posts ourselves at the outset, " Though you know the district, in three weeks' time we will be better acquainted with it than even the Boers and Kaffirs."

In November, 1902, there were many complaints in some districts of the ravages of baboons, particularly in the Waterberg, and I had to obtain leave to issue an extra supply of ammunition to our men to destroy them, as the Boers had not yet been permitted to have rifles. One resident magistrate and district commandant had issued a few, but when I learned it I was obliged to advise the district commandant not to give any licences for arms until we had orders. The baboons always knew when the good man was away, and took advantage of the occasion to drive the women and children into the house, and would then raid the crops.

Game was very plentiful in the outlying parts of the division, and as it had to be preserved, I suggested to the Inspector General that we take over the duties of game wardens in addition to our other work, as it would fit in with our patrols. The idea was not approved, however, by the government as far as the great game region along the Portuguese border was concerned, although it would have saved expense and prevented friction. It was well done under the other plan, but, as I expected, the officer in charge of that area objected to see our officers and men within it, in spite of the fact that if we did not visit it we should be unable to prevent the importation of fire-arms and fire-water for the Kaffirs. I paid no attention to the objections raised, however, and directed the officers along the border to carry on their duties of patrolling, regardless of opposition. Being firm and tactful, they managed matters in such a way that all concerned worked in harmony.

Under the new rules the whole of the low country became a preserve, managed under very stringent regulations, and throughout the remainder of the division, where game was in many places very plentiful, the game wardens and the S.A.C. divisions carried out the duty so strictly that, where there was little or no travel, wildebeeste, koodoo, hartebeeste, and other varieties of deer and antelope too numerous to mention, being undisturbed, paid little attention to the patrols, and lions seemed to be quite anxious to make our acquaintance, even encroaching upon the settlements of the frontier, and the men very often ran great risks of being devoured.

One of the game wardens under Major Hamilton was the hero of a rather remarkable adventure which I have seen described in another book, but as it occurred within the precincts of the area under the S.A.C., I must be excused for relating it. Wolhuter, a young Boer game guardian, and a comrade were returning to camp one night when a lion and lioness sprang out upon them from a thicket. Wolhuter was riding carelessly and, when his horse shied, was thrown. His companion, losing control of his horse, was carried at a furious pace along the path, pursued by the lioness, while Wolhuter was seized by the lion and dragged towards the thicket. He was in great pain, and could feel the brute's feet trampling upon him as he was drawn along the ground on his back. In this dreadful predicament, expecting his captor to make a meal of him very soon, he suddenly felt his hunting knife with his left hand. Drawing it from its sheath, he made a chance stroke, and drove it into the lion's body, behind the shoulder, killing it instantly. Being experienced in the ways of lions, he climbed a tree, and when his friend returned with assistance to ascertain what had become of him, he was found seated on a branch with the lioness watching him from below, her dead mate lying close by, its heart pierced by Wolhuter's knife. The plucky young Boer was in hospital several weeks after his adventure, where he made a good recovery.

Lions were frequently met along the Selati railway, a line which had been for the time abandoned, but on which the S.A.C. had permission to run their hand cars to reach posts in the low veldt. In the north near the Limpopo they were very bold, some of the men having to take refuge in trees and on the roofs of the sheds of Mr. Zeederburg, the former mail contractor. In another district one of the men, when trying to shoot a lion which had his comrade in its grasp, killed the poor man instead, and an officer who went on a lion hunting trip died from the effects of a mauling he received from one of the brutes.

There were other things as dangerous and more repulsive than the lion. The large rivers were infested by crocodiles, reptiles which the Kaffirs at one time regarded as sacred, and a native who killed one without the permission of his chief was promptly put to death.

Another creature which could be seen in the kloofs and noisome spots was the python, which in South Africa grows to an enormous size. Captain Scarth killed one in the Lydenberg district which measured 29 feet 6 inches. The natives do not seem to fear those snakes, however, although under certain circumstances they proved themselves to be very dangerous customers and destructive to buck, colts, calves and even larger animals, which they crush and then devour. When Scarth shot his python he heard some Kaffirs calling to him, and when he went to the spot he found a group standing near where one lay coiled like a huge hawser of pretty colours. He was so surprised at the unexpected sight that the creature had time to dart into the bushes. A few minutes later he again heard the natives crying out to attract his attention, and when he went to them he saw the python with his head waving from side to side, several feet above the bushes, and gave it both barrels. When the skin was removed the lovely colours disappeared, giving place to a dull brown.

There were many venomous snakes in the divisional area,

amongst them the maambas, brown and green. The latter
is to be found in the trees and is very poisonous. Both kill
in a few minutes, and the brown maamba is so quick that the
eye cannot follow its stroke. There were also the puff and
night adders, the renghals and the peel slang. The latter
spits at its enemy, causing temporary blindness and raising
blisters.

There are several useful antidotes for the bite of the snakes,
one of them is made up of poisons of several. When I was in
South Africa this was sold by the native doctors, and is carried
by almost all who go on hunting expeditions. Another is
in liquid form, and the dose is 21 drops for an adult ; if taken
at once it will cure, but the patient must on no account fall
asleep.

One of the most remarkable of the feathered tribe is the
honey bird, which leads to or warns one of the proximity of
a lion, a snake, or a bee's nest. This one is very well known to
all who have resided in South Africa.

My wife and family, accompanied by Mrs. R. W. Harwood
and Dr. A. C. de L. Harwood, and Mrs. Hilliam, wife of my
depot commandant, Captain Hilliam, arrived on November 22,
very much fatigued by the long voyage and the stuffy, hot
train. They were soon restored, however, and during their
stay made many friends in the Transvaal, who did much to
make their visit to the country enjoyable.

In January, 1903, Mr. Joseph Chamberlain arrived on a
visit to South Africa, and was enthusiastically received
throughout the country. While he was in Pretoria my division
furnished the escorts, and a reception was held in one of the
public parks, where a large number of ladies and gentlemen,
including Generals Louis Botha, de la Rey and Cronje were
presented.

During the same month some of the newly-appointed officials
suggested that the officers of the S.A.C. and native departments
should be more familiar with the Kaffir chiefs, but fortunately
the suggestion was not adopted. The Kaffir is not like the
Red Indian or Maori, who in their primitive state are dignified
and courteous and will take no liberties, and it does not answer
to treat him the same. Strict justice and firmness is the only

2 B

course. There was another good reason why there should be no change, the whole of the white population were against it, especially the Boers, who knew them better than anyone, and they did not believe in familiarity. If they were sometimes severe and unjust when they were in power, they had many good rules to guide their intercourse with the native population which it would not be wise to change.

The Kaffir as a labourer in any capacity is trying; under the influence of fear they will work fairly well, but in gangs it would be an unusual thing to see more than five to ten per cent. busy at the same time. As domestics in towns, both men and women are poor servants. On the locations the women do all the manual labour and work hard; the men loaf about and will not work unless circumstances compel them. Both sexes are by nature untruthful, and few are capable of gratitude for any kind act. Admonition by the cat-o'-nine-tails is the only thing understood, and as that is seldom used the Kaffir is difficult to manage. The native, of course, looks up to the white person as " baas " or " missus," and as no European will perform manual labour in that country unless he cannot help it, the employers, such as mine owners, etc., have to make the best of what they can get. White servants have been brought out from England, but as soon as they see the state of affairs they demand hired help at their work, and are then " baas " and " missus." This is not because the temperate parts of South Africa are not suitable for white labour, but because it is a black labourers' country; the white is master, and would be despised by both Europeans and Kaffirs if he lowered himself to the native level.

The best Kaffir boy that I had in the S.A.C. was a driver named Philemon, who was well educated, that is, he could read and write well, and was a preacher in the location on Sundays, and as he was able to give me some information I asked him why the Kaffirs had so little gratitude and were so untruthful. He replied that, " Nothing appeals to the native but physical pain. It is no use to treat them the same as the whites, they cannot understand it; we are spoiled by being told that we are the equals of the white people; we are not civilized, and should be taught that, until we are so, we are not the equals of the whites." Of course, as in the case of this boy, there are notable exceptions, particularly among the Zulus, and we got some good native constables from amongst them, and even in the other tribes, but then they had great supervision in the force, and that, with the fact that they occupied a high position amongst their fellows, had a good effect upon them. The Zulus are soldiers by nature and long training, and much superior in every way to the majority of the Kaffirs.

CHAPTER XIX

IN February, 1903, Major General Baden-Powell was appointed Inspector General of Cavalry in Great Britain and Ireland, and was succeeded by Colonel Nicholson, chief staff officer of the S.A.C.

When Colonel Nicholson returned from England in June and took over command of the S.A.C., I was able to report to him that, during his absence in England, I had made a complete tour on horseback of my division, inspected the different district headquarters, the outposts, men, horses, arms, accoutrements, kits, clothing, police records, all books, ammunition, messing ; had spoken to every member of the division to ascertain if he had any complaints, or if there was anything that I could do for him. I found the discipline very good, and that the removal from the division of every man who had misbehaved himself in public or had been a disgrace to the corps, had a good effect, leaving the division with as fine and respectable a body of men as anyone could desire to command. I had found officers and men keen on their work and well acquainted with their districts and the inhabitants, and the officers with a sound knowledge of the character and capabilities of the N.C.O.'s and men under their command. They knew the country so well that they could take me over any by-path, trail or mountain to any place in the district. The officers and men were respected by the inhabitants of the country, all of whom made a practice of coming to them when they were in need of advice or help. The horses were in good condition for the work they had to do, and, as directed by me in the spring, care had been taken to select places for the outposts which would be fairly free from horse-sickness, in fact, many posts were perfectly safe. In some parts of the Zoutpansberg they could be kept out at grass night and day.

I worked hard those days and rode some of the longest distances travelled on horseback. It would be tedious to give details of the tour and of the work at all the posts visited, but in each case the inspection was of the most searching character, even to the nails in the horses' shoes. To show the condition I was in, I may say that I lost only two pounds in the 1,800 mile trek, and as I rode a horse with a different pace and gait every day it made the work more difficult. No other officer could or did stay with me on those trips without a great deal of fatigue. The total mileage of my tour was 1,800 miles on horseback and 1000 by rail. This work was done over again every year.

Although I do not propose to give a detailed account of the tour, there were a few incidents and episodes that, I think, are worth recording.

At one farm, that of Mr. Shepstone, a son of the late Sir Theophilus Shepstone, at one time governor of the Transvaal, we found the owner away from home. He had invited us to stay at his place at any time when I or any of the S.A.C. officers were passing there, and he had left orders with his stalwart Zulu factotum that we were to be given the best in the house when we arrived. The Zulu met us at the door, ordered the Kaffir servants to take our horses, showed us to our rooms, and when dinner was ready announced the fact in good English. The meal was served by native girls in snow-white garments, while the big Zulu watched every move, and when we retired asked us when we should like breakfast.

During the whole of the war when the " baas " was away the Zulu had held the place, and, although there was much valuable plate in his charge, not a spoon or other article was

missing when Mr. Shepstone returned. If any commandoes
came near during hostilities, he sent the native boys round to
them to say that the British were occupying the place in force.
He certainly must have had some mysterious way of holding
the farm, for it was left untouched by Boer and Briton, and
the house was one of the best that I saw in the country parts of
the Transvaal.

Near one of our halting-places a native woman and child
were devoured by a crocodile, which was afterwards killed and
found to contain the remains of the poor creatures. I have
never been able to understand why the inhabitants of a
civilized country, with the natives under control, took no steps
to destroy those hideous, loathsome reptiles, which are so
rapacious that they will eat their own young. The natives,
especially the women and children, run great risks where the
rivers are infested by them. Cages have to be made of stakes
driven into the mud of the banks to protect the women while
they are washing clothes or getting water. The reptiles have
been known to seize mules and horses even when they are
harnessed and being driven across the fords. A short time
before he joined the S.A.C. one of the officers, at a great risk of
his life, rescued a native woman who had been seized by a
crocodile and was being taken away to its lair.

We visited the stronghold of Chief Matoppo, who at the time
was in banishment. We found the kraal situated in a wild-
looking spot surrounded by enormous, irregular rocks, to gain
an entrance between which we had to creep on all fours.
Within the enclosure there was a large, complete and clean
Kaffir kraal of many huts and one corrugated iron building,
which was perched on an eminence and dominated the ronda-
vels in the kraal. As soon as we entered we were welcomed by
Matoppo's Induna, who had charge of the chief's eleven queens,
of all ages from eighteen years and upwards, and were conducted to the big council rondavel, which was very clean like
the rest, but without any seats. These were soon provided
for us, however, and the Induna, with a large number of others,
sat on the hard mud floor, with their backs against the wall,
and after a talk, in which I explained that the S.A.C. were in
the country to protect both Europeans and natives, the

queens came into the hut on all fours, although the door was high enough for a tall man, and passed round to us large gourds full of fresh Kaffir beer, which we tasted, and it was then given to the natives. When this ceremony was over we went outside and were photographed with the queens by Jarvis and de Havilland in turn, as neither of them would miss the opportunity of being snapshotted with the dusky maidens.

The natives in this kraal, both male and female, were of very fine physique and of a rich brown colour. More perfectly proportioned people it would be difficult to meet anywhere. They seemed to be equal to the Zulus, and the men were said to be very warlike and, previous to the British occupation of the country, difficult to manage, being unwilling to pay the hut tax, which, as a matter of fact, the Boers found it almost impossible to collect, the chiefs merely handing over a few hundred pounds to the commissioner. That day was past and gone, however; we had disarmed the natives, and under our escort every hut was visited and had to be paid for promptly on the spot.

When we left the kraal we descended the hill through fine crops of mealies and Kaffir corn. The latter is a sort of millet which the natives find useful for the manufacture of their beer. We saw the eleven queens again, busy collecting and storing the grain, which they placed in egg-shaped holes in the ground, and then covered over carefully with the leaves and earth. The women were working under the direction of the eldest queen, who kept them well occupied, and it was remarkable how easily and gracefully they walked with upwards of 50 pounds on their heads.

Most of the Kaffir kraals are, for sanitary reasons, perched on the high ground of the kopjes, and, as the women carry the water to the kraal while their lazy mates loaf the livelong day, it does not matter to the men how far the kraal is distant from the wells or spruits.

When we got back to Pretoria from one part of our tour we found invitations awaiting us for a ball that was to be held that evening. We had had a hard day, including 50 miles fast riding, and had only arrived at Pretoria at 6.30 p.m., but 8.30 found us at the ball. To ride 50 miles and go to a ball the same evening at the age of 50 is another indication that I was in pretty good condition.

In other lines of work, also, there was much to do. The justices of the peace had no power to try cases and, when the resident magistrates convicted law-breakers for offences, however trifling, the guard-rooms at the headquarters of districts and sub-districts could not be used to incarcerate them even for short terms of imprisonment, but all had to be sent to Pretoria, our men having to escort them for many miles by road and train, to the great wear and tear of horseflesh on the hard trails and much worry on the trains when there were many of them. This state of affairs was brought to the notice of the law department, but that section was at that time so strongly entrenched in old customs that Lord Milner in person had to be interviewed before anything was done to mend matters. The desired changes were then made, and later on resident justices of the peace were appointed to deal with cases as in other parts of the Empire, and as time went on, as a measure of economy and to promote greater efficiency, the officers of our force, as in the N.W.M.P., were gazetted as justices, and all members of the constabulary were permitted to prosecute in the resident magistrates' courts.

It took time to effect those reforms, and they only came about through the influence of the High Commissioner after persistent efforts at first to enlist the law department had failed, even after it had been represented that it would save much worry and annoyance to farmers, who often had to ride or drive 60 or 70 miles to appear before the resident magistrate, and to constabulary troopers who had to escort Kaffirs, who were, of course, on foot, for very long distances. When these changes were brought the benefit of the system was palpable even to the law department.

The War Claims Commission finished its very important duties about the end of 1903, with only one joke recorded against them, which was that when a farmer in the south-western Transvaal applied for compensation for the loss of some pigs and fowls which had been used by the soldiers, he was awarded damages for the loss of the hogs, but not for the fowls, because the troops derived no appreciable benefit from fowls !

Although the natives had been disarmed, they could still be a menace to the farmers and isolated persons, and needed careful watching, as the latter had very few rifles. I had a very long section of the Portuguese border carefully patrolled to prevent gun-running, and we could take care of the game quite as well as the game wardens posted in the low country, who were constantly objecting to any patrols. They did not seem to recognize the fact that to prevent the natives from having facilities for murdering the farmers or starting a rebellion was quite as important as the preservation of the game and the lions and other beasts of prey, which, being undisturbed, were increasing so fast as to be a danger to the isolated settlements. Of course I paid no attention to the remonstrances of the game wardens which came to me, and kept the patrols moving in that region.

The Boers were very friendly and anxious to have our detachments near them, and they made at first a good deal of the reported risings of the natives, but all the time they knew better, and were only making excuses to get rifles to shoot game, and one cannot blame them, for they had always done so, and from the day their ancestors settled in the colony every Dutchman had the best and latest pattern rifle in his house.

In February, 1904, the question of taking a census came up. When it was decided upon and the news of it spread throughout the divisions, some evil-disposed persons, and they were many, circulated a story amongst the Boer farmers to the effect that the census was a plan of the British to cause the Dutch to be in their homes at a given date, so that the natives could fall upon them and finish the burghers and their families at one fell swoop, thus settling the political question for all time. Of course there were not many who would believe this foolish and wicked story, but there were some who did, and took to the woods and kopjes for protection on the night they were expected to be at home !

During the same year cattle and horse diseases prevailed to a frightful extent, East Coast fever and Rhodesian Redwater for the former, and the dreadful sickness for the latter.

Cattle diseases became prevalent where they had never been before, and our veterinary surgeons and those of the hard-worked and useful department of agriculture were kept busy. Ours had much of their time occupied in teaching our officers, N.C.O.'s and men how to mix and apply the wash and dip required to prevent the spread of the cattle disease. But these matters, though bad for the country, were not all; there were enemies to good-will who had come from afar to destroy the good name of their countrymen in peace as they had in war, spreading falsehood through the land, about the humane government, as they previously had when vilifying the true-hearted British officers and soldiers. Following this plague came the locusts from German East Africa. Of course the S.A.C. had to take a hand to show the farmers how to use the fungi provided for their destruction. The attempts made were useless, however, for the breeding grounds were beyond our reach and control, and, as long as the barren wastes to the west of the Transvaal are allowed to breed these pests, there will be a certainty of their periodical visits.

Following the locusts came the bubonic plague, brought into the country by rats which came by sea, and our patrols were kept busy preventing people from moving into or out of the isolation camps which were established for the sick. This disease did not last long, and the people who caught it were fortunately few. It came in during the month of March, and had entirely disappeared in a couple of months, but had great care not been taken it might have been serious.

In April there were more reports of native unrest circulated by alarmists who always saw war or rebellion in the air. Those people could never get it into their heads that unarmed natives could not make a successful rising. They had not even an assegai, and the patrols along the border were so careful that nothing in the shape of arms and ammunition could be brought in.

The native census was completed in May, 1904, and it was found that my district commands had a much better idea of their numbers than the native commissioners who were in charge of them. Captain Jarvis estimated the natives in the Zoutpansberg at 300,000 in round numbers; the native commissioner put the estimate at 250,000 ; the actual census was 309,000. When this census was over my officers made reports and maps of their districts, showing as accurately as possible without a regular survey the roads, rivers, spruits, mountain ranges, hills, kopjes, Kaffir kraals, forests, marshes, farm-houses, Kaffir locations, the resources of the districts, and the supplies available in time of trouble. These reports were made carefully and proved to be of great use to me.

On December 17, 1904, I took 200 of my men, mounted, to assist in keeping order at the obsequies of the late President Kruger. The remains had been brought from Europe, and were interred in Pretoria cemetery with great pomp. Many thousands of persons from all parts of South Africa, especially the two colonies, were present, and the leading Boer generals were there. Everything went off in a way very creditable to all concerned, and on the day following the funeral I received a very courteous letter of thanks from the Boer committee of arrangements and also from the City Council, expressing their great satisfaction with the way our duties were performed.

In August our preparations were being made to get the voters' lists of the two colonies prepared, as the work was in our hands. Politics ran high ; Het Volk meetings were being held and many persons, who were not in the confidence of the government, thought it was rebellion, but it was merely organization by the Dutch so as to be ready for the elections. At the same time some prominent Anglo-Saxons were perched on the political boundary fence, ready to change their allegiance. The worst enemies of the government were British-born persons, agitators who made it their business to fool the electorate, but, as the great Abraham Lincoln said, " You cannot fool all the people all the time," and seven years have disposed of those gentry who promised that the new government, especially if it were Dutch, would give the skilled miners, poor creatures, higher wages—they were suffering at from £50 to £100 a month !

The Dutch people had a real grievance in the Chinese question, and a handle was made of it " at home." The mines employed tens of thousands of coolies, who were subject to what was called the foreign labour department, and it, very short-sightedly, did not compel the mining magnates to take proper precautions to maintain order, with the result that it was some time before the government took steps to back up the police force of Johannesburg and the S.A.C. in their efforts for the maintenance of order.

In the homeland politicians were clamouring that the Chinese were slaves, but the truth of the matter was that they were more free than any domestic in the King's dominions, and if it had been intended that the employment of Chinese on the mines of the Rand was to be made so unpopular with the inhabitants outside the Rand that they would demand their removal from the country, the mine owners could not have done more to attain the object. The roll call at the compounds was only once a week, with the natural result that ere long there were large parties of Chinese wandering about the country, robbing houses and murdering and maiming any persons, black or white, who resisted them. Dwellings were blown up with dynamite, which those wretches soon learned how to use. They were inveterate gamblers, and it seemed to be a religion with them that money must be obtained somehow to pay their gambling losses, or death at the hands of the winners would be their portion. There were many criminals amongst them, and some, who had served in the Chinese army, were able to lead their parties in pursuit of plunder. These people were not the miserable, puny specimens that one usually sees in towns in America, working in laundries or as domestics ; they were, on the contrary, a well-built, athletic class, many of them over six feet in height and proportionally built.

This condition of affairs soon threw the whole rural population into a state of alarm, and towards the end of 1905 some of the farmers around the Rand were abandoning their homes to get further away from it. Very soon it was estimated that thousands of Chinese were wandering about the country. I think the number was exaggerated, but many thousands were out at a time, and several parties were captured as far north as the confines of the Transvaal. They made the excuse that they were on their way back to China by the overland route ! In September, 1905, the marauders had become such a menace that I had to place an extra number of posts to watch the Rand and intercept any who were going north, and eventually there were mobile troops placed around to assist the districts.

Late in 1905 a Royal Commission was appointed, at the request of a prominent member of the Inter-Colonial Council, to investigate the S.A.C. Good though the reputation of the force was, it was enhanced by the findings of the commission, and the object of the gentleman who brought the matter up was totally defeated, in spite of the fact that a large number of subalterns had been called upon to express their opinions, and their seniors and, one might say, their betters from a military or constabulary and public point of view, left out. The evidence of the people at large, and the Boer farmers in particular, was unanimously favourable to the force. They were taken haphazard, wherever found, and one and all stated that the duties of the force were well performed, the officers and men minded their own business, did not mix up with the little affairs of the neighbourhood, were moral, temperate and helpful to all.

Shortly after this it was arranged that the force should be reduced to the lowest possible limits, and my division was absorbed. I was offered the command of the Orange River Colony division of the force, its commandant having gone on leave, but, believing that he desired to return, I refused to take it.

Colonel Nicholson gave up the command at the redistribution, and I was appointed inspecting staff officer, which office I was to hold until my leave had expired. The force at this time was at its best, and before he left the colonel informed me that he considered my division as near perfection as it could be, and that it was my work which brought about that result. He said even more which it is not necessary for me to mention, and, in connection with this, I wish to say that no man can make anything perfect without the assistance of others; the main thing is to get it started in the right direction. I had done so, and had the support and assistance of as good and sound a lot of officers as anyone could desire. There were no better in the country, and I look back with pleasure and great satisfaction to the loyal support which I received.

Colonel Nicholson left behind him a good name. He was a

kind friend to the force and a capable officer. I had often the pleasure of talking over matters with him, and have had him say to me that if any of the officers or their families needed a change for the benefit of their health, his purse was at my disposal to draw upon to give them a trip "home," or if officers convalescing after illness required a rest, they could go home at his expense, or unmarried officers could come and stay with him for a time until they were better, and he asked me not to let any know the source from which the funds were drawn. I do not think, however, that I am violating a confidence at this date, and I believe distinctly in doing justice to the living as well as to the dead.

In January, 1906, their Royal Highnesses the Duke and Duchess of Connaught and Princess Patricia visited the South African Colonies. Their reception from all nationalities was most enthusiastic, and from none more than the Dutch people, who vied with those of British birth or descent to show their appreciation of the visitors.

In Pretoria there were garden parties, a horse show, reviews of the troops, a grand military tattoo and torchlight procession, which took place on the great square before the government buildings, where, owing to the removal of the old Dutch Reformed Church to another site, there was ample space for the massed bands, and other ceremonies. At that time I was very busy with the suppression of the Chinese outrages, and could not spare much time to attend many of the functions to which my wife and I were invited.

We had to consider the arrangement of a cordon of posts around the Rand and the necessity for the taking of further measures to put an end to the wanderings of the Chinese. I was requested to take charge of the work as a special case, and command posts as well as the mobile squadrons. I asked for time to think it over, as my time was almost up and I had arranged to return to Canada. I then called upon Lord Selborne in connection with that and other matters, and as he also asked me to take command I consented, on account of the importance of the duty.

I submitted to him a memorandum on the subject. I considered that the compounds were not properly supervised, and recommended that the Chinese labourers should be placed under police supervision ; that a roll, or a count, of all the labourers should be made every day and any absentees reported at once ; that telephones should be established between compounds and police posts and, if possible, along the whole chain of posts. I also recommended that the compounds be so constructed that when the labourers went out they filed out through the same channel.

The recommendations with regard to the compounds and telephones were considered impracticable. I quite understood that if wear and tear of horseflesh and men did not matter we could do without the telephones ; but to put an end to the Chinese outrages and other depredations without carrying out what I suggested about the compounds meant that we might have to maintain a chain of posts around the Rand area at great expense to the country as long as the Chinese were employed in the mines. There was no help for it, however, and as I had already a number of posts I went on with the placing of others to make the cordon complete. The Rand was so extensive that my detachments had to be posted so that they formed an irregular oval of not less than 300 miles in circumference, and on an average about 10 miles from the mines, so that the deserters could be seen by the day patrols and, if they left at night they would have a long walk from the mines to the farm-houses nearest the Rand, or to pass our chain of posts before daylight.

The detachments consisted, as a rule, of five men and averaged five miles apart, with a regular system and connections. Each one sent out patrols during the day and night. The first patrols would go out towards the Rand, and on their return the relief would patrol outwards from the line of posts for some hours, to capture any who might have passed through the line during the night, and to visit farms, orchards and plantations where some of them might be concealed, waiting for an opportunity to take some farm by surprise. Patrols had to move about at night in the vicinity of the farms and on roads leading to the Rand. They had orders to make themselves acquainted with all the farmers and storekeepers and call upon them frequently ; they were to be asked for information and were expected to report the presence of any Chinese.

When I took over the duty a number of farmers and their families were absent from their homes through fear of the Chinese, and I gave orders to have them advised that they could return and would be protected, and need have no fear after the new posts were out ; in the event of any of the farmers being away on business, they could have one of our men to take charge during their absence. It was suggested from headquarters that they could stay in the houses that they were protecting but, as the Chinese were likely to take them by surprise or blow up the houses over their heads, and a man in the house would be in equal danger, I directed the few that I placed to remain outside and move around.

This work was strenuous for all of us. I was out every morning at five or six o'clock, except when I had to be in Pretoria or at headquarters on duty, and during the time I had command of the cordon, in addition to complete tours to visit all outposts, I inspected at least 800 farm-houses and showed the occupants how they could make them secure, took the names and addresses of all, ascertained if they had firearms or if they needed any, and made typewritten reports for headquarters. When I made the complete tour of inspection round the chain of posts without seeing many of the farmers, I covered the ground at the average rate of 60 miles per day, but on my trip to call on all of the farmers as I went along I only averaged about half that speed.

On my way round I learned that there were no more popular people in the colony than the South African Constabulary. The Boers are, as all the world knows, good scouts, no better anywhere, and when they were asked if they had any suggestions to make with regard to the scouting and patrolling, they invariably stated that the men were doing splendid work, no men could do better, and that they were kind and civil to them and their families. I found the people hospitable, always ready to offer at least a cup of coffee and a slice of bread and butter and some fruit.

On one of my trips I noticed that the farmer and two little children were the only persons in sight at one of the houses, and I asked if his wife was at home, as I should like to find out her view of the trouble we were having. He replied that his wife was dead. She had left the two children with another woman and went to the front during the late war to fight beside her husband ; nothing could dissuade her from going. She wore men's clothes, fought in several of the hardest battles, and was killed in one of them ! It was a sad case, but I believe there were similar ones.

By the middle of March the mobile troops and detachments of the districts round the Rand had captured the whole of the wandering Chinese, the murderers had been brought to justice, and a great deal of skill displayed by Captain Trew and his officers and men working up the cases and prosecuting, but for all that the coolies continued their efforts, and our patrols were kept busy night and day. The neglect of our suggestions by the foreign labour department and the looseness of the discipline at the compounds made it a hopeless task to prevent the Chinese from getting out, all that we could do was by constant vigilance to protect the inhabitants from outrages. Several conflicts had occurred when arrests were being made, and coolies had to be shot in self-defence.

On my rounds the Boer farmers, anxious to keep within the law, used to ask me what they should do if the Chinese came upon their premises at any time, and I advised them that they must not on any account, or with any excuse, no matter how plausible, permit one of them to approach. They should shoot if they kept coming, either day or night, after being warned back.

The necessity for such drastic measures had been evident to me from the first, but I had given no instructions as yet to any of the Boer farmers. There had been proof already that the Chinese should be treated as burglars or highwaymen, and there was more added to what we already had in our possession when an outrage was committed on a farm on Klipriversberg, a part of the Rand patrolled by the Transvaal Town Police of Johannesburg. A large party of Chinese had attacked the house, robbed it and maltreated everyone of the occupants by breaking their limbs, and the victims, when found, were at the point of death. Had they made a fight of it all would have

2 C

been murdered.   This crime brought me a letter from the Inspector General, who had been asked by the High Commissioner how such an outrage could be committed, how it might be prevented, and if it had occurred within the area patrolled by the S.A.C.

I replied that such an outrage was quite possible under the present system of Chinese management unless every farmer was properly armed and his house made secure with bolts, bars and shutters.   In all cases where the habitation was isolated from other dwellings I advised that there should be at least two men at night, one of them, if possible, a policeman, and both well armed.   I also recommended the posting of other troops at various spots.

I pointed out that the root of the evil was at the mines.   It is well known that 20 per cent. of the coolie labourers were absent at one time from the majority of the mines on the Rand, which did not speak well for the management of the compounds.

It was clear to me that if something were not done soon to put a stop to the crimes of the coolies they would have to be deported from South Africa.

My letter bore fruit at once.   The posts suggested were placed and a mobile troop patrolled the kopjes.   The new posts were able to send men to guard the isolated farms, and all that was needed was for the discipline at the compounds to be improved and the farmers who had no arms to be supplied with them.   We could not, however, compel the mine owners to fence the compounds as I had suggested previously, and many times since, although it was decidedly their desire to retain the coolies.

On April 11, however, Lord Selborne appointed a Royal Commission, presided over by Mr. Rose Innes, K.C., Resident Magistrate of Pretoria.   I appeared before them armed with a great deal of sound information with regard to the coolies at home, in the Dominion of Canada, and in the United States, which had been collected by travellers, soldiers, missionaries and consuls.   I had my own personal knowledge of the habits, manners and customs of the coolies as coal, metal and placer miners in America, as navvies in British Columbia and the United States, and I had in my pocket the blue book containing the report of the Royal Commission which had met in 1902 in British Columbia to inquire into the Chinese question in that province. Captain Sampson, of the T.T.P., a friend of the days in Macleod district when he had a large ranch on Mosquito Creek, Alberta, was also before the commission to give evidence.

In my evidence I suggested all that I had mentioned in previous letters, except telephones, and laid stress on the necessity for fencing the mining compounds, having guards, lights, very few exits, and cells for deserters. I recommended that there should be a uniform system of passes, that the area within which the coolies could be given passes should be much smaller, and that a Chinaman misapplying his pass by going in any other direction within that area should be arrested as a deserter. I advised that revolvers or shot guns, the latter with buck shot ammunition, should be issued free to the farmers whose names I had submitted to the Inspector General, with the cost that would be necessary to put the houses in a defensible state, and informed the commission that I had personally visited 800 farms around the Rand, examined the houses, talked to the people, and knew that the rural population, and even the Kaffirs, were in a state of alarm that would not have existed in war time. I explained the merciless character of the Chinese coolie and his disregard for the sufferings he inflicted upon his victims, his slim ways, which enabled him to enter houses with such stealth in the night that the inmates would hear nothing until purposely aroused. I concluded by recommending a careful roll call and check rounds, and insisted that the trouble was aggravated by the lack of supervision at the compounds.

After this I received authority to purchase shot guns and buck shot cartridges for the farmers, but, as might have been expected, the whole of the recommendations of the board were not brought into effect. There was a roll call daily at the compounds, but, except in a very few cases, they were not fenced.

While these affairs were interesting the inhabitants of the Transvaal the war in Natal had become serious, and it was decided to have the mobile troops sent into the districts where

2 c*

our natives were numerous, such as Lydenberg, Swaziland, the Zoutpansberg, etc., and I was authorized to man the Chinese cordon with special constables selected from amongst the Boer farmers around the country, but recruits for that service came in very slowly, horses being difficult to get. It was the winter of that part of the world, and many of the farmers had their horses in the low country. In the meantime the mobile troops had to hold all their stations except the few posts nearest the mines.

The special constables were to be paid five shillings per day and their horses one shilling, but in time it was found that the men could not maintain themselves on those rates, and they were increased to a fairly good amount. The whole of the cordon was not filled with Dutch farmers until the month of July, and the mobile troops relieved and dispatched to their destinations, but many detachments of Boers had been already placed.

During this reorganization I saw much of Sir Richard Solomon, who was at the time Acting Lieutenant Governor of the Transvaal, and from him I received the officers who were to serve under me on the chain of outposts. They had been recommended to him by General Louis Botha, and were Major Pretorius and Captain Kruger, of the Boer artillery, well-trained soldiers; Mr. Keyter, of Schoongezicht, who had under him the Heidelberg commando at the siege of Ladysmith; Mr. van Dam, commandant of the Zarps or Johannesburg Police before and during the war; Mr. Kroon, a Hollander, and Mr. Beignault, a Boer, both of whom had served on commando. Of the three first named I saw most, and I formed a favourable impression of them. They were faithful workers and most hospitable. Mr. Keyter lived at a pretty spot near the kopjes about three hours' drive from Johannesburg, and I often spent the week-end with him and learned much of the doings of both sides during the war. His commando had been kept busy around Ladysmith, and he had been sent away from there to annoy Lord Roberts' advance, when it was found impossible to prevent the relief of the beleaguered city. Six thousand men were withdrawn, but there was a sufficient force left to equal Sir Redvers Buller's and endeavour to hold the line.

As we all know, and the general said, there was " no way round," and the obstacles to Sir Redvers Buller's advance were enormous. I was very naturally pleased to know what a high opinion the Boers had of Sir Redvers Buller as a fighting man. They themselves said, " It is not only the burghers who respected Sir Redvers Buller, but their wives and families ; both considered him not only one of the best of soldiers, but one of the most chivalrous of men." As Keyter said, it was impossible to turn the Boer flanks in the advance from the Tugela to Ladysmith, but in other parts of the theatre of war they had no sooner taken up a position than it was turned by superior numbers.

I had many interesting conversations with Captain Kruger, who had commanded the Creusot guns of the Boers, about everything in his experience, and found him to be a very well-informed, bright, frank young fellow. He had been trained by German artillerymen, and informed me that before the war they had very naturally told him that their army was the best in the world and their soldiers the best, and that, even after the war was in full swing, he thought it was possible that they might be right, but when he was with the Germans in the campaign against the Hereros he changed his opinion entirely, and he had no doubt that the British officer and soldier had more resource. The soldiers were well treated by their officers, which was not the case with the others ; the treatment the German soldier received was cruel in comparison, and it destroyed his initiative. To their prisoners of war, too, the British were always as kind as could be.

After the Boers were posted in the chain of outposts I was constantly amongst them, made long treks and was much pleased with the way they met my wishes. Everything was done well, the S.A.C. system being continued and found to be the best. The work was as hard as ever ; constant vigilance had to be exercised, and some of the Chinese got into the kopjes near Heidelberg, and I had to get more special constables for detachments which I had to place at least 35 miles from the Rand. The district men of the S.A.C. were kept going night and day, but outrages were kept down, for no sooner did we find the trail of the wretches than they were captured and punished. The immunity could not last long, however, for the compounds had been improved but little. There were tens of thousands of Chinese in the mines, and, although the great majority were inclined to behave well and save money, there were large numbers who gambled and would break out to rob the farms. One night the house of a Mr. Smit, of Klipriversberg, was attacked by nine of the miscreants, who had, with their usual patience, lain in some kopjes not far distant for the whole day, watching the house. Two constables from a detachment which had not yet been relieved by the Boers had been sent to guard it, and lay in the orchard watching the building. They saw two of the Chinese place dynamite cartridges, one at the end and the other at the side of the house next them, and after setting their fuses prepare to light their matches, whereupon one of the constables fired two shots, killing both. Mr. Smit, aroused by the sounds, came out rifle in hand, and the other seven were captured in the act of dragging the dead away. While the fiends were placing the dynamite cartridges one of the gang had set fire to the thatch, but the constables extinguished it before it had gained headway.

On May 30 I went with Sir Richard Solomon to the office of the Chamber of Mines, Johannesburg, and, after a great deal of discussion about all matters, it was ordered that, as I had suggested before, the area to which the Chinese were restricted would be reduced in size and posts placed round to define it. The compounds were to be enclosed ; five men to be in charge of them, and have a lock-up for delinquents, and one of them to be on gate duty all the time. The members present stated that there was a roll call, as had been arranged before at the meeting of the commission.

When everything had got into proper working order, the Chinese wanderings had been reduced to almost nothing and every marauder and deserter either on his way back to China or in prison, I sent in my resignation. I made a final tour of the chain of detachments, and said good-bye to every man of the force, Briton and Boer, and wished him good luck. All expressed regret that I was going, and many of the Boers said they were sorry, because I understood them.

I went over to see Keyter on Saturday, September 8, and was busy with him next day until ten o'clock. A number of his men were there in their Sunday dress with arms, and I asked him if they were going to church, and he replied, " No, they are going to escort you to near Klip River, and from there they will ride straight back to their posts." I thanked him for the kind thought and mounted for my last trek with the Boers. Mrs. Keyter and a friend of hers, Miss van der Merwe, came with us in a carriage, and Keyter with his men formed a strong travelling escort beyond Klip River post, about two hours' drive. Then the ladies alighted, and Keyter formed up his men on the side of the road, and addressed me on behalf of himself and his men, saying that I had come out to fight for the crown, and, that duty having been done well with the " Big Stirrups " and the S.A.C., I had worked with success to reconcile Briton and Boer, and if all would do the same there would not be an enemy of the King in the whole of South Africa. He added that I had understood the Boers and that the South African Constabulary had been by far the greatest factor of all the government departments in conciliating the Boers and teaching them what good people Britons were.

On September 18 I went to Johannesburg to visit head-quarters and settle up my affairs with the force, and the same forenoon went to the Simmer and Jack mine on the invitation of the manager and Mr. Stokes, an ex-officer of the S.A.C., who had a billet there. After lunch Mr. Stokes conducted me round the compounds, in which 4,000 Chinese lodged ; all were well cared for and disciplined under the direction of my friend Stokes, and a perfect system was maintained to prevent desertions. Those coolies were as well fed and treated as the very best I have seen anywhere, either black or white men. Large bath-rooms with hot baths were provided, ample sleeping accommodation, the food was plentiful and well cooked by steam, as that was the way the coolies desired it, and they used only three-fourths of their allowance. The kitchens were commodious and clean, in the corner of each mess-room huge boxes of tea grown in China and of their own choice were placed, and each labourer helped himself.

In addition to the regular kitchens there were others in

which the coolies could cook any special tit-bit of their own, and I saw several of them busy there. After the messing I saw the system of pay, which was by card; each labourer had two, one pink and the other white; the latter was marked at the end of the shift by the white shift boss with the number of inches that the Chinaman had drilled, and that was presented with the pink ticket at the pay office, and the value of the work done marked on the latter by a clerk. At the end of the month both tickets were presented, and the coolie paid his earnings, which were, I was informed, about double that of a Kaffir, which, from what I had observed, was a correct statement.

After seeing the compounds I visited the quarters and reading-rooms provided for the European miners who superintend the Chinese at their work. There was a very large supply of the latest papers and periodicals, and the men seemed to be comfortable and contented, earning from £50 to £100 per month.

The Simmer and Jack is the largest single gold mine in the world. There were 47 miles of underground workings, and 60,000 tons of ore were crushed every month. The yield for the previous month was £97,000 sterling in gold, and the mine had 360 stamps working steadily. The manager was an American and the underground mining engineer a Canadian. The salary of the former was £7,000 a year and of the latter £5,000 and I was informed that the deepest workings were 4,000 feet beneath the surface, and that at such great depths the mines are cooler than in any other part of the world.

It was a pleasure to go over this great property and see what could be done when a perfect system prevails. If the same could have been brought into force when the Chinese were first employed, there would have been no annoyance given to the inhabitants of the Transvaal, and the Chinese, if desired, could have been retained. I was informed before I left for Pretoria that the Simmer and Jack mine had at that date 33 years of life before it, and probably 50, when all ground is worked.

On September 30 my wife and I went to Johannesburg to say good-bye to the Earl and Countess of Selborne. Lord

Selborne was kind enough to say that I had done " marvellously good work," and thanked me heartily for it.

We returned to Pretoria next day. My wife by that time was very ill ; she had suffered for at least two months with dreadful headaches, which the worry of leaving for England had aggravated to a very great extent, and, had her mother not been on a visit to us, I should have been in sore straits. We received hundreds of kind letters from all parts of South Africa, and many came to call and say good-bye. We left on October 2 in a violent storm of rain, but many friends came to see us off in spite of the weather.

We sailed on the *Suevic* on October 7. I had thought that a sea voyage would do my wife good, but it was not so, for long before we reached England she became insensible and remained so for at least a month after we landed. She would certainly have died on the voyage had it not been that Miss Dudley, an army nurse, happened to be on board, and her care and that of my wife's mother, Mrs. Harwood, saved her life. Everyone else was most solicitous and kind ; a very pretty young German lady, Miss Hasenrahm, of Hamburg, gave up her berth, which suited my wife better than the one she was in, and others were so kind on her behalf that we owe them a lifelong debt of gratitude.

We landed in England at Tilbury Docks on November 1, 1906, and left the ship for the train, with my wife in a stretcher. There was no provision for sick people, and I had to put my wife in the baggage car amongst cans of milk for London. There were no seats, so we stood until we arrived, the monotony of the journey being broken very often by the advent of more cans of milk. Until my wife was fit to be moved I took a comfortable flat in Kensington, and the children were sent to school as soon as possible.

When I was in Africa Sir Frederick Borden, always considerate to me, had arranged that I could be permitted by the War Office to be attached for duty with the Inspector General of Cavalry, Major General Baden-Powell, who was finishing the last year of his appointment, and it gave me much pleasure to have the privilege of being with him. My wife's illness prevented me from being as much with him as I should have liked, but I took advantage of a great deal, and it was pleasant to find that he was so well thought of by every cavalry officer I met. In addition to my experience with him I took lectures and read and re-read every book which could be of use, visited Woolwich Arsenal under the auspices of Major H. Bland Strange, the son of one of my very best friends, General Strange, who showed me everything, and, as I always admired the artillery service and have kept up my studies in it, I was glad of the opportunity afforded me to go over that remarkable place.

Mrs. Harwood and the children saw a good deal of the metropolis, and when my wife was fully restored to health we had the pleasure of meeting General and Mrs. T. Bland Strange at their hospitable home at Camberley, and enjoyed a couple of week-ends there. We also met Sir George and Lady French and their daughters. It was like old times on the plains of the then wild west to meet those who had done so much for me, and I was indeed delighted to find the man who " made " the Canadian Artillery in such splendid health and taking such a deep interest in the affairs of the country.

My wife and I paid a delightful visit to my relatives in Abergavenny and Blaenavon. We stayed a while in both places and enjoyed every moment of the time. In April I visited Scotland, and with the most delightful weather made a long stay with friends. I had a glorious time. We visited every important battlefield, inspected the bottle dungeon of St. Andrew's, saw the golf course with its thousands of braw people, and, in fact, almost everything from Holyrood to the " bore stone " and the home of the Fair Maid of Perth. We visited farms, castles, picture galleries and cathedrals, just the thing I liked, and the only thing to mar the occasion was the thought that at that time my wife felt that it would not be wise for her to undertake the journey while she was not quite strong.

In London the first to call upon us was the High Commissioner, Lord Strathcona, who was so kind as to offer to write the foreword to this book. He has, since I met him in Canada, departed to his reward, full of years and honours, leaving a great and honoured name and reputation behind him. During our stay in London no one could have been more kind and sympathetic than he, and when my wife had recovered we saw much of him and Lady Strathcona, who pre-deceased him but a short time.

During the latter part of the winter Sir Frederick Borden was in London, and was so good as to give me the command of Military District No. 13, with headquarters at Calgary. In May I left England with my family for Montreal, and after a delightful trip up the noble St. Lawrence, and a short but pleasant stay in Montreal and Ottawa, I went west in time to take command of the camp of training at Calgary, which had assembled a few days before, in the last week of July, 1907.

Subsequently I was transferred to Winnipeg, and have devoted myself to the work of organizing new units, a pleasant task when the officers of my staff, the permanent force and the officers and men of the militia are so keen and work so harmoniously. The force over the whole of the western districts has increased to a remarkable but absolutely necessary extent in the last few years. Two valuable assets to the country have sprung into being and are watched over by the Departments of Militia and Education. They are the cadet movement and the physical training of boys and girls in the public schools, and the qualification of teachers for the work of instructing. They are making great progress, the improvement in the bearing and physique of the teachers and children being very remarkable. The cadets are allowed to spend a week in camp, a delightful outing for the boys, with their instructors, teachers and clergy, and under a good staff of officers, who instruct them in the best of the Boy Scout work and military drill. The physical training is compulsory in all schools in Canada, but the military training for cadet service is voluntary.

At Calgary I met many whom I had known from the days when the buffalo roamed and the city of Calgary, with its 75,000 inhabitants, was not even a name. Amongst the officers was the doyen of them all, Colonel James Walker, on whose powerful shoulders the winters of the north and the struggles with the forces of nature had no effect, whose hearty hand clasp and frank, kindly gaze said, " You can depend upon me."

The changes which had taken place during my absence of

seven years made me rub my eyes and wonder if I were dreaming. Hundreds of thousands of settlers had come into the great west. It seemed impossible that Winnipeg, with its 200,000 citizens, its fine stores, palatial residences and well-paved, wide streets, was the hamlet of 40 houses and less than 300 persons that I remembered. Regina, whose site I had driven and ridden over when the nearest habitation was the Hudson's Bay Company's post at Fort Qu'appelle, 50 miles distant, was now a railway centre, a beautiful city with parks, fine residences, magnificent public buildings, and encircled by smiling farms. There were similar changes at Moosejaw, no longer " Moosejaw bone," but a lively railway town with fine farms in every direction. Swift Current had sprung into existence and, with Maple Creek, Medicine Hat and other places, was growing fast. I was not long in visiting Edmonton on duty, and found a bustling and beautiful place, towering above the fine river, with stores and residences that would be a credit to a place a hundred years old. It was hardly credible that this was the place where we wintered in 1875, with only half a dozen poplar log houses in sight, and later, during the rebellion, only a village !

It was the same all over western Canada, and we, who had been the pioneers of this glorious change, were permitted by Providence to see the fruits of our labours and our hardships.

THE END

INDEX